Reclaiming Genders

D1488417

Reclaiming Genders

*Transsexual Grammars
at the Fin de Siècle*

Edited by
Kate More and Stephen Whittle

CASSELL
London and New York

Cassell
Wellington House, 125 Strand, London WC2R 0BB
370 Lexington Avenue, New York, NY 10017-6550

First published 1999

British Library Cataloguing-in-Publication Data
A catalogue record for this book is available from the British Library.

ISBN 0-304-33777-3 (hardback)
      0-304-33776-5 (paperback)

Library of Congress Cataloging-in-Publication Data
Reclaiming genders : transsexual grammars at the fin de siècle /
   edited by Kate More and Stephen Whittle.
      p. cm.
   Includes bibliographical references and index.
   ISBN 0-304-33777-3 (hardback). — ISBN 0-304-33776-5 (paperback)
   1. Transsexualism. 2. Transsexualism—Great Britain.
3. Transsexuals. 4. Transsexuals—Great Britain. I. More, Kate,
1965- . II. Whittle, Stephen, 1955- .
HQ77.9.R43 1999
305.9′066—dc21   98–41804
                                                              CIP

Typeset by BookEns Ltd, Royston, Herts
Printed and bound in Great Britain by Biddles Limited,
Guildford and King's Lynn

Contents

Notes on Contributors

Judith Butler teaches at the University of California at Berkeley. She's the author of *Gender Trouble* and several other publications.

Jason Cromwell is a cultural anthropologist who works as an independent scholar on issues concerning FTMs, gender, sexuality, sociolinguistics and the body. His book *Transmen and FTMs* is being published by University of Illinois Press and is due out in Autumn 1999. He has been active in the trans-community for over fifteen years.

Markisha Greaney is a receptionist in San Francisco. Since completing this chapter she has lost all interest in queer/trans theory.

Jamison 'James' Green, is a fiction writer, essayist and public speaker. He volunteers much of his time as president of FTM International, Inc., an educational organization working to improve the lives of female-to-male transsexual and transgendered people. He lives near San Francisco, California.

Roz Kaveney writes for *New Statesman and Society*, the *Independent* and the *Times Literary Supplement*. She is a former civil servant and ex-hustler (you meet a nicer class of person on the street). She co-founded Feminists Against Censorship, is Chair of G&SA (Gender and Sexual Alliance) and a former deputy-chair of Liberty (National Council for Civil Liberties).

Sandra Laframboise and **Deborah Brady** trained as nurses. They work with TG sex workers, intravenous drug users and HIV-positive people at the High Risk Project in Vancouver, British Columbia.

Gordene O. Mackenzie, author of *Transgender Nation,* is a gender activist, lecturer and writer who teaches university courses on sex, gender, politics and the media. She is currently living in Cambridge, MA, working on a book examining the gender-ambiguous body in US and international film.

Kate More has previously published on Kristeva and more recently on Nerval. In February 1997, following 'feedback' from HM Prison Service, she was suspended as a Visiting Scholar at Cambridge University because of her political involvement with transsexual prisoners. She co-edits *Radical Deviance: A Journal of Transgendered Politics.*

Diane Morgan is Senior Lecturer in Literary and Cultural Studies at University College Northampton. She is the author of *Kant Trouble: The Obscurities of the Enlightened* (Routledge, 1999), and co-editor (with Keith Ansell Pearson) of *Nihilism Now! 'Monsters of Energy'* (Macmillan, forthcoming).She has worked with Kate More for *Radical Deviance* and is currently researching a book project with her.

Jay Prosser is a Lecturer in English and American Studies at the University of Leicester. His book *Second Skins: The Body Narratives of Transsexuality* is published by Columbia University Press.

Henry S. Rubin is a Lecturer in the interdisciplinary programme of social studies at Harvard University. He transitioned while researching and writing his book *The Subject Matters: FTM Transsexual Embodiment and Subjectivity* (to be published by the University of Chicago Press).

Susan Stryker is co-author of *Gay by the Bay: A History of Queer Culture in the San Francisco Bay Area* (1996) and editor of 'The Transgender Issue', a special transgender studies issue of the queer theory journal *GLQ* (1998). Her work in progress, *Ecstatic Passages: A Postmodern Transsexual Memoir,* will be published by Oxford University Press.

Stephen Whittle, Senior Lecturer in Law at Manchester Metropolitan University, trans man and activist. Editor of *The Margins of the City: Gay Men's Urban Lives* (Arena) and co-author of *Transvestism, Transsexualism and the Law* (The Gender Trust).

Acknowledgements

Kate's dedications

My dedication is to my grandfather, a lifelong Communist and activist, to my late Uncle Gordon, whose life brought the possibility of academia into mine, and mostly to the activist community whose work this really is. I also want to remember my friends, John Miles Longden and Dave Cook, because they're dead too. As always, I owe my transition from diapers to the living: Dr Diane Morgan, Sarah Gasquoine, Dr Stephen Whittle, Kate Bornstein and my Mum. A Special Hi to Kazz, Roz and Simon!

Stephen's dedications

I would like to thank Kate More and the G&SA group (Gender and Sexuality Alliance) in Middlesbrough for proposing that this collection be made. Without their commitment to trans-theory as a way of understanding our activism and politics, it would have been very difficult to persuade others that this book not only had a place in the academy but also on the streets.

I must also thank the writers who took part in this project – being a trans academic is a hard and lonely route. Always viewed as being too subjective and too involved, it is extremely tempting to leave behind trans studies and its inevitable resultant commitment to activism, to escape into the ivory towers and to leave the troubled self behind. Considering the incredible pressure that trans people face to do what they ought to do – disappear – alongside the academic pressure to 'do something a little more serious, something a little less smutty', they have shown great strength in refusing either route.

I would like to thank all those who have gone before – all of those trans warriors who have refused not simply *to be* and who have enabled us all *to become* whoever we are. This has been a hard year, the losses to our forces have been great and I feel it is important to remember a few of those who have gone, hopefully, to some place a little kinder than this world. I wish to dedicate this book to Dee McKeller, who died while patrolling with the Q-patrol to make the streets of Houston a safer place for all trans people. Also Bill Finch, who had taken the route of a trans man in the early 1960s, but who never left the rest of us behind; he shall be missed by his friends. I also wish to remember my friend, Ben, whose untimely death could never detract from the open heart he showed to his trans parent and his parent's trans friends.

I would also like to thank and dedicate this book to those close to me who have made it possible for me to participate in its achievement. In particular, my partner Sarah Rutherford, who, over the period of our production of this book, has faced with great strength the loss of her dear mother, Marilyn. And finally Marilyn herself, who tried very hard in her life to allow us our own pathway and to support us on it when we needed her to do so. She was greatly loved and is truly missed.

This book will hopefully show us where we have been, where we are, and the road forward. Trans studies is a new encompassing discipline in which there is still a great deal of work to be done, and I am looking forward to the work of the new trans scholars of the future for whom it will, I hope, be an inspiration.

We owe thanks to *genderfuck*, *Radical Deviance* and G&SA friends and colleagues for their love and patience: Kate Baillie, Caroline Bavin, our patron – the Rt. Hon. Tony Benn, MP – Brian and Martin, Marlowe the Cat, Chris and Wendy, Jack Cummings, Simon Dessloch, Lynda Dixon, Jan Fallon, Sarah Gasquoine, Michael Gilligan, Clare Hemmings, Roz Kaveney, John Lawson, Liz, Jim McManus, Surya Monro, Diane Morgan, Zach Nataf, Averil Newsam, Kate n'Ha Ysabet, Martin Parkinson, Peter Polish, Jay Prosser, Ron, the Sarahs, Kristina Sheffield, Beryl Thompson, Matthew Windibank and Tony Zandvliet, and have a soft spot for Phaedra Kelly whom we're determined to mention! Also thanks to the ICA and Democratic Left. A special feature of edited volumes is that one encounters new computer viruses from all over the world; thanks to John Fletcher and Bernard Burgoyne for their answer to the problem of disappearing *italics*.

Introduction 1

Kate More

'**Instruction to typesetter:** *h/is, h/er, s/he, f/h-email:* This strange set of constructions, where an oblique stroke is used to introduce an approximate break in the subject between signifier/ signified, sex/gender is deliberate. Please do not correct!' (Kate More and Stephen Whittle, *manuscript for this book*)

How could one introduce punk rock without the word 'fuck' in the first sentence? How could one use Judith Butler's theory without being rhetorical, without questioning the basics? How can one not debase the authentic when engaging with postmodernism? No wonder this is the first trans-activism/trans-theory reader. Ours is a dangerous border. How many people other than myself have been sacked or suspended – or simply not tried to get jobs – for that cross-over?

Erring on the safe side for a minute (for there is something of a miracle in fourteen members of the transgender community simply getting together in a book, let alone being allowed to think through their politics), I want to ask what the relationship is between trans-activism and trans-theory. One of the reasons for this book is Stuart Feather's remembrance in *No Bath But Plenty of Bubbles*[1] of the split between the theoretical and practical wings of gay liberation. As if in response, Joan Copjec, in that brilliant and problematic book *Read My Desire,*[2] describes how the diagrams, the theoretical articulations of structuralism (which Lacan's students rejected as irrelevant and wanted to replace with a theory to take to the streets in May 1968), were not concerned with social relations, but rather with the unconscious, with desire. Far from theory being the steam from the boiling water of activism, it follows of course that desire, the unconscious, both provoke activism and are integral to it.

Unlike 1968 when people still talked in terms of 'false consciousness' and 'intellectual vanguardism' – where the 'intelligent' and 'progressive' led the way for the 'lumpen' – our use of the word 'reclaiming', synonymous with division, is knowing, deliberate. Our hope is that this book is evidence of an end to revolutionary snobbery. No one is saying that the chapter Jason Cromwell writes for us on reclaiming identity should be the party line, that we should replace one dogma, 'lesbian', with another, 'transsexual'. Far from it. The anthology merely puts the arguments, and the title of this book isn't 'Reclaiming Transsexuality' – or even 'Reclaiming Gender' for that matter. *Reclaiming Genders* implies the need to reclaim plurality, that we need the option of all strategies. And if the balance is right you will read the chapter on 'transsexual as fantasist' and take that into the chapters on visibility – remembering that the closet is a site of fantasy, a margin internalized with the secrets and possibilities of transgender identities, that we walk through life carrying not the closet, but the possibility of the closet, saying 'Shall I tell the bus driver?' And when you do read transpeople writing about reclaiming genders you'll recognize that it's absolute fantasy, but that fantasy is absolutely relevant.

In the UK most of the activism is currently associated with two groups, Press for Change and G&SA (Gender and Sexuality Alliance) and although this is a G&SA anthology,[3] the choice of editors was based on that split – Stephen representing Press for Change, and myself G&SA. The anthology itself was provoked by G&SA's grotty little xeroxed newsletter *genderfuck*, which in March 1996 took a more theoretical bent and became rather grandly, *Radical Deviance: A Journal of Transgendered Politics*, attracting the likes of Judith Butler and Hélène Cixous. It was the first attempt at making trans-theory in the UK since Gay Liberation in the early 1970s, and several of the chapters in this volume originate from *Radical Deviance*. Such a contribution justifies the inclusion in the volume of our exception, my co-editor on *Radical Deviance*, Diane Morgan – not a sex-change, nor even a tranny (my spell-checker wants 'tyranny'), but someone who read, thought, edited, wrote, stayed up late photocopying, stapling and addressing envelopes – very much a part of our community. *Radical Deviance*'s is, first and foremost, a politics of inclusion – if Diane weren't here, we would have to invent her!

Although this is an anthology of 'transsexual grammars' we have been liberal with our definitions. The word 'transsexual' used here equates with cross-living rather than cross-dressing. It has nothing to do with medical definitions; for all the flaws in a civil rights rubric, we should have the right to define ourselves, to express ourselves. I think it's important to recognize that there's a further shift in politics beyond liberalism – the age of identity politics seems finally and thankfully to be at an end. The new millennium heralds the age of 'transgender' – an umbrella term including all cross-living and cross-dressing people, in fact the whole gamut of 'gender complex' people fighting together instead of against each other. In the past we have raised all sorts of dubious boundaries: drag queens and kings were cast out as homosexual perverts, transvestites were fetishists, and perhaps most destructive, transsexuals were raised close to sanctity (unless they were gay or enjoyed sex or something). Transgender's pluralist politics – based on coalition, bringing in the gay community for the first time – offers something seriously to look forward to.

A few short weeks ago I spent five days in the dark with Diane, Roz, Jay, Susan, Stephen and no doubt others from this anthology, watching some 70 films and shorts at the First International Transgender Film and Video Festival held at the Lux Centre in London. A coalition project run by G&SA's Zach Nataf and organized by members of the various political and self-help groups, its opening night coincided with the handing-in of a long-awaited petition on transsexual rights to No. 10 Downing Street. That morning I counted a mere fifteen people supporting the call on birth-certificates – after 30 years of fighting on that issue. However much I like the fact that my birth-certificate has the 'wrong' sex on it, however much I would be annoyed if I were normalized, I nevertheless couldn't believe that people could be bored with state oppression. A few tense hours later I arrived early at the Lux – by then terrified of a flop – only to see all sorts of weirdos (rapidly including me) scrabbling for the last tickets to a 100- or 200-seater auditorium for a film that most people had already seen. By the Gala Ball on the Saturday night it seemed absolutely natural for me to combine an elegant curly moustache with a black velvet Morticia Addams dress and indeed to kiss people of all genders. In the United States, so I was told, the term 'transsexual' and the politics connected to it are already becoming passé, so I see this book as a marker for that term, a seeing-out of transsexual – not of the people, but of the prejudice.

The thing that startles is the maturity, the intelligence of transgender. Angela Mason in an interview with *Radical Deviance* said that we do not learn from our history[4] – I think that's pessimistic. Reminiscent of the think-ins of Gay Lib,[5] the first UK Radical Transgender Politics Forum eighteen months ago also had its problems, the difficult set of dynamics I note in my chapter. However, that forum was followed at Easter with one looking for solutions from cybernetics, systems theory, and which arrived at a process devised by Stafford Beer called 'syntegrity'.[6] Instead of three people like me, Roz and Stephen pontificating to 300, and the whole arrangement being held to ransom by one or two in the back row, the structure arranges groups of 30 in sets of twelve workshops, to mimic the tensile forces of an icosahedron. In theory each person should have equal input, and through each of the 30 people being connected to different workshops in different ways and by reiterating each debating topic three times, over 90 per cent of the information (according to a mathematical proof I didn't even try to understand) is shared between the participants. Sounds weird, but it means that no one gets to call the semantic shots, everyone does. Like formal poetry this is highly structured, requiring as many as one facilitator or logistician per three participants, and a number of computers to process the information and work out the algorithms, yet it's a model of democracy. One might expect this at an IBM conference, but a group of trannies?

Actually, yes. Trannies, but also (looking at the letter of invitation) queer theorists like Alan Sinfield and Mandy Merck, lesbian and gay politicians like Peter Tatchell, the avant garde like Sue Golding and Cherry Smyth and systems people like Leroy White. If sex-changes can be this organized and connected in 1998, frankly a trans politics of coalition in the new millennium has an incredible potential.

So then to sum the anthology: a pluralist grammar of trans politics – from eminent professors like Judith Butler to people like me with holes in their boots, from court cases to Lacanian sexuation tables, from the simplicity of Riki-Ann Wilchin's *Transexual Menace* T-shirt (buy one, become the organization) to running a structured cybernetic think-in at a university in London.

Enjoy!

Notes

1. Lisa Power, *No Bath But Plenty of Bubbles* (London: Cassell, 1995): 157.
2. Joan Copjec, *Read My Desire: Lacan against the Historicists* (Cambridge, MA: MIT Press, 1994): 11.
3. Press for Change have been involved with a number of books, e.g. Mark Rees, *Dear Sir or Madam* (London: Cassell, 1996), Tracie O'Keefe and Katrina Fox, *Trans-X-U-All* (1996) and Stephen Whittle, *Transvestism, Transsexualism and the Law* (London: The Gender Trust, 1995).
4. Angela Mason and Kate More in debate on 'Coalitions, common issues and hate crime', *Radical Deviance*, (1996), 2(2): 48 (Middlesbrough, London and Leeds, G&SA).
5. Cf. Power, *No Bath But Plenty of Bubbles*.
6. Cf. Stafford Beer, *Beyond Dispute: The Invention of Team Syntegrity*, (Chichester: John Wiley & Sons, 1994).

References

Beer, S. (1994) *Beyond Dispute: The Invention of Team Syntegrity*. Chichester: John Wiley & Sons.

Copjec, J. (1994) *Read My Desire: Lacan against the Historicists*. Cambridge, MA: MIT Press.

More, K. and A. Mason (1996) 'Coalitions, common issues and hate crime', *Radical Deviance*, 2(2): 47–8.

O'Keefe, T. and K. Fox (1996) *Trans-X-U-All*. London: Extraordinary People.

Power, L. (1995) *No Bath But Plenty of Bubbles*. London: Cassell.

Rees, M. (1996) *Dear Sir or Madam*. London: Cassell.

Whittle, S. (1995) *Transvestism, Transsexualism and the Law*. London: The Gender Trust.

Introduction 2

Stephen Whittle

A t the end of the last millennium those people we would now recognize as being transgender or transsexual were rarely documented, except in myth and legend, or in documents from the church courts after their trials for blasphemy or sodomy. As we enter the next millennium, the intervening one thousand years have seen transgender and transsexual people become a world-wide cultural obsession. As I sit and write this on the final day of 1997, when one might think the correspondents of the world's media should have any number of serious matters to reflect upon and even more to look forward to, I discover in today's newspaper two whole pages devoted to the selection of a transsexual woman, Dana, to represent Israel in the 1998 Eurovision Song Contest. This evening, the UK's main youth television show to see in the new year, TFI Friday, included among its features a celebration of the transition, undertaken in 1997, from one gender role to another of a young transsexual man. Why is trans such BIG news?

This introduction is by way of telling why and how this particular book was able to come about. Each year thousands of pages of newsprint, legal documentation, academic articles and textbooks are now published about the 'trans' phenomenon. Why is this book any different? For a start, it is mostly written by transgender academics who have a unique understanding of where trans studies, trans politics and trans activism are at, and the particular history that has led us to that position. Furthermore its very existence is not only a result of, but also a part of that historical process.

Ten years ago it could have been argued that the public and the media's 'Sex-Change, Shock–Horror – Naughty Vicar's Knickers' complex was a purely Western, European, phenomenon. Today that is certainly no longer the case. Almost daily, the Asian news media carry stories about the issues surrounding trans people – from the problems faced by Hijari prostitutes under Afghanistan's new fundamentalist Islamic regime to an application by a transsexual man for status recognition in the Kuwaiti courts. Similarly Latin America has not escaped. The effect of an almost continent-wide coalition between the lesbian, gay and bi communities and the trans community has been felt within the state structures of government at least in Argentina, Brazil and Colombia. In the 1990s, African governments also began to acknowledge the existence of transpeople within African cultures, recognizing that not only has Casablanca, in the far north, long been a Mecca for Europeans and Americans seeking gender reassignment surgery but also Johannesburg, in the far south, has historically been a similar centre of excellence for Africans of any colour or race, regardless of the apartheid regime of the past 40 years. These few examples are merely the tip of a much bigger iceberg. World-wide, transpeople are being seen and this book is part of that visibility.

As we move towards the end of the century and the start of the new millennium, there are unfamiliar border crossings to be faced by us all. Is this obsession with all things trans in fact the manifestation of a travel sickness suffered by those so far untainted by monumental journeys in their lives? Is it that by focusing on those people who understand and have already experienced border crossings, ordinary mortal folk will face their own travels more easily? Well if you'll believe that, you'll believe that aliens really did land at Rothwell and that Elvis is alive and well and serving fries in Birmingham! Ask transpeople and they will tell you the truth: that trans issues are only ever of any interest at all to Joe Public if Joe's daughter announces one Sunday lunch-time that she is going to change her name to Mike. Transpeople would add that, for most academics, they simply afford an interesting route to promotion and they would go on to say that for most medical practitioners, transpeople are simply a bulging purse waiting to be opened. In fact, nobody, apart from transpeople themselves, is ever going to be interested in transpeople for their own sake, or for what they might learn from the experiences of transpeople. Transpeople may be sullied with an insanity that is both fascinating and contemptible, but they are never corporeal, tangible people whom we meet. So – in reality, an 'authentic' person is never really interested in trans, because we don't exist.

The reason 'authentic' people never meet transpeople and recognize them as real people is that we have always been programmed to pass and hence disappear. If we don't pass, we are for all time to be punished for our failure to become real. Either way we are meant to hang our heads in shame. Shame at our own incurable madness, at having the blatant, unnatural greed to actually become the desired self. Whether being burnt at the stake at the hands of the medieval church as happened to

Joan of Arc for adopting male dress, and Rolandus Ronchaiai for acting and looking like a woman, or conforming to the medical models of the 1970s – which insisted that to be a true transsexual and receive the wonderful treatments, our greatest desire must be to disappear, never telling anyone of our past – either way, whether passing or not passing, the true mark of our trans status was/is the shame we have to carry with us because we are trans.

What happened in the late 1980s and early 1990s was that some transpeople underwent a huge paradigm shift (which requires its own separate history), the result of which was that they found themselves saying 'I'm fucked off with being programmed to disappear and I'm fucked off with being ashamed because I can never truly disappear. And anyway I went through all this terrible nightmare in order to live, and now I want to live life to the full, thank you very much – and if that means that I've got to learn how to sing Gloria Gaynor songs, well so be it.' Trans visibility is as simple as that: in the past ten years, transpeople have taken their lives in their hands, they have crawled out of their closets and they have made transpeople into the big news they are today. They have taken to shoving themselves down the throats of the rest of society, not just as whores on the sidewalks of Times Square, or as the tasteful 'twin suit and pearls' ladies of middle England, nor as the Lei girls who dance in the bars of Sydney, but also as biker boys (yes, they're men as well as women!), shop assistants, radical faeries, teachers, dykes, auto mechanics, stage magicians, singers, office clerks, politicians – the list is endless.

So why have we taken to the streets? The simple answer is just that we were well and truly pissed off with, in the words of Sandy Stone, being programmed to disappear. That programming had meant that we were spat at or worse, murdered (like Chanel Picket and Brandon Teena) for failing to disappear when our five o'clock shadow showed through our Max Factor foundation late one night after a hard day in the office, or when our co-workers found out that we had a 36 DD bust under our binder, T-shirt, shirt, baggy sweater and jacket on the day the temperature hit the high 80s. If we survived all that, if we did manage to disappear, that just meant that we lived our lives in constant fear of the threat of failure – of being discovered. Our dubious civil status meant that we were always known, by somebody, somewhere – we could never hide. Our fate (worse than death) was always just around the next corner. Most of us could just hope that we would be as lucky as Billy Tipton was, that we too would be already dead before we were outed! But there comes a time when looking over your shoulder just becomes too tiring, the crick in your neck gets excruciatingly painful and any attempt will be taken to relieve it. A few of us discovered then that the first, and easiest, thing to do is to stop looking over your shoulder. Tell everyone you are a freak, bore the pants off them until they really don't want to hear anymore about it and eventually you'll get some small amount of token tolerance – not much, but it would do for starters.

That policy has proven incredibly effective. Transpeople are more visible than ever and have also become more invisible than ever – we are now commonplace and hence much less interesting as the freak show! Yet we still live in a world where we still have no objectivity and our own position is always as subject (of their study) and subjective (about our own existence). Because we are subjective we can write, but only ever our autobiographies. Because we are subjects we can only ever be studied, we can never study. This book is about creating a counter discourse, it is part of the visibility we are demanding for ourselves – the reclamation of that subjectivity. We are both studying ourselves and writing the relationship between ourselves and the writing of our studies. Yet we are also studying the others who study us, we are asking not 'Why are we so interesting?' but rather 'Why do you find us so interesting?' Many of us who have contributed, who identify as trans, have written small autobiographical pieces of ourselves within our contributions. We do this because we are all activists, we know the power of not disappearing when being trans. Within the academy, we choose not to vanish, because we choose power over fear.

The book is in three parts, but they are not cast in stone. While editing, we changed the order several times to try to give the reader a way through the subject matter. We were wary of leaving the reader grasping for the rails of a lunging ship in a storm, but we do very much want the reader to explore the wide range of essays in the book. Broadly speaking, the three parts of the book take us through the historical processes that transgender and transsexual communities have themselves undergone in developing our own particular brand of identity politics. First – finding and becoming ourselves; secondly – finding our powers as a community; and finally – challenging our own understandings.

Becoming the transperson

The first chapter looks at how legal discourses ensure that transpeople can only ever be seen within the limited terms of the binary paradigms of sex and gender, and as such they can never symbolize themselves for the law. They become an insurmountable problem, always absent; the law fails them despite its apparent egalitarian approach. The essay considers the recent legal attacks made on the trans community, and how the community has shown up the inadequacies of the law's current projects. This is followed by Jason Cromwell's reclamation of trans men's history, which includes an explanation of the default assumptions that frequently make our history invisible.

Susan Stryker's essay on Lou Sullivan provides a rewriting of the history of one of the trans men's community's most important members, alongside her rewriting of the politics surrounding the 1970s and 1980s medical provision for transpeople. In Chapter 4, Jay Prosser shows us the nature of the journey the trans person undertakes, using it to show us where trans studies currently lie – at the cusp of the postmodern project, leading but always going in a different direction. Prosser argues for our referential constancy in trans studies as the example route for all cultural studies. He shows what trans theory has to offer the academy, what we have long understood and what we daily practice.

Activism and the transgender community: becoming (trans)active

Jamison Green, currently one of the more prominent trans activists in the US, starts this part but also really ends the previous part. He illustrates the dilemmas of our subjectivity, how we are nobody, just a freak show, yet how once named we regain our humanity. This is the crux of trans activism: we become the stars of the media circus in order to lose our star status. This is followed by a section on a poorly understood, and badly under-funded, area of trans activism. HIV and AIDS have by no means missed the trans community, yet our invisibility means that we are not seen when money and resources are being allocated. We have yet to see epidemic figures within the UK trans community, but as Medicare and health service funding of any sort are increasingly withheld from transpeople (on the grounds that gender reassignment surgery is purely cosmetic surgery), then more and more trans women and trans men are taking to sex work. This is not only to survive the transition period during which they may well lose their jobs, but also to fund the cost of hormones and the increasingly expensive surgery. Sandra Laframboise and Deborah Brady write of the very personal and practical route they took to try and prevent a future HIV crisis in their community.

In Chapter 7 – an interesting comparison with Jamison Green's US chapter – Roz Kaveney, Chair of G&SA, the UK group that did the first HIV work here, looks at the routes that activism can take: whether assimilationist politics or a more radical approach would be more effective in achieving civil rights for transpeople. Finally in this section, Markisha Greaney discusses the difficulties the academy places in the way of anyone it sees as being 'too subjective'. It is an experience that many of the rest of us recognize, and illustrates all too clearly the discrimination that transpeople experience within academia – that's if they ever get the chance to participate.

Post-postmodern trans-theory: into the new millennium

The first two chapters in this part look at where trans studies are going. Henry Rubin's chapter looks at the history of social studies of the transsexual from Harold Garfinkel's study of Agnes in the late 1950s through to the trans scholarship of the 1990s, of which this book is just one example. He charts the developmental route that has taken place and in particular the influence of queer theory on trans studies. Gordene Mackenzie writes about trans representation in film and gives a clear analysis of why current gender dichotomies are inadequate for understanding transpeople.

Diane Morgan then asks a fundamental question in Chapter 11 – 'What does the transsexual want from the academy?' Through her analysis of the relationship between Freudian psychoanalysis and the biological determinist experimental surgery of Steinach, she questions the relationship that can exist between the trans person and the academy. Finally Kate More precedes her interview with Judith Butler by looking at the incestuous connection that currently exists between the academy and trans, and the failure of the academy to understand the role of activism in the development of identity.

Part One

Becoming Trans

1

The Becoming Man: The Law's Ass Brays

Stephen Whittle

I have spent 23 out of my (to date) 42 years of life being known as Stephen. Prior to my adoption of the name Stephen, regardless of the name used for me by others, in my head, my day-dreams and my plans for the future I referred to myself as Peter – a name I did not retain only because other people felt it was old-fashioned. I have a beard, I wear a jacket and tie to work – not to do so would be considered inappropriate – my partner and I have four children whom we chose to have together and they all refer to me as daddy. My driving licence, passport, library card and video-club membership have only ever referred to me in the male gender. Yet my national insurance pension scheme has only ever referred to me in the female gender. If I break the law I will go to a women's prison and to cap it all I will depart this life as Stephen Whittle, female.

I frequently face a dilemma as to how I am to refer to myself in various settings. I am all too aware that I am not like most other men. For a start, if I refer to myself as a man, am I claiming some privileged position in the patriarchy? I actually do not want to claim that position and I often do not feel very privileged, having been dismissed from jobs in the past because of my otherness. I have received hate mail and been excluded from social events both public and private. I find the fact that I cannot ensure that my compulsory employment pension contributions are passed on to my partner of twenty years standing at best demeans our relationship and at worst is an almost criminal extortion of money from me. Where is my privilege?

Furthermore I have a set of skills imbued in me as a child and teenager that other men simply do not have. Apart from sewing and household cleaning skills, I listen differently and I contribute to discussions differently. My childhood, like those of many I suppose, was unhappy, but the reasons for that unhappiness were considerably different from those of most others. I know my attitude to other people and their lifestyles is one of almost excessive tolerance, as long as it involves no harm to others. I simply do not function in life with the same assumptions that other men are afforded through their upbringing and position of privilege.

In social and medical texts, my sort of man has over time been referred to as a female urning and gynandrist (Krafft-Ebing, 1893), female transsexual (Stoller, 1975) and as a 'woman who wants to become a man' (Green, 1974). More recently the common descriptor applied to me is that of 'female to male transsexual'. This is on the basis that I was born with genitalia that are regarded as female yet I have undergone a bilateral mastectomy, I take testosterone on a regular basis and I identify myself as male. Yet am I a man? I prefer to refer to myself as a trans man – my own understanding is that I am a man who was born female-bodied and, as I explain to my children, when I was big enough and old enough I explained to other people that I really was a man and I got it sorted out. This leaves me with a personally acknowledged situation that I am a different sort of man, I am a trans man with a transsexual status.

In my status as a trans man, the UK government, because I have undergone gender reassignment, acquiesces to my request to be regarded as male (and not a man) for some social purposes but for all legal purposes I will be regarded as a woman. They choose not to make my life really difficult by making international travel or a driving test embarrassing, but they refuse to allow me many of the privileges that the law affords other men. At worst they insist that I am a woman.

It is difficult to explain what being a bearded woman means to those who have never experienced that position. If I want to take out life insurance I am forced to sit in front of an insurance broker who does not know me from Adam (or Eve for that matter) and explain that I am a woman – which always raises the eyebrows. I never ever want to lose my job because the idea of sitting in the dole office waiting for the clerk to shout out 'Miss Stephen Whittle to cubicle 6' makes me feel sick. I find it appalling that one of my children might one day have to register my death and on their return to collect the certificate will find I have been identified as Stephen Whittle, female and that they will simply become 'friend of the deceased'.

The presumption that has been taken by most academic writers in the area is that I, and people like me, are demanding that we be legally recognized in the gender role in which we live. I am not sure if that is the case, and anyway, surely the role I live in is that of a trans man. I am willing to be a different sort of man, but I am not willing to be a different sort of woman because I have never been a woman. I transitioned into living as a man when I was nineteen years old; therefore, as I often explain, on that basis I never reached the exalted state of womanhood – my experience was at most that of being a different girl. But even if I was a girl my experience was significantly different from that of other girls – ask my sisters and they will verify that. My life is different: it is the experience of being a trans man. As such, discrimination has been perpetrated on me in an entirely arbitrary manner. I have lost jobs not because I do not do them well but because my life history is that of a trans man. My partner is refused my pension not because my money is not good but because I have the life history of a trans man.

Yet I am proud to be a trans man, I have surmounted great odds in life, I have had the pleasure of experiencing life in a very unique way, I have learnt a lot about tolerance and I have learnt a lot about bravery, hard work and commitment from the many other transpeople I have met. Should it be so hard to be myself, to be a trans man – and the operative word in that is 'man'. This chapter is about being a visible trans man, about obtaining my own identity and about being recognized as myself.

The transsexual? Sex sights/sites

> Transsexuals are people whose gender identity, their sense of maleness or femaleness, differs from their anatomical sex. This clash of sex and gender may cause a transsexual much emotional pain, and they must ultimately deal with this issue in some way. (San Francisco Gender Information leaflet, 1992)

What can we learn about the nature and construction of the legal culture, and the nature and construction of gender in itself, by studying the legal problems that transpire because of the emergence of transsexuality in our society? Initially difficulties lie with the semantic understanding of the meaning of the word 'transsexual'. Simplistically, as an adjective derived from the Latin, transsexual is a purely modern term in that it did not come into existence until its creation in 1950 by a populist medical writer on the phenomenon of cross-dressing (Cauldwell, 1950). It means crossing (trans) from one sex to the other. But this makes certain a priori assumptions: that we know what 'sex' is and that we know where the crossing 'from' is made 'to'.

The term 'sex' is used to denote sites of physical difference between males and females (as in 'the male sex' and 'the female sex') and in that sense it relates not just to the human state wherein the particular reference points of those sites include complex cultural and social roles (man and woman) but also to many alternative sites that we acknowledge in other species – such as cock and hen, bull and cow. The roles that are tied to these sites are apparently clear – in any species the sites of sex are based on reproductive roles[1] – but this is by no means the whole story.

In the human species the differentiation process of becoming a man or woman is a multi-step process, involving physiological, social and cultural influences. For each step there is a window in time which is a critical phase. If the window is missed then there is no backtracking. Demonstrable brain sex differences only become manifest at three or four years post-natally in the human, and the complex make-up of gender identity is a cognitive process that presupposes language development. The orientation and type of sexual activity do not necessarily belong to one gender group or another. In animal sexology, parallels to gender cannot be found, as sex acts and reproductive roles do not in themselves reveal gender roles (Gooren, 1993: 4). However, the sexual siting of human beings within the polarized groups 'men' and 'women' is not just dependent on certain physiological aspects of the body. The major societal organizing structure, having a bearing upon access and power within public and private spheres of life, is instead related to sighting, *what we see* and the cultural constructs that we place around what we see.

In relation to humanity, throughout the written and spoken words of the law we see 'man' and 'woman' used to organize many aspects of criminal and civil life – from whether a person can be charged with infanticide through to what prison they will serve a sentence in, from the category of person one is allowed to marry through to whether one can take part in certain sports activities. The placing of individuals by the law within one of the sites of sex seems to be comparatively easy for the majority of people, but there are people who challenge the conventional paradigms: transsexual and intersex people. In English law, the problem came to a head in the 1971 case of *Corbett* v *Corbett*[2] wherein the question of sex for the purposes of marriage was decided. In a sense it embodies the problems of sights and sites.

A legal position(ing)

Corbett v *Corbett* concerned the marriage of April Ashley, a transsexual woman (male to female transsexual). On the breakdown of the marriage her husband petitioned for nullity on the grounds that:

1. the respondent remained a male and hence the marriage was void and
2. the marriage was never consummated due to the incapacity of the respondent.

The judge, Lord Ormrod, decided the case on these two issues. To determine the sex of April Ashley, Ormrod devised a test based upon three factors. Sex was to be considered through chromosomal, gonadal and genital features at the time of birth. These were established as being 'male' at the time of Miss Ashley's birth. However, rather than deciding whether she was then a man, Ormrod referred back to the 1866 decision in *Hyde* v *Hyde*[3] and held:

> Since marriage is essentially a relationship between man and woman, the validity of the marriage in this case depends, in my judgement, on whether the respondent is or is not a woman. I think with respect this is a more precise way of formulating the question than that adopted in para.2 of the petition, in which it is alleged that the respondent is male. (*Corbett* v *Corbett*, 1970: 48)

One of the problems with any analysis of Ormrod's judgment is that he constantly mixed the notions of 'male and female' with those of 'man and woman'. For example, he stated in conclusion to this question:

> the respondent is not a woman for the purposes of marriage but is a biological male and has been so since birth. (*ibid.*, p. 49)

But he did not attempt to categorize Miss Ashley as a man. He argued that marriage is a relationship based on sex rather than gender, so he really needed to consider her to be a 'man' yet could not do it. Ormrod fundamentally misunderstood the sites of sex – of male and female. He did not seem to be aware that 'man' and 'woman' are anthropomorphic signifiers, and that they relate to what we see rather than where we are situated. Almost certainly Ormrod was faced with a dilemma that arose from his being unable to define the person in front of him as a man yet he felt unable, in law and because of the test he had devised, to call her a woman.

Ormrod, because of his inability to find Miss Ashley to be a woman, declared the marriage to be void, as it was not a marriage between a man and a woman. Once he had established that the marriage was void, there was no reason for him to consider the second ground: whether the marriage could have been consummated. However, he did so, and was of the opinion that 'normal' intercourse was not possible between a post-operative male to female transsexual and a man, for the difference between that and anal intercourse was a fact 'to be measured in centimetres'. Ormrod distinguished this from the earlier judgment in *SY* v *SY* (1962)[4] in which a decree of nullity, due to failure to consummate, had been refused on the grounds that a vestigial vagina could have been corrected by forming an artificial passage. Medically there is little difference between an extended vagina as in *SY* v *SY* and a wholly artificial one as in *Corbett*, just as there is little difference in any resultant act of intercourse. There is an irony in the distinction made between the two cases, in that it would seem to have been made on the basis that SY was an imperfect woman; however, nowadays it is very likely that she would have been diagnosed as a case of testicular feminization and accordingly been discovered to be a chromosomal male – in other words she would not have been a woman for the purposes of marriage on the same basis that April Ashley was not a woman. It could therefore be argued that Ormrod misdirected himself with regard to the distinguishing facts in *Corbett*, as opposed to those in *SY* v *SY*. Furthermore the construction of an artificial vagina is not restricted to transsexuals, for some women also have reconstructive surgery in acute cases of vaginal atresia (absence or closure of a normal body orifice) before they are able to have sexual intercourse. Are these people 'not women'?

The case held that a combination of hormone treatment and surgery did not, for the purposes of matrimonial law, result in a change of sex assigned to a person at birth. The sex of a person is, in law, dependent entirely upon their gonadal, genital and chromosomal sex at birth. The decision in *Corbett* has been incredibly influential, despite being from the High Court. It has been followed as precedent in other matrimonial cases such as *Peterson* v *Peterson* (1985),[5] *Franklin* v *Franklin* (1990)[6] and in the criminal law in *R* v *Tan* (1983);[7] the UK Government has supported this definition of sex in all of the 'transsexual' cases going to the European Courts. The site you sight is not what it seems – at least not in the law.

In this chapter I want to concentrate on one of our sightings of sex, man and the group contained in the legal taxonomy 'man'. If we look at the origins of the word, in Old English it refers to an adult male. The taxonomy of male is 'that which begets offspring – performs the fecundating function'. To fecundate is to render fruitful and productive. On that basis there are many human beings, infertile men, who are afforded membership of the legal group of 'men' but who are not 'men'. Furthermore we need to consider whether the taxonomy afforded means that all people who do not perform the fecundatory role are therefore women. If you are not situated at one place are you necessarily situated in the other?

Travelling

> Incorrigible beliefs show up in research about both human and animal behaviour in various ways. A common example is the assumption underlying almost all work on sex and gender that all subjects must be male or female. This shows up in the routine practice of dividing subjects into these two groups before studying them. The very act of dividing a group of subjects in this fashion prejudices the results of any further investigation, because researchers who make this their first criterion are implicitly stating that they have already determined that there are certain sex-typed differences and that they are recognisable to them without the aid of empiricism. (Devor, 1989: 2)

Correct though Devor's assertion is that researchers invariably have an obdurate belief in a duality of biological sex types and probably also in gender roles, that does not mean to say that those views have not been challenged. Some of the most eminent thinkers of the twentieth century, such as Foucault, Lacan, Baudrillard and Derrida, have produced research and ideas that look beyond the limitations of the heteropatriachal modernistic/Enlightenment paradigm that constructs a world of dualities: man and woman, heaven and hell, good and evil, madness and sanity, health and sickness, heterosexuality and homosexuality. They have challenged those basic 'incorrigible beliefs' and shattered their assumptions. In this chapter the duality of man and woman (or male and female) is addressed, and this will inevitably also call into question other dualities that co-exist alongside this notion.

The ethnocentricity of Western culture's two-sex/two-gender model is revealed through the work of many anthropologists and sociologists (see Chapters 2 and 9); this work is reinforced by the many examples in our own culture of individuals who counter the truth of the paradigm. But the duality exists as a controlling paradigm such that you cannot be situated outside of it, so within it a transsexual travels from one site to another. We cross a boundary of the imagination, a 'not really in existence border' – but, as we shall see, significant numbers of people, apart from transsexuals, do not fit within the sites of sex. To complicate matters, physically intersex people (as currently recognized by medicine) make up 2 per cent [8] of the population. Does that mean they are not in existence because they have no site in which they belong? But the physical is by no means the whole story.

Gender as it is perceived by others is called gender role. Gender identity is the total perception of an individual about his or her own gender. It includes a basic personal identity as a boy or girl, man or woman, as well as personal judgements about the individual's level of conformity to the societal norms of masculinity and femininity. The two concepts are tied together, since most people show their perceptions of themselves in their dress, manners and activities. Clothing is the major public signifier of gender that allows other people to immediately identify an individual's gender role through what they see, but there are other signifiers as well, such as mannerisms and occupational choice. For most people their gender role along with their gender identity and all the symbolic manifestations of gender will be congruent. But transpeople do not necessarily feel that they fit neatly into either the male or female role or that their behaviour is totally congruent with the rules and expectations of the society they live in.

Gender identity, it has been argued, is in fact the result of a complex interaction among three factors:

1. A sex-derivative grade, associated with genetics and hormones. An example would be the general strength differences between males and females.
2. Sex adjunctive differences, not directly associated with hormones, but with their sex-derived effects. For example the division of labour that arose from the physiological need of women to be homebound in order to breastfeed, etc.
3. Sex arbitrary differences related to issues of power and social position. For example the use of cosmetics and clothing, or the difference in access to particular activities. (Money, 1988: 77–8)

That complex interaction means that it is no longer possible to argue that either nature or nurture alone is the answer to the trans person's sense of self; it is clear that all three factors are involved in producing the complex person we call a man or a woman. The physical distinction between men and women is not absolute, as individuals are now

scientifically regarded as living on a continuum with female characteristics at one extreme and male ones at the other. This may result from
physical, psychological or social mismatches. The word 'transsexual' is
increasingly considered a misnomer, particularly by transsexuals themselves. Being transsexual is not related to any aspect of sexual activity
for the individuals who identify as such, as the physicians who treat
such people recognize; nor has it anything to do with 'crossing over',
since transsexuals and their doctors increasingly express the view that
the transsexual was always of the gender they now wish to confirm. As
early as 1967, in his foreword to Christine Jorgensen's biography,
Harry Benjamin, who pioneered research into transsexualism, was
casting doubt on the idea that transsexuals underwent sex reassignment
treatment. Rather, he forecast a view that would be upheld today by
many transsexuals: that they sought out gender confirmation treatment.
He says of Christine (who commenced living as a woman in 1952, at the
age of 26):

> But was this female gender role really new? The vivid description of
> her early life supplies a negative answer. This was a little girl, not a
> boy (in spite of the anatomy) who grew up in this remarkably sound
> and normal family. (Jorgenson, 1963: vii)

Yet the words 'transsexual' and 'sex reassignment' persist.

As we have seen, the classification of men and women, in everyday
life, follows both biological and social mechanisms. But the legal
classification (except in rare exceptions which I will refer to later) arises
solely from a biological classificatory process (*Corbett* v *Corbett*)
undertaken in a determinatory manner.

Seeing through Justice's blindfold

In 1985 Katherine O'Donovan (1985: 64–9) argued that the judicial
task of sex determination has been developed along two routes: the
essentialist approach, and the cluster approach. In the essentialist
approach the court looks to one essential feature and assigns all
individuals biologically to either the female sex or the male sex through
that feature (see Corbett v *Corbett* and the Australian case concerning
an intersexual, *C and D*[9]). The current test is one of considering three
factors only: genital, gonadal and chromosomal sex at birth. Psychological or behavioural sex is not considered relevant. However, this
apparently comprehensive test is fundamentally flawed. The reality is

that at birth, for the majority of babies it is purely genital sex (determined by the casual glance of a midwife) that is used as the determining factor of sex siting. As we have already seen, the Australian case of *SY* v *SY* referred to the status of an individual born without a vagina, yet she was to be considered a woman. What of those apparent women of whom it is discovered in later life that they have an XY chromosome base and yet androgen insensitivity has prevented the development of descended testes and a penis?

The essentialist approach is plainly inadequate and leads to a range of inaccurate sex designations, as we do not at the time of birth test the chromosomal make-up of infants, nor do we do more than a cursory examination of genitals, and we have no idea whether a child has ovaries. Currently medicine recognizes over 70 different intersex syndromes and one in every 200 children will be born with some sort of intersex matrix. For some this will never be discovered, whereas for others it will only be discovered when they attend a fertility treatment clinic in later life as they struggle to have their own children. Furthermore the work at the Netherlands Brain Bank on brain sex determination has indicated that transsexual people should possibly be included in the range of physical intersex syndromes as it supports the hypothesis that there is a brain sex difference between men and women and transsexuals have the brain sex of that gender group to which they maintain they belong (Zhou *et al.*, 1995). The essentialist approach is unable to take on board complex science that would involve being able to determine a person's sex grouping only after they were dead and their brain available for dissection.

In an attempt to deal with the complex issues involved in determining sex, some courts have developed the cluster approach, which looks to a group of similar features that then suggest that the individual fits into one sex site or another. We have seen this approach in the European Court of Human Rights cases of *D. Van Oosterwijk* v *Belgium*[10] and *B* v *France*,[11] as well as in the High Court in New Jersey in the family law case of *MT* v *JT*,[12] and several other US states. This approach allows concepts of behavioural sex or psychological sex such as masculinity or maleness to appear within the legal matrix. This approach may allow sex classification according to psychological features as well as physiological features, and may also allow personal choice to dictate rather than ascription. But it has only recently been accepted for sex determination in relation to marriage, or other areas where sex has been found to be an essential element, and only then in very limited circumstances.

We can see these limits in various jurisdictions. In Germany and Ontario in particular, the requirement in the legislation that some surgery be undergone in relation to gender reassignment before an individual is afforded status in their new sex role has led to questions in the courts concerning to what extent surgical reassignment has taken place, particularly in the case of female-to-male transsexuals. Michael Wills mentions the case of *OLG Zweibruken*, [13] concerning a female-to-male transsexual, which asks whether in order to achieve what the law calls a 'clear approximation' to the opposite sex, a bilateral mastectomy will be sufficient, or is genital surgery that includes vaginal occlusion and phalloplasty required? The case has been decided in two lower courts in favour of the female-to-male transsexual applicant, but again the state representative has appealed (Wills, 1993). Currently an application is before the Quebec courts in which a transsexual man has been refused permission to have his identity documentation changed because he refuses to undergo vaginal occlusion. [14]

In two Canadian cases, *C(L)* v *C(C)* (1992)[15] and *B* v *A* (1990),[16] female-to-male transsexuals were held not to be spouses/husbands for the purposes of marriage and family law, if the only surgery they had undergone was a bilateral mastectomy and a hysterectomy. The courts, both in Ontario, followed the doctrine in *Corbett* v *Corbett*. In *B* v *A* the parties had lived together for twenty years and on that basis had applied for a motion of financial support. Though the female-to-male transsexual (FTM) had had birth records changed from female to male, the courts held that the requirements for surgery of the Registrar-General were not the same as those required to decide if a relationship was one of husband and wife. The failure to undergo genital surgery on the part of an FTM transsexual would mean that he continued to be female and hence could not marry another female. *C(L)* v *C(C)* followed this line of thinking, and it was held that the marriage the two parties had undergone was a nullity and was void *ab initio*.

As can be seen, even in this approach there is a presumption that the law distinguishes between the private sphere of gender, and the public sphere of sex definition. Notwithstanding, in both approaches, the essentialist and the cluster, the law operates on the assumption that the two sexes are separate entities with distinct sites. Concern may be expressed that errors may be made using the essentialist approach or simply that it is inhumane, similarly that the cluster approach simply does not follow its own logic, but the premise that certain areas of the law should be organized around sexual differentiation is not queried. There are still two distinct categories – man and woman.

Tackling sex site/sight discrimination

Because there are these two categories and obvious social inequities have resulted, the law has responded by taking one of two routes. The first has been an egalitarian approach wherein it is attempted to remove all gendered/sex values from the law, what one might term the 'all men are equal' syndrome of the American Bill of Rights. In this approach we attempt to write the law as if it is unsexed or as if any sex designation holds some sort of equal value. One example of this approach exists in an obscure section of the Road Traffic Offenders Act 1988, S 25, ss 2.b (which deals with offences requiring disqualification from driving). It states:

1. If on convicting a person of an offence involving obligatory or discretionary disqualification or of such other offence as may be prescribed by regulations under section 105 of the Road Traffic Act 1988 the court ...
2. Does not know the person's sex, the court must order the person to give that information to the court in writing.
3. A person who knowingly fails to comply with an order under [the above] subsection is guilty of an offence.

One may ask what relevance it is to the court what a person's sex is in these cases. Driving disqualification has nothing to do with sex and vice-versa. But, as this is an egalitarian approach, regardless of the sex you have not disclosed, you will have committed an offence and face a fine on conviction.

The second route is that of the interventionist approach wherein we admit that 'all men are not equal', but the law will ensure instead that there is equal opportunity and equal treatment for members of different groups. The law is used in an attempt to control undesirable results of the socio-economic and political values that we give to gender and sex. Such approaches rarely attempt to provide total equality and instead limit their concern to areas deemed appropriate for the law's involvement. This is the approach of anti-discrimination legislation such as the Sex Discrimination Act 1975, wherein we provide a legal stick and judicial remedies to try to smooth out inequalities, but its involvement in social life is limited to the areas of employment, vocational training, housing and the provision of goods and services. So it becomes legal to have a stag night but not to exclude women from a motor mechanics course.

Throughout the law in many jurisdictions, we in fact see no single clearly consistent approach being taken. The two approaches frequently work alongside each other. This lack of consistency in legal approach arises, initially, because ostensibly egalitarian gestures are compromised from the start as in the statement 'all men are equal'. The supposedly neutral subject of law does not yet exist within egalitarian approaches to the law: he is both sexed and gendered male. Women are conceptualized on the basis of masculine parameters and in practice they are simply 'not men' and as such do not exist within an egalitarian approach to the law, hence the need for an interventionist approach in which their existence is at least acknowledged though it becomes objectified as different.

Living in outer space

For the feminist French analyst and linguist Luce Irigaray (1977), to have an identity that is not one's own, to be a sex that is not one, is to be excluded from the fullness of being – it is to be left precisely in a condition of dereliction. One is excluded, therefore, from the social contract within which men participate. A Rousseauesque design of the social contract inevitably fails because the abstract individual of liberal democratic theory is, as Patemen (1989) has shown, in fact a man. Irigaray is referring to women as women, women who never have their own identity. A woman's identity is defined through the social and cultural persona, women are in society but not of society. This could be seen as an echo of women in law: a woman is objectified through interventionist law, she never is the law. As such, the egalitarian project of law is doomed through its own history, and the interventionist project in law is doomed through its further objectification. Both deal in a mythical equivalency. The question is then whether there is any other form of project that can address the issue of the inadequacies of sexed/ gendered law. I would argue that the site of the trans man informs and addresses this project.

See the word for the trees

John Locke asserted in relation to the law that:

> the use of words is to be the sensible mark of ideas; and the ideas they stand for are their proper and immediate signification. (in Douzinas *et al.*, 1991: 228)

To what extent is the egalitarian project of the words in the Road

Traffic Offender's Act 1988 (RTOA) a 'sensible mark of ideas'. In the RTOA it becomes a separate offence not to acknowledge a sex classification for yourself. Is this the same thing as giving a legally incorrect classification or is the choice of sex yours, as long as you give one? Do you have to give the one that the court would recognize, and anyhow do you know what system the court would use to recognize it?

If we consider the situation of the androgen-insensitive woman, I (and medicine) refer to her as a woman, yet do we know for the purposes of the law whether she is a woman, or whether she is a man? Is the classification the one afforded on her birth certificate, that is based on a cursory glance by a midwife to see whether there is a penis or not (midwives do not actually look to see whether there is a vagina or not) – in other words part of a process that simply asserts whether someone is a 'man' or a 'not man'? Or should the law follow Ormrod's three-point test devised in *Corbett* – on that basis her chromosomes would be XY, her gonads would be undescended testes and her genitalia would include a vagina? In the civil law therefore, if the court uses the balance of probabilities test, used for ascertaining evidential proof, I suspect she would be found to be a man on a 2 : 1 preponderance. However, in the criminal court if we were to have to prove her sex, say for an offence involving soliciting, would the evidential burden of 'beyond all reasonable doubt' mean that the court would be left with no sex site that they could place this woman in?

As UK law currently stands, the transsexual man if born in Britain would be legally classified as a woman for the purposes of marriage,[17] the criminal law,[18] Social Security and National Insurance benefits,[19] immigration[20] and parenting.[21] For the purposes of employment he would be afforded the special status of transsexual woman,[22] which simply means a woman with special protection for having an identity peccadillo. If the trans man were born outside of Britain then his identity in each of these areas of the law would be dependent upon the nation state he was born in.[23] Yet the trans man would be classified on his driving licence (through the codification system) as a man. But what if the trans man is required to give his 'sex' to the court as he is facing a driving disqualification? Presumably the purpose of that disclosure is to ensure that the driving licence records of the correct person are marked up. Should he say he is a man or male, or should he say he is a woman or female? What is the requirement of the law, which would ensure that the correct person had his or her driving records amended? It is no defence to a criminal act to argue that you had no knowledge of the law, or that you did not understand it. Where lies Locke's 'sensible mark of ideas'? The logic of the law is truly at times an ass.[24]

We must accept that there are many problem areas in the law, yet striving to improve it is one of the fundamental demands of justice. There is a need to re-theorize law away from its current notional equivalency projects such as are embodied in the egalitarian definition of rape in S 142 of the Criminal Justice and Public Order Act (1994), wherein the courts had to ask whether a trans woman's vagina was a body orifice or not, or the interventionist approach of the Sex Discrimination Act 1975, in which if you fall outside the man/woman categories you are not protected. These projects simply highlight the lack that is embodied in the law.

The becoming man

The becoming man of this paper is a parody of Irigaray's notion of the becoming woman. Women in order to constitute themselves as truly social beings need to be able to represent themselves as themselves, they have to overcome the deficit of women unsymbolized as woman, they have to become woman. Similarly the project currently being undertaken by trans men is to overcome the deficit of the trans man unsymbolized as the trans man. Though the Rousseauesque social contract has produced the identity of collectivity by raising the 'I' (the individual) to the power of the homogeneous 'we', the multi-community experience derived through the identity politics of contemporary societies challenges this by effectively proposing an 'identity' that is not just logically based but is empirically and experientially based – the equivalent of the subject in psychoanalysis and postmodernism. The transgender/transsexual community is undertaking a post-postmodernist reconstruction of the self not only through theory but also through activism and its resultant inter-relationship with the law.

Of many possible examples I would like to discuss two legal challenges presented by the transsexual community to the European Courts. The first is the case of *P v S and Cornwall County Council*,[25] which was decided at the European Court of Justice in April 1996. *P v S* concerned discrimination against a transsexual employee. The European Court of Justice was asked whether discrimination against an employee because they were transsexual was contrary to the provisions contained in the 1975 Equal Treatment Directive of the European Economic Council. The court held that it was illegal to discriminate against an individual because they were undergoing gender reassignment. The result is that it is irrelevant whether P is a man or a woman, if her status is that of a transsexual man or woman then that is one 'ground of sex'. This does not mean therefore that she is outside of either the egalitarian or the interventionist approaches, but that she is contained within both – she is afforded equality because of her humanity and protection because of her difference.

The second concerns the case of *X,Y and Z* v *UK Government*,[26] which was decided in the European Court of Human Rights in April 1997. The case addressed the issue of 'fatherhood'. Fatherhood lies very close to that initial taxonomy of 'man', the person who performs the fecundatory function – yet fatherhood is increasingly becoming merely a social construction rather than a biological relationship in many circumstances. Addressing the provisions in the Human Fertilisation and Embryology Act (HFEA), the case concerned a transsexual man whose female partner gave birth to a child conceived using donor insemination, at a clinic licensed under the HFEA Authority. The paramount concern of the clinic, in the provision of treatment, must be the welfare of the child according to the regulations. The clinic, however, is obliged where a woman has a male partner to obtain the signature of that partner to a statement that he will for all legal purposes be the father of the child (to ensure that if couples later separate, the child will have a father to financially maintain it under the provisions of the Child Support Act 1991). X (rather than using the common, secretive, approach taken by many transsexual men in such circumstances) formally applied to the Registrar-General for Births and Deaths for permission to be recorded on the child's birth certificate as its father. Permission was refused on the basis that X is legally a woman, and a woman cannot be recorded as a father. Thus we see the inherent failure of both the egalitarian and interventionist approaches. Women are not equal with men and cannot be fathers, nor are they allowed the protection of the law to enable them to have the things that men are given including fatherhood.

Unlike other approaches to the European Court of Human Rights, X was not asking to be a man in law, but rather to be afforded the title 'father' as a transsexual man. He sought to become symbolized as the transsexual man – to be as other men, yet different, using the egalitarian approach, or to be symbolized as father despite being woman, using the interventionist approach. The question is one of being ascribed by the law, then of being transcribed by the law – of being written for the trans man. The European Court of Human Rights found against the applicants on two grounds. First, that there is no common consensus throughout the countries who are signatories to the European Convention on Human Rights as to whether a non-biological man can be registered as the father of a donor-inseminated child; therefore the court maintained that there must still be a wide margin of appreciation for states to act as they think fit. The second ground, however, is far more problematic. Currently the transsexual man in UK law is a 'not man' – therefore he is a woman, and the court decided that if they gave the transsexual man the status of father they would be creating a massive contradiction within the law. Can a father be a 'not man' or would a father then become 'man'? Interestingly, the court found that there was a *de facto* family relationship between the applicants, yet they failed to define the family relationships between the transsexual man and his partner or the child, leaving a highly unsatisfactory result – a family which is beyond our definition, unsymbolized and therefore not in existence.

This mirrors the failure of the law's project. Justice cannot be achieved if, for example, it becomes impossible to inscribe one's self in the letter to the court in which one has to disclose one's sex under the RTOA. That is because, in the law as it is, the self does not belong to the self. We are all inscribed onto the homogeneous 'man' without any precursors, such as masculinity or maleness: all that is required is the penis as seen by the midwife. The rest of us who lack merely become derivations. I am not trying to valorize an incommunicable mental state, or an essential trans man. But the process of becoming the trans man in law rather than the man in law is a direct counter discourse to the objectification of man by his own mechanisms. The place created undermines the essentialist approach of the judiciary, and although it bows to the cluster approach it moves beyond either by demanding a new site, a place in outer space but within the law. In his preface to *The Order of Things* Foucault says:

> Strangely enough, man – the study of whom is supposed by the naive to be the oldest investigation since Socrates is probably no more than a kind of rift in the order of things, or in any case, a configuration whose outlines are determined by the new position he has so recently taken up in the field of knowledge ... It is comforting, however, and a source of profound relief to think that man is only a recent invention, a figure not yet 2 centuries old, a new wrinkle in our knowledge, and that he will disappear again as soon as knowledge has discovered a new form. (Foucault, 1994: xxiii)

So I am aiming to become a mere wrinkle in our knowledge, but I would like to become before I disappear. What is a 'becoming man'? The dictionary says: a man who is 'befitting, that is: proper and right, who graces, adorns and embellishes, gratifies and delights our lives'. I think I do that quite successfully and I would rather not become a lost opportunity for the law.

Notes

1. Reproductive roles do not necessarily indicate reproductive capabilities in the individual within a species, as there are always significant numbers within any species who cannot reproduce for the reasons of age and fertility.
2. *Corbett* v *Corbett* [1970] 2 All ER 33.
3. *Hyde* v *Hyde* [1866] LR 1 P&D 130.
4. *SY* v *SY* [1962] 3 All E.R. 55, CA.
5. *Peterson* v *Peterson* [1985] *The Times*, 12 July.
6. *Franklin* v *Franklin* [1990] *The Scotsman*, 9 November.
7. *R* v *Tan and others* [1983] 2 All E.R. 12.
8. This figure comes from the home pages of the North American Intersex Society, *http://www.isna.org/*
9. *C and D* (Aus) (1979) F.L.C. 90–636.
10. *D. Van Oosterwijk* v *Belgium* (A/40) [1981] 3 E.H.R.R. 557.
11. *B* v *France* (A/232-C) [1993] 16 E.H.R.R. 1.
12. *MT* v *JT* [1977] 140 N.J. Super. 77.
13. *OLG Zweibruken* [1992] 47–53.
14. The transsexual man concerned refuses this surgery for several reasons, two of which are: he is concerned that his ability to obtain sexual pleasure will be curtailed by such extensive surgery, and he wishes to retain the tissues involved in case he chooses to undergo phalloplasty in the future and the tissues are needed for a urinary tract hook-up.
15. *C(L)* v *C(C)* [1992] Ont C.J Lexis 1518.
16. *B* v *A* [1990] 2 R.F.L (3d) 258.
17. *Corbett* v *Corbett* [1970] 2 All ER 33.
18. *R* v *Tan and others* [1983] 2 All ER 12.
19. *Sheffield* v *UK* Government Applic. No 22985/93 (1993) E.C.H.R.
20. *Horsham* v *UK* Government Applic. No 23390/94 (1994) E.C.H.R.
21. *X, Y and Z* v *UK* Government [1997] 75/1995/581/667 E.C.H.R.
22. *M* v *The Chief Constable of the West Midlands Police* (1996) 04/430/064.
23. For example, if born in Ontario, Canada, he would be a man for the purposes of immigration into Britain, yet he would be a woman for the purposes of marriage (see the comments earlier in this chapter on the cases of *C(L)* v *C(C)* (1992) and *B* v *A* (1990)). If born in Holland he would be a man for all purposes except (probably) the criminal law.

24. In 1981 I had my driving licence stolen. I reported it to the police and applied for a replacement. The civil service department that issued licences then went on strike. A few weeks later I was stopped for having a broken rear light on my car, and was charged with failing to produce my driving licence. During this period I received confirmation from the Driving Licence Authority that I was licensed to drive while awaiting my replacement licence. But it is an offence not to produce your licence when asked by a police officer, so I was convicted and fined. Some time later my licence was discovered by the police to have been in the police station during the said period, having been brought in among a large haul of stolen goods. I appealed on the basis of my licence having already been in police possession. My appeal was turned down *because I had not produced the licence*.
25. *P* v *S and Cornwall County Council* [1996] ICR 795.
26. *X,Y and Z* v *UK Government* [1997] ECHR 75/1995/581/667.

References

Cauldwell, D.O. (1950) *Questions and Answers on the Sex Lives and Sexual Problems of Trans-Sexuals*. New York: Haldeman-Julias.

Devor, H. (1989) *Gender Blending*. Bloomington: Indiana University Press.

Douzinas C., R. Warrington and S. McVeigh (1991) *Postmodern Justice: The Law of Text in the Texts of the Law*. London: Routledge.

Foucault, M. (1994) *The Order of Things*. London: Routledge.

Gooren, L.J.G. (1993) 'Biological aspects of transsexualism and their relevance to its legal aspects.' Paper presented at the Twenty-third Colloquy on European Law of the Council of Europe, Amsterdam.

Green, R. (1974) *Sexual Identity Conflict*. London: Duckworth.

Irigaray, L. (1977) *This Sex Which Is Not One*. New York: Cornell University Press (Trans. C. Porter and C. Burke (1988)).

Jorgensen, C. (1963) *A Personal Autobiography*. New York: Eriksson.

Krafft-Ebing, R. (1893) *Psycopathia Sexualis*. London: F.A Davis.

Money, J. (1988) *Gay, Straight and In-Between*. New York: Oxford University Press.

O'Donovan, K. (1985) *Sexual Divisions in the Law*. London: Weidenfeld and Nicolson.

Pateman, C. (1989) *The Disorder of Women: Democracy, Feminism and Political Theory*. Cambridge: Polity Press.

Stoller, R.J. (1975) *The Transsexual Experiment*. London: The Hogarth Press.

Wills, M.R. (1993) 'Legal conditions of sex reassignment by medical intervention: situation in comparative law.' Paper presented at the Twenty-third Colloquy on European Law of the Council of Europe, Amsterdam.

Zhou, J., M. Hofman, L. Gooren and D. Swaab (1995) 'A sex difference in the human brain and its relation to transsexuality', *Nature*, **378** (2 November): 68–70.

2

Passing Women and Female-bodied Men: (Re)claiming FTM History

Jason Cromwell

> Clothes play a key part in our acts of self-presentation, whether we like it or not – or recognize it – or not. (Wilson, 1990: 67)
>
> ... clothing is a necessary condition of subjectivity – that in articulating the body, it simultaneously articulates the psyche. (Silverman, 1986: 147; cited in Wilson, 1990: 69)

Females who have lived as men are often erased by androcentric, phallocentric and biological deterministic arguments, and most often subsumed under the rubric of lesbianism. This chapter provides a number of cases from the existing literature and analyses the arguments that have made and continue to make female-bodied men invisible.[1]

Based on a search of the literature, most researchers conclude that female-bodied individuals who lived as men did so for two primary reasons: socio-economic, such as better paying jobs and male privilege (Vicinus, 1992: 473; Wheelwright, 1990: 19; Friedli, 1987: 234; Perry, 1987: 96); and as a cover for their lesbianism (Friedli, 1987: 235; Vicinus, 1992: 474; Wheelwright, 1990: 19). However, many of these theorists are perplexed by female-bodied people who continued to live as men following the end of their war service or upon being discovered. For example, Martha Vicinus states: 'More troubling, because more difficult to place, were those women who either appeared "mannish" or continued to cross-dress after the wars were over' (1992: 474). The basis for their conundrum is an inability to conceive of a third possibility: female-bodied people who had a personal identity as men.

I propose that there are three types of females who lived as men: (1) those who did so for short-term gain or adventure; (2) those who did so for love; and (3) those who identified as men. There is an extensive history of all three types in the available literature. However, by leaving out the last category or by subsuming it within the other categories, the historical forerunners of contemporary FTMs (female-to-males) are made invisible or, at the very least, their motivations are obscured by resorting to socio-economic arguments and the presumption of lesbianism. If categories are limited, then those who do not fit are considered perplexing and become unauthorized beings (after Schafer, 1974: 478 cited in Magee and Miller, 1992: 69). In the following I present a number of examples from the historical literature of all three unauthorized types of female-bodied individuals.[2]

Transvestic opportunists: soldiers, sailors, pirates, criminals and frauds

Rudolf Dekker and Lotte van de Pol have documented '119 "women living as men" in the Netherlands between 1550 and 1839' (1989: xi). The majority (83) were female soldiers or sailors (*ibid.*: 9), another 22 joined the 'land army' and the remainder were civilians (*ibid.*: 10). Such individuals were able to enlist because physical examinations were not required (Wheelwright, 1990: 120). Nonetheless, the possibility of discovery in the military was extremely high (Dekker and van de Pol, 1989: 9), which leads to the observation that:

> Many archives have been lost and many others have not been researched. Moreover, we do not know how many cross-dressers left no trail behind them in written source-material. We can make a guess that this especially concerns those women who transformed themselves so successfully that they were never unmasked. For these reasons, we presume that our 119 cases are only the tip of the iceberg (*ibid.*: 3.)

In a similar vein, Julie Wheelwright states:

> It is impossible to know how many women actually chose to live as men by adopting male clothing and assuming a 'masculine' occupation throughout British history. Only those women whose identity was discovered or who, for various reasons, publicly surrendered their masquerade have come to light. (Wheelwright, 1990: 6)

Various authors have noted a number of anonymous persons who were discovered upon their deaths to have been female-bodied. Magnus Hirschfeld commented that this was a mark of their success (1966: 220). Unfortunately, their motivations for living as men will never be known. Those who were 'discovered' provided various motivations (or in many cases these were presumed) for living as men: a desire to remain with their husbands, to search for them, or to avoid detection while travelling in dangerous areas; encouragement by other people; poverty; patriotism; adventure; and a belief that it was their 'nature' (Dekker and van de Pol, 1989: 25–7). 'The decision to start dressing as a man was never for one reason alone' (*ibid.*: 27). In many cases there may have been a multiplicity of reasons.

Julie Wheelwright (1990) has documented 20 cases extensively, and referred to 35 others, of females living as males in Europe (primarily England), Russia and the United States. As the title of her book – *Amazons and Military Maids* – indicates, the majority were soldiers or sailors, some of whom kept their 'secret', and others who acknowledged that they were females throughout their military life.

One example of the latter case is Flora Sandes, who attained the rank of captain in the Serbian Army during a nationalist uprising. Sandes was born in 1876 in England (*ibid.*: 34). She originally signed on as a nurse at the age of 38, but within a couple of years was a soldier (*ibid.*: 35). Following her retirement from the army, Sandes, wearing her military uniform, carried on a lecture tour with tales of her experiences to Great Britain, Australia, New Zealand, France, Canada and the United States (*ibid.*: 103–8).

Numerous cases abound of those female soldiers and sailors who kept their secret or only revealed it when they felt it had become absolutely necessary. Among them are Christian Davies, Hannah Snell, Mary Anne Talbot, Mary Read, Anne Bonny, Emma Edmonds and Loreta Janeta Velazquez.

Christian Davies was born in 1667 in Dublin. It is conjectured that she was probably impressed by her father's friend, Captain Bodeaux, a Frenchman who was mortally wounded in battle and was subsequently discovered to be female (Thompson, 1974; Wheelwright, 1990). It seems that Davies inadvertently inherited a urinary device from Captain Bodeaux, which was a 'silver tube painted over, and fastened about her with leather straps'. (Prior to serving as a soldier, Davies married Richard Welch and gave birth to two children. Following her husband's sudden unexplained disappearance, Davies, leaving her children with her mother, dressed in her husband's clothes and joined the army as Christopher Welch. During her service Davies was wounded by gunshot; captured by the French along with 60 others, all of whom were exchanged for French prisoners; and engaged in a duel in which she wounded her opponent and was jailed for her offence. In 1703, Davies was seriously wounded in the leg and was nearly discovered during treatment. After twelve years in the army, Davies finally found her husband. She asked him to keep her secret and to treat her as his brother. While they fought side by side, Davies was struck by shrapnel that resulted in a skull fracture and a period of unconsciousness during which she was discovered to have a female body. She and Richard were reunited as husband and wife after a set of 'suitable' clothes were rounded up. She travelled with him in the army until his death, whereupon she returned to Dublin. Once home she gained notoriety as a female soldier. Davies died at 108 years of age and was ceremoniously buried with military honours.

Some female soldiers turned their notoriety into profitable stage and business careers. One such was Hannah Snell who was born in 1723. Like Davies, Snell took off in men's clothes in pursuit of her husband, who had abandoned her while she was pregnant with their first child (seven months after birth the child died) (Thompson, 1974; Wheelwright, 1990). After she ran out of money, Snell sought employment and eventually joined a regiment of soldiers as James Gray. Fearing discovery by someone she recognized, she deserted. She then enrolled as a marine on a ship headed for the East Indies. After arriving at the Cape of Good Hope, the crew marched as soldiers and were engaged in several battles. she was wounded in both legs and the groin. Not wanting 'her sex' discovered by the company surgeon, Snell told 'her secret [to a] negress whom she had befriended' and who aided in treating Snell's wounds. Snell eventually ascertained that her husband had been killed and returned to London. During a drunken moment 'she revealed the secret of her sex' to a former crew mate who, despite his promise, spread 'the story'. In need of money, Snell decided to use this to her advantage and took the tales of her career to the stage. After tiring of performing, Snell again took up men's clothes and bought a 'public house ... for which she had a signboard painted ... [and] inscribed: The Widow in Masquerade or the Female Warrior'. Snell died after a period of physical and mental ill-health in 1792.

Another female soldier who gained a modicum of notoriety was Mary Anne Talbot, who was born in 1778. In 1792, her guardian, Captain Bowen, was ordered back to his regiment and insisted that

Talbot accompany him dressed in men's clothes, calling her John Taylor (Thompson, 1974; Wheelwright, 1990). Bowen 'compelled' Talbot to enrol as a drummer in his regiment. During a siege, Talbot was wounded in the chest and back, but fearing exposure she treated herself. Captain Bowen was killed during battle and Talbot, who was determined to escape, secured a sailor's uniform and deserted. Unable to secure other work, she shipped out on a French ship in 1793. The ship and crew were captured by the British. Talbot told the ship's admiral her tale and he put her on another ship sailing to England. The admiral kept 'her secret' and Talbot sailed as a 'powder-boy,' later becoming the captain's 'principal cabin-boy' (Thompson, 1974: 88). During an engagement, Talbot was wounded in the thigh and hip, but because of the number of injured, escaped detection during a cursory examination by the ship's surgeon. Along with the other wounded, Talbot was shipped to a hospital. After four months recuperation Talbot 'was drafted as a midshipman'. The ship was attacked by French pirates, Talbot and others were captured and imprisoned. She was held prisoner for over 18 months. In 1776, following her release Talbot shipped out as a steward on an American merchant ship destined for New York. After returning to England, Talbot was accosted by a 'press-gang', and because she was without proper papers and wanted to escape, she revealed 'her sex' (ibid.: 91). She returned to her ship and also confessed to the captain, who wished to retain her services, but she declined, disembarked and returned to London. Although Talbot was advised to 'wear female dress and give up masculine habits' she continued to wear her sailor's clothes. Talbot then began to gain some notoriety as a female sailor. She worked as a jeweller and joined 'a lodge of the Odd Fellows [none of whom] knew their new member was a woman' (ibid.: 93–4). In 1797, a woman began passing herself off as John Taylor. A magistrate who knew of Talbot's whereabouts (a hospital), sent for her to confront the impostor, who was duly imprisoned. After her discharge from the hospital Talbot began wearing women's clothes. She took up parts acting on stage for a time. She was later imprisoned for debts and upon her release became a domestic servant. She died in 1808.

Not all females who lived as men received accolades for their deeds. Two such were the female pirates, Mary Read and Ann Bonny. Mary Read was raised as a boy in order to deceive her mother's mother-in-law, who gave money for the child's maintenance (Thompson, 1974). At the age of thirteen, Read was put in service as a footboy for a French-woman. When she reached the age of maturity she became a 'hand on board' a warship and later enlisted in a foot regiment in Flanders. She failed to gain a commission and transferred to a horse regiment. While with this regiment she fell in love with a Fleming comrade to whom she revealed 'her sex' (*ibid.*: 71). When the 'campaign was over' she returned wearing a dress, they were married and they opened an 'eating house', prospering until her husband's death. When money ran out she took up men's clothes again and joined a foot regiment in Holland. Unable to gain a promotion 'she took her discharge from the regiment' and boarded a ship sailing to the West Indies. During the voyage the ship was boarded by pirates, and Read was captured and taken to the Bahamas where she settled for a time. She later joined a ship on an expedition to rout Spaniards. On this ship, Read met up with Anne Bonny to whom she 'confided the secret of her sex' (*ibid.*: 73). Read also revealed 'her sex' to a young prisoner she had fallen in love with. They were later married and continued to sail with Captain Rackham.

Anne Bonny was Captain Rackham's lover, who felt threatened by her friendship with Read. To appease him, Bonny revealed Read's secret to him, which 'he carefully kept secret' (*ibid.*: 73–4). Bonny was born in Ireland and as a child had moved to America with her family. She secretly married a sailor she had fallen in love with and, as a consequence, her father disowned her. Her husband abandoned her when he realized she would not inherit her father's money and property. She met Captain Rackham and agreed to go with him to sea and to do so she 'was obliged to dress in men's clothes so as to keep her sex concealed' from the crew. When she became pregnant she was put to shore and after giving birth rejoined Captain Rackham. In 1720 their ship was attacked by the Jamaican Governor's 'armed sloop'. Bonny and Read were captured along with the rest of Rackham's crew. All were tried for piracy and sentenced to death. Read died before the planned execution 'could be carried out'. Bonny was spared execution after revealing that she was female but, nonetheless, died in prison.

Beyond piracy, other females who lived as men seemed to have equally dubious motivations, sometimes including fraud. One such case is that of Valerie Arkell-Smith who went by the name of Colonel Victor Barker. Arkell-Smith never joined the military but seems to have chosen the appellation of 'Colonel' to gain status. According to Wheelwright (1990), Arkell-Smith successfully lived as a man for six years as Barker before she was arrested on a 'bankruptcy charge' and remanded to prison in the late 1920s. Upon her release Arkell-Smith resumed masculine attire and, although Wheelwright claims that she also had lesbian relationships, Barker had told her wife Elfrida that 'there could be no normal relations' because of an injury obtained during the war (cited in Wheelwright, 1990: 4). Besides being a consummate liar, Arkell-Smith/Barker freely admitted that the prime reason she had disguised herself as a man was to make a living.

Preceding Arkell-Smith/Barker by four centuries was Mary Frith, also known as Moll Cutpurse (because of her penchant for picking pockets) who was born in 1584 (Thompson, 1974). She had careers as an astrologist and fortune teller, petty thief, pickpocket and fence for stolen goods. She is reported to have abandoned female clothes during her youth. In 1662, she published a book in which she claimed to be a hermaphrodite and had devised apparel for herself consisting of a man's jacket and woman's skirt, although she occasionally wore men's trousers. Despite her gender-mixed outfit, Frith was arrested for 'wearing man's apparel' and was sentenced to 'do penance' during a Sunday sermon. In later life she abandoned the man's jacket. Havelock Ellis considered Frith 'to have been the subject of sexo-aesthetic inversion' (1937: 8). She died at the age of 74. An acrostic based on her name reads:

> Merry I lived and many parts I played,
> And without sorrow now in grave am laid.
> Rest and the Sleep of Death doth now sure ease
> Youth's active sins and old ag'd increase.
> Famous I was for all the Thieving Art,
> Renowned for what old woman ride in cart;
> In pocket and Placket I had part.
> This life I lived in Man's disguise;
> He best laments me that with laughter cries.
> (Thompson, 1974: 28).

Although no ditties were composed in honour of Civil War soldiers such as Emma Edmonds and Loreta Janeta Velazquez, their war exploits were many, including battles and spying on enemy troops. Edmonds's birth name was Sarah Emma Evelyn Edmonson. She was a Canadian, born in 1841 (Hall, 1993: 74). Edmonds was influenced to join the army after reading the book *Fanny Campbell, The Female Pirate Captain, A Tale of the Revolution*, which had been given to her by a 'grateful' pedlar (Hall, 1993: 75; Wheelwright, 1990: 14). In her biography, Edmonds wrote that reading the book 'inspired! [me and that] ... each exploit of the heroine thrilled me to my fingertips. I went home that night with the problem of my life solved' (cited in Hall, 1993: 76). While she was quite young her father decided to 'marry her off' to an older man. Although she agreed, it was only out of obedience and before the wedding she executed her escape with the help of her mother's friend. In 1858 she was informed that her father had learned of her whereabouts. She cut her hair, put on men's clothes, began calling herself Franklin Thompson, and began living as a man. Prior to her military career, Edmonds/Thompson was a successful travelling bookseller. In 1861, as Thompson, Edmonds enlisted in the Union army. Two years later, while afflicted with a serious case of malaria, Edmonds deserted in order to avoid 'being exposed as a woman if placed in hospital' (ibid.: 83). After her recuperation, Edmonds resumed wearing women's dresses. While the war was still going on, she wrote her book *Nurse and Spy*, which was published in 1864 and was a partially fictionalized account of her war exploits.

Loreta Janeta Velazquez, dressed as a Confederate soldier with a heavily padded coat, a wire mesh undershirt she had devised and an 'artificial beard and mustache', was known as Lieutenant Harry T. Buford (Hall, 1993; Wheelwright, 1990). Velazquez has been described as an 'opportunistic' soldier who was not assigned to a regiment 'but sought combat assignments or commissions' (Hall, 1993: 107–8). As Buford she was accompanied by a 'black servant' who was unaware that she was female. In her memoirs, Velazquez wrote that she had been inspired by Joan of Arc and had 'wished that [she] was a man' (ibid.: 109). She later decided that:

> To be a second Joan of Arc was a mere girlish fancy, which my very first experiences as a soldier dissipated forever ... convincing me that a woman like myself who had a talent for assuming disguises ... [and] had it in her power to perform many services of the most vital importance, which was impossible for a man to even attempt. (cited in Hall, 1993: 113–14)

Resuming women's clothes, she embarked on a career as a military spy. Following a successful foray to Washington, DC, Velazquez put on her soldier's uniform and was assigned to a 'detective corps'. She was 'arrested on suspicion of being a spy' and protested vehemently in order to prevent detection of her physical sex. She was successful in her efforts and was released. However, the following day she was arrested 'on suspicion of being a woman'. She tried to maintain through several interviews that a mistake had been made, but eventually confessed. She was convicted and sentenced to a short jail term.

Following her release, she enlisted as a soldier and obtained a transfer as a commissioned officer. During burial duties Velazquez was badly wounded in the right arm. Following her recuperation, she resumed female dress and once again became a spy. Some 'documents were traced back to her [and she was] arrested' (*ibid*.: 123). Using fake British citizenship papers, the British consul intervened and she was released. She once again resumed wearing her uniform, passing as Buford, and headed for Richmond. She was again arrested 'on suspicion of being a woman in disguise'. While being held prisoner, she took the prison superintendent into her confidence. He championed her cause, 'interceded' on her behalf, and she was officially assigned to 'the secret service corps'. On return from an assignment 'she was again arrested on a charge of being a woman in disguise'. By this time tales of her exploits had become known and 'crowds gathered to see the Confederate heroine' (*ibid*.: 125).

After things settled down, Velazquez resumed her career as a Confederate spy, exchanging women's clothes for her uniform as situations dictated. After some time she began playing both sides of the war by spying on both. In part her 'double agent' exploits were for self-protection, as the Union authorities were pursuing her as a spy. Unwittingly, she was assigned by the Union 'to catch' herself. She was given 'instructions on a general plan for capturing the female agent' and was surprised by what they knew of her spying expeditions. As opportunity would have it, her brother invited her to accompany his family to Europe. She saw her chance to escape and accepted both the Union's assignment to catch the female spy and her brother's invitation. Under pretence of pursuing the spy, she went to New York and waited for her brother. They sailed to England almost immediately. Following her return from Europe, Velazquez travelled through the devastated South and then went to South America. In 1876 her memoirs were published and at some time in the 1880s she seems to have disappeared, leaving no record of her death.

From a transgender perspective it is possible to see Velazquez as a female-bodied man. The use of a heavily padded coat, a self-devised wire mesh shirt, and artificial whiskers are equivalent to contemporary FTMs' 'tricks of the trade' which include (but are not limited to) chest bindings, crotch padding, and stage make-up for creating beard lines. Further, Velazquez was recorded as saying she had wished she were a man. While this statement is probably not uncommon among many females, most do not go to the extent that Velazquez and FTMs do in order to fulfil their desire. Even so, I have included Velazquez among the transvestic opportunists because her cross-dressing was episodic rather than constant; and, when opportunity forced her hand, she used her femaleness to her advantage rather than keep her female body a secret.

Although there are hundreds of females who served in wars, most of them escaped detection or died on the battlefield only to be discovered in death. Like other females who lived as men, whether temporarily or for the majority of their lives, their motivations are not always clear. Some like Davies, Snell and Talbot joined the army or navy in search of lost husbands, others like Bonny to accompany a lover, and still others, like Read, Edmonds and Velazquez, did so for adventure.

Many of the tales of female men seem fantastic. Those who served in the military often suffered wounds so severe that they led to death; and many individuals were captured and imprisoned. Both wounds and capture frequently lead to 'discovery'. Although for many their cross-dressing ended following either the end of their military service or their discovery, some continued to dress as men throughout their lives. Such was the case with Angélique Brulon, who was born in 1771, served in the military for seven years, received three wounds, and was awarded 'the Cross of the Legion of Honour' of France, and wore her uniform in civilian life until her death (Gilbert, 1932; Wheelwright, 1990). For others, dressing as men was a lifestyle choice. For example, Queen Christina of Sweden, who abdicated her throne in 1654, declared her independence and 'to demonstrate [it] she abandoned the female, and adopted a male, attire . . . [and] took the name of Count Dohna' (Gilbert, 1932: 95). She was 'always strangely attired, partly as a man, partly as a woman, sometimes completely as a man, but never entirely as a woman' (*ibid.*: 101). This was to be true until her death in 1689. Another lifestyle choice seems to be that of Charlotte Charke, whose 'narrative' of her life was first published in 1755 in London. Charke's narrative is frequently discounted as less than truthful for as the editor (who remains anonymous) of the second edition proclaimed: 'Ungrammatical, insanely inconsequent, braggart and fantastic, the *Narrative* is not literature ... If the swagger has a quaver in it, it is against her will: barefaced beggar that she is, it is your purse she asks, never your pity ...' (Charke, 1827: 10). Besides acting on stage in both female and male roles, Charke also lived as a man for much of her life (Bullough, 1976: 490).

Female husbands and passing women: women who posed as men for love

Sometimes females disguised themselves as men in order to have relationships with women. They took on male roles not just for better-paying jobs, but also to live with their lovers without being subject to public scrutiny, much less scorn. Such is the case with Mary East, Delia Hudson/Frank Dubois and Cora Anderson.

Mary East was born around 1715. During the 1730s East met a woman with whom she formed a relationship (Thompson, 1974; Katz, 1976). A decision was made that one of them would assume a male identity and they would cast their lot together – 'drawing lots' it was decided that Mary would be the man. She assumed the name James How. They ran several successful businesses together for eighteen years until a woman recognized How/East and began blackmailing her. In 1764 or 1765, How's wife died. The blackmailer increased her demands and threatened bodily harm. How/East told a friend about being blackmailed and 'how she had posed as a man for many years'. With How/East's friend's assistance the blackmailer was arrested. She then resumed wearing female clothes and the use of her birth name. She died in 1781.

On 30 October 1883 the *Milwaukee Sentinel* headlined a short article: 'Disguised as a Man. An Illinois Wife in Masculine Attire Woos, Wins and Marries a Wisconsin Maiden – An Extraordinary Story.' Thus began Milwaukee's newspaper coverage of the story of Frank Dubois. Dubois's birth name was Delia; she was married for fourteen years to S.J. Hudson, and they had two children (*Milwaukee Sentinel*, 31 October 1883: 5). Marital differences were cited as the cause of her leaving her husband (*Milwaukee Sentinel*, 30 October 1883: 5). Her husband went in pursuit of her and, through an acquaintance of both, located her in Milwaukee. However, when she saw him approaching, she locked him out, refused him entry, and after he left, she took off. During the prior eight months she had been posing as a man and employed as a handyman and labourer, and had married Gertrude Fuller. A few days after Dubois disappeared Gertrude joined her. One news account reported: 'there is some unknown bond of sympathy which tempted them to their marriage and subsequent actions' (*Milwaukee Sentinel*, 1 November 1883: 8). During the following two days, the papers carried stories stating that the pair had not been found (*Milwaukee Sentinel*, 2 November 1883: 8; 3 November 1883: 3). By 4 November, Gertrude Dubois was located, but Frank, on learning that men had come to see him, took off leaving Gertrude behind (*Milwaukee Sentinel*, 4 November 1883: 2). The next two days, short stories were carried in the *Milwaukee Sentinel* (5 November 1883: 3; 6 November 1883: 2), but Dubois was not reported found until the end of the month, at which time she was arrested and confessed (*Milwaukee Sentinel*,

28 November 1883: 3). The final outcome of Dubois's case is unknown. It is difficult to surmise from the newspaper accounts exactly what Hudson/Dubois's motivations were for her male disguise. However, she had been 'courting' Gertrude for several months (while still living with her husband) prior to their marriage (*Milwaukee Sentinel*, 31 October 1883: 5).[3] Thus it seems likely that the ruse was for love.

Thirty-one years later another case of two married women would also be a sensation in Milwaukee newspapers, which also mentioned the case of Hudson/Dubois and her strange disappearance (*Milwaukee Sentinel*, 5 May 1914: 20; 6 May 1914: 3). Cora Anderson went by the name of Ralph Kerwineo (also spelled Kerwineio) and passed as a man for thirteen years (*Milwaukee Journal*, 14 May 1914: 8). She twice lived with women as husband and wife, both of whom knew that she was a woman posing as a man (*Milwaukee Journal*, 4 May 1914: 2). Her first wife stated that they had married 'in a spirit of fun' and she was fully aware that Cora was a woman. Part of her decision to pose as a man had to do with her being part Potawatomie-Cherokee Indian and feeling that she could make better money as a 'dark-skinned man' than as a woman. Another part of Cora's decision involved her love affair with the woman who became her first wife (*Milwaukee Sentinel*, 3 May 1914: 2). Mamie White who first posed as Anderson's wife stated, 'We wanted to be together, so we rented a room and the people with whom we lived never doubted that we were man and wife' (*ibid.*). But Cora had met someone else and White was 'dumbfounded when [Cora] told me that she had proposed marriage to her new found friend' (*ibid.*). Marriage to the new friend and White's jealousy were the cause of Ralph being discovered to be Cora (*Milwaukee Sentinel*, 5 May 1914: 2). White had informed the police that Cora was masquerading as a man. Anderson was charged with 'disorderly conduct' but the charges were dropped after her promise to return to female attire (*Milwaukee Journal*, 7 May 1914: 10). She also turned her career as a man into an opportunity by writing a series of newspaper articles about her adventures as well as commentaries on men's social behaviours (*Milwaukee Journal*, 13 May 1914: 7; 15 May 1914: 10; 24 May 1914: 7).

Female-bodied men: by nature and character, a man

According to Dekker and van de Pol, in at least one case history it is possible that the individual was a transsexual 'before the introduction of the word by modern science' (1989: 69). Not unlike contemporary female-to-male transgender people, Maria van Antwerpen (aliases Jan van Ant and Machiel van Antwerpen) stated when asked to what sex 'she' belonged, 'By nature and character, a man, but in appearance, a woman.' Antwerpen further commented, 'It often made me wrathful that Mother Nature treated me with so little compassion against my inclinations and the passions of my heart' (*ibid.*: 68).

Another who seems to have followed her heart is Catalina de Erauso who was born in 1592 and was, at an early age, put into a convent. At the age of fifteen, she fled from the convent and after making a suit of clothes from her habit and petticoat, she dressed herself as a man (Gilbert, 1932; Thompson, 1974). Dressed in this manner, she was variously employed as a valet, a cutpurse (briefly), a page, and then as a sailor on a Spanish galleon that sailed to South and Central America. Once she reached the Americas, she joined the army as Alonso Diaz Ramérez de Guzman. Erauso served for a number of years until, 'severely wounded', she was forced to reveal her physical sex and she was subsequently discharged. In 1624 she returned to Spain and continued to wear her military uniform. Two years later, she was granted permission by Pope Urban VIII 'to continue to wear men's clothes' (Thompson, 1974: 37; Gilbert, 1932: 169). She later returned to America and became a courier until she was 'taken ill' and died in 1650. Even while in Spain, Erauso's story became known and she was treated as a curiosity (Perry, 1987: 86). It is possible that she should be categorized as a female-bodied man who, given the century in which she was born, could only 'construct for herself a male persona that would completely obliterate her identity as a woman' (*ibid.*: 94). Erauso is said to have left the convent because she 'wanted to live as a man' and is reported to have found a way to 'dry up her breasts' (*ibid.*: 89). While Mary Perry declares that Erauso's 'life suggested that anyone with a choice would choose the adventure, the freedom, the exhilaration of being a man' (*ibid.*: 96), another possibility is that Erauso identified as a man.

The detailed account of Erauso's life seems to be the exception rather than the rule. Although many females, including Deborah Sampson as Robert Shurtliff, fought in the Revolutionary War (Medlicott, 1966: xv; Wheelwright, 1990: 52), the records are scarce and less well documented than later cases. However, there is an extensive history of females living as men beginning in the 1850s. One of the most famous cases is that of Calamity Jane, who was born in 1847 and died in 1901. In 1877, Jane is reported to have abandoned 'the society of women forever, and joined the male sex' (Horan, 1952: 176). According to one of her biographers, 'She was completely devoid of a female figure. Her body was slim [but] it is difficult to obtain a reliable physical description of Jane. Her pictures show her to be more of a man than a woman' (*ibid.*: 172–3). Although James Horan seems extremely doubtful about many of Jane's exploits, he states: 'There is no doubt that Jane was tragically miscast by nature in sex. There is little doubt she should have been a man. [Men] accepted her as one of their own kind' (*ibid.*: 172).

A less famous case, but one which was recently brought to our attention by a fictionalized account of his life in film, is that of Little Jo Monoghan who was born around 1857 and died in 1903. Monoghan arrived in a small Idaho town in 1868, where he staked a mining claim, herded sheep, broke horses and became a homesteader, working a sawmill and horse ranch on his property. Thirty-five years later at his death it was discovered that Monoghan had a female body (Horan, 1952: 305–10).

Often it was only upon death that an individual was discovered to have had a female body. Such is the case with James Barry, James Allen, Nicholas de Raylan and Murray Hall. James Barry (née Miranda) was born around 1795. He enlisted in the military and in 1819 became a staff surgeon. In 1827, he was promoted to surgeon-major (Ellis, 1937: Thompson, 1974). In 1851, Barry was made deputy inspector-general and seven years later became inspector-general of hospitals. Although he was a very brusque and stand-offish person, Barry had a very successful career. Because of his diminutive size and beardless appearance some acquaintances speculated as to Barry's 'true sex'. Some concluded that he was a woman and others that he was a hermaphrodite. Some who knew Barry referred to him with male pronouns, while others used female ones. Some clearly suspected, while others remained clueless, including Barry's man-servant. However, it was not until his death in 1865 that an autopsy determined that Barry was female-bodied. Barry was not known to have had sexual relationships of any kind.

James Allen (birth name unknown) was not discovered to be female-bodied until his death in 1829. He was married for 21 years to a woman named Mary (Thompson, 1974). Together they bought and ran an inn successfully 'for a time' until they were robbed. They sold the inn and moved to London. Allen died because of an accident on the job, at 42 years of age. Allen's wife stated that she did not suspect that he was anything but a man, but that when she made attempts at intimacy with him he feigned excuses such as illness (Thompson, 1974: 136; Duberman, 1986: 24, 27). He wore a binding around his chest and always wore layers of underclothes, supposedly to protect him from getting cold. Upon examination of his body it was found that his 'breasts, which were moderately full, were forced, by the compression of the bandages, under the armpits' (Duberman, 1986: 28). Allen's wife had come to believe that James was a hermaphrodite and swore that she was ignorant of his having a female body.

In 1906, Nicholas de Raylan died from tuberculosis at the age of 33 (Katz, 1976: 250–1). He had been a private secretary 'to the Russian Consul', and had fought in the Spanish–American War (Savitsch, 1958: 6). He was 'married twice', divorcing his first wife after ten years. His second wife was devoted to him. Both of his wives 'were convinced that their husband was a man and ridiculed the idea' that he was female. He wore self-constructed genitalia consisting of a 'penis and testicles made of chamois skin and stuffed with down' and held in place by a waistband (Savitsch, 1958: 7; Katz, 1976: 251). Eugene de Savitsch considered Nicholas de Raylan a homosexual because of his having female organs and female object choices (1958: 10). Savitsch clearly equated the possibility of changing sex with males only, although he was aware that females also wanted to change their sex (*ibid.*: 86). He states, 'When we refer to the change of sex operation, we mean here the surgical procedure by which the external appearance of the male genitalia is changed to that of a woman' (*ibid.*: 53). He mentions no possibility of such operations for female-bodied people, thus it is improbable that Savitsch would recognize de Raylan as an FTM who fashioned his own male genital apparatus.

Murray Hall lived as a man for over 30 years (*San Francisco Daily Call*, 1901: 11). He held memberships in 'the General Committee of Tammany Hall, . . . [and] the Iroguois [*sic*] Club', he was also a friend of a prominent New York senator, and an active worker in his political district (Katz, 1976: 232); he was the owner of 'an intelligence office' in New York City. Hall was 'married twice' and his last wife 'kept her [*sic*] secret' until his death. Hall was not discovered to be female-bodied until his death following breast cancer. He refused medical treatment for his cancer because he feared his secret would be discovered. Hall even kept his secret from his adopted daughter. Hall's acquaintances and friends were shocked to learn that he was physically female, but they continued to use male pronouns in speaking about him. The following are examples: 'During the seven years I knew him I never once suspected he was anything else than what he appeared to be.' 'Suspect he was a woman? Never. He dressed like a man and talked like a very sensible one.' 'If he was a woman he ought to have been born a man, for he lived and looked like one' (cited in Katz, 1976: 234). His death certificate lists him as being 70 years of age although his friends thought him to be in his fifties. During the inquest into his death one witness, after referring to Hall as 'he', was asked, 'Wouldn't you better say she?' To which the witness replied, 'No, I will never say she.' Despite his friends' convictions as to Hall's identity, the coroner ruled that he was female and his death was from natural causes. The response to Hall's life and death is reminiscent of the 1989 death of Billy Tipton (see pp. 52–7).

It was not only death that exposed female-bodied men; sometimes it was poverty, accident, or wrongdoing. Such were the cases with Albert Cashier, Charley Wilson and Johann Bürger. Albert Cashier (née Jennie Hodgers) served for three years 'in the 95th Illinois Infantry Regiment' (Hall, 1993: 20; Wheelwright, 1990: 140). He was 18 years of age when he enlisted in 1862. Cashier was born in 1844 in Belfast, Ireland. He came to the US as a stowaway. In 1911, after living as a man for over 50 years, his secret was discovered following an accident in which his leg was broken close to the hip. Upon examination a doctor 'discovered' that Cashier was female-bodied. Cashier prevailed upon his employer and the doctor to keep his secret. They agreed and Cashier was admitted 'to the Soldiers' and Sailors' Home in Quincy, Illinois, taking the commandant into their confidence' (Hall, 1993: 21; see also Wheelwright, 1990: 146). Oddly (but then considering the time, perhaps not) the admission papers referred to Cashier's 'senility' and 'weakened mental facilities' (Hall, 1993: 21), rather than his broken leg.

Along with other Union soldiers Cashier is listed on the Vicksburg 'monument to Illinois soldiers who fought there' (ibid.; 22). During his 3-year military career, Cashier participated in 'forty battles and skirmishes and was never wounded'. Following the war, Cashier returned to Illinois and worked as 'a farmhand and handyman' in several Illinois towns. In 1890, Cashier applied for a soldier's pension but refused a required 'medical examination' and was denied the pension. Eventually a pension of twelve dollars a month was granted in 1907 (Hall, 1993: 24). Wheelwright puts the amount at '$70/per month' (1990: 140).

Cashier's secret finally leaked out two years after his accident in 1913. The same year he was judged 'insane' and consigned to a state mental hospital. The commitment seems dubious at best, considering that 'the symptoms' included memory loss, times of noisiness, insomnia and feebleness. His story was picked up by numerous US newspapers. Former comrades referred to Cashier without apparent hesitation as a man and 'stressed his bravery and fortitude'. One comrade who visited Cashier at the hospital reported that he had 'found a frail woman [sic] of 70, broken, because on discovery, she [sic] was compelled to put on skirts' (Hall, 1993: 25; see also Wheelwright, 1990: 147). In 1915, Albert Cashier died six months after being confined to the mental hospital. He was 71 years of age and was buried 'with full military honors, wearing her [sic] Union uniform, and she [sic] was buried in a flag-draped casket. The inscription on her [sic] tombstone ... reads: ALBERT D. J. CASHIER, CO. G, 95 ILL. INF' (Hall, 1993: 26).

Charley Wilson (née Catherine Coombes) was born in 1834 (Thompson, 1974). He worked 'for over forty years' as a man, in various trades including dockworker, sailor, printer, decorator and painter. In 1887, 'a little, old, grey-haired man dressed in a neat suit of clothes, wearing a black bowler hat, and carrying a small bag, walked into the Rochester Row Police Station' seeking help (ibid.: 147). Charley was eventually taken to the men's ward where he was instructed to undress for a bath in the presence of two others. He asked to speak with a doctor and ward matron, whom he told he was physically female. His confession resulted in his being moved to the women's ward where he was provided with a woman's dress. As his story unfolded he revealed that he had been married for a short time to a man who abused him. Wilson assumed men's clothes and sought work as a painter, a trade he had learned from his brother. While living in the poorhouse, Wilson is reported to have said: 'If I had the money I would get out of here in men's clothes and no one would detect me, but at present I cannot work on account of my fractured ribs' (ibid.: 150). Furthermore, he 'never reconciled [himself] to living and dressing as a woman' during the remainder of his life.

Johann Bürger (née Anna Mattersteig) was arrested during 1908 'on charge of abduction and as being a woman' (Katz, 1976: 252). He declared in court that it had not been his intent to break the law as regarded his manner of dress and his 'abduction' of his companion. He further declared that he 'felt herself [sic] wholly like a man' and was certain that nature had made a mistake.

Another person who was convinced that he was a man is Alan Hart (née Alberta Lucill Hart) who was born in 1892 near Portland, Oregon. He graduated from college in 1912 and went on to medical school, graduating in 1917 (Katz, 1976). His diploma from medical school has his name as Alan Lucill Hart (Brown and Morris, 1995). After Hart's repeated requests a doctor performed a hysterectomy around 1916 (Katz, 1976). A year later he married a woman who was 'fully cognizant of all the facts' (*ibid.*: 277). His first wife, whose name was Inez Stark, left Hart in 1923. Hart had a very successful career as a roentgenologist (X-ray technician) and developed a method for early detection of tuberculosis. He also was a successful novelist (*Dr. Mallory, The Undaunted, In the Lives of Men*, and *Dr. Finley Sees It Through*) and wrote a medical book, *These Mysterious Rays*, about 'X-rays, radium, and ultra-violet therapy' (Katz, 1983: 517)

Hart's novel *The Undaunted* is semi-autobiographical. One of its characters, Sandy Farquhar, 'included some elements of Hart's own experience' (Katz, 1983: 518). The doctor who treated Hart noted that he 'was recognized by a former associate . . . Then the hounding process began . . .' (Katz, 1976: 276). Farquhar is described similarly:

> He had been driven from place to place, from job to job, for fifteen years because of something he could not alter any more than he could change the color of his eyes. Gossip, scandal, rumor always drove him on. It did no good to live alone, to make few acquaintances and no intimates; sooner or later someone always turns up to recognize him. (Hart, 1936: 257; cited in Katz, 1983: 521)

Farquhar 'went into radiology because he thought it wouldn't matter so much in a laboratory what a man's personality was. But wherever he went scandal followed him sooner or later' (Hart, 1936: 522; cited in Katz, 1983: 522). Farquhar is also described as having what is immediately recognizable by FTMs as body dysphoria:

> He remembered the first entry in the little book, made when he was twenty. 'My body is an incubus [nightmare] and my fears are born of it. But it is possible for the possessor of a defective body to remain unbroken by the disasters that overcome it because he has it always in his power to escape his servitude, his subjection, to his body'. (Hart, 1936: 196; cited in Katz, 1983: 520)

Unlike his character, Sandy Farquhar, who eventually commits suicide, Hart had a successful and happy life. Two years after Inez left him, he married Edna Ruddick and they lived happily together for 37 years until his death in 1962 (Brown and Morris, 1995: 2). In Jonathan Katz's discussions of Hart, he adamantly insists Hart was 'clearly a lesbian, a woman-loving woman' (Katz, 1976: 277); yet he seems surprised that Edna refused his attempts at contact (Katz, 1983: 522).

Default assumptions, or the Billy Tipton phenomenon[4]

Ironically, Katz has stated: 'Too often, academics act as if to name something is to know it' (1976: 211). Not only does he identify Hart as a lesbian, he also includes Bürger, De Raylan and Hall under the rubric of 'lesbian transvestites', based on their cross-dressing, cross-living, and having had female lovers. He acknowledges that Bürger may have thought of himself as a man and that such an identification 'is commonly labeled a[s] transsexual' today (*ibid.*: 252). But he states that the label 'is so loaded with traditional assumptions connecting gender and "masculinity" and "femininity" as to render it of the most controversial and doubtful character' (*ibid.*). Furthermore, in his 1983 work, in a footnote concerning another reference to 'transsexualism', Katz refers to Janice Raymond's *The Transsexual Empire*, as 'The most profound, extended critique of the medical concept' (1983: 662). The failure of his argument, like other critics (e.g. Raymond, 1979; Garber, 1989, 1992; Tyler, 1989), is in relying on 'eminent' authorities rather than consulting transpeople themselves, who even as early as his published works (1976 and 1983) were rejecting and bypassing the so-called medical empire as well as rejecting the sexist demands made by them.

Katz is also guilty of operating, like others, all too frequently on what Douglas Hofstaeder (1982) calls 'default assumptions'. He defines 'default assumptions' as something that holds true in the 'simplest or most natural or most likely possible model' concerning any particular topic or subject: 'the critical thing about default assumptions is that they are made automatically, not as a result of consideration or elimination' (Hofstaedter, 1982: 18). To some degree or another, we all make default assumptions. For example, when we see what appears to be an effeminate man or a butch woman, we make an assumption that they are gay or lesbian, respectively. There are a number of default assumptions about both contemporary FTMs and their forerunners.

It is a default assumption that females do not become men. Related to this are other default assumptions: (1) females become men only to take advantage of male privileges or as a cover for their lesbianism; (2) depending on the author's perspective, females quit assuming male identities in the mid-nineteenth or mid-twentieth centuries; (3) females who live as men are women who cannot accept their lesbianism; (4) females cannot become men; and (5) cross-dressing/living is equivalent to homosexuality. The foundation for all of these assumptions is that genitals equal sex which equals gender.

These default assumptions can be illustrated in some recent

newspaper articles concerning the movie *The Ballad of Little Jo*. Maggie Greenwald, the director, states: 'I stumbled upon some information about the real Little Jo Monihan [*sic*], about whom almost nothing is known except that she lived as a man and nobody had discovered the truth about her until she died' (Kahler, 1993: 17). The default assumption here is that the *truth* is that Monaghan was female and thus *really* a woman. Greenwald vividly reveals her default assumptions when she concludes in the interview: 'Women discover themselves – and this is so much a part of feminism – that they don't have to be fake men; to be strong; to be powerful ... Jo becomes a woman not a man. She passes through a phase to survive, ultimately to be a woman' (*ibid.*: 20). As discussed above, Monaghan lived as a man and no one knew otherwise until his death, but 'ultimately' he was a woman.

Another default assumption is made when Greenwald states, 'It would only be extreme incidents that would make a woman decide to live her life as a man' (*ibid.*: 17). These 'extreme incidents' always involve socio-economic explanations. In the case of Monaghan, an out-of-wedlock child was born and Monaghan was disowned by her family. According to one male movie reviewer, 'With no family to depend on, Josephine [note the use of Josephine instead of Little Jo], had to find either a husband or a pimp. Instead she decided to pass for a man and live on the edge of Western society' (Ulstein, 1993: 11). For those familiar with television's *Dr. Quinn, Medicine Woman* – who was not married for several years into the series and, once married, was not economically dependent on her husband and not a prostitute – the producers obviously forgot that a woman in the Old West had limited choices.

One article accompanying a review of *Little Jo* is headlined: 'Women posing as men pursued better opportunities' (Lee, 1993: 11). Quoted in this article is Julie Wheelwright, who states, 'very often it was a pattern of women in working-class occupations who would take on male attributes to further their careers' (*ibid.*). Referring back to *Dr. Quinn, Medicine Woman* for a moment, she is clearly a feminine woman in a male occupation. I do not know if the television show is based on any real persons, but I do know that many females pursued so-called male careers without changing their sex (e.g. Elizabeth Blackwell, Angie Debo, Elsie Clews Parsons, as well as all of the Protestant missionary women). I call this default assumption 'the Billy Tipton phenomenon'. The same article even uses Tipton as an example of career opportunism, stating, '[I]n 1989, when Billy Tipton died in Spokane, it was revealed that the American jazz pianist and saxophonist – who had married and was the father of three adopted children – was in fact a woman. She apparently began appearing as a man to improve her chances of success as a musician' (*ibid.*).

Another default assumption is that females cannot be men. Concerning Billy Tipton and others, one writer stated, 'One look usually convinces viewers that these people were quite clearly women' (Lee, 1993: 11). Yet, no one in Billy Tipton's life knew him as anything but a man. Always, as in the headline mentioned above, females who live as men are considered to be 'posing', or living 'a charade', or 'masquerading' as a man. In other words, they are not taken seriously. For example, after stories were published about Christian Davies, Hannah Snell, Emma Edmonds and Loreta Janeta Velazquez they were discounted as impostors and flagrant liars (Wheelwright, 1990: 27, 123, 137–40). Excuses and rationalizations are made as to the 'whys' of their lives.

People say they can understand a woman wanting to be a man because of the cultural privileges that males in our society have. But they cannot understand a man wanting to become a woman. Therefore, a male who becomes a woman must have a *real* need and a *condition* that is treatable. A man who becomes a woman is a transgender and/or transsexual issue. A female who becomes a man is a socio-economic issue – and feminists will rally to 'her' cause and, in doing so, deny FTMs their reality (Bonnie Cromwell, 1991, personal communication).

It is a default assumption when people conclude that Billy Tipton was posing as a man in order to be a musician. It is a default assumption when someone concludes that a female lived as a man for economic and social reasons or when in a relationship with a woman as a cover-up for lesbianism. For example, Wheelwright (1990) makes the following statements:

1. 'During the course of their entry into the masculine world many became so immersed in their male identity that women became "the other" in their eyes' (*ibid.*: 10).
2. 'Cross-dressing for women often remained a process of imitation rather than a self-conscious claiming of the social privileges given exclusively to men for all women' (*ibid.*: 11).
3. 'Women who entered male occupations, passing as men or known to their workmates, often coped with the contradictions of their position by developing a strong male-identification' (*ibid.*: 11–12).
4. 'It is, however, clear that women expressed a desire not for the physical acquisition of a male body but for a male social identity' (*ibid.*: 12–13).

There are two primary assumptions in all of these statements. First, Wheelwright presumes to know what was in the minds of these individuals. Second, she assumes that none of the individuals she discusses could have possibly conceived of themselves as men (that is, she leaves out the third possibility). Hence, from her perspective, (1) they should not have seen women as 'the other'; (2) they could only imitate men and so were unconscious of their claim to social privilege; (3) because they entered male jobs they developed a male identification and this had to be a conflict; and (4) these individuals did not clearly express a desire for physical transformation.

However, to rephrase Katz, to name something is not necessarily to know it; moreover, to refuse to name something may effectively render it invisible, but it does not make it impossible. By looking at some of these individuals as females who identified as men, their 'troubling behaviour' is explainable. To wit, (1) women would be 'the other'; (2) it was not imitation and (whether it is seen as sexist or not) they believed they had a right to male privilege just as other men did; (3) they did not develop a male identification as a result of entering male occupations, they entered them because they were male-identified; and (4) many did express a desire for physical transformation in the only language they had, which was discounted, ignored, or interpreted as a desire for male power and privilege. On this latter point, Wheelwright interprets Davies's urinary device and Velazquez's wire mesh shirts as a sign that their 'masculinity was only artificial' (1990: 59); however, they can also be interpreted as aides that enhanced their masculinity and affirmed their male identification at a time when no other choices were available to them.

But what about cases where choices are available? To begin with, the continuing response to Tipton's life poses many questions. If he were impersonating a man only in order to be a musician, why keep the secret from everyone after his career ended? Why, for that matter, keep it secret from closest friends and family at all? At the very least, making his secret known to others could have been an interesting inside joke. Why did he marry a woman? Why did he lie about his ability to have sex with her? Why lie about his genitals being crushed in an accident? Why did he 'always wear a t-shirt and belt with an [athletic] cup on the outside of his underwear? (*People Magazine*, 20 February 1989). Why did he adopt three children and be their father? Why do his adopted sons continue to insist that he was a man and their father? One of his sons has said, 'He did a helluva job with us. He was my dad' (*ibid.*).

It is ironic that many lesbians would have rejected Tipton while he was alive and yet claim him as a part of their history after his death. For example, it is highly unlikely that he would have been invited to the Michigan Women's Music Festival.[5] Does this mean that 'anatomy is not destiny' while one is alive, but 'anatomy is destiny' after death? It seems this must be the case. Why else would people begin to use female pronouns after Tipton died and it was discovered his body was female? Tipton did not have surgery to alter his sex and he certainly lived during a time when it was available. However, this is true for many FTMs because the results (especially for genital surgeries) are risky, aesthetically not very good, and quite expensive. Tipton left no written explanation for the actions of his life. He left instead a life lived for over 50 years as a man and tried to take his secret to the grave. Does his life as a man have no meaning?

Billy Tipton's life speaks for itself. A person does not spend 50 years of their life living in fear; hiding from the ones they love and live with; going to extreme measures to make sure that no one knows what their body is or looks like; and they do not die from a treatable medical condition (bleeding ulcer) – *if* they are simply a woman living as a man so they can take advantage of male privileges. It is unfortunate Tipton left no written statement about the 'whys' of his life. When someone like Tipton dies or is discovered they are discounted as 'not real men' or 'unreal men'; and despite having lived years of their lives as men, they are turned into lesbians.

Recently transpeople have begun to object to people they see like themselves being turned into women and lesbians. In 1993, Candice Brown and Ken Morris began a campaign in Portland, Oregon to have Alan Hart recognized as a man. They formed the Ad Hoc Committee of Transsexuals to Recognize Alan Hart. The committee petitioned the political group, Right to Privacy (RTP), to drop the name Lucille Hart for their annual fund-raising awards dinner. RTP had been using the name since 1982 because they wanted to recognize an Oregonian lesbian pioneer (a default assumption based on equating cross-dressing/living with homosexuality). In October 1995, the committee passed out 400 fliers to the hundreds of people attending the benefit. They also wore buttons proclaiming: 'HIS NAME WAS ALAN HART'. RTP failed to respond to their campaign, but the committee pressed on. In December, they requested transpeople to send faxes, e-mails and letters with the same message as that printed on the buttons to RTP's Portland office. In January 1996, members of the Ad Hoc Committee from Oregon and Washington met with representatives of RTP. This meeting resulted in Brown and Morris being invited to RTP's board meeting in February. The following month RTP dropped Hart's former name and agreed to choose a more appropriate one.

Long before Brown and Morris formed their committee, Louis G. Sullivan, a female-to-male transsexual, who died in 1991, was active in reclaiming the lives of female-bodied men. He collected numerous clippings from San Francisco and Milwaukee newspapers as well as references in books on females who lived as men for all or part of their lives. It did not matter whether they were described as transvestites, female husbands, or mannish lesbians. The earliest of these is dated 1870 and concerns a female who committed suicide dressed in men's clothes (*San Francisco Daily Morning Call*, 1 January 1870: 10). There are no details of this person's life, however. Sullivan collected other newspaper clippings which detail the lives of several individuals following their 'discovery': Delia Hudson/Frank Dubois, Cora Anderson/Ralph Kerwineo, James Barry, Murray Hall, to name just a few (as discussed earlier). He also wrote a biography of Jack Garland (Sullivan, 1990a) based on newspaper accounts of his life, and included summaries of these peoples' lives as well as many others in his book, *Information for the Female to Male Cross Dresser and Transsexual* (Sullivan, 1990b). According to the newspaper accounts these individuals assumed men's ways in order to increase their chances of employment and to draw better wages, for adventure or to travel unfettered, as well as to 'marry' women. But seldom were the individuals allowed to speak for themselves; therefore, with the exception of a few rare cases it is difficult to say with any certainty what motivated these individuals to assume the status, role and lifestyle of men. Some individual motivations may have been as the news accounts report, but for others there may have been a belief that they were men with female bodies.

Conclusion

Some distinctions can be made between the three types discussed above. The transvestite females are distinguished by temporarily living as men, or by their episodic nature, as well as by the individual returning to women's apparel. Where possible, the distinction is based also on the individual's statements about their motivations. However, sometimes these must be taken with a grain of salt, not only because the person may have been trying to protect herself from possible prosecution, but also because of the reporter's possibly skewed perspective.

Female husbands and passing women tend towards more permanent status of living as men and often range from a few years to a lifetime.

Statements by both parties involved as to the nature of the relationship are also important in establishing whether or not they were lesbians. However, denials of sexual intimacy must be weighed with caution, especially as society's awareness of lesbianism became more acute and the chances of condemnation and prosecution became more real for all parties involved.

It is at this juncture that the distinctions between lesbians and female-bodied men becomes unclear. First, it is not uncommon for female-bodied people to have relationships with women. Second, it is not uncommon for female-bodied men to not engage in sexual relationships with their female partners. Although at the body level it would seem that sexual intimacy between the couple would indicate a lesbian relationship, it is not the case from the mental and emotional levels for individuals who did not (or do not) identify as women. Nonetheless, three criteria can be used for determining if an individual had a male identification:

1. Did the individuals make statements that (contrary to their physiology) they are men or always felt themselves to be men?
2. Were attempts made at body modification (e.g. padding of clothing, binding of breasts and devices used in place of male genitalia) and did the individual pursue or have whatever surgeries were available (e.g. Hart's hysterectomy)?
3. Was there an attempt to live a better part of their lives as men or an undertaking of a lifetime of living as men; and were there efforts to take the secret of their female bodies with them to the grave, or if 'discovered' did they try to find a means by which the secret could be kept?

If these criteria are met, then seemingly perplexing behaviours can be better understood as behaviours appropriate to male-identified female-bodied people.

Because it is difficult for some people to conceive of someone who is female-bodied but who does not identify as female, it is easy to find their behaviours perplexing. But being perplexed does not justify making assumptions based on gynocentrism or androcentrism, using biological deterministic arguments, and subsuming relationships under the rubric of lesbianism. As Lorraine has so cogently stated:

Human beings ... are intentional agents whose consciousness of themselves and the world they live in form an inextricable feature of everything they say, think, or do. (1990: 3).

Discounting, ignoring and misinterpreting individuals' statements about themselves or the actions undertaken during the course of their lives may render them invisible, but it does not mean that they identified as women nor does it mean that they were (are) lesbians.

Notes

1. Parts of this chapter are included in my chapter, 'Traditions of gender diversity and sexualities: a female-to-male transgendered perspective', in Sue-Ellen Jacobs, Wesley Thomas and Sabine Lang (eds), *Two-Spirit People: Native American Gender, Sexuality, and Spirituality* (Urbana: University of Illinois Press, 1997), pp. 119–42.
2. By necessity this chapter only skims the surface of the available data. A book from an FTM perspective is required to cover the gamut of female-bodied people who transgressed their historical categories. At least one FTM is currently involved in such a project.
3. Interestingly, Hudson as Frank Dubois was arrested and charged with assault and battery in March of 1883 without being discovered to be female (*Milwaukee Sentinel*, 8 March 1883: 5).
4. Much of the following section was presented at the 1993 'Southern Comfort' conference and portions appeared in a letter to the editor of *Seattle Gay News* (18 August 1989: np) and was published in *FTM Newsletter* (1994: 4–5) and reprinted in *Cross-Talk* (1995: 15–16, 23) and *Boy's Own* (1995: 6–9).
5. In 1991 male-to-female transpeople were excluded from participating in the Michigan Women's Music Festival. Beginning with the 1992 festival transgender activists have held protests and information tables outside the gate of the festival location. Since 1995 MTFs have been allowed to attend if they are post-surgical.

References

Brown, C. and K. Morris (1995) *The Alan Hart Story: A Typical Transsexual Tale*. Unpublished paper.

Bullough, V.L. (1976) *Sexual Variance in Society and History*. Chicago: University of Chicago Press.

Charke, C. (1827 [1755]) *A Narrative of the Life of Mrs. Charlotte Charke, Written by Herself*. London: unknown publisher.

Cromwell, J. (1989) 'What about Billy's life as a man?', Letter to the Editor, *Seattle Gay News*, 18 August.

Cromwell, J. (1993) 'Default assumptions or the Billy Tipton phenomenon'. Paper presented at Southern Comfort Conference, Atlanta (October).

Cromwell, J. (1994) 'Default assumptions or the Billy Tipton phenomenon', *FTM Newsletter*, 28: 4–5.

Cromwell, J. (1995a) 'Default assumptions or the Billy Tipton phenomenon', *Cross-Talk*, **67**: 15–16, 23.

Cromwell, J. (1995b) 'Default assumptions or the Billy Tipton phenomenon', *Boy's Own*, **18**: 6–9.

Dekker, R.M. and L.C. van de Pol (1989) *The Tradition of Female Transvestism in Early Modern Europe*. London: Macmillan Press.

Duberman, M.B. (1986) *About Time: Exploring the Gay Past*. New York: Gay Presses of New York.

Ellis, H. (1937) *Studies in the Psychology of Sex, Volume 2*. New York: Random House.

Friedli, L. (1987) ' "Passing women": a study of gender boundaries in the eighteenth century'. In G.S. Rousseau and R. Porter (eds), *Sexual Underworlds of the Enlightenment*. Manchester: Manchester University Press.

Garber, M. (1989) 'Spare parts: the surgical construction of gender', *Differences: A Journal of Feminist Cultural Studies*, **1**, 3: 137–59.

Garber, M. (1992) *Vested Interests: Cross-Dressing and Cultural Anxiety*. New York: Routledge.

Gilbert, O.P. (1932) *Women in Men's Guise*. London: Bodley Head.

Hall, R. (1993) *Patriots in Disguise: Women Warriors of the Civil War*. New York: Paragon House.

Hart, A. (1936) *The Undaunted*. New York: W.W. Norton.

Hirschfeld, M. (1966 [1938]) *Sexual Anomalies and Perversions*. London: Encyclopedic Press.

Hofstadter, D. (1982) 'Default assumptions', *Scientific American*, **247**, 5: 18, 22, 26, 30, 36.

Horan, J.D. (1952) *Desperate Women*. New York: G.P. Putnam.

Kahler, F. (1993) ' "The Ballad of Little Jo": Maggie Greenwald's feminism and a rich consciousness', *Seattle Gay News*, 10 September: 17, 20.

Katz, J. (1976) *Gay American History: Lesbians and Gay Men in the U.S.A.* New York: Thomas Y. Crowell.

Katz, J. (1983) *Gay/Lesbian Almanac*. New York: Carroll & Graf.

Lee, L. (1993) 'Women posing as men pursued better opportunities', *Seattle Post Intelligencer: What's Happening*, 10 September: 11.

Lorraine, T.E. (1990) *Gender, Identity, and the Production of Meaning*. Boulder: Westview Press.

Magee, M. and D.C. Miller. (1992) ' "She foreswore her womanhood": psychoanalytic views of female homosexuality', *Clinical Social Work Journal*, **20**, 1: 67–87.

Medlicott, A. (1966) 'Introduction'. In *The Female Marine or Adventures of Miss Lucy Brewer*. New York: Da Capo Press.

Milwaukee Journal (1914, 4 May) 'Writing life's last chapter': 1–2.

Milwaukee Journal (1914, 7 May) 'Girl-man now is free again': 10.

Milwaukee Journal (1914, 14 May) 'Man-girl in a legal tangle': 8.

Milwaukee Sentinel (1883, 30 October) 'Disguised as a man': 5.

Milwaukee Sentinel (1883, 31 October) 'Romance and Reality': 5.

Milwaukee Sentinel (1883, 1 November) 'The mysterious husband': 8.

Milwaukee Sentinel (1883, 2 November) 'The dual personage': 8.

Milwaukee Sentinel (1883, 3 November) 'Strange stories – whereabouts of 'Dubois' and his young "Wife"': 3.

Milwaukee Sentinel (1883, 4 November) 'Found at last': 2.

Milwaukee Sentinel (1914, 3 May) 'Milwaukee "man" clerk proves girl': 1–2.

Milwaukee Sentinel (1914, 4 May) 'Girl masquerader refuses to talk': 1.

Milwaukee Sentinel (1914, 5 May) 'Presto! Ralph Kerwineio now Miss Anderson': 1–2.

Milwaukee Sentinel (1914, 5 May) 'Sex concealment revives memory of Waupun "Man"': 20.

Milwaukee Sentinel (1914, 6 May) 'Sex concealment revives memory': 3.

People Weekly (1989, 20 February) 'Death discloses Billy Tipton's strange secret: he was a she': np.

Perry, M.E. (1987) 'The manly woman: a historical case study', *American Behavioral Scientist*, **31**, 1: 86–100.

San Francisco Daily Call (1870, 1 January) 'Suicide of a woman': 10.

San Francisco Daily Call (1901, 18 January) 'Lived as a man, dies as a woman': 11.

de Savitsch, E. (1958) *Homosexuality, Transvestism, and Change of Sex*. Springfield: Charles C. Thomas.

Silverman, K. (1986) 'Fragments of a fashionable discourse'. In T. Modleski (ed.), *Studies in Entertainment: Critical Approaches to Mass Culture*. Bloomington: Indiana University Press.

Sullivan, L. (1990a) *From Female to Male: The Life of Jack Bee Garland*. Boston: Alyson Publications.

Sullivan, L. (1990b) *Information for the Female to Male Cross Dresser and Transsexual*. Seattle: Ingersoll Press.

Thompson, C.J.S. (1974) *The Mysteries of Sex: Women Who Posed as Men and Men Who Impersonated Women*. New York: Causeway Books.

Tyler, C. (1989) 'The supreme sacrifice? TV, "TV", and the Renée Richards story', *Differences: A Journal of Feminist Cultural Studies*, **1**, 3: 160–86.

Ulstein, S. (1993) ' "Jo" views the West through a woman's eyes', *Seattle Post Intelligencer: What's Happening*, 10 September: 11.

Vicinus, M. (1992) ' "They wonder to which sex I belong": the historical roots of the modern lesbian identity', *Feminist Studies*, **18**, 3: 467–97.

Wheelwright, J. (1990) *Amazons and Military Maids*. London: Pandora.

Wilson, E. (1990) 'Deviant dress', *Feminist Review*, **35**: 67–74.

3

Portrait of a Transfag Drag Hag as a Young Man: The Activist Career of Louis G. Sullivan

Susan Stryker

I n 1961 Lou Sullivan was a 10-year-old girl living in the suburbs of Milwaukee, Wisconsin; in 1991 he was a gay man dying of AIDS in San Francisco.[1] Sullivan has been posthumously lionized by the transgender movement that took shape in the years since his untimely death at age 39 – and rightly so. He became a transgender activist within the Gay Liberation movement in the early 1970s, was one of the first community-based historians of transgender people, and helped to establish the organized FTM community in the United States. After receiving his AIDS diagnosis in 1986, Sullivan selflessly devoted his final years to overturning what he perceived to be homophobic biases in the provision of medical services to FTM transsexuals who identified as gay. If he were alive today he would undoubtedly be one of the leading voices on transgender issues.[2]

The detailed journals Sullivan left of the 30 years between 1961 and 1991 provide one of the most complete and compelling autobiographical accounts of a transsexual life ever recorded, and as such they are among his most important legacies as an activist. They offer a privileged glimpse into the inner life of a person who defied considerable odds to actualize a 'transhomosexual' identity – the very existence of which was denied by the medico-psychotherapeutic professionals who had assumed responsibility for managing transgender lives.[3] In achieving what he himself called 'my own interpretation of happiness',[4] Sullivan exemplified the Foucaultian concept of 'counter-discursive identity formation', which has proven so important for understanding the development of other communities based on sexual identities.[5] Contrary to what much of the existing scholarly literature on transgender phenomena suggests, many transsexuals – like many homosexuals – have formed a personal sense of self not only *through* particular scientific discourses of sexuality, but *in opposition* to them.[6]

In this chapter, I draw upon Sullivan's journals to offer a brief summary of his career as a transgender activist. In doing so, I seek to demonstrate how transsexuals have struggled to resist aspects of medicalization that rob them of personal agency and autonomy even while they seek access to the technologies of re-embodiment, and to link this struggle to other forms of queer resistance to heteronormative oppression.

'Looking toward transvestite liberation'

Sullivan's activist career began in 1973 at the University of Wisconsin's Milwaukee campus (UWM), where he worked as a secretary in the Slavic Languages Department and participated in the Gay People's Union (GPU). Sullivan published his first political essays that year in the *GPU News*, offering some of the earliest critiques from a transgender perspective of the emergent gender ideology that condemned transvestites and transsexuals as political reactionaries. The first of these essays, 'A Transvestite Answers a Feminist', developed out of conversations Sullivan had with a co-worker who had recently become involved in the women's movement (S. Sullivan, 1973). The other, 'Looking Toward Transvestite Liberation', was widely reprinted in the gay liberation press (S. Sullivan, 1974).

Because Sullivan still lived publicly as a woman during this period of his life, was attracted to men, and dressed full-time in men's clothing, he described himself as a 'heterosexual female transvestite'. Sullivan had a very queer notion of heterosexuality, however. He had made masculine psychical identifications since early childhood, and his sexual desires were directed primarily towards gay men – especially effeminate, cross-dressing gay men. 'My heart is with the drag queens', he had written in his journal in 1970 at age 19, 'But where do I fit in? I feel so deprived and sad and lost. What can become of a girl whose real desire and passion is with male homosexuals? That I want to be one?' (22 November 1970). Based on this sense of his own gender identity and sexual orientation Sullivan sought – and gained – inclusion in the men's rather than the women's caucus of the GPU. Initially dismissed as a confused eccentric, Sullivan rapidly won the respect and friendship of many men in the GPU who eventually welcomed him into Milwaukee's gay male night-life.

Sullivan deeply identified with the drag queens he met in the city's gay bars. He saw in them a reflection of his own situation as a masculine subject who presented a feminine image to the world. By participating in gay male culture, Sullivan learned to take more pleasure in the artifice of gender and to feel less trapped by womanhood. He sometimes acted like a female-bodied drag queen who engaged in complex, multi-layered performances of gender – going to a Lou Reed concert with his drag buddies, for example, while dressed as Alice Cooper. At other times he used butch drag to pass as male. Dressed as a boy, Sullivan would travel to Chicago to loiter around gay bathhouses and offer patrons quick and anonymous oral sex, or to visit the Hellfire Club, a celebrated gay men's S/M bar. On his first trip to the Hellfire, Sullivan was amazed at how 'un-hard the scene was. It was fun. We're all girls pretending we're big shot boys' (18 January 1974).

In some respects, however, Sullivan's immersion in Milwaukee's gay drag scene was merely compensatory, a way of understanding himself by analogy. He had never met another FTM, not to mention another gay-identified FTM. A lone pre-operative MTF transsexual and his drag queen friends were all the transgender community Sullivan was able to find for himself in Milwaukee in the early 1970s. Sullivan consequently read voraciously, trying to discover some FTM figure with whom he could identify in a less convoluted manner. He learned of many 'passing women' and other female-bodied people who lived significant portions of their lives as men, but he failed to find any mention of gay FTMs in the historical literature. In his darker moments, he feared that the total lack of gay FTM visibility meant he was either delusional about his own sense of self or else utterly alone in the world. Still, Sullivan searched. He published biographical sketches drawn from his research in the *GPU News* and, later in the 1980s, in transgender community publications. Many of these vignettes were eventually incorporated into Sullivan's pioneering self-help book, *Information for the Female to Male Cross Dresser and Transsexual*, which after nearly twenty years remains an initial point of contact with the FTM community for many biologically female gender-questioning individuals (L. Sullivan, 1980).

Sullivan's San Francisco transition

Sullivan left Milwaukee for San Francisco in 1975 to accompany a boyfriend who had been accepted into a doctoral programme at UC Berkeley. San Francisco had far more transgender resources than Milwaukee, and Sullivan soon learned of support groups and therapists specializing in 'gender dysphoria' at the Public Health Department's Centre for Special Problems (CSP). He was disappointed, however, at the lack of services geared specifically towards FTMs. He complained of the CSP group that 'of course it's all M-F TSs. After thinking about it I decided not to join the group – there's just so much I can't say in a M-F group, there's a point where my "feeling just the same but in the opposite direction" no longer does me any good, no longer answers my questions' (5 August 1976). He settled instead on seeing a therapist privately.

The day after Sullivan scheduled his first therapy appointment, a story broke in the Bay Area press about Steve Dain, a high school teacher in Emeryville (between Oakland and Berkeley in the East Bay) who had transitioned from female to male. As one sympathetic article noted, 'What puzzles most people is that Dain is not seeking a new identity in a new locale' after transitioning (Anspacher, 1976). Rather, he had simply reported to work at the school district where he was tenured and requested a new teaching assignment, since he felt that it would be inappropriate to continue serving as the girls' gym coach. Dain's decision to transition in a community in which he had already established a prior identity did in fact signal a change in how transsexuals tried to build post-transitional lives for themselves. Dain's attempt was not entirely successful, in that his former principal reacted phobically and had him arrested for creating a public disturbance. Although Dain won a series of lawsuits stemming from the arrest, he ultimately left his teaching position to pursue a successful career as a chiropractor.[7]

Sullivan followed the case with rapt attention, and screwed up his courage to contact Dain – the first FTM with whom he had ever communicated. 'My greatest desire is to meet and talk to some one who has gone through this change', Sullivan wrote. 'I so badly need peers, and as I am sure you know, there aren't a hell of a lot of F-Ms around'.[8] Dain responded promptly and warmly, promising to meet with Sullivan 'after things settle down'. He supported Sullivan's decision to pursue therapy, but offered words of wisdom. 'Remember – only you will be able to answer the questions you ask yourself, so listen for your answers as you share your feelings with your counsellor.'[9]

Inspired by his contact with Dain, Sullivan took his first serious steps towards obtaining surgical and hormonal sex-reassignment in

November 1976 by requesting, completing and returning an application for admission to the Stanford Gender Dysphoria Program in Palo Alto. Almost immediately thereafter, however, Sullivan suffered a severe crisis of identity and resumed living as a feminine heterosexual woman for the next three years. Although at the time he experienced the decision to 'go back' as a form of failure – an admission to the world that his masculine identifications and transsexual desires were indeed delusional – those last three years as a woman were crucial to the formation of the man he would eventually become. He became involved in a feminist consciousness-raising group, took classes in auto mechanics to break down self-limiting gender stereotypes, and worked to overcome feelings of self-hatred due to internalized misogyny. He held a job as a woman but spent a substantial amount of his private time cross-dressing and cruising the Castro. After being picked up one night in the summer of 1979 by a drunk gay who wanted to take Sullivan home until he said 'I'm female', Sullivan wrote in his journal 'I assured him I wouldn't have gone anyway because he wasn't femme enough for me' (18 July 1979).

Sullivan carved out a unique place for himself as a heterosexual female transvestite in the Bay Area's transgender community between 1977 and 1979, during which time he began educating organizations geared to MTFs about FTM concerns. After Sullivan became treasurer and newsletter editor of one such group – Golden Gate Girls – they changed their name to Golden Gate Girls/Guys (GGG/G) and became one of the first 'co-gender' transgender organizations in the nation. It was through GGG/G in 1978 that Sullivan first met another person who identified as a female-to-male cross-dresser.

Nineteen seventy-nine proved to be a momentous year in the process of Sullivan's transition from woman to man. Late in 1978 he had been profoundly shaken by the death of his youngest sibling in a car crash. Suddenly confronted by the spectre of mortality, Sullivan discovered previously untapped emotional reserves – he resolved to live more fully in the present and to find greater comfort and happiness in his own life. One unexpected consequence of this changed perspective was that Sullivan broke off his troubled, on-again/off-again relationship with the man with whom he had come to California, who had always felt ambivalent about Sullivan's masculinity. Sullivan soon realized that his urge to present a masculine image to the world was always greatest when he was not involved with a man. He wrote, 'I think it is because when I am alone I have no man to pretend to be, no man to live through vicariously' (3 October 1979). He recognized that 'in my need for a man in my bed I detach myself from my body and my body becomes his', but that when he was not in a relationship, 'in my search for the perfect male companion I find myself' (21 August 1979).

After the break-up, Sullivan turned more to other transgender people for companionship and validation. He was beginning to make contact with others who identified similarly to himself, and was flattered at the requests he was beginning to receive for articles and opinion pieces in the transgender community press. He was also thrilled by the 28 responses he received after placing a personal ad in the *Advocate* that read 'Bisexual Men: Slim serious female 28 who has passed as a man part time since 1973 identifies w/ gay men, wants companionship, romance.' Most importantly, he discovered within himself the ability to insist that he was in fact a gay FTM – even if the so-called experts denied such a thing existed. He began thinking seriously again about surgical and hormonal transition, although he was acutely aware that he might be denied access to medical services because of his sexual orientation. Fortunately for Sullivan, transgender medical services were at that very moment undergoing a significant reorganization that would allow him to achieve much of what he sought for himself.

Sullivan had met local San Francisco psychotherapist Lin Fraser at a GGG/G meeting in January 1979. She reintroduced him that September to Steve Dain, and from that point onward Sullivan's transsexual career progressed rapidly. 'It was like looking at my own future, or in a mirror', Sullivan wrote excitedly in his journal the day after meeting his FTM role model. Dain 'said I had a perfect right to be a gay man if that's what I want', and that it 'pisses him off that those Docs think you've got to fit a prescribed mould'. Sullivan also noted that Dain was counselling 'an 18 yr. old female who says she feels like a gay man and who hits Castro Street – so we *do exist!*' (28 September 1979). A few days later Sullivan wrote, 'I can see the pieces of my life falling into place and am extremely optimistic about my future' (30 September 1979). In December, armed with an endocrinology referral from Lin Fraser to a sympathetic doctor in private practice, Sullivan began injecting testosterone. Within a matter of months, he had obtained a driver's licence with his new masculine name and gender designation. The following summer he underwent a bilateral mastectomy by yet another doctor in private practice and began living full-time as a man. His last remaining desire was to undergo phalloplasty, which was still relatively unavailable outside a few major clinics.

Friends in the transgender community told Sullivan that the clinics 'wouldn't touch [me] with a ten-foot pole ... because I don't have the typical transsexual story they want to hear', but he resolved once again to contact the Gender Dysphoria Program in Palo Alto (formerly affiliated with Stanford University). Sullivan applied for phalloplasty surgery in the spring of 1980. He was rejected. Judy Van Maasdam, an administrative assistant to Dr Donald Laub who had worked her way into a position of considerable responsibility in the programme, wrote to Sullivan to say that 'we have decided that we cannot be of assistance to you' because 'the history which you presented was not typical for the majority of persons who, in our program, have made successful adjustments with gender reorientation, and who have been helped, not harmed, by sex reassignment'.[10]

Sullivan responded to this institutionalized homophobia in a manner that demonstrated his political sensibilities:

> When I applied to your program, I knew I had an 80% chance of being rejected, but felt it was important to add my special circumstances to your list of statistics. ... It is unfortunate that your program cannot see the merit of each individual, regardless of their sexual orientation. The general human population is made up of many sexual persuasions – it is incredible that your Program requires all transsexuals to be of one fabric. I had even considered lying to you about my sexual preference of men, as I knew it would surely keep me out of your Program, but I felt it important to be straightforward, possibly paving the way for other female-to-males with homosexual orientations – and we do exist.[11]

Decentralization of transgender health-care

The vagaries of Lou Sullivan's transition initially present a confusing picture – on the one hand, he met with remarkable support from a handful of gender dysphoria specialists, while on the other hand he encountered incomprehension and opposition from one of the longest-established gender identity clinics in the world. This seeming contradiction can be resolved by understanding how Sullivan's experience was structured by a significant shift in the organization of transgender health care services in the United States during the late 1970s and early 1980s.

Sullivan would have found it more difficult to obtain non-black-market hormones and chest surgery outside the context of a major gender dysphoria clinic had he begun his process only a year earlier.

For more than a decade prior to Sullivan's transition, most transsexuals had gained access to hormones and surgery through university-based gender identity clinics – the first of which was established at Johns Hopkins University in November 1966, followed soon thereafter by ones at the University of Minnesota, UCLA, Stanford University and elsewhere (Green and Money, 1969). The consolidation of transsexual medicine in high-profile clinics affiliated with major research institutions and controlled by eminent social-scientific experts in human sexuality was itself a response to an earlier *laissez-faire* approach to transsexualism in the years immediately following Christine Jorgensen's advent to celebrity. Between 1952 and 1966, transsexual surgery and hormones were available on demand to patients, based on ad hoc arrangements with surgeons and endocrinologists. Many transsexuals were quite pleased with this state of affairs, but others fell victim to unscrupulous doctors who left them maimed and ill-equipped for post-surgical life.[12] The shift to centralized university-based gender identity programmes thus in part reflected an ethical concern among some medical and psychotherapeutic professionals that transsexual clients could be better served if the proper authorities developed objective criteria for managing their care. This shift also reflected assumptions that scientific experts knew better than transsexuals themselves what was in their own best interests.

The shift embodied a great many other cultural concerns as well. The rise of the gender identity clinic can be seen as a typical instance of 'big science' at the height of the Cold War – an attempt at the social-scientific regulation of culture through academically sanctioned expert opinion, an anxious effort to control potentially destabilizing social expressions of sexuality and gender in the context of sexual revolution and a burgeoning feminist movement. Transsexual candidates at these clinics were subjected to rigorous psychometric and sociometric testing, and were compelled to spend months or years proving to their self-appointed guardians' satisfaction that they could live in their 'gender role of choice' before being allowed access to hormones and surgery. The obvious if unstated goal of these programmes was to produce transsexual men and women who conformed to heteronormative gender conventions, including the visual appearance of a conventional female or male morphology.

Even though the establishment of a nation-wide network of university-based gender clinics had been privately funded and co-ordinated in large part by the wealthy FTM transsexual Reed Erickson, the clinic system always served the needs of MTFs more adequately than it did those of FTMs.[13] This was particularly true of the clinical bias towards the production of conventional morphology, since MTF genital surgeries have long been far more cosmetically and functionally satisfactory than FTM genital surgeries, and many FTMs prefer to forgo 'bottom surgery' entirely. This was true as well of the bias against homosexually oriented transsexuals. While the revelation of MTF lesbian desire could indeed result in denial of surgery, specialists generally acknowledged that a minority of MTF trans-sexuals lived as lesbians post-transitionally.[14] They flatly refused, however, to believe that gay FTMs existed. Thus, although the easier access to hormones and surgeries outside the major clinics that became available around 1980 proved significant for all transgender people who somehow contested heteronormativity but nevertheless sought to alter their bodies, this development was especially important for FTMs and 'transhomosexuals' – doubly so for gay-identified FTMs like Sullivan.

Two landmark events around 1980 fundamentally changed the landscape of transsexual medical services in the United States. First, in 1979, the Harry Benjamin International Gender Dysphoria Association (HBIGDA) – the professional organization that has assumed responsibility for managing the lives of transgender people – came into existence and issued its 'Standards of Care: The Hormonal and Surgical Sex Reassignment of Gender Dysphoric Individuals' (Denny, 1994: 633–48). These standards effectively codified the treatment protocols developed in the big clinics over the previous decade. Second, in 1980, the third revised edition of the American Psychiatric Association's Diagnostic and Statistical Manual (DSM-IIIR) first listed 'gender identity disorder' (GID) as an official psychopathology (*Diagnostic and Statistical Manual*, 1980). These were not unrelated events. The inclusion of GID in the DSM was in fact the result of lobbying by the same people who formed HBIGDA's membership. Recognition of GID as a bona fide psychopathology created a situation in which they could better assert their professional competence based on their area of specialization, and thus gain greater status in the eyes of their peers. With the development of bioethical standards and inclusion in the bible of psychiatric diagnosis, 'gender dysphoria' had finally arrived as a legitimized research field (Irvine, 1990).

These new developments helped decentralize transsexual medical services that had been consolidated during the post-1966 period by expanding the 'gate-keeper' role of HBIGDA-affiliated psychotherapists working in private practice. Once an 'industry standard' had been established for access to hormones and surgery, the days when clinics attached to major universities dominated transgender health care were clearly numbered – indeed, many clinics began shutting down in the late 1970s, or spinning off from their bases of institutional support and re-establishing themselves as private enterprises. In their place arose smaller, more specialized surgical and endocrinological practices in which psychotherapists served as virtual front-office staff responsible for screening transsexual clients. As arbiters of widely accepted professional bioethical standards, psychotherapists offered the doctors a measure of protection against charges of malpractice that might stem from performing irreversible procedures on patients who later proved ill-suited for the transition. The new arrangements also permitted doctors to schedule fewer consultation hours with their potential clients and thus to devote more of their time as practitioners to more remunerative activities. This trend towards more intensive specialization and less general practice reflected broader developments in the US health care industry, and was not limited to the reorganization of transsexual medicine.

These new arrangements created new challenges for transgender people struggling to exercise a measure of autonomy over their own identity and embodiment, but they offered new opportunities as well. With the crucial decision to grant surgical and hormonal access devolving more fully upon a 'second tier' of practising psychotherapists rather than upon an élite cadre of clinical specialists, more transsexuals who presented atypical histories or desires were able to get what they wanted for themselves through the personal relationships they established with sympathetic individual psychotherapists.

Building community and recovering history

Lou Sullivan was among the first transsexuals in the United States to follow this new path and to help popularize it for others. His priority in this matter stemmed in part from the fact that as a gay FTM he had a greater stake in searching out alternatives to the older model of service provision. However, due to his geographical location in San Francisco, Sullivan also found himself at an epicentre of institutional change in the management of transgender health care. As a result of his years of work in the Bay Area's transgender community, Sullivan had developed extensive personal contacts with many of the professionals who were instrumental in establishing the new decentralized approach to transsexual medical services. This included his therapist Lin Fraser, a charter member of HBIGDA, as well as Paul Walker, principal author of the HBIGDA Standards of Care.

Sullivan and Walker, who was also gay, had become friends in 1979 when Sullivan began working as the first and only FTM peer counsellor at San Francisco's Janus Information Facility (JIF) – a transgender referral service and clearing-house supported by the Erickson Educational Foundation (EEF) and administered by Walker. It was here that Sullivan produced the first edition of his *Information for the Female-to-Male*, which was distributed by JIF along with other self-help literature developed by the EEF. In his role as a peer counsellor, Sullivan was able to disseminate at the grass-roots level his positive experiences with accessing transsexual services outside the context of major gender identity clinics. He thereby helped steer prospective clients into the new networks for transgender medical services that were just beginning to emerge in the context of the HBIGDA Standards of Care.

Through *Information for the Female-to-Male* and his voluminous correspondence with gender-questioning female-bodied people throughout the English-speaking world, Sullivan helped lay the foundations for what would become a thriving FTM community by the 1990s. By the mid-1980s, Sullivan was in touch with hundreds of FTMs, and he socialized with many who lived in the Bay Area. In August 1986, Sullivan wrote in his journal about watching the movie *Mystery of Alexina* (based on the story of the famous French hermaphrodite Herculine Barbin) and running into 'a black FTM gay man, Chad, (who I met last year at the FTM picnic as "John,") [who] was with his white FTM lover. ... All of a sudden I have a million FTM contacts' (8 August 1986).

In spite of informal community events like the above-mentioned picnic, there was as yet no formal FTM organization on the West Coast – indeed, only two such organizations had ever existed in North America, Mario Martino's Labyrinth Foundation in New York and Rupert Raj's Metamorphosis in Canada. Sullivan's community-building efforts took on greater focus in October of that year when he helped organize FTM, the San Francisco-based support and advocacy group that has since become the largest such organization in the world. Sullivan recorded a conversation in his journal that can serve as a point of origin for the San Francisco FTM group:

Another great thing that happened is that John G., a 'well-known' F-M phoned me to say he'd like to get a female-to-male group going and someone suggested he call me, because I might want to, too. I was so flattered that he'd call ME. . . . I'm very excited by the idea of calling a gathering of F-Ms just to talk to each other, exchange information, and just 'be there' for new F-Ms coming out, and John seems particularly interested in steering them *away* from Judy and Laub, and toward [some of the more sympathetic doctors in private practice]. I'm very excited – oh, already said that. But I *am*, and about maybe even getting a small newsletter going. (4 October 1986)

Sullivan quickly became the driving force behind the San Francisco FTM support group, and the founding editor of the *FTM Newsletter*. He continued to serve in a leadership position in the group until shortly before his death in 1991.

Without quite recognizing it himself, by 1986 Sullivan had blossomed into a major presence in the transgender community. He not only helped establish the most prominent FTM support organization in the country, but became a pioneering historian of FTM identity. Sullivan's historical activism was in fact deeply interconnected with his physical and social transition from woman to man. In June 1979, while in the throes of breaking up with his long-time lover and beginning to re-examine the possibility of pursuing hormonal and surgical alterations to his body, Sullivan had attended a lecture and slide show at the San Francisco Women's Building called 'Lesbian Masquerade: Some Lesbians in Early San Francisco who Passed as Men'. The lecture, presented by community-based scholar Allan Berubé on behalf of the Gay and Lesbian History Project collective, struck Sullivan like a bolt from the blue. Although he had researched 'passing women' while writing for the *GPU News* between 1973 and 1975, Sullivan had gradually lost interest in the topic during the period when he was consciously identifying as a woman. He was thunderstruck by the new level of historical knowledge that had begun to emerge from the first wave of gay and lesbian studies in those few intervening years, and was inspired anew to search for gay FTMs in history. This rekindled hope of finding transgender forebears with whom he could identify in fact helped sustain Sullivan in his decision to transition hormonally and surgically.

Sullivan soon developed a far-reaching critique of the prevailing gay and lesbian interpretation of transgender lives – just as six years earlier he had developed a critique of anti-transgender feminist gender ideology. The orthodox view in the first generation of gay and lesbian community-based scholarship, exemplified by such work as the San

Francisco History Project's (1989) 'She Even Chewed Tobacco' or Jonathan Katz's *Gay American History* (1976) was that transgender people passed as the 'opposite' sex in previous eras either in order to enact same-sex desire within a profoundly homophobic culture, or (in the case of female-to-male passing) for purely economic reasons. Feminism and gay liberation supposedly obviated these motivations and made transgender practices seem politically suspect. Sullivan recognized that homosexually orientated transgender people like himself flew in the face of this interpretation, and he found in the figure of Jack Garland a historical antecedent for his own situation. Garland was a widely beloved lay social worker in San Francisco's impoverished Tenderloin neighbourhood who was discovered to be female upon his death in 1937. Berubé and the History Project represented Garland in their work as a lesbian, but Sullivan knew from his own research that Garland (like Sullivan himself) preferred to be involved with men. Sullivan suggested to Berubé that Garland's case represented something more complex than a lesbian passing as a man to avoid homophobia – he was rather a person who had gone to extra-ordinary lengths to be perceived as a man by men in order to enact homosexual desire. To his credit, Berubé invited Sullivan to become involved with the Gay and Lesbian History Project rather than dismissing him as a deranged crank. As a result of that encouragement, Sullivan eventually published a book-length biography of Garland (L. Sullivan, 1990), and in the process helped found the Gay and Lesbian Historical Society of California (GLHS). Thanks in part to Sullivan's early influence, the GLHS now has remarkably rich archival collections of transgender material.

Living and dying like a gay man

> It really hasn't hit me that I am about to die. I see the grief around me but inside I feel serene and a certain sense of peace. My whole life I've wanted to be a gay man and it's kind of an honour to die from the gay man's disease. I'm going to take a special pleasure in informing Judy Van Maasdam – I'll write something like 'your clinic decided that I couldn't live as a gay man but I am going to die like one.' (7 January 1987)

As 1986 drew to a close, Lou Sullivan was filled with optimism for the future. The new FTM group was off to a good beginning, work on his biography of Jack Garland was progressing steadily and he had finally managed to find a doctor who would perform genital surgery. After months of worrisome complications his testicular implants finally seemed to be taking and his new scrotum was healing nicely. He had recently started his own typesetting business and had just moved into a new apartment. A relationship with a gay lover had recently come to an abrupt end, but even that seemed to offer him a fresh beginning.

Sullivan first noticed some shortness of breath on 2 December while moving furniture into his new apartment. A nagging cough persisted throughout the month, but he thought it was just a mild flu or bronchitis. At a meeting of the Gay and Lesbian Historical Society on 28 December, a friend who happened to be a nurse told him it sounded like 'walking pneumonia' and suggested that he see a doctor immediately. The next day Sullivan made an appointment for New Year's Eve with his regular physician. By the 30th, however, he felt as if he couldn't breathe at all and had his sister take him to the emergency room of UCSF hospital. The immediate diagnosis: acute *pneumocystis carinii* pneumonia, an opportunistic illness commonly associated with HIV infection. Sullivan was rushed into intensive care, and the next day blood tests confirmed what the doctors had already concluded. Lou Sullivan had AIDS.

Sullivan was dumbfounded. He had had very few sexual partners and none of them had ever gotten sick. He had no idea how he had become infected. Evidence from his journals seems to suggest, however, that Sullivan was probably exposed to HIV in the summer of 1980. After being on testosterone for over six months and completing his mastectomy, Sullivan had spent that summer revelling in his new-found ease in passing as a gay man. He frequented San Francisco's many gay sex clubs and bathhouses, taking special pleasure in sucking off any number of men in 'glory holes'. Sullivan's timing was truly tragic. San Francisco in the summer of 1980 – a year before the AIDS epidemic became visible but years after it had begun – was probably the worst place in the world at the worst time in history to be having lots of unprotected sex with gay men. A few weeks after his orgiastic fling Sullivan wrote in his journal about having a bad case of the flu. He was most likely sero-converting, though at the time no one would have known that a sudden flu-like illness was a symptom of AIDS. Sullivan apparently remained asymptomatic for five-and-a-half years, until the prolonged stress of his genital surgery activated the HIV infection.

Recovering his health and adjusting to his status as a PWA occupied most of Sullivan's attention for the first few months of 1987, but he gradually returned to as normal a life as possible. He was determined to finish his biography of Jack Garland, and also had hopes of publishing his journals. Then he found a new cause to devote himself to in June, when an FTM friend told him about a recent scientific article on 'homosexual and heterosexual gender dysphoria' in which the authors blithely mentioned that they had dropped from their statistical analyses a single gay FTM they had encountered in their investigations because they didn't know how to 'fit him in' (Blanchard *et al.*, 1987). Sullivan was outraged. 'I must write them to protest such an overlooking and censoring of our existence! These are all pressing concerns of mine – things I need to accomplish before I die' (24 June 1987).

A few weeks later, Sullivan's friend Paul Walker returned from a sexological meeting in Holland with the exciting news that Dr Louis Gooren had reported several gay FTMs had recently begun attending support groups in Amsterdam – the first 'official sighting' of the heretofore nearly mythical creatures. In the discussion after Gooren's presentation several other sexologists confessed that they, too, had had sporadic contact with other gay FTMs in Europe and the United States. Gay FTMs were suddenly one of the hottest topics in gender dysphoria research, and Sullivan was ecstatic. 'I am so delighted this is finally happening, and deep down am proud to have been one of the ground-breakers who can honestly report I've never wavered in my desire to be a gay man – and I've done a hell of a good job reaching my dream, through no help from the so-called experts' (30 July 1987).

Not content to sit back and simply let sexual science take its course, Sullivan launched a campaign to orchestrate as many 'field sightings' of gay FTMs as possible. Based on all the contacts he had established through JIF and the *FTM Newsletter*, he was in the perfect position to steer gay FTMs towards gender dysphoria professionals now only too eager to pay attention to their stories. For Sullivan, documenting the existence of gay FTMs was not simply a matter of participating in a taste-test of sexual science's flavour of the month. It was a project that became a way of validating his own life before he died, as well as a way of helping others like him avoid the experience of anguished seeking that he himself had suffered. Sullivan wrote that 'a big fear of mine is that I will die before the gender professionals acknowledge that someone like me exists, and then I really *won't* exist to prove them wrong' (30 July 1987). Consequently, after contacting a senior professional specialist on FTMs, Ira Pauly, Sullivan arranged to lecture Pauly's students at the University of Nevada–Reno Medical School. The lecture was videotaped and – given Pauly's reputation and Sullivan's charismatic zeal – it made a substantial impression among gender dysphoria professionals. Sullivan subsequently attended one of the biennial HBIGDA meetings, where he impressed many of the other participants with his intelligence and candour.[15]

Sullivan also contacted Eli Coleman of the University of Minnesota Gender Identity Clinic and Walter Bockting, who had been working with the Dutch gay FTMs, and arranged to be interviewed. Their 1988 case study of Sullivan was considered a landmark article in the specialized field of gender dysphoria research (Coleman and Bockting, 1988). Over the next few years Bockting and Coleman became leading proponents within HBIGDA of recognizing the existence of gay FTMs and, by extension, acknowledging that gender identity, social role and sexual orientation were not linked in any deterministic manner. The simple fact that gay FTMs existed, they claimed, called into question dominant theories of gender transposition and the development of homosexuality (Coleman and Bockting, 1989).

While Bockting and Coleman's proposition that transgender people could configure identity, desire and social role in multiple and potentially non-heteronormative ways might seem intuitively obvious to anyone versed in the queer theory of the 1990s – or who knows it to be true from their own experience of life – their thinking represented a radical departure within an incredibly normativistic field of social science. By the 1989 meeting of HBIGDA, however, their position had become widely accepted and was the focus of several presentations.[16] Gender identity specialists explicitly embraced the possibility of using the power of modern medicine and sexual science to actively produce and enable socially intelligibly homosexual lives. This was a rather remarkable accomplishment for which Lou Sullivan could claim considerable behind-the-scenes credit. Without this change in the conceptualization of transgender identity among the medical and psycho-therapeutic professionals who control access to surgical and hormonal re-embodiment technologies, there would be far fewer transhomosexuals today, and the queer movement of the 1990s would have a substantially different feel.

Sullivan was determined not only to change professional attitudes towards transhomosexuals, but to change practices. He wanted to see sexual orientation removed from the diagnostic criteria for gender identity disorder in the DSM – for access to hormones and surgery, in other words, to be 'orientation blind'. Sullivan corresponded with members of the group working on revising the definition of GID for the forthcoming DSM IV, letting his views be known. Though he did not live to see it, the DSM IV did drop sexual orientation subtypes within the GID diagnosis. However, as Dr Ray Blanchard (who participated in the DSM-IV GID revisions working group) contends, this change had virtually nothing to do with Sullivan's activism, and as Blanchard further points out, the DSM III-R definition of GID was in fact capable of accommodating the existence of gay FTMs. The problem, as Sullivan's experience demonstrates, was that transhomosexuals were denied sex-reassignment procedures at the level of individual clinics and individual medical practitioners. The crucial change, therefore, was in professional opinion about the suitability of self-professed transhomosexuals for surgical and hormonal reassignment. In this regard, Sullivan certainly played an important role. According to Blanchard, Sullivan's main contribution was in

> bringing the existence of gay-identified FTMs to the attention of clinical authors who were in a position to disseminate this information more widely among health care professionals. This may indeed make it easier for gay-identified FTM transsexuals to get sex-reassignment surgery without having to lie about their histories.[17]

Blanchard's assessment of Sullivan's role gives voice to a key assumption in the social scientific approach to transsexualism – it is clinical specialists who speak, know and act as deliberative agents. Transsexuals are merely the objects of discourse, the subject spoken about, deliberated over, and acted upon. This attitude has been typical not only within the clinical literature on transsexualism and other transgender phenomena, but also of cultural studies conducted by scholars who generally tend to critique the way institutionalized power renders silent those upon whom it operates. In her recent monograph, Bernice Hausman goes so far as to claim that transsexuals' desire and agency can be read simply and directly through the discourse of their doctors (Hausman, 1995:110). As Lou Sullivan's story demonstrates, however, the relationship between transsexual agency and medical discourse is complex rather than simple. At least for non-heteronormative subjects, it is a situation of struggle rather than a place where power is effortlessly aligned with the project of caring for one's self.

For all he managed to accomplish, Sullivan's strategy for self-care was basically reformist. He managed to appear within the social-scientific discourses on transgender identity as a gay man but did not challenge the power-laden 'language games' that constituted the means of that appearing – social-scientific expert opinion retained the position of speaking the truth of his existence. It is ironic that Sullivan died not knowing that by his example he had helped inaugurate a transgender political movement that would present a far more radical challenge to the social-scientific establishment than anything he ever seemed to have imagined. While it remains impossible to speak of a single unified transgender movement with clearly articulated goals, it is certainly true that one aim of many activists is to do for gender identity disorder what gay liberation did for social scientific accounts of pathological homosexuality – that is, to make transgender people themselves, rather than their self-appointed clinical caretakers, the ultimate authority about transgender lives.

Rest in peace

Lou Sullivan's biography of Jack Garland was published to favourable reviews by Alyson Press in 1990. It, as well as the third edition of *Information for the Female-to-Male*, remains in print. Sullivan died on 6 March 1991 of an AIDS-related illness while surrounded by friends and family members. Members of the FTM support group made a panel in his honour for the NAMES Project AIDS Memorial Quilt.

Notes

1. A note on pronouns: I use the masculine personal pronouns 'he', 'him' and 'his' and the proper name 'Lou' when referring to Sullivan throughout this article. I chose this manner of representing him in deference to the identity that he achieved, and that he felt was the best representation of himself to others. I am not attempting to deny that Sullivan had another name and answered to other pronouns for 29 of his 39 years, nor am I advocating any simplistic notion of transsexual gender essentialism.
2. Most sources for Lou Sullivan's life and career are found in the Louis Graydon Sullivan Collection (seven linear feet), on deposit in the San Francisco History Room of the San Francisco Main Public Library, by special arrangement with the Gay and Lesbian Historical Society of Northern California. I processed the Sullivan Collection for archival use and prepared the collection description, and am therefore familiar with Sullivan's life and work in some detail. My familiarity with the documentary sources is the basis for some of the unattributed generalizations I make about Sullivan in this article. I have presented other unpublished work on material in Sullivan's childhood journals, and am in the process of preparing a biographical monograph on Sullivan's life and career that draws extensively from his unpublished journals.

3. 'Transhomosexual' is a term coined in Clare (1984) and further elaborated in Clare (1991), Clare and Tully (1989), and Tully (1992).

4. Lou Sullivan journal, 20 June 1966. Subsequent citations of the journal appear in the main body of the text, in parenthesis following the quoted material.

5. Jennifer Terry (1991) offers a superb explication and application of counter-discursivity.

6. Bernice Hausman (1995) offers perhaps the most recent significant example of scholarship on transgender phenomena that views transsexualism strictly as a product of medical discourse, with no room for transsexual agency or counter-discursive struggle. For an ethical critique of this tendency in much of the social-scientific literature on transgenderism, see James L. Nelson, 'The silence of the bio-ethicists: the cultural politics of managing gender dysphoria', and for a critique of inappropriate uses of discourse analysis, see Henry S. Rubin, 'Phenomenology as method in trans studies', both forthcoming in *GLQ: A Journal of Lesbian and Gay Studies*, 4, 2 (1998), which is published simultaneously as Susan Stryker (ed.), *The Transgender Issue* (Durham: Duke University Press, 1998).

7. For other press accounts of the Steve Dain story, see Rassmussen (1976a, 1976b) and Malaspina (1976).

8. Sheila (Lou) Sullivan to Steve Dain, 9 August 1976, Louis Sullivan Collection.

9. Steve Dain to Sheila (Lou) Sullivan, 19 August 1976, Louis Sullivan Collection.

10. Judy Van Maasdam to Sheila (Lou) Sullivan, 12 March 1980, Louis Sullivan Collection.

11. Lou Sullivan to Judy Van Maasdam, 22 March 1980, Louis Sullivan Collection.

12. On early transsexual history, see Bullough (1975) and Meyerowitz (1998). For accounts of badly managed surgeries, see Vivian Le Mans (pseud.), *Take My Tool: Revelations of a Sex-Switch* (1968); packaged and marketed as a piece of cheap pornography, Le Mans's book is actually a remarkable autobiographical narrative produced by a male-to-female transsexual that covers the period 1940–68 and offers some unprecedented glimpses of working-class transsexual life.

13. For a brief mention of Reed's behind-the-scenes role, see Harry Benjamin, 'Introduction', in Green and Money (1969). For more detailed information see the Erickson Educational Foundation Newsletter.

14. Caricatures of transsexual lesbians figure prominently in the running argument advanced in Janice Raymond, *The Transsexual Empire: The Making of the She-Male* (Boston: Beacon, 1979). For a less hysterical account, see Feinbloom (1976).

15. Louis Sullivan Correspondence with Ira Pauly, 1987–9; Louis Sullivan Collection.

16. See, for example, Holly Devor, 'Sexual behaviour of female-to-male transsexuals'; Ira Pauly, 'Female to gay male transsexualism'; Ira Pauly, 'Sexual preference of female to male transsexuals'; and Walter Bockting and Janke Poortinga, 'Sex roles of homosexual men and male-to-female transsexuals: a comparison'.

17. Personal communication, Ray Blanchard to Susan Stryker, 2 July 1993.

References

Anspacher, C. (1976) 'Sex change uproar in Emeryville', *San Francisco Chronicle*, 7 August: 1ff.

Blanchard, R., L. Clemmensen and B. Steiner (1987) 'Heterosexual and homosexual gender dysphoria', *Archives of Sexual Behaviour*, 16, 2: 139–52.

Bullough, V. (1975) 'Transsexualism in history', *Archives of Sexual Behaviour*, 4, 5: 561–71.

Clare, D. (1984) 'Transhomosexuality', *Proceedings of the Annual Conference of the British Psychological Society*, 6, University of Warwick.

Clare, D. (1991) 'Transsexualism, gender dysphoria, and transhomosexuality', *Gender Dysphoria*, 1, 1: 7–17.

Clare, D. and B. Tully (1989) 'Transhomosexuality, or the dissociation of sexual orientation and sex object choice', *Archives of Sexual Behaviour*, 18, 6: 531–6.

Coleman, E. and W. Bockting (1988) ' "Heterosexual" prior to sex reassignment – "homosexual" afterward: a case study of a female-to-male transsexual', *Journal of Psychology and Human Sexuality*, 1, 2: 69–82.

Coleman, E. and W. Bockting (1989) 'Homosexual and bisexual development in female to male transsexuals', paper presented at Harry Benjamin International Gender Dysphoria Association.

Denny, D. (1994) *Gender Dysphoria: A Guide to Research*. New York: Garland.

Diagnostic and Statistical Manual of the American Psychiatric Association (1980) 3rd rev. edn. Washington, DC: American Psychiatric Association.

Feinbloom, D., et al. (1976) 'Lesbian/feminist orientation among male-to-female transsexuals', *Journal of Homosexuality*, 2, 1: 59ff.

Green, R., and J. Money (eds) (1969) *Transsexualism and Sex Reassignment*. Baltimore: Johns Hopkins University Press.

Hausman, B. (1995) *Changing Sex: Transsexualism, Technology, and the Idea of Gender*. Durham, NC: Duke University Press.

Irvine, J. (1990) *Disorders of Desire: Sex and Gender in Modern American Sexology*. Philadelphia: Temple University Press.

Katz, J.N. (1976) *Gay American History: Lesbians and Gay Men in the United States*. New York: Avon.

Le Mans, V. (pseud.) (1968) *Take My Tool: Revelations of a Sex-Switch*. Los Angeles: Classic Publications.

Malaspina, R. (1976) 'Sex-change teacher arrested at school', *Oakland Tribune*, 3 September: 1.

Meyerowitz, J. (1998) 'Sex-change and the popular press: historical notes on transsexualism, 1930–1955', *GLQ*, 4:2.

Terry, J. (1991) 'Theorising deviant historiography', *differences: A Journal of Feminist Thought*, **3**, 2: 55–73.

Tully, B. (1992) *Accounting for Transsexualism and Transhomosexuality*. London: Whiting and Birch.

Rassmussen, M. (1976a) 'Sex-change teacher', *San Francisco Chronicle*, 9 August: 1ff.

Rassmussen, M. (1976b) 'Sex-change furor: Emeryville teacher arrested', *San Francisco Chronicle*, 3 September: 1ff.

Raymond, J. (1979) *The Transsexual Empire: The Making of the She-Male*. Boston: Beacon.

San Francisco Gay and Lesbian History Project (1989) 'She even chewed tobacco: a pictorial narrative of passing women in America', in M. Duberman, M. Vicinus and G. Chauncey (eds), *Hidden from History: Reclaiming the Gay and Lesbian Past*. New York: Penguin.

Sullivan, L. (1980) *Information for the Female-to-Male Cross-Dresser and Transsexual* (2nd edn, 1984; 3rd edn, 1990). San Francisco: Janus Information Facility.

Sullivan, L. (1990) *From Female to Male: The Life of Jack B. Garland*. Boston: Alyson.

Sullivan, S. (1973) 'Looking toward transvestite liberation', *Gay People's Union News* (Milwaukee).

Sullivan, S. (1973) 'Looking toward transvestite liberation', *GPU News*: np.

4

Exceptional Locations: Transsexual Travelogues

Jay Prosser

I spent half of my life travelling in foreign places ... I have only lately come to see that incessant wandering as an outer expression of my inner journey. I have never doubted, though that much of the emotional force, what the Welsh call *hywl*, that men spend in sex, I sublimated in travel – perhaps even in movement itself, for I have always loved speed, wind and great spaces ... (Jan Morris, *Conundrum*, 1986)

These notes are the marks of a struggle to keep moving, a struggle for accountability. (Adrienne Rich, 'Notes Toward a Politics of Location', 1986)

The voyage out

Border crossing has become *the* trope for the end of our millennium. As we come closer to that instant in which the last three digits in the calendar year will return to ominous zeros, boundaries are increasingly figured as there to be transgressed, limits as there to be pushed past. Homi K. Bhabha has dubbed the *fin de siècle* 'the moment of transit' (Bhabha, 1994: 1), and Elaine Showalter's work on the equivalent nineteenth-century period suggests border crossing and an intensification of the 'longing for strict border controls' (Showalter, 1990: 4) in response as germane to a century's heightening consciousness of its ending in general. In her recent analysis of *fin de siècle* culture, Rita Felski has suggested that the subject who has been elected to figure this transgression of boundaries is the transsexual or transgenderist. Eroding the borders between male and female, sex and gender, precisely because perceived as a subject in transit, the transsexual/

transgenderist promises the end of both sex and history as grand narratives. Constructed as the very *'fin'* of the *'siècle'* itself, we might say, postmodernism's avatar, the transsexual/transgenderist captures how modernity's 'hierarchical logic of binary identity and narrative totalisation gives way to an altogether more ambiguous and indeterminate condition' (Felski, 1996: 338). 'Trans' eases our transition into the next millennium.

Felski's essay marks an important intervention into this romanticization of intermediacy and indeterminacy. She suggests that such a representation erases the specific material differences of transsexual and transgendered (among other gendered) lives – and indeed her own refraining from attempting a distinction between transgender and transsexuality should be understood as an illumination of their non-differentiation in postmodernist thought. For example, Baudrillard's 'elevation [of transsexuality] to the status of universal signifier ("we are all transsexuals") subverts established distinctions between male and female, normal and deviant, real and fake, but at the risk of homogenising differences that matter politically: the differences between women and men, the difference between those who occasionally play with the trope of transsexuality and those others for whom it is a matter of life and death' (*ibid.*: 347). Even though her concerns are more far-reaching, this insistence on situated gendered histories, on the disjuncture between referential and figurative transgendered/transsexual subjects, should make Felski's essay a touchstone of current transgender studies. It provides good theoretical and political reason for us to describe the locatedness and embodiedness of transgendered and transsexual subjects, for we as those subjects to lay out both our differences over and against the postmodern universalization of 'trans' into signifier of *différance*, and our differences from each other.

The subject of transgender difference in relation to identity borders is already a concern in transgender studies. It is being articulated most substantially – and the trope of the border figured most prominently – around the relations between butch lesbian and female-to-male transsexual identities, perhaps because nowhere do queer, transsexual and transgender identities verge on each other more closely. As Gayle Rubin has argued,

Some butches are psychologically indistinguishable from female-to-male transsexuals, except for the identities they choose and the extent to which they are willing or able to alter their bodies. Many FTMs live as butches before adopting transsexual or male identities

... The boundaries between the categories of butch and transsexual are permeable. (Rubin, 1992: 473)

The permeability between butch and FTM has led at once to a recognition of the shared territory of these identities, and a sense of the need to specify each, to articulate the differences between them. If butch and FTM can be so 'psychologically indistinguishable', what drives the FTM to reconfigure his soma in ways that the butch does not? What resides in, what is the status of, that 'exception'? What is specific to the transsexual's transition, what to the butch's location? The very proximity of these subjects demands that we consider the differences between them and calls for an exploration of their border zone.

The practices of affiliation and specification, of communion and differentiation – and the exchanges between butches and FTMs in particular – are not without their points of dispute. Dispute surely characterizes the workings of any border, whether geographic or metaphoric. In fact the very existence of a border signifies the recognition of territory that is not sufficiently overtly differentiated. In my own contribution to the exchange on butch/FTM borders, in a strategic attempt to distinguish transgender narratives from a generic queerness, I have critiqued queer theory for erasing the specific differences of transgender lives. Queer theory has institutionalized itself through the figure of transgender, significantly contributing to the postmodern troubling 'trans', but in so doing it has often sublimated the experiential grounds for this figure: the real-life experiences of transsexual and transgender subjects. In a reading of Leslie Feinberg's *Stone Butch Blues: A Novel*, I deployed one queer theorist, Judith Halberstam, to exemplify this queer sublimation of transgender. I argued that Halberstam's enlistment of female-to-male transsexuality as a figure for lesbian postmodernism failed to sustain the material irreducibility of transgender and transsexual experience to queer theory. In continuation of our exchange, Halberstam has elucidated how the terms of my distinction in turn effectively erased other subject locations, in particular that of the 'queer butch', the 'transbutch' or the 'female-to-butch' (the 'non-op transgender person') – those female-embodied subjects who identify as queer and transgendered.[1] In her new taxonomy of these specific 'female masculinities', moreover, Halberstam demonstrates that non-queer transsexuals or transgender-ists by no means have a monopoly on gender dysphoria, and that the grounds of any distinction between transsexual and butch are contestable. Because of the absence of an agreed-upon border, a stable dividing line, the project of defining butch and FTM, of differentiating and marking distance between them, is fraught (as the first two essays in our exchange evidence) with the danger of blocking the other's right of passage. As Halberstam neatly puts it:

> when theorized from the perspective of the FTM, the stone butch becomes pre-FTM, a penultimate stage along the way to the comfort of transsexual transformation; however, when theorized from the perspective of the butch, the stone butch becomes a non-surgical and non-hormonal version of transgender identification and does away with the necessity of sex reassignment surgery. (Halberstam, 1998)

Distinguishing between FTM and butch can make the stone butch appear a pit-stop for FTM, and by the same token for the stone butch the FTM may appear an excessive step beyond.

Yet the differences between these subjects are surely not simply circumstantial: the butch is emphatically not an FTM who fails to transition simply because she fears surgery (for instance) but a transgendered subject in her own (distinct) right. The necessity of explaining the differences between butch and FTM therefore remains, and the problematic would seem to revolve around notions of movement and location. How to say where one is coming from without refiguring the location of the other into a place that is either uninhabitable or superfluous, a place that is there either to be passed *on* (abandoned: this is butch for the FTM) or *passed* on (refused: this is FTM for the butch)? How to recognize communal ground without inserting oneself so fully into the other's space as to occupy, even colonize it? The question of the 'identity border' takes (appropriately) this double-sided form: how to identify with the other without incorporating him or her, and how to differentiate oneself without repudiating the other's location. The importance of both practices of affiliation and specification to transgender studies is paramount, to the extent that I would suggest that they are equally definitive of this moment of the inception of transgender studies. In its academic form at least a discursive effect of queer studies, in particular of queer studies's own institutionalization through gender-crossing, cross-dressing, gender-troubling patterns, transgender studies nevertheless in its very articulation as transgender studies constructs itself as an area distinct from or within queer studies. Naming itself as such (in evidence in the special issues of journals, in conferences and special panels, in this anthology even), transgender studies demands recognition of its specificity even as it acknowledges its genealogical debt to and political affiliation with queer. At an Oedipal moment not unlike queer theory's first articulation in, say, Eve Kosofsky Sedgwick's presentation of queer theory as different from but in debt to feminist theory, caught between dependence and independence, the relation of transgender to queer is necessarily complex.[2] If specification has a paradoxical value within transgender studies – both conciliatory and aggressive, both necessary for affiliation and on some level complicating this – this contradiction has everything to do with the tension that characterizes the origin of transgender studies, its dependent and independent relation to queer studies.

'Movement is all' (Halberstam, 1994: 226) and 'specificity is all' (Halberstam, 1998): combining Halberstam's pithy statements from her two essays on the butch/FTM border provides one way to negotiate a moment requiring both affiliation and differentiation between transgender subjects. Each of Halberstam's assertions indexes one half of the double-sided task of current transgender studies. 'Movement' is the dynamic of identification necessary for affiliation: in identifying with the other, one moves (transitions) across ostensible differences to establish common ground. As a methodology and a politics, indeed precisely as a movement, transgender depends on this identification and affiliation. On the other hand 'specificity' describes the practice of identifying oneself: recognizing difference – a process that does require some degree of fixing or locating oneself. Specification puts a much needed brake on movement that is incessant, a sliding into the other. Although logically there may seem to be a contradiction between movement and location, I want to configure their practices, and concomitantly those of affiliation and specification, as interconstitutive of each other and of transgender studies. The cessation or deferral of claims to identity difference is often seen as foundational of post-identity politics. Indeed, I think such a belief is intrinsic to the queer project. Halberstam for instance argues that a truly radical politics is arrived at not through representation of our difference but through a recognition of what we have in common, namely larger political combatants; there is an anxiety that differentiating from each other 'internally' will detract from this worthy external focus. Yet in a movement such as transgender that functions in part as an attempt to specify previously assimilated or unarticulated identities (female-to-male transsexual and Halberstam's transbutch may serve as examples of assimilated and unarticulated respectively), some degree of location, of subject definition and differentiation, is not only necessary but the base of a politics based on difference. One cannot affiliate without recognizing difference.

Identity is inarguably violent work. As Judith Butler and other theorists of identity working out of psychoanalysis so cogently show, identification, whether with an ideal or with an embodied subject, is inextricably entangled with disidentification. To claim an identity for myself is by implication to disclaim others. By representing myself as a transsexual man, inevitably I remove myself from the category of butch (a disidentification from a prior identification). Even though this removal from butch may not be intended as a circumscription of the other, invariably it entails some form of differentiation against the other, a differentiation that is almost a propulsion: what we might think of as at least some transsexual men's pushing off from butch – the transsexual men who have come through a butch trajectory. Identity for oneself is always a problem of the other, of dislocating the other, of some degree of displacement: 'how is it that only through the other can I be myself, *only in the place* of the other can I arrive at a sense of self?' (Fuss, 1995: 4; my emphasis). Identity's violence resides in this rule of dislocation: that only in the place of the other can I be myself. But in this occupation of the place of the other also resides the very encounter with the other that allows affiliation. Identity leads unavoidably to fraught relations between you and me; but it does not follow from these entanglements and tensions, and above all from claims to difference, that identity need be the bar to belonging, affiliation, and our collective political action. Rather locating ourselves, even as it depends on dislocation from other (sometimes each other's) moorings, can be the very mobilizing force of our movement.

I will return to this apparent paradox about location and movement in closing. As a way of shifting the theoretical dialogue into another register (one closer to my current critical home), the body of this essay seeks to elaborate concerns about transsexual specificity – of location, borders, mobility and the other – more obliquely and more literarily (but also more literally) through an examination of the subject of travel in transsexual autobiography. I am interested in the theme of transit in transsexual autobiography, both as a figure for transsexual transition and as a literal journey undertaken. What is the relation between the voyage (literal and figurative) and transsexual subjectivity? What is specific about the notion of the journey or transition to transsexuals and why do some autobiographies border on travelogues? How does the representation by transsexuals of themselves in transit compare to the postmodern representation of the subject as transitional? And finally what might the figures of journeying and location in transsexual autobiography contribute to this debate about specificity and movement, location and transition, within transgender as a field of study and a political movement? In between my readings of transit in transsexual autobiographies, I interweave moments from my own trajectory as a transsexual man: mementoes intended to suggest my present difference from, as well as my continued ties to, my past as a stone butch.

JFK [Airport], several years before I begin hormone treatment. I pass through the security gate. Keys, change, belt: predictably, I set off the bleeper. The guard scrutinizes me for a good moment: 'Say something', he says. I know what he's really looking for but am still without a ready quip: 'Like what?' I say. He has his sign now: 'Over there', he directs me. His walkie-talkie points me decisively away from my girlfriend towards the man being patted down by the male frisker: the men's line.

Transit zones

Transsexual autobiography is produced out of a specific and stable subject location. The autobiographical act is dependent on and reaffirms the conception of the transsexual as a categorical – discrete and identifiable – subject. As Georges Gusdorf has demonstrated, one of the key conditions of autobiography is that the writing subject conceive of him- or herself as different, as separate – as a subject – and for transsexual autobiographers this exceptionality consists precisely in their transsexuality. All transsexual autobiographers, by virtue of the fact that they write as transsexuals – hence the titles: the story of a transsexual, the journal of a transsexual and so on – write out (and write themselves out) under the rubric of transsexuality; all such autobiographies are dependent for their production and circulation on the autobiographer's recognition of his or her status as a transsexual. In those few cases in which the autobiographer's signature is known for something other than his or her transsexuality – April Ashley and Caroline Cossey for modelling, Renée Richards for tennis – the autobiography is almost invariably prompted by the subject's outing as a transsexual. Thus even these public figure autobiographies depend on the subject's specific and stable location as transsexual.

As the subject of the autobiographies is transsexuality, the account of becoming or being a transsexual typically occupies the entire narrative.[3] The recounting of transsexuality is structured and delimited by the conventions of autobiographical narrative as indeed transsexuality, since its beginnings in sexology's case histories of sexual inversion, has been constructed through the conventions of autobiographical narrative in the clinician's office.[4] Through its inscription as autobiography (first the oral, then the published account), transsexuality in fact appears as a narrative: a plot typically beginning in childhood recognition of cross-gendered difference and ending, again typically, with the transsexual achieving some marker of becoming (becoming a man or a woman, although not infrequently becoming a transsexual living as a man or a woman), some degree of closure. If followed, the strictures of narrative – primarily that narrative has a beginning and an end, that it is progressive and connective – shape the account of transsexuality. Those autobiographers who challenge the conventions of transsexuality do so therefore by simultaneously rupturing the conventions of narrative, the best example of this coincidence being Kate Bornstein's *Gender Outlaw: On Men, Women, and the Rest of Us*. Opposing transsexuality's telic structure (that it has a gendered outcome at all) through fragmenting the telic conventions of narrative into Barthesian-like vignettes, *Gender Outlaw* is on both counts our first postmodern transsexual autobiography. But in virtually all other autobiographies the dynamic works the other way – from fragmentation to incorporation, where incorporation is both wholeness of narrative and embodiment of subject – and the narrative is driven by the attempt to make sense of the transition, to forge a cohesive story out of rupture.

Importantly then as narrative, autobiography allows the transsexual to make connections between past and present: it traces the trajectory of *how I got here*. Sandy Stone has critiqued transsexual autobiographers for representing 'sex change' as instantaneous and subscribing to a gendered binary: 'They go from being unambiguous, albeit unhappy men, to unambiguous women. There is no territory between' (Stone, 1991: 286).[5] I suggest that in fact transsexual autobiography's key function is to narrate this 'territory between', to document the move between gendered locations. Although Stone is right to point to sex reassignment surgery as the significant turning point in most autobiographies – a convention that surely reflects the convention of the medical narrative of transsexuality – transsexual autobiography is less fixated on a singular instant of sex change, offering up instead other less determined episodes of becoming. To take the autobiography of Canary Conn as an example: while Stone cites Conn's remarks: 'I'm not a muchacho ... I'm a muchacha now – a girl' (Conn, 1974: 310; cited in Stone, 1991: 286) as indication that the subject conceives of the preceding surgery as the magical moment of sex change, in actuality

Conn's narrative presents her transsexuality as a process of becoming, a progressive narrative flagged by multiple turning-points. Most prominently, the letter coming out to her parents, the decision to live as a woman and take the name Canary, the first stage of her sex reassignment surgery, and her acceptance as a woman by her family during her visit home, serve as turning-points marking Conn's progressive transformation to womanhood. Necessarily as narrative, autobiography staggers transition over time.

If narrative performs an integrating and delineating function, this is surely a key reason why many transsexuals write autobiographies (or record their transitions through other media: photographic, video, cassette or on the Internet). The record enables the transsexual to trace a route to constructing identity; or in the case of the autobiographical narrative written retrospectively, to retrace the movement. This desire to perceive a progressive pattern of becoming underlies the pervasive metaphors of journeying or voyaging in the autobiographies. As some titles alone evidence – Raymond Thompson's *A Girl's Journey to Manhood*, Mario Martino's *Emergence*, and Duncan Fallowell/April Ashley's and Nancy Hunt's *Odysseys* – autobiographies may explicitly cast the transsexual life as a journey, transition as movement in between. The centralization of the metaphor in the autobiographical title equates the autobiography with this journey. The journey or odyssey is as much the writing as the transition, for it is the writing that enables the subject to configure transition in terms of beginnings, ends, progression and connection; it is narrative that maps the territory between. When Feinberg uses Robert Frost's 'The Road Not Taken' as the epigraph for hir *Journal of a Transsexual*, it is both s/he and hir text that take the road 'less travelled by' (Feinberg, 1980: 1): the *Journal* describes a subject who, having begun the female-to-male transition, has broken it off and now wishes to be read as a 'very masculine woman'. The text, titled *Journal of a Transsexual* yet written under Feinberg's female name – Diane Leslie Feinberg – literalizes this urge to be 'read' as a woman. Jan Morris describes her 'journey from the start as a quest, sacramental or visionary, and in retrospect it has assumed for me a quality of epic' (Morris, 1986: 170). 'Epic' here similarly refers as much to the autobiography as to the transsexual transition: the narrative writes the transition as a heroic voyage in search of a true self. Finally, when Conn summarizes the last photograph in her narrative with the legend, 'A Happy End to the Greatest Voyage', the metaphor seeks to mark closure both to her transition and to her narrative (Conn, 1974: np). Through the retroactive workings of autobiography, transsexuality appears as a journey towards a specific gendered location: a voyage through text and sex.

That autobiography is a journey into the self is a truism, but for the transsexual who undergoes radical social and corporeal relocation, it is a particularly compelling one. The journey figure endows the life with direction and structure. Voyages like narratives conventionally have points of departure and destination, beginnings and ends. If Morris describes transition as a path out of non-belonging after some forty-odd years as a man –

> [Transsexuality] is one of the most drastic changes of all human changes, unknown until our own times, and even now experienced by very few, but it seemed only natural to me, and I embarked upon it only with a sense of thankfulness, like a lost traveller finding the right road at last. (Morris, 1986: 104)

– the image signals that her decision to take hormones appears, again in retrospect, as a move in the right direction. The life/narrative is a journey because there is a need to depart from somewhere (to get away from a specific body/place) and to arrive somewhere else (a place more habitable). The journey, in other words, brings into relief the importance of gendered location, the fact that that gendered location makes a difference to these autobiographical subjects. The metaphorics of the journey evokes a notion of transit with connotations different both from the incessant and desultory movement idealized by postmodern representation (the impossibility of finding a place) and from the militarized incursions and defence tactics that worry the figure of 'border wars' (behind which is the dream of a place undivided). A more appropriate analogical frame for the transsexual's writing of transition as journey may be that of immigration: the subject conceives of transsexuality as a move to a new life in a new land, allowing the making of home, precisely an act of translation.[6] According to this metaphor, gendered borders can be both helpful markers in the progression of the subject's route (in arranging sex reassignment surgery, Morris writes that she 'had reached the frontier between the sexes ... it was time for me tentatively to explore life on the far side' (Morris, 1986: 116); she needs to mark something left behind and something crossed into) and restrictive checkpoints to identity that, as *Stone Butch Blues* suggests, some subjects do not fully cross. Indeed, Feinberg's earlier *Journal of a Transsexual* captures in fine detail the ways in which movement can be restricted for the transgendered subject who does not make the transsexual passage (does not pass and does not pass on), in which literal places and acts of journeying between them are dangerous. Feinberg is taunted on the street, harassed in a café, made to feel discomfort in the women's bathroom, chased through parking lots, punched on the subway. Certainly 'no place like home' for hir transgendered body in the world as for *Stone Butch Blues's* fictional Jess, Feinberg writes: 'I remember to keep moving at all costs' (Feinberg, 1993:7). But (to recall my earlier argument on *Stone Butch Blues*) the fact that there is no place like home only fuels the urgency of establishing a specifically transgendered community. This is the goal, as I see it, of Feinberg's textual and activist work, evidenced in hir writing most recently of a specifically transgendered history, *Transgender Warriors*. For the subject with no cultural home, all the more reason for struggling to create one (for indeed, can one even be a subject without a cultural home?); by the same token, for the transsexual who feels dis-located in sex, all the more reason for constructing the transition through the autobiography as a journey towards a gendered home.

Appropriately, as a travel writer who has published over a dozen travel books, Morris pushes the metaphor of the journey to its catachrestic edge. For Morris, genders are like countries, transition a journey across what she conceives to be their quite different terrain. Born on the borders of England and Wales, Morris constructs her 'Januslike' (Morris, 1986: 131) geographic predicament as symbolic of her gendered predicament; the state of being in-between leads to the longing to belong somewhere:

> I pined sometimes to be a member *somewhere*. Just as, in possessing these two landscapes of my childhood, I had felt myself to belong to neither, so I felt now that I belonged to no segment of humanity. (Morris, 1986: 39, emphasis in original)

Feeling out of gendered place is brought home in particular physical locations, most prominently during an expedition to Everest that, as James, Morris covers for the London *Times*. Out of joint with what she perceives as a characteristically masculine endeavour to master place for the sake of it, Morris claims that 'Everest . . . emphasized once more my own inner dichotomy' (*ibid.*: 87):

> this elusive prize, this snatching at air, this nothingness, left me dissatisfied, as I think it would leave most women. Nothing had been discovered, nothing made, nothing improved. (*ibid.*: 84)

By suggesting a binary of men's and women's experience of place (men relishing battle with the void, women desirous to find or produce something within it), Morris seeks to authenticate her cross-gendered identification and map her progression towards becoming woman. The construction of genders as different locations and locations as differently gendered is in fact foundational to *Conundrum*'s trajectory. For instance, Venice and Oxford are imbued with seductiveness, serenity, gentleness and beauty, and portrayed as feminine: 'a kind of ossification of the female principle ... of all that I would like to be' (*ibid.*: 98). Africa in contrast represents for Morris absolute ambivalence. Associated in its foreignness with the masculine – 'I found the black African as incomprehensible as a man in the moon' (*ibid.*: 99) yet as much impacted with her perception of the racial other as the gendered other ('the fetishes ... the edible slugs, the tribal savageries ... the empty history ... Black Africa seemed everything I wanted *not* to be' (*ibid.*: 98–9) – Africa appears as her place of disidentification just as Venice and Oxford appear as sites of identification. Morris thus maps her duality onto the world, making of literal locations autobiographical figures, ways for telling the transsexual self.

Morris's anthropomorphization of locations and her characterization of her autobiographical self through location admittedly read as products of a rather grandiose autobiographical ego. But Morris's tendency to write her transsexuality onto the world is bound up with how she materially experiences her transsexuality as different in different locations, an experience of difference that in turn reveals a more complex mapping of gender than simply Self versus Other. If Venice represents hypostasized femininity for Morris, this cannot be divorced from her experience of her femininity in that city, her experience as a transsexual woman, a male in transition to womanhood. She is convinced that the blind woman who begs by the Accademia Bridge to whom she returns whenever in the city can somehow 'read' her by her handshake – while she is still James – as a woman, and her feminization of Venice is inextricably enmeshed with this incident. The encounter signposts self-realization as much as self-reflection (she is not a woman yet), and Venice comes to stand for the feminine for this reason: because it marks the progression in Morris's identity as a transsexual. By the same token, Morris's ambivalence towards Africa is surely correlated to her experience of her gendered ambivalence in Africa where her transsexuality now that she is in transition appears readable, her in-betweeness a recognizable albeit esteemed condition. These incidents of experienced transgendered difference serve to suggest the degree to which she conceives of her transsexuality as culturally specific: gender is by no means a universalized binary (with no territory between) after all. In fact Morris's mappings elaborate the binary or duality of genders by using the borderlands of her birth locale to figure her transsexuality at the outset of *Conundrum* (the Janus-like border), into a culturally variable set of zones where gender is not a case of either/or and transsexuality is not a case of immediate or singular crossing but a question of local reading. As Morris writes on how the world reacts to her transition,

> Americans generally assumed me to be female ... Englishmen ... found the ambiguity in itself beguiling ... Frenchmen were curious ... Greeks were vastly entertained. Arabs asked me to go for walks with them ... Japanese did not notice. (*ibid.*: 111–12)

What remains intact for Morris is the figure of the voyage for transsexual transition, of transsexuality as a journey and the idea of progression. Transsexuality, Morris is certain, enables her to arrive at where she imagines she should have been, a kind of pre-destination: 'I had achieved Identity' (*ibid.*: 163). Moreover, while acknowledging that the experience of gender may be more nuanced on arrival – that as a transsexual woman who has lived as but never felt like a man she cannot quite say what it is to be a woman or a man – Morris presents transition as a borderland crucial for her to pass through. In so doing, she underscores the cultural uninhabitability of these nuanced, borderland zones, the territory between. Appropriately, the incident that Morris uses first to exemplify her passage through this gendered transit zone takes place in the transit zone of customs at an airport – that peculiarly unterritorialized but highly policed zone in between countries:

> I approach the security check. Dressed as I am in jeans and a sweater, I have no idea to which sex the policeman will suppose me to belong ... I feel their silent appraisal down the corridor as I approach them, as they search my sling bag I listen hard for a 'Sir' or a 'Ma'am' to decide my course of conduct. Beyond the corridor, I know the line divides ... An awful moment passes. Everyone seems to be looking at me. Then 'Move along there, lady, please, don't hold up the traffic' ... and instantly I join the female queue. (*ibid.*: 110)

That Morris may not stake a claim in the location of woman in any uncomplicated way does not undo her recognition of the fact that, culturally speaking, there is no occupied middle ground, that the territory between remains precisely that. As the Lacanian dictum is so wonderfully literalized by this scene, the subject must line up on one side or the other of the divide; the imperative of gender demands that s/he take a place, that s/he not 'hold up the traffic'. Not surprising then that so many transsexual autobiographies frame this transit zone, the transition itself, as a transitional phase: a space to move beyond rather than to keep moving in. On this count transsexual autobiography falls dramatically away from a postmodern celebration of incessant 'trans', for the very purpose of sexed *reassignment* is, in contrast, to take a place.

Renée Richards also coincides her metaphorical transsexual journey to womanhood with a literal transition: her sea passage from the USA to Europe towards Casablanca for sex reassignment surgery. Although Richards will return from Casablanca as Dick Raskind, unreassigned, dick/Dick intact, marry a woman, have a child and attempt one more time to live as a man, the transatlantic crossing from New York to Genoa serves as the point of significant gender crossing from man to woman in *Second Serve*. It is on this ship that Richards feels herself for the first time no longer to be acting a woman but to be one:

> As the *Michaelangelo* steamed through the quiet Mediterranean waters, I felt myself sinking more and more into the persona of Renée. It was not a role anymore. I felt myself to be a woman, and except for the much atrophied genitals between my legs I really was one. (Richards, 1983: 222)

Like Morris complicating any gendered binary and tracking the territory in between, Richards figures the transition as less from man to woman than from performing woman to being woman. Brilliantly punning on the notion of passage and crossing, Richards writes: 'The *Michaelangelo* was my transitional vehicle' (*ibid.*: 219). Once again, transsexual transition (the territory between) appears to the autobiographical subject as a move towards home, the very point of the journey; although as Richards's figure underscores, it is a complex move: like the movement of the autobiographical narrative itself, both backwards and forwards, a voyage out that is at once a return home:

> What I had moved toward as I sat watching the ship's wake spread into the Mediterranean was like a homecoming, a return to reality rather than an escape. (*ibid.*: 222).

If the metaphor of voyage has such appeal to transsexual autobiographers in their writing of transition, it is because of this lure of the return home, this *nostalgia* (*nostos*: the return home); of course home is always an imagined construct, as Benedict Anderson (1983) and other thinkers of nationalism have shown. For the subject who conceives of himself or herself as dislocated in the world and dislocated from sex, the lure of home, precisely because of its unrealized status, cannot be underestimated. What is exceptional about transsexual autobiographers (in addition of course to their transsexuality) is their incredible mobility as a group, the space their narratives assign to relating accounts of trips taken, moves made across the world and back again, new territories explored. In addition to Morris's and Richards's voyages for instance, Katherine Cummings's (1992) autobiography charts a move from Australia to the US and eventually home again; Erica Rutherford (1993) moves from Scotland to South Africa to the US and then on to Canada; and Ashley from Liverpool to Paris, Spain, and Rome and eventually back to England. These narratives present themselves as much as travelogues as transsexual autobiographies, detailed accounts of geographic journeys. In this regard they suggest a close relation between geographic and gendered movement, as if, as Morris's epigraph to this chapter suggests, physical journeying were a sublimation of the quest for a gendered home. Appropriately therefore, it is only when the shores of home are reached – gendered and geographic – as they almost inevitably are in these very teleological narratives, that the voyage out can be written.

Is there anything more material, however, to the connections between transsexuality and the trip abroad?

When I left New York to return to live and transition in London, I was gender ambivalent: passing as a man in the world, but at work – wherever I was known – a butch woman. On arriving in England, I got my passport and work papers changed to male and began my life immediately as a man, finally, it felt, gender coherent.

When I tell this to one of the psychiatrists at my gender identity clinic (he asks how long I've been living as a man), he guffaws: 'So you transitioned mid-Atlantic?' Actually: yes. Or at least as soon as we hit the tarmac. Sex change, you might say, came with the territory.

Foreign parts

At the moment it enters the popular lexicon and becomes a cultural phenomenon, transsexuality begins with a trip abroad and a return home: George Jorgensen's trip to Copenhagen and her return to the US as Christine. Much of the popular press was caught up with the journey and the locale as part of the transsexual phenomenon: 'Ex GI Turned Woman Flying Home for Yule'; 'Blonde Beauty Who Used to Be a Man Eagerly Awaits Trip Home' (headlines cited in Jorgensen, 1967). Transsexuality in the popular imagination, not surprisingly given that the Jorgensen story followed so soon after the Second World War and involved one of America's 'own boys', became laden with ideas of the journey and foreignness. Transsexuality appeared an act of translation: of self to other, or of self through other. In his *Emergence*, Martino, one of the few earlier female-to-male transsexual autobiographers, recalls his father joking about the Jorgensen story: 'Imagine going abroad and coming back a broad!' (Martino, 1977: 40) The 'joke' runs together the foreignness of transsexuality, of Jorgensen (whose family was originally from Denmark), of the geographical location of her sex reassignment surgery, and of (man becoming) woman. Abby Sinclair's 1965 autobiography *I Was Male* reveals that 'going to Denmark for that operation' (Sinclair, 1965: 9) became a code for sex reassignment surgery, as if the location abroad were crucial to the form of transformation. From its beginnings as a cultural phenomenon – which the Jorgensen story surely marks – transsexuality is linked with the trip abroad and the idea of foreignness.

For the perpetuation of this association evidenced in the autobiographer's figuration of herself as a voyager, there is a more prosaic reason: for many following Jorgensen, the trip abroad was necessary to obtain sex reassignment surgery. Before such surgery became legally practicable in the West, as French *travesti* Coccinelle points out in her 'interview' in Mario Costa's 1960 *'Coccinelle': Reverse Sex*, for many transsexuals wishing for surgery journeying abroad presented the only option. A large proportion of early male-to-female transsexual autobiographers made the trip to Casablanca to Dr Burou, the French gynaecologist who pioneered the male-to-female surgery still practised today. The English *travesti* Ashley, on seeing the results of Coccinelle's surgery, was inspired to become one of Burou's patients in 1959. Even when sex reassignment surgery became routinely practised by clinics and hospitals in the US and the UK, the demands of the medical establishment could still force the transsexual to make the trip to Burou, and his clinic in Casablanca remained a mecca for male-to-female reassignment. Her treatment halted in the US when diagnosed by sexologist John Money as a transvestite, Richards is forced to make the trip to the clinic in the late 1960s, and Morris after her in 1972 when she is told she must divorce her wife if she is to receive surgery in the UK. Both, like Ashley and others before them, must journey to 'foreign parts beyond the law' (Morris, 1986: 127).[7]

But as with any voyage in transsexual autobiography the visit to Casablanca is anything but prosaic. In Ashley, Morris and Richards, Casablanca is heavily figurative: a site of romantic transformation, product of the autobiographer's conceptions of otherness and the East. Stone has already noted – and begins her 'Manifesto' brilliantly recreating – the 'wonderfully "oriental"' (Stone, 1991: 281) tone of Morris's account of her 'sex change' in Casablanca, and indeed all these accounts are not merely oriental but orientalist. The East is mythicized as a place of magical transformation, even transcendence for the Western subject. Hearing 'the limpid Arab music' and smelling 'the pungent Arab smells', Morris constructs Casablanca as a 'city of fable, of phoenix and fantasy, in which transubstantiations were regularly effected, when the omens were right and the moon in its proper phase' (Morris, 1986: 136). The night before her surgery, Ashley likewise evokes Casablanca as mysterious and portentous:

> I went out to the balcony and absorbed the city – it was a balmy evening, pregnant with omens. A young boy stared at me from across the street, a monkey on his shoulder, a fixed smile on his face like a pagan doll. (Fallowell/Ashley, 1982: 85).

The simile of pagan doll doubles strangeness on strangeness, and indeed if sex reassignment surgery appears as conversion in these narratives, it is anything but Christian: Burou the surgeon is a 'magician' (Morris, 1986: 134), a 'wizard' (Morris, 1986: 136; Fallowell/Ashley, 1982: 73). Following what had by then become a transsexual autobiographical convention, Richards also approaches Casablanca as an enchanted place of transfiguration: a place to work not something magical (man to woman) as in Morris but something more real (unsexed spirit into woman):

> In the back of my mind hung an image of Casablanca, exotic and white, shimmering in the African sun. There I would surrender my dual nature and my days as a hermaphroditic spirit would be finished. At last I would know the pleasure enjoyed by ordinary mortals – to be one entity. (Richards, 1983: 228)

Strikingly, when they actually see it, all three autobiographers remark on the ordinariness of the clinic itself: all are clearly surprised by its unexceptionality in the midst of what they take to be – what they wish to be – this exceptional location.

What is at the root of this urge to write Casablanca as exceptional site of transformation? I would suggest that in order to mark sex reassignment as a crucial gendered turning-point – in some sense, a transsexual boundary or border – Casablanca is orientalized and exoticized. The orientalization of Casablanca, the rich descriptions of the place itself, function as a metaphorical device for the subject's feminization. Already famed as louche capital of the East as captured by the Bogart/Bergman eponymous film of 1942 – a film that Ashley refers to in her account of her trip as if her experience of the geographic place were inextricable from this Hollywood representation – Casablanca appears as gender gateway: a path of escape to integral female difference through which the subject wishes to mark her passing. Drawing on a founding myth of the West about the East's femininity, the autobiographer suggests that simply by being in this locale she undergoes feminization. Before she has even had the surgery, Morris inserts herself into such a feminized frame. She represents Burou's clinic as a harem: Madame Burou is described as an 'odalisque' (Morris, 1986: 137), the walk from the office to the surgical area as 'like going from the seraglio to the eunuch's quarters' (*ibid.*: 138), as if merely to evoke the East is to effect demasculinization. After the surgery, for both Ashley and Morris the location becomes part of the reassignment experience: Ashley declares: 'I am a woman in Casablanca' (Fallowell/ Ashley, 1982: 88), Morris that she is 'sex-changed in Casablanca' (Morris, 1986: 140) – again as if the specification of being 'in Casablanca', as if that simple addition of location, authenticates the transformation from male to female. If 'going to Denmark' meant to become a transsexual in the public eye, to be 'in Casablanca' in transsexual folklore is to be in some sense already transformed, to be already woman. Geographic location again forms a way for troping the transsexual transition, part of the autobiographical frame.

It is therefore apt and fascinating that Richards's decision not to go through with sex reassignment surgery in Casablanca is represented as a moment of disorientation: of disillusionment simultaneously with transsexuality's narrative and with the East. Journeying from Genoa in her Maserati after her transatlantic crossing, Richards consciously approaches Casablanca through the layers of its construction in transsexual folklore; it is precisely her consciousness of the constructedness of the place and her own voyage that makes her hesitate before Burou's clinic:

> Before me were the steps up which Bambi had travelled, as well as the other Parisian travestis. Here was the reality about which I had been dreaming, yet it still had the quality of a dream. It stood shimmering in the heat, wavering like a mirage. Perspiration began to dampen the sleeves of my dress; slowly a thought began to penetrate. This whole trip had been a fantasy: on the boat it was F. Scott Fitzgerald; in Italy it was Fellini. (Richards, 1983: 246–7)

What makes her retrace her steps to the hotel away from the clinic is the sense of the irreality of the voyage. The narrative or figurative dimension of transsexuality has become indistinguishable from its literal transition; she doubts her ability to distinguish between the trope of transsexuality as a grand odyssey and the actual journey itself. This disorientation is experienced as feeling out of place on many levels: feeling out of place as a transsexual; feeling out of place as a woman; feeling out of physical place on the steps of the clinic; feeling out of place in the Orient with all that the Orient has come to signify during her trip (geographic and transsexual):

> I became *disoriented*. I felt that, somehow, I was no longer worthy to be a woman, though I certainly was not a man. I was something horrible – something in between – something like a monster. (*ibid.*: 247; my emphasis)

To be caught in between, to be out of place is for Richards a terrifying experience; not to be able to cross both the space of the steps up through the clinic door and what Richards conceives of as the space between sexes, is truly shattering:

> Up until that moment of truth in front of the clinic, I would have said confidently that I was a woman trapped in a man's body; but I had stood paralysed, not fifty feet from the remedy and had been unable to cross the remaining space. The only identity that I could clearly claim was that of a failure. (*ibid.*: 248)

Unable to claim not only the identities of man or woman but that of transsexual, no longer able to fit herself into that transsexual trajectory (to be 'a woman trapped in a man's body'), onward movement seems impossible and she must make a return: both a return to being a man and a return home to New York.

The episode that precedes her journey back serves to confirm that Richards's disorientation is a disorientation in the orientalist sense. After her retreat from the clinic, she escapes to Marrakesh and has what she represents as a particularly seedy and threatening encounter with an Arab who is sexually interested in what Richards despises about herself: her gendered intermediacy (not being able to cross). While she finds his insistent approach a general turn-off, what renders him particularly repulsive is the skin disorder that covers his body: 'Spotted all over his torso and legs were warty sores. I had seriously thought that I might be able to service this man in some way' (*ibid*.: 251). After he fails in his attempts to have intercourse with her ('I could feel lesions on his skin' (*ibid*.: 252), Richards returns to her hotel room to wash him off: 'I scrubbed myself raw. The memory of those sores haunted me. Who knew what they were?' (*ibid*.: 252). A true marker of her disorientation, of her disillusion with the Orient, she describes the sores as 'manifestations of an African disease' (*ibid*.: 252). The Orient's promise to cure her disease has instead become manifest as a disease that threatens to infect her: a true falling out of place. After this incident Richards hurries West back to New York. Eventually for her, foreign parts must be removed at home. (Richards eventually has her surgery performed in the hospital of her childhood home in Queens, New York.)

The construction of Casablanca in transsexual autobiography as other represents the subject's attempt to convey how sex reassignment surgery makes a gendered difference. It entails the transformation of the self through the production of an other: an other that dramatically layers racial difference over gendered difference. Richards's provisional turning back from womanhood as it is inscribed in her autobiography is a propulsion of a constructed racial other: a failure to incorporate the other. When the subject does go through with surgery as do Morris and Ashley, the exoticization and eroticization of Casablanca mark the autobiographer's translation into her personal narrative of what remains in the medical narrative of transsexuality the significant moment of transition from male to female: it signals her move into differently gendered terrain and her incorporation of the other, again the gendered layered over by the racial. Through portraying the locale as other and identifying with this other, the autobiographies stage – in not unproblematic terms – the integration that surgery itself may be seen in the narrative of transsexuality to effect: an integration between gender identity and sexed body: between what has been identified by the subject herself as self (gender) and other (sex).

But importantly not all stories tell this narrative; for some this integration remains exactly a foreign fantasy.

My Chinese grandmother was born to abandonment in the south-eastern village of Swatow. Although wealthy and land-owning, her parents wanted not girls but sons: signs of their good fortune. That the little girl they had instead had developed smallpox after her birth was a compounded sign of their misfortune; her lack of value, her undesirability, was writ large on her skin. They left her therefore to fate, placing her in a basket beside a river – like Moses I used to think, struggling to find a foothold in this strange narrative terrain. The baby was discovered by a fisherman, who took her home to his wife. A childless couple, the fisherman and his wife decided to keep the child (a fairytale, I used to think) and my grandmother grew up down the road from her natal family, knowing – or rather surely not knowing – where she really belonged.

She married young and when her farmer husband died of cancer of the penis, she found herself repeating her own history. She abandoned her own daughter to go to Singapore to work as an ayah. She never saw this first child again: a fact, my mother says, she always refused to discuss. In Singapore she remarried, this time to a Persian Jew (himself a product of generations of geographic displacement) and had six more children. My mother was the first. She was also the first to leave Singapore – and her mother – for the West.

On this side of my family, becoming has involved acts of migration: departures that are simultaneously real and metaphoric; violent abandonments unpredictably caught up with gendered meanings, disownments (or appropriations) responsible for overwhelming feelings of non-belonging.

I left England because closeness wouldn't allow me myself. It was only as my mother's son that I found I could return home.

Getting out of here

I want to go home more than Dorothy. (Claudine Griggs, *Passage Through Trinidad*, 1996)

So much has male-to-female transsexuality in autobiography become intrinsically associated with a trip abroad that one of the most recent transsexual autobiographies published, *Claudine Griggs's Passage Through Trinidad: Journal of a Surgical Sex Change*, as its title suggests, is written explicitly (and self-dramatizingly) as a travelogue: a minutely detailed account in the form of journal entries of a trip to Trinidad, Colorado, for sex reassignment surgery. Even though Griggs's geographical journey hardly constitutes a trip abroad (her home is in Irvine, California), like Casablanca for Ashley, Morris and Richards, Trinidad is constructed as a place of transfiguration, not merely physical but mythic. To be sure, for many transsexuals – male-to-female and to a lesser extent female-to-male – since 1969 Stanley Biber's clinic at Mt San Rafael Hospital in Trinidad has become a place for transsexual pilgrimage: we might say the latter-day Casablanca, or as it has been dubbed, the 'sex-change capital of America' (Tayman, 1991: 220). For Griggs as much as for her predecessors going to Casablanca, the trip to Trinidad is A Voyage in that legendary sense:

> the journey to Trinidad is everlasting, since an altered body inevitably brings with it an altered life experience. Trinidad delivers one onto a different path, and it delivers the realisation that the previous path is closed forever. There is a postscript of desire to wander both and then choose the better, regret that one did not travel to Trinidad much sooner, sorrow that one travelled to Trinidad at all, fear that one might have failed yet to undertake this journey. (Griggs, 1996: vii)

Yet as the slippage and eventual slide into abstruseness in the last sentence suggests (regret that one did not go sooner, sorrow that one went at all, fear that one has not yet made it), the trip to Trinidad is for Griggs ambivalent and this definitive ambivalence clogs and stalls the narrative of *Passage Through Trinidad*, its very passage. What, we are asked to consider, is Griggs seeking to pass *through* in Trinidad? On the one hand Trinidad represents departure from transsexuality. Griggs hopes that sex reassignment will effect the integration of body into her gendered self as a woman – ('I ... seek only to alter my body to fit my mind' (*ibid*.: 37) after living seventeen years as a woman without surgery).[8] This integration will in turn allow her to leave behind her transsexuality, to pass in body and thus pass through it. On the other hand as the account painfully evidences, the experience of sex reassignment, of being in the 'sex-change capital of the world' (*ibid*.: 39) and attended to as a transsexual, in effect only serves to inscribe in her a deeper consciousness of her subject location *as a transsexual*. Ironically, she can no longer sublimate her consciousness of being a transsexual which she had been able to do while passing as a woman pre-operatively:

> For almost 15 years I gave up trying to find a surgeon, I disclosed to almost no one that I am transsexual; I've existed at work, at home, at school, in the shopping mall, grocery store, bowling alley, golf course, library, on the freeways, on the sidewalks, every place but the bedroom and the doctor's office, Mondays through Sundays, year after year, with no one apparently knowing that I am not just a girl down the street. Now, in the last couple of days, I've had to confront the fact that I am transsexual with a dozen people I've never previously met ... I lecture myself, insisting that I should have long ago squelched my hatred of being transsexual: but here in Trinidad, Colorado, everyone I meet reminds me that I am what I hate. (*ibid.*: 38–9)

Imagined as a move forward in her transition, surgery is actually experienced as a traumatic move back into the past: 'It was very hard for me to be transsexual again, like a terrible regression of sorts' (*ibid.*: 129). This paradox – that Griggs's journey, an attempt to leave behind the transsexual self she cannot come to terms with, only serves to reinforce transsexual as identity; *that transsexual is both the site of her departure and arrival* – makes *Passage Through Trinidad* an emotionally draining read. It is particularly draining because of the painful material this circularity encompasses: a laborious account of the pain and discomfort involved in Griggs's recovery from surgery. A passage into physical and psychic pain rather than through it, the book describes minutely the vomiting, constipation, thirst, boredom, catheter discomfort and dilation difficulties that follow Griggs's surgery. The level of detail is relentless, excruciating:

> I unfasten the sanitary napkins in front and expose the genitalia. As gently as possible, I wash around the inner thighs, hips, and belly button. The delicate touch of the warm washcloth is painful; the skin itself seems to burn with the slightest pressure. Still, resolutely, I am convinced that it doesn't hurt as much as yesterday, so I continue gingerly blotting the bruised tissue, slowly moving closer and closer to the genitalia, rinsing the washcloth several times as it stains from residual Betadine and blood. (*ibid.*: 68)

Each day – with such entries at intervals sometimes of every two hours –

describes the same routine of pain/recovery, bodily ingestion/expulsion.

Because the only 'place' in this claustrophobic account is Griggs's sick/recovering body (the circularity means it's hard to tell the difference between sickness and recovery), the reader cannot help but feel cheated – cheated for Griggs but also as a reader, cheated by the narrative – when her story doesn't follow the transsexual narrative, when it doesn't go from fragmentation to bodily integration: when it doesn't reach 'home' as its chapter titles promised it would ('Decision', 'Arrival', 'Hospital', 'Pain', 'Routine', 'Visitors', 'Progress', 'Freedom', 'Anticipation', 'Release', 'West', 'Home'). For there is a final chapter, a kind of appendix aptly titled 'Aftermath' that, appearing in the form of Griggs's responses to Stanley Biber's follow-up questionnaire, makes clear that surgery has not delivered the subject from her transsexuality at all but only impacted her irremediably in it. Griggs writes that for her surgery has

> solidif[ied] the realisation that there is essentially no cure for transsexualism; it is a disorder that can be treated, but there is no procedure possible to make me a natural female. I will never be the person I envision I would have been if I had been born female: I can never return to 1953 and start life again; I can never have the childhood of a little girl, the adolescence of a young woman, the family experience of a young bride, wife, mother; I can never have a social history undivided by the change of life from man to woman. (*ibid.*: 202)

Surgery enables no return journey back to this place of a past that should have been. For her reader as much as for Griggs in closing, this realization that surgery has been her rite of passage not out of but more fully into transsexuality is a truly traumatic one; the *Journal* ends with the author extremely depressed, even, so it seems, contemplating suicide.

How are we to read the account of a transsexual trajectory that doesn't find a home of some sort? In spite of its generic and generic departures, *Stone Butch Blues*, as I have argued, found home in transgender, precisely in a gendered borderland: Feinberg felt at home in her body even though she did not become a transsexual man; and the narrative spins out in a series of dreams a specifically transgendered albeit imagined home. But home in the sense of both body and community altogether eludes transsexual Griggs in *Passage Through Trinidad*. Not only has her sense of herself as 'just a girl down the street' evaporated because of her trip, not only does she no longer feel at home even *at home*, it is not clear that after surgery she feels any more at home in her body. We must acknowledge the reality of the home that Griggs really desires: to have been born female; to have had the cultural life and sexed attributes of a natal woman. Yet at the same time we must admit the fundamental irretrievability of this home; there is no reading that can get her back there, no deconstruction that can chip away at the solidity of this absent presence of the past at the heart of this narrative. Given this double-bind – precisely that there is *no place* like home for some transsexuals – we need to develop critical paradigms for making sense of the subject who is traumatized by having to make any gendered movement at all: by the very fact of her transition and of being a transsexual.

Perhaps the key to developing such models for reading is contained in Griggs's own recognition of the specificity of her transsexual narrative: a bordered location, a place that keeps her in much as she wishes to get out. Paradoxically, the identity she sought surgery to depart – transsexual – Griggs implicitly admits in writing her account is the only 'home' she has. If she cannot conceive of herself as 'real woman' (*ibid.*: 210), the very publication of her *Passage Through Trinidad: Journal of a Surgical Sex Change* – even while its title studiously avoids use of the category – suggests that Griggs herself realizes that this transsexuality is the most secure location, the exceptional place to which she can (and indeed in the end, must) lay claim. Hopelessly unreconciled to this transsexual location in the present, transsexual narrativization (narrativization as a transsexual) is nevertheless the only way that Griggs may keep hold of her past. She never was that little girl; but her pining for this girlhood even as a little boy means that she was always transsexual. As current transgender writings continue to assume that transsexual – by virtue of that 'trans' movement – is ipso facto queer, Griggs's narrative suggests the worthiness of holding onto transsexuality as a specific identity category. Even for Griggs, transsexual provides a way of making sense of absences – else why write the narrative? Queer theory has denounced any identity between being and seeming, any continuity between fantasy and reality, so effectively that any subject who desires them appears theoretically atavistic, a kind of ontological dupe. But is such a subject with these desires – are these desires at a particular moment in transsexual subjecthood – necessarily a political cop-out, or is this figuration rather a sign of the way in which queer itself has become a not-always-useful categorical imperative?

The politics of transgender location

If five years ago Stone's seminal essay signalled Janice Raymond's transsexual empire 'fighting back', are we now with the burgeoning of transgender studies and the proliferation of different transgendered identities seeing that empire break up? If so, what are the implications of this fragmentation? Should we try to cement over our differences or can we articulate those differences *and* form affiliations with other subjects and methodologies? If the break up of empires in the first half of the century connoted all things positive (independence, the right to self-definition, and freedom from occupation by the other), the breakup of empires at the *fin de siècle* hardly presents a model for our cultural work. Rather today decolonization appears to lead inexorably to internecine struggles over issues (ethnicity, religion, territory) around which individuals previously peacefully cohabited. Hence perhaps the fear of borders and boundaries that pervades current cultural theory: the fear reflects back what is real about our historical moment. Are there any other models or moments for politics formed out of bordered differences to which we might turn?

At a moment in feminism perhaps analogous to the queer present with its diversification into transgender studies and bisexual studies, Adrienne Rich presented her 'Notes Toward a Politics of Location'. By 1984, the year of Rich's essay, feminism had become a powerful political movement and a rich set of academic methodologies. Yet for some feminists the project of addressing the differences within feminism seemed to jeopardize a common goal. There was anxiety that the sex debates around lesbianism, pornography and sadomasochism (epitomized by the Barnard conference in 1982: see Carole Vance, 1989), and the specifications of black and other feminists of colour (Cherríe Moraga and Gloria Anzaldúa's *This Bridge Called My Back* appeared in 1981, Barbara Smith's *Home Girls* in 1983), were signs of a terrible fracturing of feminism's collectivity: an end to its very capacity to function as a movement. It was to this anxiety that Rich's essay spoke.

Rich helpfully specifies the rather formidable category difference into a more homely but still mobilizing notion of location. To sustain a political movement, she argues, it is crucial to write one's location: a location not just in body but in categorical positioning. To locate myself in my body is not to describe my bodily experiences but to recognize how this body takes its place in the world in relation to other bodies:

To write 'my body' plunges me into lived experience, particularity: I see scars, disfigurements, discolorations, damages, losses, as well as what pleases me. Bones well nourished from the placenta; the teeth of a middle-class person seen by the dentist twice a year from childhood. White skin, marked and scarred by three pregnancies. (Rich, 1986: 215)

To locate in my body is not, then, to speak from an infinitely indefinable, incessantly shifting, indeterminable 'I'. To fall into these 'in-'s is surely to evade what Rich calls 'accountability', to get caught up with our own linguistic deferral and forget our embodiedness (and forget that some subjects can't forget it). Rather to locate myself in my body is to recognize the location I have in the world as a definable, discrete subject: a subject whose differences from the other are physical, material, social. For instance, Rich locates herself categorically, narrates herself progressively thus: a woman, a white woman, a white middle-class woman, a Jewish white middle-class woman, a North American Jewish white middle-class woman. Political accountability consists in naming and recognizing the specificity of our location and what we are not. We cannot have a movement that occults or assimilates the trajectory that has brought us to the place we are now. For Rich this 'Recognition of our location, *having to name the ground we're coming from*', forms not the threat to but the basis of the feminist movement (*ibid.*: 219; my emphasis). Indeed Rich suggests that there cannot be a movement without specificity, as she also crucially suggests that there cannot be specificity without difference. There *is* a tension in representation around location and movement. Paradoxically a movement requires some degree of location; it cannot be founded on the individuated, infinitely plural subject. It must be staked in claims to sameness and difference, to definition. Inevitably, this act of definition and representation will bring into relief our differences, perhaps even causing rifts and exclusions:

> *You cannot speak for me. I cannot speak for us.* Two thoughts: there is no liberation that only knows how to say 'I'; there is no collective movement that speaks for each of us all the way through. (*ibid.*: 224; emphasis in original)

But without this tension between us, and between what we have in common and what we do not, there can be no *movement* at all. We need to acknowledge the territory between us in order to cross it.

At the *fin de siècle*, at this moment of its origin, transgender studies faces a cross-roads – prematurely so. We can ride the crest of postmodernism, joining its celebration of mobility; after all if Felski is right, we have already come to figurehead this movement and in this sense we are offered a ready-made point of entry into cultural theory. In depending wholly on this join, however, we pay the price of our own dislocation. This form of postmodern theory does not allow for both the differences between speaking as an embodied trans subject and the representation of this trans by the other, and the differences between our multiple subjectivities. Accountability, as I understand Rich – that is politics – must be grounded in examined difference, not in difference's deferral (*différance*). Thus I prefer what I see as our other option: to take our cue from an earlier moment of difference in feminism perhaps via Rich's intervention, and carve out a space in which we specify our locations, name the ground we're coming from and in narrating our journeys articulate what we have left behind and where we are *not* going even as we say where we are. We risk showing to the other that his or her resting place is the very point of our departure, that perhaps we are moving in completely different directions. But it seems to me that this is the act of differentiation that sparks the friction and debate that are anyway (in the form of our exchanges) the driving force of our transgender movement.

Postcard to J-Boy

When I'm having sex with someone, I'm thinking that I have a penis most of the time. And the dildo kind of ruins that for me. Because it's not one. And it is clumsy to wear a dildo. It's easier for me to have sex with someone and imagine I have a dick, than it is to wear a strap-on that lets me know I don't have one. (J-Boy)

Being a stone butch was a very disembodied thing for me ... there is very little of my body that can be touched, and it's because I feel this is not my body. It's a very painful place to be ... [In transition] I saw that something on the other side could be possible. (Jay) (Both cited in Heather Findlay, 1995)

Dear J-Boy
Some months into my transition I was invited by an old college friend to a dinner party. Among the guests were Helen, a butch friend of mine, and Colette, a French woman whom I had known some ten years earlier. Helen I had seen recently; Colette not but she had, I understood, been apprised of my transition.

When I arrived at the party Helen rushed over with visible relief: 'At last', she said. 'Now you can be Jay.' It turned out that Colette had approached Helen, certain that she was me: 'You must be Jay.' Colette had looked not for a face that resembled mine (or that was mine) but for someone 'readable'. Apparently looking for a woman who wanted to be a man she had found a butch woman.

The crossing of Helen's and my lines was not over for the evening. At dinner we found ourselves seated next to each other (there seemed to be a queer corner to the U-shaped table: I was, I noted, right on its edge, verging onto one of the straight legs). Both sporting recent haircuts, both wearing dark jackets and pants (though I wore a tie), Helen and I were told throughout the evening that we looked like twins. 'It's to show people the options', Helen quipped with the customary speed: 'You can be a butch dyke ... or you can be a man.'[9]

It's nice here, J-Boy: it almost feels like home. Though you're certainly close to it, so that you might feel the difference of this place, I sometimes wish you could be here.

Jay.

Notes

1. For Halberstam's original essay on female-to-male transsexuality which sparked the dialogue, see her 'F2M: the making of female masculinity' (1994). For my critique see my 'No place like home: the transgendered narrative of Leslie Feinberg's *Stone Butch Blues*' (1995). For Halberstam's response to my critique of her essay see her 'Transgender butch: butch/ FTM border wars and the masculine continuum' (1998). I am grateful to Halberstam for making this latter work available to me in manuscript, for her permission to cite it here, and for her ongoing generous conversation with me.
2. See Axiom 2 in Sedgwick's *Epistemology of the Closet* (1990) : 27–35.
3. There are exceptions. Autobiographies that make of transsexuality a secondary theme include Erica Rutherford's *Nine Lives* (1993) and Jayne County's *Man Enough to be a Woman* (1995): the first an account of a painter, husband and father, the second of a punk performer. As the title to County's autobiography suggests, however, for both texts transsexuality remains the commercial raison d'être.
4. The relations between transsexuality, narrative, and autobiography are more complex than I have space to articulate here. For a detailed discussion of transsexual autobiography and its origins in the case histories of sexual inversion see respectively Chapters 3 and 4 of my *Second Skins: The Body Narratives of Transsexuality* (New York: Colombia University Press, 1998). Sections of this chapter are drawn from the second part of this book.

5. From this pattern of dichotomous and instantaneous transformation Stone excepts Jan Morris's *Conundrum*. Because her discussion of transsexual autobiography (the first of the texts as a body of work) is an appurtenance to her important formulation of transsexual subjectivity (another first in cultural theory), Stone's reading is based on four autobiographies only.

6. This metaphor is elaborated by one anonymous transsexual interviewee cited in Bryan Tully:

> [Transsexuality] is a bit like going to another country, to become a naturalised citizen. You don't know how you will blend in but you must plan to provide yourself with all the accoutrements from the land you are coming from, or else you will end up in a defective state ... Rather than being an immigrant, one is returning home like a Jew ... You can divide up transsexuals into the immigrants who see the new world ahead rather like El Dorado, the refugees who get bundled into that new state without good preparations, and the defectors who have tried very hard to be good citizens, even pretend that they are, but deep inside they are yearning and waiting for a bolt-hole opportunity. (Tully, 1992: 208–9)

Judith Shapiro similarly attempts to find in the multiple meanings of 'naturalisation' a new metaphor of trajectory for thinking about transsexual transitioning:

> (1) a status acquired in the way foreigners acquire citizenship, (2) a change in gender that entails a change in the body, which we associate with the domain of nature, and (3) a recognition of the transsexuals' own experience of sex change as validating what they believe to be their true nature. (Shapiro, 1991: 260)

7. Historically there has been no equivalent mecca for female-to-male surgery because no one has pioneered phalloplasty successfully to the extent that Burou did vaginoplasty.

8. Griggs writes that, since the surgeon with whom she had scheduled gender reassignment fifteen years earlier lost his licence for gross malpractice, she had been terrified by the thought of surgery and had never looked for another surgeon.

9. For her hilarious rendition of this anecdote and a meditation on the effects on one butch of her transsexual mate's transition, see Helen Sandler, 'From butch to bloke', *Diva* (April 1996): 66.

References

Anderson, B. (1983) *Imagined Communities*. London: Verso.

Bhabha, H.K. (1994) *The Location of Culture*. London: Routledge.

Billings, D.B. and T. Urban (1996) 'The socio-medical construction of transsexualism: an interpretation and critique'. In R. Ekins and D. King (eds), *Blending Genders: Social Aspects of Cross-dressing and Sex-Changing*. London: Routledge.

Bornstein, K. (1994) *Gender Outlaw: On Men, Women and the Rest of Us*. New York: Routledge.

Butler, J. (1993) *Bodies That Matter: On the Discursive Limits of 'Sex'*. New York: Routledge.

Conn, C. (1974) *Canary: The Story of a Transsexual*. Los Angeles: Nash.

Cossey, C. (1992) *My Story*. Winchester, MA: Faber.

Costa, M. (1960). *'Coccinelle': Reverse Sex*, trans J. Block. London: Challenge Publications.

County, J. with R. Smith (1995) *Man Enough to be a Woman*. London: Serpent's Tail.

Cummings, K. (1992) *Katherine's Diary: The Story of a Transsexual*. Port Melbourne, Victoria: Heinemann.

Epstein, J. and K. Straub (eds) (1991) *BodyGuards: The Cultural Politics of Gender Ambiguity*. New York: Routledge.

Feinberg, D.L. (1980) *Journal of a Transsexual*. New York: World View.

Feinberg, L. (1993) *Stone Butch Blues: A Novel*. New York: Firebrand.

Feinberg, L. (1996) *Transgender Warriors: Making History from Joan of Arc to Ru Paul*. Boston: Beacon Press.

Fallowell, D./Ashley, A. (1982) *April Ashley's Odyssey*. London: Cape.

Felski, R. (1996) 'Fin de siècle, fin de sexe: transsexuality, postmodernism, and the death of history', *New Literary History*, 27: 337–49.

Findlay, H. (1995) 'Modern stone: what is stone butch now?', *Girlfriends* (March/April): 20, 21–2, 44–5.

Fuss, D. (1995) *Identification Papers*. New York: Routledge.

Griggs, C. (1996) *Passage Through Trinidad: Journal of a Surgical Sex Change*. Jefferson, NC: McFarland.

Gusdorf, G. (1980) 'Conditions and limits of autobiography'. In J. Olney (ed.), *Autobiography: Essays Theoretical and Critical*. Princeton: Princeton University Press.

Halberstam, J. (1994) 'F2M: the making of female masculinity'. In L. Doan (ed.), *The Lesbian Post-modern*. New York: Columbia University Press.

Halberstam, J. (1998) 'Transgender butch: butch/FTM border wars and the masculine continuum'. In *Female Masculinity*. Durham, NC: Duke University Press. Also in *glq: A Journal of Lesbian and Gay Studies*, 4 (2), 1998.

Hunt, N. (1978) *Mirror Image: The Odyssey of a Male-to-Female Transsexual*. New York: Holt.

Jorgensen, C. (1967) *Christine Jorgensen: Personal Autobiography*. New York: Erikson.

Martino, M. with Harriet (1977) *Emergence: A Transsexual Autobiography*. New York: Crown.

Moraga, C. and G. Anzaldúa (eds) (1983) *This Bridge Called My Back: Writings by Radical Women of Color*. New York: Kitchen Table.

Morris, J. (1986) *Conundrum: An Extraordinary Narrative of Transsexualism*. New York: Holt.

Prosser, J. (1995) 'No place like home: the transgendered narrative of Leslie Feinberg's *Stone Butch Blues*', *Modern Fiction Studies*, 41, 3–4: 483–514.

Raymond, J. (1979) *The Transsexual Empire: The Making of the She-Male*. London: Women's Press.

Raymond, J. (1994) *The Transsexual Empire: The Making of the She-Male*. Reissued with a new introduction on transgender. New York: Teachers College Press.

Rich, A. (1986) 'Notes toward a politics of location'. In *Blood, Bread, and Poetry: Selected Prose 1979–1985*. New York: Norton.

Richards, R. and J. Ames (1983) *The Renée Richards Story: Second Serve*. New York: Stein.

Rubin, G. (1992) 'Of catamites and kings: reflections on butch, gender, and boundaries'. In J. Nestle (ed.), *The Persistent Desire: A Femme–Butch Reader*. Boston: Alyson.

Rutherford, E. (1993) *Nine Lives: The Autobiography of Erica Rutherford*. Charlottetown, PEI, Canada: Ragweed.

Sedgwick, E.K. (1990) *Epistemology of the Closet*. Berkeley: University of California Press.

Shapiro, J. (1991) 'Transsexualism: reflections on the persistence of gender and the mutability of sex'. In J. Epstein and K. Straub (eds), *BodyGuards: The Cultural Politics of Gender Ambiguity*. New York: Routledge.

Showalter, E. (1990) *Sexual Anarchy: Gender and Culture at the Fin de Siècle*. New York: Viking.

Sinclair, A. (1965) *I Was Male*. Chicago: Novel Books.

Smith, B. (ed.) (1983) *Home Girls: A Black Feminist Anthology*. New York: Kitchen Table.

Stone, S. (1991) 'The "Empire" strikes back: a posttranssexual manifesto'. In J. Epstein and K. Straub (eds), *BodyGuards: The Cultural Politics of Gender Ambiguity*. New York: Routledge.

Tayman, J. (1991) 'Meet John, er, Jane Doe', *Gentleman's Quarterly*, 61: 220–7.

Thompson, R. and K. Sewell (1995) *What Took You So Long? A Girl's Journey to Manhood*. London: Penguin.

Tully, B. (1992) *Accounting for Transsexuality and Transhomosexuality*. London: Whiting.

Vance, C.S. (ed) (1989) *Pleasure and Danger: Exploring Female Sexuality*. London: Pandora.

Part Two

Becoming (Trans)Active

5

Look! No, Don't!
The Visibility Dilemma
for Transsexual Men

Jamison Green

T ranssexual people usually wish to be perceived and taken seriously as members of the gender class in which they feel most comfortable. Transsexual men are able to integrate into mainstream society through employment and social relationships; their natural masculinity (enough by itself in many cases), combined with the external effects of testosterone, renders them virtually undetectable in most social situations. Cultural tolerance for a wide variety of adult male 'looks' (appearance styles) and behaviours is also a factor in the success of many transitional men. Billy Tipton is just one modern example of a transgendered person who was accepted as a man among his peers without benefit of hormones or surgery. But what happens to the transsexual man who 'comes out' and admits to having been born female?

Many of us have been 'outed' because of unfortunate medical situations or indiscreet friends or family members. A few of us have been used as grist for the insatiable media mill as we have fought to retain employment in places where we originally represented ourselves as female, or have been sued by disgruntled ex-spouses. And some of us have chosen to make ourselves visible as FTMs – men who were born with female bodies, not 'women who became men' – because we have realized that the isolation individual men like ourselves experience can lead to poor self-esteem and ill-informed choices with respect to treatment in medical, legal and social arenas.

I am one of the growing cadre of men who have chosen to make ourselves available to assist transsexual and non-transsexual people in understanding the experience of transsexual men. I have inched my way out of the transsexual closet with considerable trepidation, and many people in my life have no idea of my transitional past because I choose not to disclose it to them. I have found that when a man elects to reveal his transsexual history or status, results are mixed, varying according to situation – but generally the experience has struck me as being somewhat like joining another species.

I started doing educational work regarding gender and transgender issues in 1989 at the request of Steve Dain and Lou Sullivan, both of whom were too busy (and, in Sullivan's case, too ill) to continue to do some of the college and university classroom lectures and question-and-answer sessions they had been doing regularly for several years. There was no remuneration for these sessions, which would last an hour or sometimes two, and with travel time could often take three or four hours. I soon realized that taking time away from my employer to give classroom lectures meant that I was actually losing money in the service of education. In other words, we sometimes pay for the privilege of telling our stories. Sullivan also referred me to a speaker's bureau operated by a large San Francisco transvestite club, through which I participated in numerous panel presentations for classes in which the professor wished to clarify the difference between transvestites and transsexual people. Through these panels I learned that these presentations can be a valuable form of therapy. It can be worth every penny it costs to receive the validation I feel when I am sincerely thanked for sharing my personal story, especially when the exchange has proven enlightening for even one person in the audience. And yet, as I listen to each panel of cross-dressers, transgenderists and transsexual people reciting our oh-so-similar litanies of struggle and change, there seems to be a self-centeredness, even a pathetic quality of self-justification to so many of our public 'confessions'. We say we want to be invisible, yet we beg to be acknowledged. Stepping in front of the class we become laboratory rats, frogs in the dissection tray, interactive multimedia learning experiences.

'How old were you when you first realized you were a frog, Mr Green?'
'How did your parents react when you told them you were a frog?'
'Do you date? Do you tell your partners you're a frog?'
'So, how does it work? I mean, uh, can you, like, do it?'

No one has really ever suggested that I am an actual frog – but these are essentially the questions that are most frequently asked. Of course, these questions are expected. I often sit in the audience as if I were a student until the professor announces that apparently the guest speaker will be late or has forgotten (unless the class is so small that the professor recognizes me as a stranger and quizzes me with her eyes, hoping I am there to take this class period off her hands, or unless my visit is a repeat performance and the professor knows me on sight). Then I rise up from within their midst, students gasping and murmuring around me: 'It was sitting next to me and I didn't know!' 'Oh, my God.' 'I never would have guessed.' 'He looks so normal!' It's fun to fool them, at first. It's validating, reassuring. It's educational. I get to show them that they never know who might be transsexual, that transsexual people are just like anyone, just like them. I am an object lesson.

I started out, like most transsexual speakers, just telling my story and leaving time for questions. Over the years I learned the most effective way to tell my story quickly, whetting the students' appetites, planting certain concepts in their minds and leaving more time to respond to their questions rather than lecturing. I do this because when they see me think on my feet, when I can use spontaneous humour, when I am vulnerable to them, then they see me most completely as a human being. They come to trust me. I find this trust ironic because it grows very quickly out of their original expectations that I will not be what I seem, or that they would be able to tell that I am trying to be something that I am not. When I am successful, it is because they let go of their preconceptions and their prejudices, they realize that they can exist without those crutches of belief, that they can move through the world without fear and without certainty and still the world goes on. Nothing really changes when they acknowledge the existence of transpeople (transsexual and transgender people) and realize that we are not inherently monsters or perverts. Nothing really changes except that their compassion quotient expands exponentially. Nothing really changes except each of the students goes away with a little piece of me that they can own and mould and reinterpret as they wish.

I lose a bit more control of the use of my own story every time I tell it. Every time I lecture a class of 200 students, 200 more people in the world know – or think they know – something about my genital organs, even if I never talked about them. They learn more about me in one hour than my co-workers who see me every day will ever know – unless my co-workers sign up for Human Sexuality.

It's one thing to confine one's public confessions to the educational arena (as a guest lecturer), a world contained within the ivy-covered walls and ivory towers of inquiry and theoretical exploration (unless you are seeking tenure – see Chapter 8). It's quite another to venture into the political arena where theory and practice become one and there is little tolerance for exploratory gestures. Here you must act, advance, thrust and parry, and be prepared to compromise. There is no hanging back, no way of just checking in and then retiring. Once you have stepped into the ring, it's you and the bull: there is no escape without everyone knowing you did not have the spine for it. And they'll know why you didn't have the spine: regardless of what you tell them, it will be because you are a trans person. It's one thing to present yourself to a university class – where they know they must behave themselves in front of their professor, where they know they can be critical in private, on paper, in their intellectual analysis of some mutilated creature's pathetic display of narcissistic neediness. It's quite another to offer yourself up, uninsulated, as fodder for politicians and journalists who have no reservations about expressing their distaste for our ilk, and no reason whatsoever to care about us or our issues. It will take much more than a personal story and an attitude of 'specialness' for having lived on both sides of the gender fence to find any compassion in these hardened souls.

And why should we even be trying to talk to politicians and journalists? Such behaviour is completely at cross-purposes with the stated goals of medical and psychological treatment for transsexual people. That treatment is supposed to make us feel normal. We are not supposed to want attention as transsexuals; we are supposed to want to fit in as 'normal' men. We are supposed to pretend we never spent 15, 20, 30, 40 or more years in female bodies, pretend that the vestigial female parts some of us never lose were never there. In short, in order to be a good – or successful – transsexual person, one is not supposed to be a transsexual person at all. This puts a massive burden of secrecy on the transsexual individual: the most intimate and human aspects of our lives are constantly at risk of disclosure. Every time a transsexual man goes into a public (or even private) toilet he is aware of his history; every time he makes love with a partner; every time he seeks medical care; whenever he is at the mercy of a governmental body or social service agency, he is aware of his history – or aware of any anomalies in his body – and must consciously be on guard against discovery. And this is supposed to be the optimal ground of being for a successful person? I think not.

This burden of secrecy is reinforced by myriad social conventions and institutions that support rather than challenge individual prejudice concerning the existence of transsexual people. There are doctors who will not admit they provide services to us. Insurance companies deny medical coverage for conditions relating to 'sex reassignment' or 'surgical sex change' (which can be extrapolated to mean any medical condition once one's transsexual status is known). Some governments or governmental agencies will not allow us to change our identity records to ease our passage through life. Employers are free to dismiss us because they feel that who we are is just too 'disruptive'. It is easy to see how a non-transsexual could feel justified in treating transsexual people with disdain or disgust. So long as their ignorance and prejudice protect them from expressing basic human courtesy to transpeople, non-transsexuals will continue their persecutions.

Yet all these obstacles have not stopped us. All this disapproval has not prevented – will not prevent – the existence of transsexual men and women. It is easy to see how transsexual people are typically justified in their desire to circumscribe knowledge of their past or present lives. And yet as more of us become visible, those whose livelihoods or relationships depend on maintaining secrecy may feel tempted to disclose themselves and take a stand, while they are simultaneously alienated from those who are doing so because their own circumstantial constraints compel them not to act. This inner conflict may breed the very same low self-esteem that activists are attempting to alleviate. The individual who is not able to reconcile his desire to help the nascent trans community with his own need for confidentiality and security may isolate himself further from the only people who share his experience, or he may actively oppose community-oriented efforts.

Can one accomplish anything for the trans community while remaining closeted? I do believe so, certainly. But I think many – not all – transpeople who want to remain hidden will resist making any blatant pro-trans noises for fear of calling attention to themselves. Having stepped out of the transsexual closet myself, I occasionally wonder when certain of my friends – both trans and non-trans – will feel the pressure of my growing notoriety and decline to be seen with me. I wonder who knows about my transsexual past, and who doesn't. Have my co-workers seen me on television? Have acquaintances seen my photo on the cover of San Francisco's queer community newspaper when it was on the streets for two weeks? Would they say anything about it if they had? Have my friends told their friends about me; is that why people seem so eager to be introduced to me? Are they kind, or are they curious? Is it me that people seem attracted to, or is it the exotic trans phenomenon?

Walking down the street in San Francisco or New York City, Boston, Atlanta, Portland, Seattle, London, Paris, Rome, no one seems to take any special interest in me. I am just another man, invisible, no one special. I remember what it was first like to feel that anonymity as testosterone gradually obliterated the androgyny that for most of my life made others uncomfortable in my presence. It was a great relief to be able to shake off layers of defensive behaviours developed to communicate my humanity from inside my incategorizability. It was a joy to be assumed human for a change, instead of stared at, scrutinized for signs of any gender. Now, whenever I stand up in front of a class or make any public statement in support of transgender or transsexual people, I am scrutinized for signs of my previous sex, knowing my gender is reinforced by my male appearance. No one notices me on the street, yet I have been on television and in films, my photograph has appeared in several national (US and internationally distributed) magazines, and I have been asked for commentary and interviews that have appeared in many more publications. In some cases I am identified as transsexual, and in others there is no indication as to my transsexual status. In some cases, my appearance in a publication has had nothing whatsoever to do with transsexualism (I do have other areas of expertise). And I have a lurking suspicion that I would not receive the attention I do (for non-transsexual-related accomplishments) if I still retained the androgynous appearance that I had for the first 40 years of my life. In fact, I know that androgynous people such as I was have often been passed over as subjects and spokespersons on such topics as women in non-traditional jobs because we didn't appear acceptably gendered, and this applies equally to pre-transition female-to-male people and post-transition male-to-female people.

Now, however, people are quite comfortable with my male presentation. My psyche seems to fit nicely into male packaging: I feel better; people around me are less confused, and so am I. So why tell anyone about my past? Why not just live the life of a normal man? Perhaps I could if I were a normal man, but I am not. I am a man, and I am a man who lived for 40 years in a female body. But I was not a woman. I am not a woman who became a man. I am not a woman who lives as a man. I am not, nor was I ever a woman, though I lived in a female body, and certainly tried, whenever I felt up to it, to be a woman. But it was never in me to be a woman. Likewise, I am not a man in the same sense as my younger brother is a man, having been treated as such all his life. I was treated as other than a man most of the time, as a man part of the time, and as a woman only rarely. Certainly I was treated as a little girl when I was young, but even then people occasionally assumed I was a little boy. I always felt like something 'other'. Can I be just a man now, or must I always be 'other'?

The tremendous sense of relief that transitioning men feel marks what is probably one of the most satisfying periods of their lives. While immense challenges arise during transition, and while there may be a sense of urgency to complete the process that can obliterate all other external concerns, the sense of growing into one's self – of really becoming who one is at last – is so rewarding that it may erase the long-standing pain of being misunderstood concerning one's gender. The transition itself opens so many windows on the gender system that we may be compelled to comment on our observations, which could not be made from any other vantage point than a transsexual (or sometimes transgender) position.

An even further irony is that once a man is no longer visibly transsexual – that is, once his previous androgyny has been transformed to unquestionable masculinity – he may no longer be of interest to the press. I have had reporters at public events look right through me when directed to me as an expert or knowledgeable source. They do not wish to interview me because I do not look like a transsexual. Only after they somehow find out that I am a trans person are they interested in me, and then not for my expertise, but for the tingling quizzicality they can enjoy while they stare at me, hardly hearing a word I say, and wonder how someone so male ever could have been a woman.

Seeking acceptance within the system of 'normal' and denying our transsexual status is an acquiescence to the prevailing binary gender paradigm that will never let us fit in, and will never accept us as equal members of society. Our transsexual status will always be used to threaten and shame us. We will always wear a scarlet T that marks us for treatment as a pretender, as other, as not normal, as trans. But wearing that T proudly – owning the label and carrying it with dignity – can twist that paradigm and free us from our subordinate prison. By using our own bodies and experience as references for our standards, rather than the bodies and experience of non-transsexuals (and non-transgendered people), we can grant our own legitimacy, as have all other groups that have been oppressed because of personal characteristics.

Transgendered people who choose transsexual treatment, who allow themselves to be medicalized, depend on a system of approval that grants them access to treatment. That approval may be seen as relieving them of their responsibility – or guilt – for being outside the norm. They then become either the justification for the treatment by embodying the successful application of 'normal' standards; or they become the victims of the treatment when they realize they are still very different in form and substance from non-transsexual people, and they still suffer from the oppression they wished to escape by looking to doctors to make them 'normal'. By standing up and claiming our identity as men (or women) who are also transpeople, by asserting that our different bodies are just as normal for us as anyone else's is for them, by insisting that our right to modify our bodies and shape our own identities is as inalienable as our right to choose our religion (though not nearly as inexpensive or painless), we claim our humanity and our right to be treated equally under law and within the purviews of morality and culture.

Gender and genitals comprise a stronghold of control binding all people to a social order that has serious difficulty tolerating diversity or change. Somebody's got us by the balls and they don't want to let go. Who is that somebody? Who is so afraid of losing control? What are they going to lose control of? What is preserved by denying the legitimacy of transsexual (and transgendered) people? What is destroyed by acknowledging us? Is it the right of succession? Is it the right to own property? Is it the ability to know whether to treat another as an equal, an inferior, or a superior human being?

In the introduction to the 1994 edition of *The Transsexual Empire*, Professor Janice Raymond postulates the reason why 'there are not as many female-to-constructed male transsexuals'. She writes that for women:

the construction of gender dissatisfaction has been medicalized through promotion of breast implants, hormone replacement therapy, infertility hormones and reproductive procedures, and plastic surgery. (Raymond, 1994: xiv)

She also points out that:

Maleness is not so easy to come by, especially because the majority of vendors (professionals) are males themselves and more discomfited in giving it away. (*ibid.*: xv)

These are very female-centred positions, and don't allow any space for variant opinions. Raymond states that the medicalization of transsexualism prevents the destruction of stereotypical gender roles and reinforces sexism (*ibid.*: xvii). It is Raymond herself (in collusion with some of the doctors she so vehemently objects to) who has put us into gender boxes. Her dogmatic insistence that it is impossible to change sex and that transsexuals never move beyond gender roles are blatant reactionary responses to what she perceives as threats to female bodies, feminism and feminist politics – everything upon which she bases her own identity concept. Raymond's brand of feminism cannot survive without rigid gender roles, and especially not without the objectification and vilification of men as actors in either male or female roles.

Bernice Hausman (1995) also takes on the medicalization of gender, asserting that transsexuals are expert at the arts of impersonation, producing gender as the real of sex, though gender does not 'exist' (Hausman, 1995: 193). She claims that transsexuals are unable to accept and accommodate themselves to the sexual meanings of their natural bodies, and the demand for treatment is made to accommodate a cultural fantasy of stable identity (*ibid.*). She even takes gender away from homosexual people by claiming that 'gender is a concept meaningful only within heterosexuality and in advocacy of hetero-sexuality' (*ibid.*: 194). Yet, as Judith Halberstam has pointed out, '... lesbians are also turned on by gendered sexual practices and restricted by the limiting of gender to bio-binarism'. (Halberstam, 1994: 225). Refreshingly, Halberstam states:

> The breakdown of genders and sexualities into identities is in many ways ... an endless project, and it is perhaps preferable therefore to acknowledge that gender is defined by transitivity, that sexuality manifests as multiple sexualities, and that therefore we are all transsexuals. (*ibid.*: 226)

Halberstam goes so far as to say that 'There are no transsexuals'. And while I believe this last remark to be nobly intended, I must disagree with it if for no other reason than to acknowledge my own transformation. At least Halberstam's position gives us all individual voices. While Raymond wants us to take sides and rage against each other until someone dies, Hausman's effort to obliterate the discussion by dismissing the entire concept of gender renders us all speechless.

Gender is a form of communication, a language that we all use to express and interpret each other socially. For most practical purposes, however, the majority of our society have not learned how to separate sex from gender, and the use of the terms interchangeably (most commonly the substituting of gender for sex in an effort to avoid intimations of impropriety) only muddies the waters. The middle-of-the-road American sees a masculine woman or a feminine man, and he doesn't care who they actually sleep with. He's already figured out that they're queer, and he's ready to kill to protect mom and apple pie. The signifiers that matter are not necessarily the clothing, or the genitals (which are not visible), or the sex partner (who may not be present or apparent), but the qualities of character and non-genital physicality, as well as aspects of personal expression that may be cultivated or innate, that give the 'reader' an idea of the subject's masculinity or femininity, which the reader then may choose to apply to his understanding of the subject's maleness or femaleness, extrapolating further to define the subject's sexual orientation or activity. Thus gender is both expressed and interpreted, but it may not be interpreted as gender when the signals are mixed, that is when the body and the gender do not conform to the reader's expectations. Everyone uses gender to communicate, as much as we use our clothing, our posture, our vocabulary, our tone of voice. The fact that gender is problematic for some theorists as well as some transpeople is no justification for an attempt to mandate it out of existence.

Like Raymond, Hausman uses the fact of sex reassignment surgery as part of her argument against it, citing descriptions of surgery and post-operative pain in transsexual autobiographies. Hausman notes that the admission of pain serves 'to undermine the text's primary argument that the subject was really meant to be the sex he or she must be surgically fashioned into' (Hausman, 1995: 167). The implication is that if there is pain, then there is something unnatural about the body's situation. More faulty logic. Not all transsexual people experience undue pain with their surgeries. Not all non-transsexual people are pain-free, whether or not they have had any surgery. To embrace another two arbitrary extremes that can also co-exist in one physical body, both athletes and disabled people can attest to the pain that sometimes accompanies self-actualization. I don't see how the quality of being pain-free confers a greater veracity on a subject's experience.

Hausman says that to advocate the use of hormones and surgery in the service of gender identity: 'one must accede to the facticity of gender and its status as the master signifier of sex. In other words, one must believe in the simulation as real' (ibid.: 193). The abstraction from broad experience that makes this kind of theory possible is reinforced by the exercises in self-justification that are most transsexual autobiographies (Denny, 1994).[1] The distance established by the printed page still allows most readers to perceive the transsexual subject as object, as less than human, or certainly dismissable. Rarely do transsexual people represent themselves as active agents in their own transformations. They are compelled to change. They always knew something was wrong. There's that binary thinking again: if something is wrong, it must be made right. Is it so surprising that transsexual people would seem to apologize for themselves in a world that has vilified and ostracized them?

What we need to understand, and why female-to-male visibility is necessary in order to bring the point home, is that what we experience is not something wrong, but something different. If Hausman sees gender as the mirage doppelgänger of sex, and sex as 'the real', she can have no context in which to comprehend those of us who experience our own reality differently. To me, my gender never was the signifier of my sex; my gender was, and is, the social expression of myself that I was unable to change to conform to the expectations others had of my sex. I tried hard to be a non-conforming woman. I believed the feminist line that biology is not destiny. Now I feel as if I'm being told by Gender Studies theorists that biology is not destiny unless you are transsexual. I cannot say that I was a man trapped in a female body. I can only say that I was a male spirit alive in a female body, and I chose to bring that body in line with my spirit, and to live the rest of my life as a man. Socially and legally I am a man. And still, I am a different kind of man. I am not trying to encroach on the identities (or physical space) of women (so Raymond's argument holds no weight, especially her position that maleness is hard to come by). I am not worried about 'passing' for male or 'getting caught'. I am not concerned that men won't accept me, because my experience has been that they do. I am not worried about fabricating a past: I accept my past. I have continuity in my body, and the 'real of sex' for me is the way I express myself, as both a gendered and a sexual body.

Look! No, don't! Transsexual men are men. Transsexual men are men who have lived in female bodies. Transsexual men may appear feminine, androgynous or masculine. Any man may appear feminine, androgynous, or masculine. Look! What makes a man a man? His penis? His beard? His receding hairline? His lack of breasts? His sense of himself as a man? Some men have no beard, some have no penis, some never lose their hair, some have breasts. All have a sense of themselves as men.

Look! No, don't! Don't notice that I am different from other men unless you are ready to acknowledge that my uniqueness is the same difference that each man has from any other man. If transsexual men want to disappear, to not be seen, it is because they are afraid of not being seen as men, of being told they are not men, of being unable to refute the assertion that they are not men. All men fear this. In this way, all men – trans and non-trans – are the same. Many non-trans men have never thought about it because they have never had occasion to conceive of a situation in which their manhood would be called into question. But if they stop to think about it, I would venture to guess that all men would cling tenaciously to their self-concept as men, even if they lost their penis (though the loss of this unique organ would very likely be a serious threat to a man who had not examined his sense of self). One thing all men understand is that they are not women. This is also true for transsexual men, even though they have lived in female bodies. As soon as a transsexual man reveals his trans status, he is examined for vestiges of 'woman' that may then be used to invalidate his maleness, his authenticity, his reliability. Look! No, don't! What is true, what is false? What is a 'real' man?

I am real; I am an authentic and reliable man. I am also a transsexual man. I am a man who lived for 40 years in the body of a woman, so I have had access to knowledge that most men do not have. Invisibility has been a major issue in my life. Throughout my childhood and young adulthood I – my identity – was, for the most part, invisible. I was always defined by others, categorized either by my lack of femininity, or by my female body, or by the disquieting combination of both. The opportunity to escape the punishing inadequacy imposed on me by self-styled adjudicators of sex role performance was one I could not ignore. I simply will not accept a similar judgement of my masculinity. And I have yet to meet someone who could look me in the face, who could spend any time at all in conversation with me, who would deny my masculinity now the way they would dismiss it before as 'just a phase' or 'inappropriate behaviour for a girl'.

The fact is that the known biological aspects of sex difference – which we call natural and think of as immutable – are no more immune to change than the psychosocial manifestations of sex difference – which we call gender and cultural, and understand to be mutable (Hubbard, 1998: 46). One of the most difficult things for me to reconcile about my own transition was my movement out of a place in lesbian culture and into a white heterosexual embodiment. Let me emphasize: Not all transsexual men have lesbian histories, and not all transsexual men are heterosexual. Nonetheless, my personal politics are quite closely aligned with queer culture, so I am again a different sort of heterosexual man. I am not afraid of homosexuality, though I do not practice it. Many gendered and heterosexist social constructs collapse like cardboard sea-walls against the ocean of my transsexual reality.

Academics are afraid of being called essentialists,[2] but I am not afraid of saying that as an artist and as a human being I am motivated to express both the core and essence of my being-ness, and I will stand by the truth of my experience and the logic of my analysis. If phrases like 'male energy' are too vague and ethereal (Raymond, 1994: xxi), what are we to do with phrases like 'the real of sex'? My experience of myself, corroborated by other functioning, self-actualized adults (both hetero-sexual and gay and lesbian) who have known me much or all of my life, is that I seem far more comfortable to myself as a man, more 'natural', and more acceptable to them. Not that they didn't love or accept me before my transition to manhood, because they did. Some of them were resistant, even fearful concerning my change. But they rode the wave, and most of us have landed together, still friends, still relatives, still intrigued by the possibilities in life.

There: was that the self-justification part, or was it evidence, testimony on behalf of myself and other transsexual men? When I state the facts of my experience, listeners or readers get to choose whether or not the tone they perceive is one of self-justification. It all comes down to attitude. In my transition I lost only two friends. I have gained countless more since then. And I have learned something about responsibility, about duty, and about what civil rights really means. I've learned how discrimination really works, and how class, race, sex – and gender – distinctions are used to empower some and disempower others. I've learned that power is relative, while strength is internal. Before my transition I was just a middle-class white transgendered female, ostensibly a woman and therefore lesbian (in my sexual intimacy), trying to make my way in the world, climbing the career ladder, building my relationships, enjoying my hobbies and pastimes, hoping that someday I would be recognized as a literary, musical, and photographic artist. During my transition I learned about shame, fear and hatred. I also learned what courage is. Since my transition I am just a middle-class white man, ostensibly male, who happens to be heterosexual (in my sexual intimacy), trying to make my way in the world, climbing my own career trellis, building my relationships, enjoying my hobbies and pastimes, working towards someday being recognized as a literary, performing, and photographic artist.

Look! No, don't! It all comes down to attitude. If you accept me – if you can acknowledge that I am a man, even a transsexual man – then you can accept that life has variation, life is rich, you don't control it, you experience it. You can still analyse concepts, you can still have opinions, you can even disagree with me. And if you don't accept me, well, then you don't. But as you go through life categorizing and qualifying, judging and

evaluating, remember that there are human beings on the other end of the
stick you're shaking, and they might have ideas and feelings and
experiences that are different from your own. Maybe they look different
from you, maybe they are tall women with large hands, maybe they are
men who have given birth to their own children, maybe the categories
you've delineated won't work in all cases. Look! No, don't! Transsexual
men want to disappear because we are tired of being forced into
categories, because we are beyond defending ourselves.

Look! No, don't! Transsexual men are entering the dialogue from
more perspectives, more angles, than were ever theorized as being
possible for them. Maybe if we are ignored we will go away. Maybe if
we are continually not permitted to speak, not allowed to define
ourselves, not given any corner of the platform from which to present
our realities, then we will disappear and refrain from further
complicating all the neat, orderly theories about gender and sex.
Maybe if no one looks at us we will be safe.

At first I thought my transition was about not being looked at any
longer, about my relief from scrutiny; now I know it is about scrutiny
itself, about self-examination, and about losing my own fear of being
looked at, not because I can disappear, but because I am able to claim
my unique difference at last. What good is safety if the price is shame
and fear of discovery? So, go ahead: Look!

Notes

1. I must admit that I have not read many autobiographies by male-to-female
    transsexual people, but I have read every one published through 1996 (by
    commercial publishers) written by female-to-male transsexual people, and
    I have been almost uniformly disappointed to find that every explanation
    sounds like self-justification, like a liturgy of cause and effect, like
    rationalization, even when it's the truth. People doubt, people wonder.
    People who cannot imagine the experience transsexuals have will probably
    always think of it as something false or deluded. This is why I have found
    educational public speaking to be so effective: people have a direct
    experience of my physical presence and my gender expression, and it
    becomes true for them in a visceral way they do not easily dismiss or forget.
2. Raymond reacts against such charges (1994: xx–xxi).

References

Denny, D. (1994) 'Review: two transsexual autobiographies', *Journal of Gender Studies*, Summer.

Halberstam, J. (1994) 'F2M: the making of female masculinity'. In L. Doan, (ed.), *The Lesbian Postmodern*. New York: Columbia University Press.

Hausman, B.L. (1995) *Changing Sex: Transsexualism, Technology, and the Idea of Gender*. Durham, NC: Duke University Press.

Hubbard, R. (1998) 'Gender and genitals: constructs of sex and gender'. In D. Denny (ed.), *Current Concepts in Transgender Identity*. New York: Garland.

Raymond, J. (1994) *The Transsexual Empire: The Making of a She-Male*, 2nd edn. New York: Teachers College Press.

Author's Note

This chapter was written in 1996 and presented at the Second International Congress on Sex and Gender Issues, King of Prussia, PA, on 21 June 1997.

6

Testimonies of HIV Activism

Kate More and Sandra Laframboise with Deborah Brady

Talking Heads
Kate More

Asked about my experience of HIV activism, I'm always reluctant. I haven't got HIV. I didn't meet many trannies with HIV. I've never done sex work. There are other people who could write this. Sex workers, people with HIV. Sometimes I get introduced as the 'HIV Woman' and I either go all technical and talk about preventative strategies and studies in Vancouver, or – sublime to the ridiculous – go on about being hassled by a group of hustlers, as Roz would call them,[1] over the difference between a Wonderbra and an Ultrabra. Have I got this right – an Ultrabra pushes silicon-enhanced boobs together and a Wonderbra is for magicking up boobs from nowhere? Before and after? Before and instead of?

What I don't tell people is how pissed off I got at travelling up to the group and being told to butt out in lots of little ways, and once or twice in rather bigger ways. And yet when I come across a bloody-minded Community Policeman, Rape Crisis Centre, Women's Refuge or Duty Social Worker I get to a place which is so angry and so personalized that it's *me* that's being crushed under the 'proper procedures' – these people have the power to wipe out my very being, and my feeling is, they know it.

We did an HIV leaflet that was somewhat well-known. We produced others, but this was the well-known one. The text comes later (pp.141–4), but you had to see it. The cover was a phone-box sex worker card with a naughty lady spanking the botty of a half-nude man (p. 142). The card advertised 'TG HIV Info (from a Merciless Mistress!)' – well, maybe you had to be there. The HIV professionals thought it bent the distinction between us and them too much. Outside of our local area, we gave it out a couple of times in bars down in Leeds and got accused of campaigning against the local rape crisis centre, which has just shut down. They thought we would want fewer services. We went to our council and said, 'These services are funded by the taxpayer, which includes the TS taxpayer. You are paying trained counsellors to turn away rape victims because we aren't politically correct! ... on the basis of some early 80s political doctrine that no one believes any more. Do you realize how close to rape of rape victims that is?' It was a litany, 'You are telling people who have been raped that they aren't real women ... you are following an ideology which said that "all transsexuals rape women's bodies by turning the real woman's body into an artefact".[2] Taxpayers are paying you to call rape victims "rapists".' I couldn't believe it. I still can't believe it.

We were told, by the council, that the only way we could get rape support in our county was to organize a rape crisis centre for men, women and TSs, which would cost exactly £92,000. This was the cost of the present crisis centre. We decided to read that advice as saying that competition was the only way to convince the current centre to be more pluralist, but maybe our local RCC had their enemies too. We got legal advice from a Queen's Counsel hired by the Equal Opportunities Commission that we should take the RCC to court as a test case and when 'P', who is a friend, was so successful in *P v S and Cornwall County Council* we thought we could just present them with the ruling and point out how the Sex Discrimination Act applied to the provision of goods and services, which applied to them. When they knew they were in the wrong – legally – they would find a way forward.

Of course a friendly letter from our lawyer, herself an ex-RCC lesbian, met with a response from their, no doubt, ex-RCC lesbian lawyers saying 'go walk'. The RCC hired rooms in our building and when our post started being discovered in the *Ladies*, opened and on display to the general public or just empty envelopes, and when the allegations began to freak us, the police, and everyone else, out, Cleveland County Council intervened and redirected our mail through them.

After a while Cleveland County Council's HIV Unit experienced a tug-of-love fracas over their photocopying machine, and Health Promotion stopped being able to talk to, and photocopy for clients, and the council's various funding committees decided, uniquely, to hold discussion of our grant applications *in camera* and the Chief

Executive intervened directly to prevent the council adopting an Equal Opportunities policy we had sponsored, on the basis that we were trouble-makers and no other council in the UK had a policy, so they didn't need one – even if one of their highly paid systems people had been a TS and had left to become a bar-maid, before committing suicide. And then irony of ironies, the [right-wing] government abolished the council because it was too progressive. After five separate grant applications were turned down, and the council's HIV Unit was privatized amid allegations of corruption – that was when we gave up doing HIV work.

We had taken law, HIV and counselling courses and so carried on doing indirect work, setting up a case law archive (the only one in the UK), and training and leafleting solicitors, running a free newsletter, writing to MPs (all of them). We rang round the country's Community Policing policy units (all of them – twice); we talked to the Police Complaints Authority about the conflicts between PACE[3] and intimate searches of TSs; we went into prisons, and lobbied when people were raped or murdered, raising trans issues on community and national policing forums, even starting one for County Durham and joining the Parliamentary Forum on Transsexualism; we kept saying, 'The largest study in the UK, by Charing Cross Hospital no less – "Fifty-two per cent of male-to-females: victim to violence".' After one of our ring-arounds ACPO[4] minuted the custody suite issue. But no one seemed to be implementing even an ACPO minute. The policy was a secret even from some custody suites. When enough pressure was brought to bear on the police, the first crucial policy was finally adopted. We couldn't believe it, no general catch-all phrase including the crucial three words, 'sex', 'gender' and 'sexuality', no recording system for TG hate crime, no mention of the term 'transphobic' to label bad behaviour – actually it used phrases like 'officers may have to deal with them', and it took outrageous liberties with definitions – it conflated the umbrella term 'transgender' with 'transsexual' – in effect medicalizing and bracketing all trannies into the heteronormative, and then conflated 'transsexual' with 'intersex' – everyone is either a transvestite or a hermaphrodite, fetishist or bearded lady, all those old, straight, stigmatized categories. It was a categorization that denied trans agency, made us seem safe. But it was based on the ACPO minute, and it was policy! They just decided to ignore us and take the easy option. We kept up a dialogue with the, if I remember rightly, 63 rape crisis centres in the UK for over two years. Sent them leaflets and copies of our newsletters and journal. We even surveyed them. Only one RCC before the survey, Brighton – in a town that has more TSs per head than any other in the UK – could be said to be accepting of transgender. I spoke to all of the RCCs on the telephone at least once, and was invited to give talks at perhaps a dozen of them. I don't think a single TS had ever, knowingly, been invited into a RCC before then. Something like 16 accept some sort of TS now. We have to cherish these small victories.

When we were looking for grants we also needed to produce some figures, so along with a multiple choice hate crime survey (which we twisted people's arms to fill in), based on the Stonewall one, which criminally excluded trans, we did a first rough-and-ready attitude survey of the lesbian and gay community, and one of telephone sex workers. We knew nothing about surveys and statistics of course. We went into gay venues on HIV promotion evenings and sent a team out into the club asking everyone to support the Press for Change birth-certificate petition. The least provocative thing we could think of. If they hesitated, we told them they could sign themselves as 'Mickey Mouse – The White House' if they liked. Made a note of how many men and women said no. It was terribly unsophisticated. We averaged the results of each team member. Scene lesbians in Cleveland hated our guts. The gay men were unexpectedly supportive. It was something like 1-in-8 refusals compared with 1-in-61. One gay man knew the correct address on Pennsylvania Avenue. His name was Ronald MacDonald.

We went down to Brighton to do the sex worker survey – went around phone-boxes collecting an example of each card, irrespective of whether advertising as a TS or not, and logged how many phone numbers offered sex from transpeople: 1 in 4 – we didn't believe it ourselves until a real survey in Amsterdam a year later came up with 70 out of 300, approximately the same. These days, after that woman was multiply stabbed in Soho, it's really rare to advertise in phone boxes.

News Flash: London Sex Worker Murdered[5]

The body of Robyn Brown, a 23-year-old transgendered sex worker was found partially clothed on 1 March in her West End flat: Flat b, 6 Gosfield St, London W1 from where she worked, advertising through cards in Soho telephone boxes. The post-mortem, carried out at Guy's Hospital, showed that she had died of repeated stabbing. Robyn, who, the police reported, was born as James Brown, and also used the names Gina, Gemma and Errol, was last seen alive by a friend at half past six on Friday evening (28 February 1997). The lead officer, DS Brian Morris told us that he has been pursuing enquiries with friends, associates and family, to whom she was open about her work. He particularly focused on any arguments she may have had on the evening of the attack and described it as 'a vicious and brutal murder'. Several knives have been taken away from the scene for forensic examination, but so far the murder weapon has not been identified. The police are looking for help from the gay and TG community, who can call free and anonymously on (0800) 555111.

Sex workers from the community told us they believed Robyn had a drug-related criminal record and said that she worked with her post-op TS girlfriend. However, drugs are common in this community and those questioned clearly came away from meeting police believing that the murder was being treated as drugs-related, and it is therefore unclear where this idea comes from. Police are reported to have talked to community sex workers respectfully, a notable change in attitudes since the Kings Cross rapes of the mid-1980s. There has, however, been criticism of both the limited scale of the inquiries and of poor liaison by police, contacting none of the usual NGOs.[6] One sex worker said, 'The police didn't contact me, or anyone I know, and I know everyone.' It was felt that this might be partly responsible for some of the recent panic. Since the murder at the end of February there have been at least two reports of attacks on London-based TG sex workers, one to G&SA and the other to GALOP,[7] it being unclear if this was the same incident or if it was reported to the police. Neither was an attempted stabbing. The police said they knew nothing of these reports.

Enquiries made by NGOs proved unhelpful; GALOP reported difficulties with one officer's attitude to confidentiality. The officer stated that the victims of these attacks could not be assured confidentiality if the result was prosecution. This was because of new legal requirements that can force disclosure of all non-sexual attacks. GALOP supplied the appropriate police telephone number to their caller, but were not convinced that the incident would be reported. G&SA offered to relay details anonymously to their caller, but this was declined.

These criticisms follow quickly on the heels of those arising from a recent ruling by Mr Justice Hooper at Reading Crown Court which, although finally closing a 27-year-old loophole created by the Corbett case, by making vaginal rape of MTFs a crime, also, controversially, found the accused not guilty of raping the 46-year-old TS sex worker (on Christmas Day, 1995). Roz Kaveney, G&SA's Chair and Deputy Chair of Liberty, said that after *R v Tan* it was 'clear that the judiciary considers TG sex-workers to be asking for it'. In *R v Tan* (1983),

Gloria Greaves, a TS S/M mistress working in the Victoria area of London, argued that as she never had sex with her slaves she didn't perceive that she broke the law. The judges, however were determined to prosecute her, finally applying an ancient and mostly unused offence, that of keeping a 'disorderly house', which had been designed to outlaw cock-fighting.

The London-based transzine *girly* added to the controversy, recalling another TG prostitute's death: Maxwell Confait was strangled and h/er house set on fire on 21 April 1972 in Doggett Road, Catford. Three youths between the ages of 14 and 18, including a Turkish Cypriot with poor English and another with a mental age of 8, were taken into custody and, under examination by Detective Chief Superintendent Jones and Detective Inspector Stockwell of Lee Road police station, confessed. After several appeals these were found to be unsafe convictions and several years later Paul Pooley, the son of Dick Pooley who founded the prisoners' rights organization PROP, stated that he had seen the murder being committed by a man called Douglas Franklin. Franklin had been Confait's lover/protector when both were serving time in Wormwood Scrubs. Sir Michael Havers, then Attorney General, ruled that neither Pooley nor Franklin would be prosecuted, on the grounds that although one or the other was guilty, if it came to court, each would incriminate the other. The three boys were released after over three years in custody. One had been sent to Rampton, the notorious high-security mental hospital.[8]

Further controversy was created by the *Pink Paper*. Robyn Brown's murder was reported briefly in the 7 March issue under the headline, 'POLICE HUNT SOHO TRANNY'S KILLER' and described her as a 'transvestite', although she appears to have worked under different names and identities depending on the clientele she served. The use of the pejorative, 'Tranny', the article's use of 'he' and the transvestite tag, drew considerable criticism from NGOs and community policing groups alike. Someone who knew Robyn told me, 'Gina would never have put up with that crap, she was queer, Girl!'

The High Risk Project Society, Vancouver, BC
Sandra Laframboise with Deborah Brady

When I decided to clean up and walk away from seventeen years of prostitution, addictions and bikers, I found nothing more frustrating than not being able to find any services specifically addressing the needs of transgender people. For the next four years I lived secretly among the heterosexual community with a fear of being discovered, rejected and ostracized, which later proved to be a blessing in disguise and the driving force behind High Risk Project.

Like many of my sisters and brothers I have felt like a freak of nature, and had a sense of not belonging anywhere. 'Where do I go?' and 'What do I do?' were some of the many questions I was faced with when I cleaned up. When on the streets I was accepted and validated, and was able to escape from the realities of being transgender. I did not need to adjust to the real world, and the expectations of others. In the straight world we were abandoned, forgotten, and we occupied a social status reminiscent of that of the lepers of earlier times. In the real world there was no human rights protection, and no dignity for the transgender. When I cleaned up, I entered a world where many services treated me like a man, even though I had sex-reassignment surgery sixteen years ago; a world where even the professional had little understanding of the transgender experience.

So I hid in religion for those four years and became worldly religious, going around the bars and preaching the gospel of our Lord Jesus Christ through the Salvation Army. I began a long road of facing buried emotions of anger, pain and resentment. The healing began with an understanding of what self-esteem was all about. I dealt with the guilt of letting the world dictate to me their view of who I was supposed to be. Because I didn't fit their model of binary gender I was not supposed to exist, to think or to feel, yet I feared most the rejection of those for whom I did not exist, and became a people 'pleaser' and lost myself.

One day an angel in disguise told me she had a dream and saw me in a white uniform and talking to a lot of people. She asked me if I had ever thought of going back to school and pursuing a career. I immediately felt frightened and thought it impossible – a self-defeating attitude that many of us assume so well. I applied to college and was immediately accepted into the psychiatric nursing course at Douglas College in Vancouver. During that period of time I gained self-confidence about myself and realized that something needed to be done about this awful lack of support sensitive to the transgender community. I left the Salvation Army to follow up my own roots, which are Native American and more specifically Cree Metis. I discovered that I had a history and that I had traditions, which I now value dearly and practise to the best of my capabilities. I also took the risk of teaching the students all about transgender issues. I began in the psycho-social section and explained to my classmates the dilemmas of being transgender through my life experience (as limited as that was then). In the section on medical surgery I brought in a lot of pictures and did some teaching about the surgical procedure and the care required. Needless to say, this process was excruciating, as it polarized the classroom and I began to face the pressures of being out. At times it felt very lonely and depressing, but the voice inside me kept telling me that I was on the right track. By the end of my studies I had launched a gender discrimination case against a fellow student and won the case. As a result, Douglas College now has a comprehensive sexual harassment policy that is considered a model policy in Canada. This prepared me to fight for my rights in other areas, and become an advocate and role model for other transgender brothers and sisters.

When I graduated as a Registered Psychiatric Nurse I felt that there was a mountain of work and activism needing to be done. I immediately began to search for support groups for transgender persons. I found a local association called Zenith Foundation and became affiliated with them. However, I still felt inadequate as there was nothing addressing specifically the needs of ex-sex-trade workers. The High Risk Project (HRP) was in its infancy, having been conceived by two members of Zenith, and they invited me to join. This was exciting for me as it dealt specifically with the street transgender community. HRP was initiated by an ex-street worker and an HIV-positive member of our community as a support group serving a hot meal to street transgender people one night per week. When I joined I realized the importance of this service and the need to expand to more than a support group. I immediately began networking with service providers, and presented my cause as a holistic nursing care plan for street transgender people. To my amazement I found a lot of support in the 'trenches'. Community workers and nurses had long wondered how to reach the transgender community, and had recognized that the specific needs of the transgender person required a peer-driven model. I was given a space free of rent. I knocked on doors and received free food. I solicited for peer volunteers and created the first Canadian transgender drop-in centre addressing in a minimal way the health issues of our sisters and brothers.

By then the other two original founders of HRP had left as they didn't have the energy or the time I was willing to invest. I continued to look for volunteers and found Deborah Brady my faithful assistant. She had a way with words that I didn't have and helped me refine on paper what I had conceived in reality.

We then gave notice of separation from the Zenith Foundation and incorporated ourselves as a non-profit charitable organization in January 1995. Deborah helped me write the programmes and the budgets and we began to lobby the government with every intention of going ahead full steam even though we didn't have monetary support. We ran the drop-in programmes with money from our nursing jobs.

In that process we were able to educate the public through media exposure, and professionals, lay people and government officials with whom we came in contact. In 1994, the government adopted a policy of moving a major portion of health care back into the community and away from the big institutions. The government began extensive community consultation and invited all marginalized fringe groups to participate and made an extra effort to include those who have been the most disadvantaged. Needless to say we jumped on this opportunity and went to every public meeting we could and made sure that our name was heard and recorded. Yes! We were laughed at. People questioned us and patronized us, but nevertheless we continued on. Deborah went to some meetings while I went to others and we rallied very important bureaucratic supporters on our side and established ourselves as credible care givers. We weren't pointing the finger specifically at any person or institution, nor did we try to attribute blame for the lack of services, but rather we stressed that systemic discrimination results when it is assumed that gender is binary, and those of us who are neither or both do not fit. We then said, 'let us help you understand us because we have the solution'. Thus our model 'transgender people for transgender people' began.

Six months later we received government funding and we are now operating a full drop-in centre employing two persons and serving 93 members who are engaged in the sex trade or IV drug use or are HIV-positive. Deborah and I have remained full-time volunteers, working with missionary zeal to improve the programmes and services. Drop-in programmes include a free hot meal Monday to Friday, laundry and shower facilities, a food bank, plus member-controlled entertainment and safe space. We assist with advocacy, referrals and peer counselling/support. Two peer support groups have formed and meet on a weekly basis. Our street outreach worker gives out condoms and provides a presence on the streets. A group of peers is developing an educational curriculum for 'gender sensitivity training' to combat transphobia.

We have just finished a six-month research project sponsored by the British Columbia Law Foundation, which studied our dilemma in respect of Canadian human rights and health legislation. Our legal brief that is about to be published will make extensive recommendations to the government. We have published three pamphlets: *Transsexual Basics*, *Transgender HIV*, and an informational pamphlet on the *High Risk Project*.

In conclusion I would like to say that if you feel there is nothing out there for you, take a look at what *you* are doing to ensure that there is a place for you. 'Transgender people for transgender people' means that those of us who are able need to act to change the climate of intolerance and misunderstanding that pervades our social structures. Nobody can properly do it for us, we have to do it for ourselves. Ultimately, the transgender experience is only understood by those with the transgender experience.

UK HIV Leaflet: From a Merciless Mistress[9]

Although Aids and HIV is not yet an issue for UK transsexuals to the extent that it is in the United States and Canada, many of the high-risk behaviours associated with the virus elsewhere are common and increasingly so here.

UK Male-to-female transsexuals often engage in prostitution and associated with this unprotected receptive anal intercourse pre-operatively either to earn the money to buy surgery, or because social attitudes and discriminatory case law make it extremely difficult for us to get ordinary jobs. Like many marginalised groups often left to depend on the state, drug and alcohol abuse is an increasing problem.

In Vancouver a study of 40 m-to-f street-involved transsexuals reported severe social difficulties including homelessness, discrimination, rejection by others, physical abuse, racism, homophobia (sic) and sexism. Of the 40, 85% practised unprotected receptive anal intercourse, 90% prostitution, and 62% injection drug use with needle-sharing. Of the 28 who had had an HIV antibody test, 14 (50%) were reactive.

In Australia it was found that the hostility of gay and straight communities towards TSs made them effectively invisible. This in spite of significant numbers of positive tests. No attempt at HIV/Aids provision was made for TSs in the first ten years of the epidemic there.

Until recently it was believed that most HIV-positive TSs in this country had either brought the virus from North America, had been the recipient of a blood transfusion in continental Europe, or had practised unprotected receptive anal intercourse, but it is now recognised that some types of gender reassignment operation,

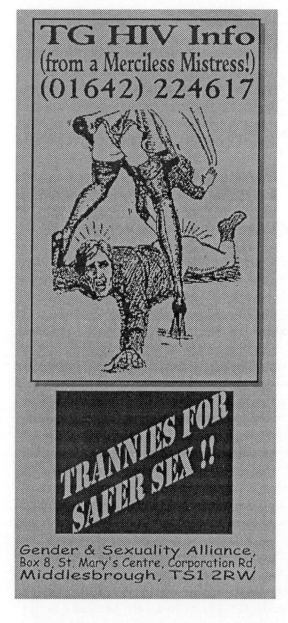

TG HIV Info
(from a Merciless Mistress!)
(01642) 224617

TRANNIES FOR SAFER SEX !!

Gender & Sexuality Alliance,
Box 8, St. Mary's Centre, Corporation Rd,
Middlesbrough, TS1 2RW

particularly where part of the colon or bowel is used to substitute for penile tissue, are very high risk. This substitution of bowel is often done in cases of genital mutilation, or where penile tissue has atrophied because of long-term preoperative hormone use.

If you are awaiting surgery you can improve the condition of your penile skin by masturbation. Strapping tissue away is also to be avoided.

Safer sex using condoms and plenty of KY jelly is, however, also essential for those with ops using penile tissue as the virus can get into the blood-system via intravaginal hair follicles during sex. It is believed that the action of the penis pulls the hair from its follicle allowing semen-to-blood contact. According to some authorities this risk may be lessened by carefully douching with a diluted depilatory cream such as Immac.

Post-operatively sex or active and adequate dilatation are essential, as is vaginal hygiene using an anti-fungicidal agent (such as Betadine) once a week. The sensitive area around the vagina and clitoris can be cleaned with baby wipes which usually contain a mild antiseptic such as cetrimide. Showering is more hygienic than bathing. The use of tampons is not recommended. It is advisable to temporarily cease being sexually active, at least vaginally, if you have any tissue damage or if you have had a recent vaginal prolapse. If in doubt seek medical advice from a GP or preferably your surgeon.

Although some colonic ops do lubricate, m-to-fs should always use a *water-based* lubricating jelly such as KY, Sensilube, Wet Stuff or Boots Own, as there is not usually enough vaginal moisture to overcome tightness at introitus (when the penis begins to enter your vagina). Lube also reduces the likelihood of getting vaginal cuts and tears and therefore the risk of contracting the virus, especially when using NHS-issue perspex dildos!

Even post-op, m-to-fs may (like many biological women) have an ejaculatory fluid and though this is lower risk than cum (or even pre-cum) it may still carry the virus. This is most relevant to oral sex or in a lesbian relationship when sharing dildos etc. as the ejaculate must penetrate a partner's skin, body fluid to body fluid – less likely in receptive sex.

F-to-ms must all, by now, be aware of the dangers of phalloplasty – the pressure exerted during intercourse has caused penile stiffeners to puncture the bladder, and this may result in death. F-to-ms using a 'Herb' or other similar penile prosthesis need to remember that if you pee through it, you can transmit a virus through it. Treat it like any other penis – keep it clean and wear a condom!

It's important for both sexes to know that if you use dildos to have vaginal and anal sex in the same session you should use condoms and change them between orifices (this is also the best way to keep rubber dildos, which are porous, clean). Never share a dildo with your partner unless you use and change its condoms. You should always clean a dildo after use.

Oral sex can be made safer with dental dams (which come in three thicknesses and two flavours, vanilla and bubble-gum!) or by cutting a latex glove or a condom open and tonguing through that.

Generally speaking both f-to-m and post-op m-to-f transsexuals are at high risk from others carrying the virus, they are less likely to infect their partners, via sex at least. If you find that you are HIV positive this does not mean that you do not need to tell them! It is not true, by the way, that you cannot get the op if you are HIV+.

Being aware of HIV risks is one thing, changing your behaviour is another. We are one of the communities *most* resistant to behavioural change. Peer pressure may be the only successful method, so if you know a friend who is not practising safer sex, even as a serial monogamist, don't just worry, tell them how worried you are!

A big issue in the TS/TG sex work community is exclusion from Rape Crisis services, which is political and not the same as exclusion from well-woman clinics (m-to-fs don't need cervical smears, and so often aren't called, even if this means they don't get important breast cancer screening). In the past reputations for hostility surrounding some rape crisis centres have effectively prevented access to all rape services, including those run by the Police and NHS. Sex workers are also resistant to Police-run services in their highly criminalised part of society.

In the past we have only been able to recommend the St Mary's Centre (NHS service) available for those living in Greater Manchester. They can give you confidential HIV and pregnancy testing in-house, and also provide long-term support and counselling. They are aware of the special needs of f-to-m rape victims. Although we are actively working on this issue and may be able to arrange more local support for you, if you are close to Manchester, we can arrange for someone to accompany you and a safe place for you to be seen from.

Notes

1. Roz Kaveney. Not politically correct but I ended up talking of 'the girls', which seemed to be the noun of choice.
2. This is a slight paraphrase of a statement by Janice Raymond from her book *The Transsexual Empire* (London: Women's Press, 1980). If this seems an extreme characterization of the separatist women's movement stance from the 1980s, see K. More (1996), 'Transsexuals and the radicalness of separatism', *Radical Deviance*, 2, 1: 6–14.
3. The Police and Criminal Evidence Act.
4. Association of Chief Police Officers.
5. This section is based on an article in *Radical Deviance: A Journal of Transgendered Politics*, 2, 4: 131.
6. Non-governmental organization.
7. London's Lesbian and Gay Policing Group.
8. Information about Maxwell Confait was supplied by Ben-the-Wendy, author of the *girly* article.

9.   Although this is the text of the first TG HIV leaflet we know of in the UK, dating from perhaps the end of September 1994, there was another early one produced in France by PASTT (Prévention-Action-Santé-Trans-sexuels-Travestis, 23, rue Chateau Landon, 75010 Paris), and work done in Australia (for instance at the Australian Gender Centre, 75, Morgan St, PO Box 266, Petersham, NSW 2049) and at the High Risk Project in Vancouver, Canada. The credits following are from the last funded version produced: 'Leaflet funded by Cleveland County Council Equal Opportunities Department, and produced by "Legislate for Excess" @ G&SA, in association with Cleveland County Council HIV Unit, Billingham. (Text revision: May 1995/Phone-box Sex Worker Card Design printing – November 1996).'

7

Talking Transgender Politics

Roz Kaveney

Preamble

The more I think about it, the more I realize that there is a need for a thorough-going discussion of the implications of a specifically transgendered politics, and the way, specifically, that it seems likely to blow wide open traditional transsexual politics. For a long time, because there was so little sense of community among even transsexuals, let alone a broader community of transgendered people, it seemed churlish to complain about the fact that the reformist agenda being promoted by some heterosexually identified, politically mainstream transsexuals did not make all that much sense even in its own terms; that it ran the risk of betraying a lot of transsexuals, let alone any (transgendered) one else. The reformist agenda has become a victim of its own success; it is, I fear, time for some of us to rock the boat.

Much of what follows derives from a list of six axioms on which I believe any workable transgender and transsexual politics has to be based. It is my belief that these are self-explanatory and non-negotiable; they are assumed as such in what follows. They are:

1. Display solidarity with all of our transgender (including transsexual) brothers and sisters.
2. Build alliances by getting involved as ourselves in other areas of politics.
3. Don't let journalistic and intellectual attacks on our community go unanswered; we can have and keep the intellectual and moral high ground.
4. Be creative, be smart, be ourselves and don't let anybody tell us who we are and what we do.
5. Refuse the pathological medical model – we are not sick, just different.

6. Refuse those politics – heterosexism, body fascism – that work against all the above, but most especially against no.1.

These are not outrageously radical suggestions; they do not go on about oppression or elevate victimhood, nor do they necessarily criticize elements of our community. They are, I would argue, versions of the basic maxims of any group on the margins, of any group that needs to ensure its freedom and its self-respect. It is not my intention to accuse anyone of being in possession of false consciousness; I imagine that most of us would regard my maxims, stated in the abstract, as acceptable. And yet a lot of the political, social and cultural strategies considered normative and acceptable by large parts of the transgender community are intrinsically opposed to these maxims. I would argue that, inasmuch as this is the case, those strategies are counter-productive.

In all that follows, transgender is used as an overall and inclusive term, in which transsexual is included along with a lot of other self-naming categories and, presumably, other categories for which no name currently exists. I entirely reject the tendency on the part of some people inside and outside the community to use it simplistically and inaccurately as a synonym for transsexual (usually defined by those who adopt this usage as self-recognizing in a medically or pathologically defined identity, seeking full surgical reassignment and seeking full assimilation in a revised gender role through invisibility), implicitly consigning all other groups to the supposedly inferior category of transvestite.

General position

Some of what follows is a polemic against specific political proposals; much of it is a critique of stock attitudes and language that have characterized our internal dealings. Gayle Rubin[1] has suggested that it is dangerous for marginalized groups to try to buy respectability by casting out other communities or a section of their own; historically, those radical transgendered people who worked with the lesbian and gay movement were victimized in precisely this way. It would be ironic if, at precisely the moment when this tactic has been renounced by lesbians and gay men, and they are prepared to work with us again, we were to adopt it ourselves either at their expense or that of sections of our own community.

Instead, we should adopt multi-objective long-term campaigns based on political alliances with other sexual minorities and other groups of the marginalized and oppressed, and abandon the explicit and implicit attitudes that go hand-in-hand with reformist selling out of our own transgendered brothers and sisters. I am not trying to impose my own brand of PC, but just suggesting that words have not only direct meanings but connotative meanings, the standard pile of garbage that ways of putting things bring in their trail.

Passing: invisibility versus acceptance

The reformist transsexual agenda often sets up, as part of its argument, a largely false dichotomy between 'people who pass' and the inferior capacity of 'people who don't pass'. This automatically knocks a hole in the concept of solidarity, of course; some of us are the sheep and some of us are the goats – and who wants to identify themselves as a goat or as in solidarity with goats? Whenever and wherever this discourse appears, there is the implicit assumption that the rights of those who pass are either somehow more important than the rights of those who do not or that, at least, they are the only rights that can be practically defended in the political and journalistic area and so have to be prioritized.

In pre-political days, which I, at least, am old enough to remember, the community had its own way of conjugating the verb 'to pass', which went 'I pass all the time; you pass just about enough of the time; she or he is a perfect disgrace with whom it is an embarrassment to be seen'. And, of course, none of us really know that we have passed all the time and for as long as we fetishize the model of passing as the only way to be accepted as who we are, for just that long our self-esteem will be under threat from any small child or gutter journalist who feels like having a go.

Even those of us who do pass, most of the time, or even almost all of the time, must, just as much as those of us who perhaps do not, learn to value ourselves as who we are – and that includes valuing not only our maleness and our femaleness but our transsexuality as well. One of our principal enemies is shame, and setting ourselves up to be disciplined by anyone who wants to name us and shame us is not healthy.

And, to touch directly on policy matters, how does changing our birth certificates and passing and disappearing into the wider community free us from discrimination and oppression? Some bigots, some of the time, will spot us, or think they spot us, and be able to discriminate against us, or anyone else they think is one of us, with impunity, arguing in self-defence that they were doing no such thing. If there is no document that states who we are, our right not to be discriminated against as TS disappears. The possibility, or even probability, that someone passes most of the time is no defence for them on the rare occasions when they do not. You are only as safe as ✔ your roughest day.

I have always thought that the idea of disappearing invisibly and living without any contact with one's past life whatever was the sort of self-damaging stuff that some doctor was always going to turn out to have suggested in the first place. We are all of us dependent on other people and on our own pasts – any of us who are interested in doing anything in the world are always sooner or later going to bump into our pasts, so we might as well confront them. This is a personal view, but the campaign for personal invisibility has always struck me as entirely perverse and self-hating. As we used to say in GLF days, we're here – get used to it.

It is less important to pass than to be accepted. If being transgendered is valued as a human variation, then many problems disappear. And it is more likely to be valued if we value it ourselves – being out and proud and prepared to defend ourselves is probably rather less risky than being in the closet, ashamed of our pasts and relying on a piece of paper.

Transgendered people come in all sizes, shapes and flavours; we also exist in four dimensions. One of the reasons for having a big conceptual box like transgender in which to put ourselves is that we are so varied; another is that we each of us are prone to vary across time. Often, to describe oneself simply is to describe a particular moment, to say who we were in a particular year. It is a matter of prudence not to burn bridges that we may, as individuals, find ourselves in need of sooner or later.

Far too often, individual transgender autobiographies, particularly transsexual ones, come across as conversion narratives in which one used, for example, to be a heterosexual transvestite, or a drag hustler, or a radical queen, or a butch, but has transcended this forever and moved into a radically different state. Similarly, activists who have come out of hustling, or drinking, or self-hatred, often talk as if their current state has nothing to do with that which it has set aside. 'I once was lost, who now am found/ Was bound, who now am free'. Even a butterfly, whose tissues have more or less gone into meltdown, has some somatic features in common with the caterpillar and chrysalis it once was; we talk as if we are changed, changed utterly.

(This also tends to reinforce transference onto any doctors with whom we have to have dealings, and strengthen the medical model. Chris Straayer posed, during the First International Transgender Film Festival, the question of why, in such films as *The Christine Jorgensen Story*, the normal expectations of the biopic were reversed and the patient acquires protagony (protagonist status). I suggested that it is because such films are conversion narratives, and in them doctors become cognate with divine grace.)

It is because we exist in a time when it is peculiarly perverse to want to cut ourselves off entirely from our individual histories. Our pasts may well have been experienced in an entirely negative and painful way, but identity is in part memory. To abandon those skills we learned in transition, or in our pre-transition past, or to abandon those people, transgendered and otherwise, who gave us support, in the name of an entire revision of ourselves, is to confront an unfriendly world with one hand tied behind our backs. To recommend this as a part of our politics is to betray ourselves. I would never try to prevent anyone pursuing this as an individual goal, but they should not expect encouragement to do so at the expense of the rest of the community, or to be regarded any longer as normative.

Single goal: is it even what we need?

I accept, reluctantly and pragmatically, the superficial attractions for some people of a single-goal campaign aimed at social integration through invisibility. I am cynical enough about the way things work in practice to suspect that many of the advantages suggested by its advocates are in fact illusory or retrograde even in respect of their own stated goals. We cannot claim freedom from discrimination as transsexuals by denying that we are transsexuals. Disappearing into invisibility is escaping, and escaping is running away; and it will fail as a defence from oppression and naming and shaming the moment that someone guesses. They don't have to know, only to guess, which is going to be hard cheese for tall, rugged women and short plump men.

Advocates of invisibility-seeking political strategies often have the intellectual honesty to posit possible negative consequences – except that where they say 'might' and 'could', I would say 'will'. Some of us remember the way that well intentioned doctors used to be even tougher than they are now when it comes to deciding what is appropriate behaviour in our gender of preference and making access to surgery and other aids to transition dependent on meeting their requirements.

I remember when one of my friends had her surgery put back two years because she turned up to see Dr John Randall wearing jeans. I remember when convictions for drug possession or hustling were enough to get people turned off NHS waiting lists altogether. The extent to which this was a matter of social discipline is borne out by the fact that the same people were allowed to see the same doctors as private patients. Do we really want to empower civil servants in this way, enabling them to decide which of us gets new documents and which do not on possibly entirely arbitrary grounds of how we dress, what we do for a living and with whom we sleep?

One of the standard criticisms of our community by lesbian and gay theorists such as Raymond and Altman[2] has been that the medical institutions dedicated to gender reassignment are a control mechanism whereby weaker brothers and sisters are filtered out of the lesbian and gay community and into an entire gestalt of social gender control. It would be a serious political mistake on our part to give retrospective aid and comfort to those theorists by accepting constraints on our own diversity, by allowing doctors or anyone else to tell us who we are and ought to be. Contrary to what we are being told by New Labour, rights are not a trade-off with responsibilities. Our right to equality, and our right to what medical assistance we may need to seek that equality, are not contingent on our jumping through hoops.

And of course this particularly applies to those of us who, in order to be politically active, are to that extent out as TS in the first place. I would have thought it improbable that those of us who have been out to the extent of appearing on television or in the newspapers would necessarily be considered priorities for this revision of paperwork. We are, it could be argued, out of our own free will, having decided that defending the rights of our community was more important, as indeed it is, than our integration into a normative society.

To identify the goal of integration into society with disappearing into that society is inconsistent with pursuing any further goals whatever. Those of us who do not accept that particular model of TS and TG goals are going, I assume, to be expected to be workhorses for all future campaigns for the welfare of the whole community.

Bad outcomes

There is also the possibility, if we divert all our energy and all our resources into the single issue of birth certification, that we will lose; that the argument that official documents recording matters of fact have of their nature to be immutable will be held to be more important than our welfare. Do we want to put all of our eggs in that basket?

It may be the case that EU legislation will force ID cards on us; I am personally opposed to this, and will continue to object to it. However, it is quite likely that, should ID cards be imposed, they will make the use of birth certificates when applying for jobs pretty much a thing of the past. In practical terms, it is going to be more important that ID cards match up with our needs and desires than that birth certificates do. It is to be hoped that the Home Office will be as flexible over identity cards as it is over passports. It would be entirely wrong for a particular section of transsexuals to campaign on this issue in a way that deprived other transgendered people of important rights by asking the Home Office to be less flexible rather than more.

And, of course, there is no guarantee that the certification reform would be in and of itself much help in a lot of real situations. You can change your birth certificate in Spain, I believe, but, while you can contract a marriage, your marriage remains voidable by challenge.

Marriage: copping out? selling out?

The only context in which our right to marry is going to exist safely is one that those TSs who identify as simplistically heterosexual are not going to like very much. It is one in which the right to marry, to have one's long-term relationships certified by a rite of passage and the granting of legal recognition, is extended to all couples irrespective of sexuality or birth gender.

At present, there is an imperfect separation of civil marriage as it affects pensions, child-rearing and tax, from the sacraments and rites of Christianity and other religions. When, as seems likely, the special legal position of the Church of England, and of Christianity in general, is removed as part of an ongoing process of constitutional reform, there will be no further need for this to be the case, or for arbitrary dogmas and decrees about the true purpose and nature of sexuality to be guaranteed by law.

I find it unacceptable that those TSs who identify as heterosexual should want their right to be wed to be at the expense of those of us who identify as lesbian and gay; as things stand, we could get married, but only on unacceptable terms. And why should we be asking for a reform that involves special favours when campaigning for an egalitarian marriage law enables us to remain in solidarity with other groups?

Gays, lesbians and solidarity

Speaking for myself as one of the significant minority who identify as lesbians, dykes, gay men and transfags, I slightly resent the assumption that we will always stand in the background or stay away from meetings with MPs who might throw a wobbly at the idea of our existence. We can't be shovelled under the carpet like that – they are, after all, bound to find out sooner or later. The same applies to those of us who have variously disreputable pasts; we are entitled to equal civil rights not for being straight or pretty or respectable or quiet, but because human rights are inalienable. It is true – and moreover I say it all the time – that one catches more flies with honey than with vinegar, but like all proverbs that will only take us so far. As I have said before, human rights are not supposed to be a reward for good behaviour.

While we are at it, indeed, I have also to say that those of us who are straight-identified should not be quite so nervous about forming alliances with lesbians and gay men. A lot of our community are, or at one stage in their life tried to be, lesbians and gay men, and a lot of us have them as a significant part of our affinity group. They have, most of the time, the same enemies as we do; the enemy of my enemy is my friend and we must all hang together or we shall all hang separately. Do you think Dr Adrian Rogers of the Conservative Family Campaign makes a distinction, or that queer-bashers care?

Of course, there is a long history of oppression of our community by the lesbian and gay community – I know all about this, because I was there. The fact that they were persuaded by briefly fashionable damn silly ideas into doing stupid and vicious things is no excuse for our being stupid enough to refuse useful alliances because of damn silly ideas on our side of the question. We need the alliance, basically; and the new pluralism of the 1990s makes that possible. It also makes it possible to have it on equal terms – a lot of people are ashamed of the past, and we no longer have to apologize for ourselves to most of them, or justify our differences from them, when doing business with them. This is a historic opportunity and it would be dumb to pass up on what might not last if we neglect it, or betray it.

Medicals

An increasing number of jobs involve a medical for medical insurance, in which questions are asked about past extended medical stays. It is by no means certain that the obligation to make full and frank disclosure excludes reassignment surgery, particularly in the case of those of us who had bad post-operative complications. An altered birth certificate will not protect us from dismissal for giving false information in the medical or from the voiding of medical insurance and pension rights on those grounds. I don't pretend to know what the answer is to that particular problem, but it is one with which we are going to have to deal sooner or later – again, our need to deal with this is not served by focusing one single issue of dubious utility. It will not go away because we choose to lock our pasts in a cupboard.

Burn-out: a disadvantage of multi-issue campaigning?

The issue of burn-out is an important one – the fact that we are in the struggle for equality for the long haul does not mean that any of us has individually to be in that struggle for the long haul without let up. None of us is actually indispensable. If we put a lot of our energy into advocating reforms that benefit other groups as well as our own, if we make alliance-building one of our priorities, we ensure that the weight of campaigns is spread.

If, for example, we favour not a bill that seeks to make discrimination against us illegal, but a bill that makes discrimination on a wide set of grounds illegal, and ensure that our interests are specifically included in such a bill, then and to that extent we are behaving with political maturity. If we do not get involved and visible in, say, campaigns around a Bill of Rights, our interests are certain to get neglected or misunderstood, because other people do not live with them in the same way. If we go on campaigning on a broad front, we will be visible, which means that we will automatically recruit new campaigners as we go. When I co-founded Feminists Against Censorship, it was with a view to sticking with it just long enough to achieve short-term goals; after that, I dropped out and left it to newer people to keep going. I was not, much as it pains me to admit it, indispensable.

Against birth certificates

The single-issue campaign in favour of re-certification is objectionable because it is of little practical utility. It cuts us off from participating in reforms that could benefit us and that are being advocated by groups that are prepared to defend our rights, but that are not interested in fighting for what they regard, with some justice, as a solipsistic and retrograde campaign of interest only to us.

Such a campaign has, as one of its premises, the assumption that our acceptance into society should be on society's terms rather than occurring as part of a more general process of persuading society to be a deal less hung-up on other people's business. This premise is implicitly divisive of our community since it creates a hierarchy of those who wish to integrate into society in terms of traditional gender roles, and believe that they can do so, over those of us who do not. Being in solidarity with each other as a community is inherently opposed to privileging one section of the community over another.

To be specific, the remarks one hears from time to time, usually from the pro-re-certification faction, about unnamed MTFs who 'look like truckdrivers' are a darkening of counsel, which serves nobody's long-term interests. I would have hoped that at this stage in the 1990s, body fascism would be a thing of the past, but it was noticeable, in von Praunheim's *The Transexual Menace*, that there was an unspoken privileging of, for example, the thin and beautiful over the fat and homely – to the extent, indeed, that where the thin were allowed the dignity of conversion narrative biographies, the fat were only allowed to ooze oceanically about their current state of mind.

Human rights do not depend on good behaviour; they also do not depend on perfect teeth, hair and nails, or on good dress sense, or on a trim waist or a bushy beard. I am repelled by the fact that we have let the medical model and the heterosexist, looksist agenda that goes with it, persuade us to despise each other and, by doing so, ourselves. We should be, to the extent we can manage, in solidarity with each other, because we need to look after, and be looked after by, each other. And if this is a mixture of hippie sentimentality and old-fashioned leftist moralism, what is so great about the self-aggrandizing individualism of the Thatcher years or the communitarian bullying of New Labour, that we should discard those things?

Final comments

Health care issues are perhaps the one area where we are asking for rights that to a real extent appertain to us and us only. By us, in this context, I do not, let it be clear, mean transsexuals only; other groups of transgendered people have a right to those medical procedures that they need and desire. My own view, which I accept is a highly contentious one, is that a useful analogy is with the defence of abortion rights. Reassignment surgery, like abortion, is directed at enabling individuals to take charge of their lives and to defend their potential; it also involves the permanent closing off of particular avenues of possibility – it is always a serious matter. I would argue, in fact, that the right to own one's own body and one's own mind is intrinsic to the very notion of personal liberty.

Protection from harassment as individuals will almost certainly come about through bills that promote protection generally, into which we have merely to input our particular needs. There is no point in doing this for just a section of our community or believing that undergoing certain medical procedures ought to buy us particular immunity from harassment and assault.

I would add to this the question of defending ourselves as a community from the libels of some feminists on the Left and from the Moral Right; this is a matter of arguing back and not letting the issue drop. We have to be prepared to confront and oppose and reply. Sometimes, but not all of the time, this can be done in co-operation with other groups under attack; sometimes other groups will rush to our defence unasked – this is a good thing and means that sometimes we should be prepared, at least as individuals if not as a community, to return the favour or even anticipate it. We have also to avoid those easy answers to questions about why we exist at all, which offer major hostages to fortune.

Political activity is only partly about ideals; it is also about winning. The struggle for the political and civil rights of minorities can only be fought partly on the basis of demonstrating to people that we are oppressed and that they ought to do something about it. It is also fought by getting together with other minority groups and finding, or creating, common ground in terms of measures that benefit as many people, including us, as possible. Normalizing ourselves in society at large may be one goal; another goal is to normalize ourselves in the worlds of politics, the arts and intellectual discourse. Those of us who are on the Left need to remind other left-wingers that we are here, and have rights, and have made a contribution; those of us who, for whatever strange reason, are of the Right, will presumably do the same thing.

It is regrettably the case that, in the past, we have asked for our rights on the basis that we are poor pathetic unfortunates who need help. This is disempowering. Actually, of course, we are a community with a lot of remarkable, strong, intelligent, creative and gifted people in it – the reason why we need our rights is that to be denied them cuts us off from our gifts and deprives society of them. The argument for the availability of surgery is not, as it happens, that we are going to go mad without it, but that we will never achieve our full potential without it.

We are not wimps and we should not adopt campaigning strategies or goals that make us look like wimps.

A multi-issue approach, which fights for the rights of our whole community rather than a particular section of it, is the only one that will, in the long term, guarantee us something approaching equality and something like acceptance by society on our own terms. Our situation is to a serious extent not one soluble by any sort of quick fix; the quick fix of re-certification of birth and recognition of marriage proposed as a single-issue approach is peculiarly divisive, futile and redundant. We need to participate in the struggle for comprehensive across-the-board anti-discrimination measures and ensure that any such laws specifically include us; we need to join in the struggle for the option of all long-term partnerships to be recognized; we need to join the struggle for an ethic of fair and decent treatment for all in a just society. Why cry for the moon when we can have the stars?

Postscript: transgender as human variation

We need to move away from models of the transgendered condition that pathologize it towards one that express it as part of a standard range of human variation. Even were it to be the case, as some scientists have suggested, that some transgendered people prove to have in common certain features of brain structure, there is no reason to assume that there is only one transsexuality or transgenderedness, or that there are not a variety of routes to the same condition.

Indeed, the evidence of history and anthropology would imply that there is such a variety. In some cultures, transgendered status is simply recognized as a personal attribute; in others, it is achieved as a by-product of religious ecstasy; in yet others, it is an available response to particular social and economic circumstances such as being the daughter and only child of a family whose possessions – herds, say – can only be cared for by someone with customary male status.

In a similar way, the altered state of consciousness in which the body is experienced as not fully connected with the mind is one that may be the product of brain lesions, or of taking certain drugs, or as the desired end result of religious meditation. There is no particular need to pathologize even the first of these three if it does not, ultimately, prevent the individual from functioning; the latter two are clearly not pathological states, though identical with the first which some would hold to be.

Accordingly, we are perhaps best advised to hold back from

attempted medical explanations, both because they are not necessarily accurate for each and every individual and because, if generally accepted, they could be used, like the similar attempts to explain male homosexuality in terms of genetics and brain structure, by those, like the former Chief Rabbi of Britain, who would advocate genetic engineering to eliminate sexual deviance. It is my conviction that such programmes would not work, but the attempt to make them work would undoubtedly involve a massive loss of human rights.

If we rely on the idea that we are sufferers from a genetic malfunction to excuse our pathologized condition, those of us who exist in spite of attempts to eliminate us, as a kindness, before birth will perforce be accused of existing out of sheer malign perversity. Again, a politics of being proud of our status as a creative human variation is, in the long term, a strategy far more likely to win us acceptance.

In his *Consciousness Explained* (1992), Daniel Dennett postulates that consciousness is nothing more than a control mechanism for keeping track of endlessly self-revising sensory drafts, is, to use a metaphor, the tune played between the notes. It can further be logically argued both that Dennett's model of the senses is a limited one – he assumes the standard five and ignores the possibility that, for example, balance and self-maintained body image might be senses within his meaning, and that selfhood might be further constructed upwards from moments of consciousness, identity upwards from selfhood.

Accept these possibilities, and variant modes of consciousness, selfhood and identity, from religious ecstasy through moments of sudden creative insight to transgenderedness, become explicable not as reductive pathologies, but as part of the rich harvest of the evolution of the human brain. In this perspective, and perhaps also in the very different attempt to use the Lacanian psychoanalysis that has so often been used against us – two intellectual strategies that appear at odds, but that some are trying to reconcile – lie positive explanations of our sense of transgendered self considerably less likely to lead to disaster than reductive biologism.

Notes

1. Gayle Rubin, 'Thinking sex', in Carole Vance (ed.), *Pleasure and Danger* (London: Routledge and Kegan Paul, 1984).
2. See Raymond's *The Transsexual Empire* (London: Women's Press, 1980) and Dennis Altman's *Homosexual: Oppression and Liberation* (London: Angus & Robertson, 1972).

8

A Proposal for Doing Transgender Theory in the Academy

Markisha Greaney

Introduction

> As with males theorising about women from the beginning of time, theorists of gender have seen transsexuals as possessing something less than agency. . . . The people who have no voice in this theorising are the transsexuals themselves.
>
> (Sandy Stone, 'The *Empire* Strikes Back: A Post-transsexual Manifesto')

Who gets to do theory in the academy? Not me.

As a white, male-to-female transgendered dyke, I have not been allowed to participate in the professional production of critical theory for reasons that have nothing to do with my intellectual ability and everything to do with the discomfort people like me evoke in graduate school admissions committees. Even within the emerging field of queer theory, I seem queer in ways that trouble the academics who, in practice, decide what queer theory is and who queer theory is for in the choices they make about who they train to do it. This paper is essentially a plea from an academic without an academy and implies a larger critique of the academic community itself for perpetuating the conditions that produce my enforced silence.

Too much queer theorizing as practised by academic lesbians and gays privileges 'homosexual' – to wit, the non-transgendered homosexual – as the synonym of the term 'queer', a reductive move that deprives the term of its original, primary meaning of 'different, unusual, odd, or strange' *as well as the contextually dependent nature of these meanings*. What is lost is the term's radical potential to point towards the ever-shifting scenes of subjective transformation and to thereby be mobilized and redeployed by successions of other marginalized peoples.

Foucault seems to have understood this point similarly. As David Halperin points out in his essay on the roots of queer theory and queer politics in Foucault's work on sexuality, homosexuality is significant for Foucault primarily to the extent that it represents for him

> a historic opportunity to open up new relational and affective potentialities, not in virtue of qualities intrinsic to the homosexual, but because the position of the homosexual 'off-centre,' somehow, together with the diagonal lines which the homosexual can draw through the social fabric, makes it possible to bring to light these potentialities. (Foucault, quoted in Halperin, 1995: 67)

As Halperin notes, 'Foucault saw homosexuality not as a newly liberated species of sexual being but as *a strategically situated marginal position from which it might be possible to glimpse and to devise new ways of relating to oneself and to others*'[1] (*ibid.*: 68; emphasis mine). Transgender identification and embodiment open up such potentialities – ones that destabilize the bases from which relation and affect take their bearing. If non-transgendered homosexuality is critically interesting to Foucault because it is queer, 'off-centre, somehow', then transgendered homo/sexualities should be all the more interesting because they are queerness squared – they exponentially rather than arithmetically increase the complexities of embodied, desiring subjectivity.[2]

In the wake of Judith Butler's book *Gender Trouble* (1990), the rhetoric of 'subversion' and 'trouble' has become *de rigueur* among non-transgendered lesbian and gay queer theorists, but to those of us queers who are consistently left out of queer theory and its production, this rhetoric has a decidedly hollow ring to it. There seems to be a certain amount of hypocrisy and question begging going on here. What gets to count as 'good' trouble or subversion? Just how much trouble and subversiveness are these theorists willing to advocate? As long as they stop short of advocating gender anarchy, they are, perforce, setting limits, drawing lines. Academic queer theorists have yet to realize that they are drawing these lines – contextually speaking – in precisely the same places as their more conservative adversaries are drawing them – that is, right between what they are comfortable with and what they are not comfortable with.

Thus, queer practice within the academy, both intellectually and in terms of institutional politics, has not resulted in a broad-based mobilization of variously marginalized peoples, but rather has only displaced the relatively static and oppressive boundaries of academic institutional culture to the extent necessary to accommodate gender-normative lesbians and gays at a level of mutual comfort for themselves and for the institution. Non-transgendered lesbian and gay academics have effected closure in their theorizing of the queer, a closure that is reflected in graduate department admissions, as well as in who is hired and tenured to teach in these departments. The openly transgendered – as well as many other different, unusual, odd, or strange people – need not apply. The academy remains as closed to us as it once was to the openly homosexual.

Who gets to do theory in the academy? Let me cite one particularly irritating example of someone who does. While myself and other transgenders, intersexuals, male lesbians, queer butches, FTM fags and a rainbow of other alternatively sexed/gendered people are routinely ignored or appropriated, a non-transgendered academic like Jacquelyn N. Zita gets to publish a paper in an anthology of lesbian philosophy musing on the possible existence of male lesbians ('My mind crawls uneasily with the question . . .'), ultimately dismiss them as oxymoronic and therefore a clear indication that something is fundamentally 'wrong' with postmodernism, and then tell us in contributor's notes that she has 'a male lesbian kitten named Sunshine'[3] (Zita, 1994: 129, 255).

As Zita's article demonstrates, even in that rare moment when transgendered subjectivities are considered at all, it continues to be not in the form of a much-needed analytics of how we already exist, but, rather, as a question of if we exist, along with the more insidious, unstated question of if we should exist. Who gets to say what sexualities and identities are possible? And when will 'the love that dare not speak its name' allow us to speak our names?

As an undergraduate in the late 1980s and early 1990s, I came of age intellectually during the burgeoning discourses of queer theory in the academy. Initially, I was intensely closeted and socially isolated, painfully aware that it was by mere virtue of my genital configuration that my having a lesbian subjectivity was an undebatable impossibility to the theorists of the day, let alone to my colleagues in women's studies classes. Groping for a language at a time before 'transgender' had gained some currency as an umbrella term for gender queerness, I began inventing my own words to describe myself, unaware that there were others who had coined similar terms. I began thinking of myself as a 'non-operative transsexual' and, somewhat more satisfyingly, as a 'male lesbian'. The term 'lesbian', I theorized, referred to my identity and the structure of my desire, while the term 'male' acknowledged my physical difference from other lesbians and the profound paradox I was faced with.[4]

Voraciously, I continued devouring theoretical texts, trying to find some mention of myself, or at least some allusion to my possible existence. My unique subject position became for me a kind of litmus test: as long as I existed – and I preferred to assume that I did – any theory that could not accommodate the possibility of my existence was already flawed and inadequate. Though I never did quite find myself articulated specifically in these theories, I did begin to see that it was within the framework of postmodern queer/feminist theories that I actually could begin to situate myself. What was so frustrating to me then (and still frustrates me to this day) is that even these theorists utilizing and celebrating this kind of framework ventured nowhere near serious considerations of transgendered subjectivities and their potential for pulling the theoretical rug out from under any theorizations that are tacitly built upon unproblematized notions of what genital configurations mean, as well as how they have come to these meanings in the first place.

In spite of what I was beginning to gain intellectually from theory, I nevertheless found myself in an ever-deepening state of confusion, loneliness and emotional distress. It was in this condition that I began coming out privately to my professors, who confirmed to me that my thinking was very provocative and represented a timely intervention in many current debates. They encouraged me and actively guided me further along the path I had already begun to set for myself.

It soon became clear to me that I could not wait for others to articulate my particularities in their discourse; I had to do it for myself. I felt I had something challenging and unique to offer the enterprise of critical theory. Judith Butler could speak blithely about 'imagining alternatively gendered worlds' (1990: xiii), but I felt I had already been living in one, and could submit a map of an occupied terrain.

It was at the height of my intellectual fervour in this undertaking, inspired by Sandy Stone's work and full of the exhilarating thrill of theoretical possibilities that no one else seemed to see, that I found myself on the verge of graduating. Loath to leave the academy at such a crucial time, I consoled myself with the thought that I was about to actually begin *living* my theories, and that getting into graduate school to continue my theoretical work would be relatively easy. In 1993, the year following my graduation, I drafted the following application essay.[5]

Statement of Purpose: Application for Graduate Admission

Although my interests cover a wide terrain of critical theory, my main concern is queer/transgender theory.

Academically, my theorizing of gender was nurtured within the women's studies programme at a major university in California. In an early paper submitted to Sandy Stone, I invented and proposed the term 'non-operative transsexual' (as opposed to the pre- or post-operative transsexual) as a way of rethinking the relationships between body, gender identity and sexuality. This was not simply an academic exercise – it was also an urgent plea for an acceptance of new categories and an attempt to come to terms with critical questions in my life: *Should/must I get a sex change operation? Aren't there any other alternatives? How am I going to live my life?*

Inspired by Stone's 'The *Empire* Strikes Back: A Post-transsexual Manifesto' (1991), I set up an independent research project with her with the intent of taking up her challenge to write a 'counterdiscourse' that would provide a 'deeper analytical language for transsexual [/transgender] theory' and to thereby *write myself into the discourse.* My research with her culminated in a paper titled, ' "Kabuki Trouble": Sexual Subversiveness on and off the Kabuki Stage' (Greaney, 1992), and in May 1993 I presented a version of this paper at the international 'Queer Sites' conference at the University of Toronto.

In 'The Technology of Gender', Teresa de Lauretis (1987) claims that from the first time we check the square next to the M or F on an application form, we officially enter the sex-gender system and engender ourselves as men or women. While she notes that checking the M box for women would be like 'cheating' or 'erasing ourselves' and checking the F box for men would have 'quite another set of implications', it is precisely this set of implications that I want to address. It is precisely from this point that my theorizing begins because, as a male to female transgender, I *want* that F to stick to me, in de Lauretis's phrase, 'like a wet silk dress' (1987: 11–12).

In other words, what I am asking is this: What if we – feminists, queers, and transgenders – all started checking the 'wrong' boxes? How will patriarchy deal with us if we displace, invert, subvert and proliferate this seemingly eternal M/F binary? What if we fuck (with) this system? After all, just what else are we to do with this sex-gender system? On the other hand, is this a call to sexual chaos and anarchy too radical for feminists? Perhaps this strategy would end up being more beneficial to anatomical men than women. If so, does that mean, as Jane Flax asks, we are doomed to keep 'hanging' complex social meanings and structures on anatomical differences? (Flax, 1990: 148). While I, too, ask why it is we do just that, I also have to ask *just where else are we to hang these meanings and structures, and who will get to decide?*

Science and technology are opening up new arenas for exploring these issues. I am fascinated with Donna Haraway's cyborg theory and her incessant themes of irony, boundary confusions, 'permanently partial identities and contradictory standpoints', and 'potent fusions and dangerous possibilities' (Haraway, 1991: 154). With many other postmodern theorists glorifying similar themes, I can't help but wonder why there has been so little mention of transgenders who, to my mind, *already are the very embodiment of these themes.* Haraway's cyborg manifesto, I submit, implies a transgender manifesto (the promise of chimeras?). One of her questions, 'How can our "natural" bodies be reimagined – and relived – in ways that transform' (*ibid.* 3) is implicitly central for transgenders.

In addition to musing about cyborg genital configurations and the contestable meanings they may have, I am also interested in what is happening over the Internet. Sandy Stone, for one, contends that 'In cyberspace the transgendered body is the natural body' (Stone, 1995: 180). 'Checking the "wrong" box', it would appear, is rather commonplace over the net. Stone's forthcoming work promises to be definitive both in transgender theory and in its relations with cyborg/transhuman theory.

I am particularly excited with Judith Butler's work because she is one of only a few feminist theorists whose work opens up a space for trans/gender/fuck theory. In *Gender Trouble*, she advocates the loss of gender norms and claims that this would proliferate gender configurations, destabilize substantive identity and deprive the naturalizing narratives of compulsory heterosexuality of their central protagonists: 'man' and 'woman' (Butler, 1990: 146). I ask: Who better to do just that than the transgender? I am eager to wreak the 'erotic havoc' she alludes to.

Other feminist theorists I am interested in include Diana Fuss. I would like to show how her deconstruction of the essentialism/constructionism debate has ramifications for other binaries, particularly the man/woman and homo/hetero binaries that the transgender throws into radical question. However, while it is true that the transgender is my main concern, I am interested in more than simply adding the terms 'trans' (and 'bi') to the sign 'gay/lesbian theory': I wish also to take Fuss up on her call for a 'theory *of* marginality, subversion, dissidence, and othering' (Fuss, 1991: 5; original emphasis). Jane Flax's (1990) work appeals to me as well because she is not only a theorist, but a practising analyst who finds 'undecidability' inadequate for her very real patients. While I, as a postmodernist, may also be accused of glorifying open texts and decentred selves, I must also live in the 'real' world. I am thus interested in how Flax finally responds to her patients. I am acutely sensitive to her theory/practice dilemmas because I myself am at once theorist/therapist and subject in crisis (of representation).

I have a host of questions I would like to pursue: How are the medical establishment, the Department of Motor Vehicles, the International Conference on Transgender Law and Employment Policy, feminist theorists, popular media, and transgenders themselves currently converging and diverging to construct the transgender? How have the constructions of 'genetic' (non-trans) women and men provided the conditions of possibility for the birth of the transgender? How will constructions of the transgender reinform (transform?) constructions of 'women' and 'men'? What can transgenders learn from gay/lesbian theories? politics? cultures? How will the appearance of a transgender speaking as a transgender challenge and further complexify current theories of the subject? What are the implications for a theory of trans*racial* identity?

I am concerned with rhetoric and obsessed with text. I am interested in Wittgenstein's language games, Austin's speech acts, Butler's notions of expropriation, and the connection of the latter with hypertext theories of 'the reconfiguring of author-reader relationships' (Landow, 1994). I also maintain a passion for music (my undergraduate major) and an interest in its relations with linguistics and rhetoric.

Finally, while as a transgender I ask, 'How shall I live my life?', as a postmodern theorist I also ask, 'How shall I write?' I too often find that the 'opposite' of what I want to claim may also be true, that so many of the words I use are so contestable I no longer know which ones to put within quotes, and that I need simultaneously to deconstruct what I am constructing, constantly interrogating what motivates my deployments. Furthermore, I find that purely theoretical writing can't move me in quite the same way as such writers as Audre Lorde, Joan Nestle, Leslie Feinberg and Gloria Anzaldúa have moved me with their writings. What I need – and have already been developing in a text of over thirteen hundred pages of writing I call (borrowing from Lorde) 'meta biomythographical theory' – is a new way of writing theory. Ultimately I wish not merely to convince, but to move others as they have moved me.

Conclusion

But it has been downhill since those last optimistic months as an undergraduate. After coming out as a transgender, I have gone from graduating cum laude with the praise and support of my professors to disillusionment, rage and periods of paralysing depression caused by perpetual under-employment, bouts of homelessness and – most demoralizing of all – estrangement from the very academic community that had produced me as an academic subject.

My first academic slap in the face came when requesting letters of recommendation. One early supporter, a professor who initially guided and encouraged my theoretical project, declined to write a letter for me even though she had offered to do so while I was an undergraduate, prior to my transitioning. She offered no explanation for withdrawing her support. This was devastating not only academically – I needed three letters of recommendation and she was one of only three professors familiar with my work and situation – but also devastating on a personal level as well. Apparently, while 'male lesbians', 'non-operative transsexuals', and 'transgendered subjects' might be interesting topics for office-hours discussion, she was not willing to endorse either me or my work to her peers once I declared my intent to seriously pursue transgender studies within a prestigious graduate programme.

This painful experience with my former mentor exemplifies my larger experience with the academy. I was given these celebrated theories and encouraged to utilize them to pursue my own queer agendas, but once I began to embody and manifest some of the potentialities envisioned by these theories, I was abjected, abandoned and ignored. I still have not found a graduate programme that will accept me to do the work I want to do.

Part of the problem is that there is currently no place in the academy where 'transgender theory' as such has an institutional footing, and there are very few interdisciplinary programmes in which the kind of work I envision could conceivably be supported. Add to this such pragmatic considerations as finding compatible faculty members, meeting admittance requirements, being able to afford tuition costs and feeling relatively safe and comfortable as a transgender in the campus environment, and my graduate school options seemed very few, indeed. I settled upon three possibilities, and for three years in a row was rejected by all of them. One programme rejected me a second time when I reapplied the following year.

Except for one school that couldn't even be bothered to address me with my correct name and pronoun (in spite of the fact that all my application materials and supporting documents quite clearly reflected my current name and gender), I assumed that the rejections stemmed from some personal failing. If I read more books, wrote more articulately, and presented myself better, I would surely be found worthy of admission. Upon inquiring as to the reasons behind the rejections, however, I began to realize this was not the case. The professor with whom I had the highest hopes of studying, for instance, quite candidly informed me that my rejection was 'purely political', and that it had nothing to do with my abilities or potential. In a terribly disillusioning conversation, she explained that her department was very conservative despite her presence there, and that my proposal was too scary, radical and 'trendy' for her colleagues. All she could suggest was to make my proposal more conventional, and to keep searching for a sympathetic faculty member elsewhere.

But by this time, even if that were possible, it was too late. Due to ongoing problems finding employment as a transgender, I had defaulted on my undergraduate loans, resulting in a hold placed on my academic records to prevent me from submitting further applications. Three weeks after that final rejection, in March 1996, I was committed to a hospital for suicidal depression.

Who gets to do theory? Not me.

My hope is that this paper will call attention to the glaring absence of – and urgent need for – spaces within the academy for transgender theorizing, for theorizing by transgenders themselves, and for 'out' transgenders within the academy to mentor this intellectual endeavour in the emerging generations of students. This not being the time for subtlety, I am offering myself in this essay as an ideal candidate for doing transgender theory. I hereby challenge the academy to re/consider me – and my question: Who gets to do theory?

Acknowledgements

I would like to thank Sandy Stone and Judith Jack Halberstam for their academic support and guidance. I am also deeply indebted to R.C. Williams for housing and supporting me throughout much of my precarious existence for the past few years, as well as for his continued belief in me, which had outlasted my own. Most recently, I am indebted to Susan Stryker for providing me with a quiet space in which I could rework this article, as well as a theoretical 'jump start' of sorts for an academic theorist who has been 'out of the loop' for over four years now.

Notes

1. This wonderful phrase is, to my mind, a far more productive way to define 'queer' than its current reduction by academic 'queers' to mere signification of non-transgendered homosexuality. An understanding of 'queer' in this sense has far-reaching implications that I should like to be in a position to develop further at a later date.

2. In an earlier writing of this paper for another publication, I was directed to Halperin's quotes by Susan Stryker, who noted how well they fit with what I was trying to say. With the deadline looming, I did not have time to read Halperin's entire essay and sufficed myself with only a small section of his text. Upon completion of my paper, however, the venue of its publication changed, and a new deadline afforded me enough time to obtain and read Halperin's entire essay. I have been astonished at its relevance to my own arguments here.

   At this point, having neither time nor academic environment in which to extend this paper adequately in light of Halperin's essay, I regret that I can only encourage the interested reader to (re)read Halperin's text alongside my own with transgender concerns in mind. One highly productive strategy, for instance, would be one of rhetorical supersedence, supplanting instances in Halperin's text of non-transgendered homosexuals with transgenders and instances of non-transgendered heterosexuals with non-transgendered homosexuals, as in the following:

   > The history of the ongoing struggles for [transgender] emancipation and [transgender] liberation has consisted largely in the story of how [transgenders] fought to wrest from [non-transgender-identified homosexuals (as well as non-transgender-identified heterosexuals)] control over such matters as who gets to speak for us, who gets to represent our experience, who is authorised to speak knowledgeably about our lives. (Halperin, 1995: 56–7)

   My thanks to Stryker for directing me to Halperin's work.

3. Although I find it unworthy of engaging with more fully than I do here, I cite Zita's text as one of many examples of the kind of (often patronizing) ignorance transgenders face from the 'experts' in positions of power – i.e., non-transgendered theorists, professors, doctors, psychologists, Hollywood movie writers, and so on.

4. Although my self-identification as a male lesbian turned out to be a transitional one – having not identified as a male lesbian (or male anything, for that matter) in quite some time – I nevertheless retain strong protective feelings for that identity and that part of my past. I now see that terribly tenuous and fragile male lesbian space I once occupied as a crucial part of my dyke formative years, and, as such, a part of myself that I have tender feelings for.

5. Slightly edited for this chapter.

References

Butler, J. (1990) *Gender Trouble: Feminism and the Subversion of Identity.* New York: Routledge.

Butler, J. (1991) 'Imitation and gender insubordination'. In D. Fuss (ed.), *Inside/Out: Lesbian Theories, Gay Theories.* New York: Routledge.

Cohen, E. (1991) 'Who are "we"? Gay identity as political (e)motion (a theoretical rumination)'. In D. Fuss (ed.), *Inside/Out: Lesbian Theories, Gay Theories.* New York: Routledge.

de Lauretis, T. (1987) 'The technology of gender'. In *Technologies of Gender: Essays on Theory, Film, and Fiction.* Bloomington and Indianapolis: Indiana University Press.

Flax, J. (1990) *Thinking Fragments: Psychoanalysis, Feminism, and Postmodernism in the Contemporary West.* Berkeley and Los Angeles: University of California Press.

Fuss, D. (1989) *Essentially Speaking: Feminism, Nature, & Difference.* New York: Routledge.

Fuss, D. (1991) 'Inside/out'. In D. Fuss (ed.), *Inside/Out: Lesbian Theories, Gay Theories.* New York: Routledge.

Greaney, M. (1991) 'The Native American berdache and the "non-operative transsexual": towards a case for the "non-biological sex change"'. Unpublished paper submitted to Professor Sandy Stone, Department of Sociology, University of California, San Diego.

Greaney, M. (1992) '"Kabuki trouble": sexual subversiveness on and off the kabuki stage'. Unpublished paper submitted to Professor Sandy Stone, Department of Sociology, University of California, San Diego.

Halperin, D. (1995) *Saint Foucault: Towards A Gay Hagiography.* New York: Oxford University Press.

Haraway, D. (1990) *Primate Visions: Gender, Race, and Nature in the World of Modern Science.* New York: Routledge.

Haraway, D. (1991) *Simians, Cyborgs, and Women: The Reinvention of Nature.* New York: Routledge.

Landow, G.P. (1994) 'What's a critic to do? Critical theory in the age of hypertext'. In G.P. Landow (ed.), *Hyper/Text/Theory.* Baltimore: Johns Hopkins University Press.

Stone, A.R. (1995) *The War of Technology and Desire at the Close of the Mechanical Age*. Cambridge: The MIT Press.

Stone, S. (1991) 'The *Empire* strikes back: a post-transsexual manifesto'. In J. Epstein and K. Straub (eds), *Body Guards: The Cultural Politics of Gender Ambiguity*. New York: Routledge.

Zita, J.N. (1994) 'Male lesbians and the postmodernist body'. In C. Card (ed.), *Adventures in Lesbian Philosophy*. Bloomington and Indianapolis: Indiana University Press.

Part Three

Thinking Transsexualism into the New Millennium

9

Trans Studies: Between a Metaphysics of Presence and Absence

Henry S. Rubin

A s part of the initial research for this article, I visited my local video store to rent *Paris Is Burning*, the well-known film that portrays the ball culture of Chicano and black underclass MTFs and drag queens in New York. Made in 1987 and 1989, the film purports to document 'gay life'. That *Paris Is Burning* has been received as a gay film was brought home to me in my exchange with the shaven-headed gay clerk at the video store who, after some initial confusion, winked and smiled at me though I offered no sign of being a gay man. My invisibility as a transsexual man to this clerk along with the gay frame of the film left him only one semiotic option; I must be an unmarked gay man. Leaving aside the possibility of a pornographic orientalism, there could be no other reason for me to rent the video.

This simple exchange in the video store started me wondering at the rapid rise of the category 'transgender'. When *Paris Is Burning* was released in 1991, the term 'transgender' had yet to gain cultural relevance, so by default, it was a documentary of 'gay life'. And yet, the aspirations of the *Paris* MTFs to attain realness is at odds with the values of gay drag culture.[1] Gay drag culture operates on a tension between appearance and reality where performers reveal that they are parodying the real. The realness that the trans women in *Paris* aspire to makes no such distinctions and resists the impulse of parody. Today, it might be more appropriate to think of *Paris Is Burning* as a trans film.

In this chapter, my intention is to provide a context for scholarly work that approaches texts, films, and social life *as* trans phenomena. To do this, it is necessary to provide an intellectual history of the scholarship on trans over the past 30 years. This work has been situated at the interstices of the fields of sociology, feminist studies and queer studies. I intend to trace the trajectories of this scholarship in order to shed some light on the tensions that structure present sociological research and cultural criticism as trans studies emerges as a distinct field of scholarship.

Let us begin with A. A for Agnes. In 1951, the child who was to become Agnes was twelve years old and began experimenting with her mother's Stilbestrol – hormone replacement therapy that had been prescribed for her panhysterectomy. Agnes stole money from her mother's purse and had the prescription filled and refilled throughout her adolescence until she arrived in 1958 in Los Angeles at the UCLA Department of Psychiatry to see Dr Robert Stoller and company. After seven years of oestrogen, Agnes appeared to the doctors as 'convincingly female. She was tall, slim with a very female shape. Her measurements were 38–25–38'[2] (Garfinkel, 1984: 119). Agnes wanted only one thing – to become the woman she knew herself to be. In the course of the intake examinations, Agnes spoke with Stoller, Dr Alexander Rosen and also with sociologist Harold Garfinkel for 35 hours of tape-recorded and transcribed interviews. These interviews form the basis of an extraordinary article by Garfinkel titled 'Passing and the managed achievement of sex status in an "intersexed" person (part I)'. Agnes got what she wanted from Stoller and Garfinkel – her sex reassignment surgery. In return, Garfinkel got more than he bargained for. As is apparent from the title of the article, in the 35 hours of taped interviews Agnes presented herself as a real woman who claimed 'I've always wanted to be a girl; I have always felt like a girl; and I have always been a girl but a mistaken environment forced the other thing on me' (*ibid.*: 130). At the same time, Agnes never mentioned and explicitly denied ever taking oestrogen. Garfinkel and Stoller believed that Agnes was intersexed until five years after her surgery when she casually told Stoller that she had ingested Stilbestrol at an early age. The original article was published in 1967 with an appendix that served to jolt the readers in much the same way as Agnes' revelation surprised Stoller and Garfinkel.

As an origin story, the tale of Agnes and Harold is remarkably productive. The article and its appendix take up more than a quarter of a classic volume of *Studies in Ethnomethodology* – increasing the immense appeal of a school of sociology that is directly concerned with the social construction of reality and providing an alternative to the positivism of Talcott Parsons which swept through sociology in the middle years of this century. Ethnomethodology is the study of the individual's methods of naturalizing the reproduction of the social fabric, for example, gender. In addition, the revelation of the appendix turned the article into two. Read as a text on an intersexed individual who had to manage her physical appearance, it spoke to the gender work that is performed universally by all in culture. Read again as an article on a transsexual who managed her identity even to her health care providers, the piece speaks to the unique labour of someone who was always at risk of losing herself if her labours were unsuccessful.

Garfinkel's text and the responses to it generate and structure the themes that continue to occupy trans studies. As I have already noted, Garfinkel was intrigued by Agnes' insistence that she was (in his terms) 120 per cent female and that she claimed what scholars in the 1990s would call an essential female identity, despite her anatomy. Garfinkel observed the various essentialist rationalizations that Agnes deployed in order to preserve her sense of herself.

[S]he insisted that her male genitals were a trick of fate, a personal misfortune, an accident, above all 'it was beyond my control' whose presence she never accepted. She treated her genitals as an abnormal growth. Occasionally she would speak of them as a tumour. With genitals ruled out as essential signs of her femininity, and needing essential and natural signs of female sexuality, she counted instead the life-long desire to be a female and her prominent breasts. (Garfinkel, 1984: 130–1)

And yet, she was fully aware that she had a difference from other women that needed to be managed. For instance, Garfinkel notes that Agnes knew she had to manage her history. 'I just never say anything at all about my past that in any way would make a person ask what my past life was like' (ibid.: 148). Garfinkel's ethnomethodology and his research methods (interviews) allowed him access to Agnes's essentialist world-view. These were described in a value-free manner, rather than critiqued or celebrated. However, Garfinkel does contrast Agnes with revolutionary homosexuals.

It was no part of Agnes' concern to act in active alteration of 'the social system'. Instead she sought her remedy as an adjustment to it. One could never consider Agnes a revolutionary or a utopian. She has no 'cause' and avoided 'causes' as one frequently finds among homosexuals . . . Challenges to the system were for Agnes not even so much as hopeless risks. She wanted 'in'. The credentials committee was at fault. (ibid.: 177)

The essentialist rhetoric of transpeople has, as we shall see, come under attack from feminist and queer studies with the result that transsexuals and others are assumed to unproblematically reproduce hegemonic gender ideals. Because Garfinkel's ethnomethodology was informed by the sociological tradition of *verstehen* that is committed to interpretative understanding, rather than the Marxian tradition of critique, Garfinkel limits his comments on revolutionary identities to this single paragraph. In the main, Garfinkel's work stays attuned to what he might call the achievement of an ascribed identity. That is, *how* one becomes what one always already is.

Throughout the text, Garfinkel makes comparisons between Agnes and other 'deviant' identities. He notes that Agnes identifies as a woman, not as an intersex person, transsexual, transvestite or homosexual.

'I'm not like them', she would continually insist. 'In high school I steered clear of boys that acted like sissies ... anyone with an abnormal problem ... I would completely shy away from them and go to the point of being insulting just enough to get around them ... I didn't want to feel noticed talking to them because somebody might relate them to me. I didn't want to be classified with them'. (*ibid.*: 131).

Garfinkel also does work to contrast Agnes with homosexuals and transvestites. In his introduction of Agnes to his audience, Garfinkel tells us that she is dressed in form-fitting clothes appropriate to a girl of her age, class and race. She does not wear garish clothing or make-up. These comments and Agnes's own disidentification from drag queens, transvestites, homosexual men and others articulates another theme in trans studies: the cultural and historical relationships between these identities. A male-bodied person in a dress or a female-bodied person in a tie has multiple meanings across different epochs and (sub)cultures. And individuals inhabiting these identities, as well as the 'experts' who make decisions about trans lives, depend upon a process of 'othering' to ascertain the truth about those bodies. Teasing out the commonalities and identifying the differences among these subject positions is another aspect of Garfinkel's text.

Two other related issues emerge from Garfinkel's text for me. First, upon reading the article, I made the note that 'I saw myself'. Despite the fact that the article was derived from interviews with a trans woman, I was able to locate and identify myself in relation to Agnes.

Paradoxically, my identification with Agnes was tempered by the realization that this piece has set a standard for the scholarship that followed, such that the MTF experience is centred and the FTM experience is largely invisible or at best, cast as a mirror image.

Second, what comes through in Garfinkel's text is a sense of Agnes's subjectivity, though this was not necessarily Garfinkel's intention. As Michael Lynch and David Bogen point out:

> 'Agnes' and the other personages in the story perform a kind of colloquy that surpasses, reflexively comments upon, and at times stands in judgement of the 'author' and 'his theory'... The various personages in Garfinkel's text are often at odds with one another and with 'him' about 'his research'. Agnes sometimes refuses to respond to his interrogations, and she expresses suspicion and even contempt for the theoretical auspices of the research. Garfinkel, in turn, sometimes remarks that Agnes was dissembling, being evasive, or being resistant. (Bogen and Lynch, 1991: 275)

As Jennifer Terry points out in her essay 'Theorising Deviant Historiographies', archiving historical texts like the one co-authored by Garfinkel and Stoller, often entails reading between the lines to 'explore the production of a counterdiscursive deviant subjectivity, forged in conflict with medico-scientific discourses which pathologise homosexuality [and trans]' (Terry, 1991: 55). 'This historiographic practice does not cleanse homosexual [or trans] subjects of character-istics which could be called "self-hatred" or "self-degradation", replacing them with utopian and heroic qualities like "liberated" and "self-determining"' (ibid.: 71). That Agnes's subjectivity squeaks through the cracks between Garfinkel and Stoller's words demands further attention. There are 35 hours of taped and transcribed interviews that are begging for just such a trans rereading.

In this original text are a series of oppositions that have structured inquiry into trans phenomena. On the one hand, transsexuals and other transpeople have been viewed as exemplars of the universal work of all people in culture who must do gender work. On the other hand, trans folk are subject to particular risks and to the possibility of failure, which make this gender work unique. A second theme found in the story of Agnes is the function of essentialist rhetorical strategies to transpeople. This contrasts with the ethnomethodological use of trans phenomena to illustrate the principles of social construction. Likewise, Garfinkel's piece establishes an opposition between performativity and realness.

The article also sets the terms for the debates about the historical and cultural border wars between various identities now called 'transgender', including gender-inverted gays and lesbians. That Garfinkel's piece focused on Agnes, a male-to-female trans, has centred future scholarship on an MTF model, relegating FTMs to 'mirror image' status, or simply rendered invisible. Finally, Agnes' subjectivity as a trans woman surfaces only unintentionally. Garfinkel's work is ambiguously caught between a metaphysics of presence and absence that repeats itself at each turn:

Presence	Absence
specificity of transgender work	universality of doing gender
realness	performativity
essentialist	social construction
different from homosexuals	queer
different from each other	transgender
interpretative understanding (*verstehen*)	critique
MTF	FTM
trans subjectivity	trans as representation of gender achievement
Stability of gender categories	Instability of gender categories

I shall argue, in the next section, that Garfinkel's ambivalence between these terms largely drops out of the next wave of scholarship on trans phenomena. In the main, theories about gender from Suzanne Kessler and Wendy McKenna's *Gender: An Ethnomethodological Approach* (1978) to Judith Butler's *Gender Trouble* (1990) and *Bodies that Matter* (1993) emphasize the terms of absence. More importantly, the secondary research that utilizes these theoretical master works, tends even more strongly to dogmatic (mis)readings of these texts. As a result, trans scholars on the cusp of the first wave of research *by trans on trans* have been calling for correctives that invoke the terms of presence.

Gender: An Ethnomethodological Approach by Suzanne Kessler and Wendy McKenna is a feminist reinterpretation of Garfinkel that privileges the terms of absence.[3] *Gender's* influence is huge, even making its way into Kate Bornstein's popular book, *Gender Outlaws: Men, Women and the Rest of Us* (1994). Like Garfinkel's text, *Gender* is an ethnomethodological examination of gender with an entire chapter devoted to transsexualism. It also has a chapter devoted to cross-cultural studies and an appendix. The appendix consists of letters from Rachel, an MTF friend of the authors, which are intended to suggest that the letters 'could have been written by any woman' and in order to suggest that 'a sense of femaleness is accomplished by filtering material through a female gender attribution. The tone is experienced as "feminine" ... because the letters are seen as female authored' (Kessler and McKenna, 1978: 214). Gender attribution is described by Kessler and McKenna as the process of deciding whether someone is male or female. This process is, they assert along with Garfinkel, more than merely a process of genital inspection limited to transpeople. It is a universal form of interaction between individuals who present themselves as gendered and those who read for gendered cues. This is the work of gender.

Again following Garfinkel, *Gender* outlines eight rules that constitute what the authors call the 'natural attitude'. Transsexuals, they argue, might be seen as violators of two of these rules; gender is invariant and there may be no transfers from one gender to another. But they claim that transsexuals maintain the natural attitude through a concern with passing and through essentialized narratives, which assert that the transsexual is always already the gender that he or she transitions into. Also, the legal and especially the medical establishments participate in the renaturalizing process through sex reassignment, which alleviates the ambiguity of the transsexual mind/body split. According to Kessler and McKenna, the construction of genitalia that correspond with the transsexual's gender identity precludes a challenge to the rule that genitals are the essential sign of gender (women have vaginas and men have penises).

In their opening remarks to the chapter on transsexualism and again throughout the appendix, Kessler and McKenna tell us that 'our interest in transsexuals is not in terms of transsexualism, per se, but only in terms of what transsexualism can illuminate about the day-to-day social construction of gender by all persons' (*ibid.*: 112). So although the authors include Rachel's letters in order to give us a greater sense of 'who she is and how she expresses herself' (*ibid.*: 214), their concern is not with developing a picture of trans subjectivity, but rather with shedding light on the 'normal' by way of the 'pathological'. Notably, they choose to exhibit Rachel because she is 'a good ethnomethodologist', or an 'articulate' transsexual. This adjective, deployed also in reference to an FTM, is used to describe transsexuals who are properly reflexive about the social construction of gender.

Presumably other transsexuals, especially those who are essentialist, are not so articulate.

Unlike Agnes, who was defensively adamant that Garfinkel see her as always having been female and not misunderstand the things she told him (not interpret her past as being the past of a male), Rachel allows us to see how she is constructing gender at the same time that she credibly displays it to us (Kessler and McKenna, 1978: 215).

Hence we have Kessler and McKenna replying to Garfinkel: Our transsexual is better than your transsexual because she is attuned to the terms of absence that substantiate our universalizing, constructionist theory. This text appropriates an uncut (I mean uncensored) transsexual subjectivity in her own words, but only for the purposes of illuminating the constructedness of gender. Garfinkel's text has less of Agnes's own words, but gives more credence to her subjective self-understandings.

Kessler and McKenna continue to obscure the specificity of trans gender work when they report on the difficulties that their transsexual interviewees had with the questions they posed about learning to be gendered. Questions such as: What did you need to learn to be considered a man or a woman?

> At first we assumed that our questions were poorly phrased; then we thought that our interviewees were just being evasive. Finally we concluded that their non-responses were informative. We decided this by asking these same questions of non-transsexual males and females. They could not answer them either. (*ibid.*: 124)

This is followed by the revelation that those FTMs and MTFs who *could* answer their questions were suspected by the researchers of not being authentic transsexuals or not being authentic men or women. This section of their text is troubling on several counts; first, that the transsexuals might have been evasive, or for what reasons, is dismissed. Second, the authors have an expectation that all transsexuals hold the same ideology and are therefore homogeneous. Finally, if the transsexual interviewees did break the rules of gender by vocalizing a social constructionist perspective, they were considered by the researchers themselves as illegitimate.

This is the Catch-22. The terms of absence that Kessler and McKenna privilege require of transsexuals a reflexivity about the social construction of gender and yet, as they claim, 'doubt about gender attribution can be generated by a failure to exhibit all aspects of the natural attitude in interaction, even with those [like the authors] who under certain circumstances can bracket the natural attitude' (*ibid.*: 124). There is, it seems, a basic incompatibility between the terms of absence and the desire of (at least some) transsexuals to be considered legitimate men and women or even legitimate transsexuals.

This feminist reinterpretation of ethnomethodology leads down a treacherous path for transsexuals. At the time of *Gender*'s publication, one of the implicit goals of feminist scholarship and of the movement was the elimination of gender, or at least of gender roles. Kessler and McKenna do not supply a blueprint for a future society, and they explicitly reject an androgynous world. But they do make several statements that suggest that what they are after is a world that can tolerate gender ambiguity. They are explicitly critical of the diagnostic category 'transsexualism' because

> It is a category constructed to alleviate ambiguity – to avoid the kinds of combinations (e.g. male genitals–female gender identity) that make people uncomfortable because they violate the basic rules about gender ... In a society that could tolerate lack of correspondence, there would be no transsexuals. There would be men with vaginas and women with penises or perhaps different signs of gender. Similarly, if men could wear dresses there would be no transvestism. (*ibid.*: 120)

That Kessler and McKenna can make this statement is enabled by their looking through the transsexuals. Because transsexual subjectivity remains largely absent from their account, they can argue that transsexualism would whither away after the feminist revolution (analogous to some Marxian claims that women's inequality would be alleviated by a class revolution). This also enables them to dismiss the claims of Robert, an FTM who believed he would still want the change in a more tolerant society; 'we believe that it was not because he did not feel like a woman that he had to get surgical and hormonal treatment, but rather because he did not feel comfortable having a vagina and breasts when other people who had vaginas and breasts seemed so different socially and psychologically from him' (ibid.). What is dismissed by Kessler and McKenna is the relevance of body dysphoria to trans folk. This is consistent with a particular feminist emphasis on gender roles, rather than identities and bodies.

Kessler and McKenna's chapter on cross-cultural studies brings the discussion to the relationship between transsexuals and other transgender formations. Their cross-cultural chapter focuses on a comparison between the berdache and transsexuals. The authors are to be commended for pointing out the difficulties of anthropological research that rests on cross-cultural translation. Using the reports of the anthropologists is a tricky business and they point to several pitfalls. The greatest of these is the attempt by field workers to make sense of berdache using Western, industrialized categories of gender 'deviance'. 'Although some berdache were homosexual, and some homosexuals were transvestic, and some transvestites were hermaphroditic, to treat these gender-based categories as identical is to obscure crucial distinctions' (*ibid.*: 25). However, Kessler and McKenna favour the berdache over the transsexual in several passages. The berdache do not take hormones or have surgeries. Gender attributions of berdache (and one assumes non-trans) are not made according to genitals, but rather on the basis of gender role (as hunter or weaver and or on). Ultimately, Kessler and McKenna appreciate the berdache because s/he is a third sexer who undermines the binary opposition of male/female. 'The transsexual phenomenon does not undermine the dichotomy of gender; it reinforces it. The berdache, in contrast, may not have been considered a special type of man or woman (one who had crossed over categories) but rather a third type of person' (*ibid.*: 27).

Kessler and McKenna's ethnomethodology is informed by feminist principles, some of which have continued to hold sway and some of which have fallen away. The deepest feminist mark on their work is the resistance to body modification, which is central to the transsexual project. This resistance is understandable from a point of view that recognizes the immense patriarchal pressure on women to modify and cultivate their bodies to please the male gaze. Unfortunately, a transsexual desire becomes misread through this perspective as body mutilation. Kessler and McKenna's choice of the berdache over, for instance the hijras of India, is deliberate. Hijras perform self-mutilations that are closer to, although still not the same as, transsexual surgeries. The choice of the berdache allows Kessler and McKenna to assume a critical position *vis-à-vis* transsexuals.

Nonetheless, the feminist re-reading of Garfinkel offers a critique of the beauty imperative that transsexual women face in much the same way as non-trans women.

There is some suggestion that not only must one be normal, but it helps to be attractive. A clinician during a panel session on transsexualism at the 1974 meeting of the American Psychological

Association said that he was more convinced of the femaleness of a male-to-female transsexual if she was particularly beautiful and was capable of evoking in him those feelings that beautiful women generally do. (*ibid*.: 118)

In addition, Kessler and McKenna point out that the imperative to be heterosexual after transition also accords with the natural attitude. These two criticisms have provided ammunition to transsexual lesbians, transsexual gay men and transsexual women who do not conform to stereotypical notions of female beauty. Likewise, Kessler and McKenna attend to FTMs in a way that Garfinkel did not, although little emphasis is placed on theorizing the differences between FTMs and MTFs. In what can only be described as wishful thinking, they tell us 'Science will soon be able to construct perfectly functioning penises. Because of this we will never know what would have been the long-range repercussions, in concepts about gender, of having a group of men in society who do not have penises' (*ibid*.: 120). It is close to twenty years since this statement, yet phalloplasty remains an untenable option for most and unsatisfactory for those who can afford it. The 'long range study' is feasible, but this is not the real intent behind the statement. Ultimately, Kessler and McKenna would prefer it if FTMs and MTFs would elect a non-surgical option, like the berdache, as this would violate the natural attitude and provoke a challenge to hegemonic gender ideals. In this feminist rereading of Garfinkel, a shift in methodology from the register of *verstehen* to critique paints transsexualism (as opposed to other transgenders) as false consciousness.

Now let us turn to more recent scholarship in queer theory, specifically Judith Butler's work, which has become an equally productive set of texts. Butler's two books, *Gender Trouble: Feminism and the Subversion of Identity* and *Bodies that Matter: On the Discursive Limits of Sex*, have generated an immense literature in a very short period of time – some of the best (and the worst) of which is focused on the gendered component of sexual identities. Butler develops Esther Newton's ethnographic work on drag, recasting it in the terms of her discipline, rhetoric, and heavily reconstituting it via the linguistic turn in continental philosophy. In *Gender Trouble*, Butler counters some lesbian, feminist and gay critiques of drag queens (as misogynist imitations) and of butch/femme styles (also criticized for imitating heterosexual roles). Instead of asserting that these styles are not imitative, she invokes the rhetorical notion of (re)iteration to suggest that drag performances are parodic imitations that reveal that all gender is performative. Drag is a practice that parodies the very notion that there is an original. Gender always already is a copy without an original. In addition, Butler troubles the very idea of an interior gender identity, instead suggesting that gender identity is imposed or constructed from the outside in. With all of this, she sounds very close to Kessler and McKenna.

A great deal of the secondary material that flowed after *Gender Trouble* took Butler's two main theses to mean that there is no such thing as gender or that our (feminist/queer) goal should be a world without gender and that a subjective sense of gender identity was illegitimate. These are patent misreadings of Butler and though all of us know that a text is measured not so much for its intent, but for its effects, Butler published *Bodies That Matter* as a 'rethinking of some parts of *Gender Trouble* that have caused confusion' (Butler, 1993: xii). Butler writes:

> This is not the same as censoring or prohibiting the use of the 'I' or of the autobiographical as such; on the contrary, it is the inquiry into the ambivalent relations of power that make that use possible. ... In this sense, the argument ... does *not* entail that we ought never to make use of such terms ['sex', 'race', 'gender'], as if such terms could only and always reconsolidate the oppressive regimes of power by which they are spawned. On the contrary, precisely because such terms have been produced and constrained within such regimes, they ought to be repeated in directions that reverse and displace their originating aims. [*ibid.*: 123)

Obviously, a significant difference between Butler and Kessler and McKenna is the former's emphasis on 'drag' as opposed to 'transsexuals'. This is a difference on two levels; first, Butler's notion of drag comes out of gay and lesbian communities and does not emerge out of a consideration of transsexuals. Looking backward, we can say that Butler's notion of drag is pulled from what Leslie Feinberg has called the overlap of two circles of communities: gay/lesbian and transsexual. This is the transgendered or 'queer' space that has emerged of late. But I think it is significant that at the time of Butler's writing, this space was largely considered gay/lesbian and that the examples she uses (drag queens, butch/femme and so on) are marked as gay. Because Butler's work has been influential in the formation of this space and because I want to show the power moves that constitute this space so as to critique some transgender formations, I maintain a conceptual distinction between transgender work and gay/lesbian gender work. Butler's theory is centred on the terms of gay/lesbian gender work. Second, despite these origins, Butler is not concerned with identities or categories of people. Rather, her interest lies with certain gender practices that are not specific to a single identity, but can be applied (she hopes) to all the work of gender everywhere. Butler's universalism places her along with Kessler and McKenna in favouring the terms of absence, though for different reasons.

Because of her universalism, Butler does not distinguish between transgender work, non-transgender work and gay or lesbian gender work; they are all versions of drag. Yet she casts herself in opposition to Marilyn Frye, Janice Raymond and bell hooks who 'place drag on a continuum with cross-dressing and transsexualism, ignoring the important differences between them' (ibid.: 126). Here we see that Butler *does* have some specific parameters to 'drag', which allow her to make distinctions between 'subversive' drag and 'hegemonic' drag or drag that 're-idealizes' and 're-naturalizes' gender performance. She warns, in *Gender Trouble*, that 'parody by itself is not subversive, and there must be a way to understand what makes certain kinds of parodic repetitions effectively disruptive, truly troubling, and which repetitions become domesticated and re-circulated as instruments of cultural hegemony' (Butler, 1990: 139). She also reminds us that the context of the reiteration is especially relevant: 'What performance where ...?' (ibid.). In *Bodies That Matter*, Butler alternatively suggests that what determines the 'subversiveness' of drag is critical reflection: 'drag is subversive to the extent that it reflects on the imitative structure by which hegemonic gender is itself produced and disputes heterosexuality's claim of naturalness and originality' (Butler, 1993: 125). So, we are not so far from Kessler and McKenna's good trans/bad trans typology.

This is where Butler turns to an analysis of the MTFs and drag queens in *Paris Is Burning*. She starts out with this ambivalent characterization of the film:

> There is both a sense of defeat and a sense of insurrection to be had from the drag pageantry in *Paris Is Burning*, that the drag we see ... is one which both appropriates and subverts racist, misogynist, and homophobic norms of oppression. ... This is not first an appropriation and then a subversion. Sometimes it is both at once; sometimes it remains caught in an irresolvable tension, and sometimes a fatally un-subversive appropriation takes place. (ibid.: 128)

In her discussion of the participants, she has little to say. She tells us they are Latino or African-American 'men' (her quotes), and leaves aside the differences between the drag queens and the MTFs. After rehearsing the basic categories of the drag balls, Butler examines the standard of measurement by which the performances and 'performers' are measured: 'realness' – 'what determines the effect of realness is the ability to compel belief, to produce the naturalised effect. ... Significantly this is a performance that works, that effects realness, to the extent that it *cannot* be read' (*ibid.*: 129). This causes Butler a significant degree of dismay. For Butler, the performative strategy that is subversive is that which exploits the tension between appearance and bodies. Drag makes visible the seams of the performance.

Butler then considers two of the performers: Venus Xtravaganza and Willi Ninja. Her choice is curious and confusing to me. Venus, a light-skinned trans Chicana who wants to marry a white man and live in the suburbs, is compared to Ninja, who 'can pass as straight' (*ibid.*: 130). Ninja, a gay man, is derided for producing heterosexual videos with Madonna, while Venus is regarded more carefully. She passes and Butler is hard on her for wanting suburban life, yet Butler points to Venus's unsuccessful passing (she is vulnerable and murdered because of her pre-operative status) as a sign that Venus presents a challenge to heteronormativity. Here again, ambiguity and showing the seams of gender performance is coded as being transgressive. Violence, either homophobic or transphobic,[4] is one sign that indicates that a drag performance is subversive. Akin to Kessler and McKenna, when the transsexual subject side-steps surgery and 'lets it all hang out' then Butler can sympathize with her plight. What would happen to Butler's comparison case if she had chosen one of the MTFs who was post-operative to contrast with Pepper Labeija who claimed she imperso-nated women, who cried when her mother burned her mink coat, but had never been a woman because she had never menstruated? *Que es mas macho? Que es mas politico?*

Butler's ambition is to create a complex notion of drag that does not reduce to a one-to-one correspondence between any particular identity and revolutionary practice. This certainly takes us beyond Kessler and McKenna, but the effects of the text are, as I already pointed out, stronger than the author's intentions, with the result that the equation, drag equals ambiguity in performance, has rendered trans desires for realness and legibility 'unseemly' to queer theory.

This brings us up to the 1990s, where we begin to see the emergence of trans scholarship by transpeople. Sandy Stone's reply to Janice

Raymond, 'The *Empire* strikes back: a post-transsexual manifesto' (1991), is a ground-breaking piece that re-envisions the terms of queer theory with an eye towards the specificity of transgender work and towards trans subjectivity. Stone's stance is that sexologists and transsexuals have combined to spin an intricate web of intertextuality, so that the essentialism which MTFs use to ground their transsexual desires is mostly a result of patients giving the health care providers what they expect.

> Initially, the only textbook on the subject of transsexualism was Harry Benjamin's definitive work *The Transsexual Phenomenon* [1966]. ... It took a surprisingly long time – several years – for the researchers to realize that the reason the candidates' behavioural profiles matched Benjamin's so well was that the candidates, too, had read Benjamin's book, which was passed from hand to hand within the transsexual community and they were only too happy to provide the behaviour that led to acceptance for surgery. (Stone, 1991: 291)

This claim by Stone suggests that transsexuals were strategically essentialist. This interpretation rests on a queer theorist's antipathy to essentialist rhetoric, while preserving some integrity for transsexual subjects who are not as stupid as they may have seemed to feminists and queer theorists. But Stone is torn between her two allegiances: to queer theory (and to her theoretical (m)other, Donna Haraway) and to her transsexual community. So although she claims that the 'people who have no voice in this theorising are the transsexuals themselves' (*ibid*.: 294), the end result is that Stone views this sort of rhetoric and some transsexuals' desire to pass as complicity. Stone values the queer strategy of revealing the seams of gender and reprimands passing transsexuals for 'failing to develop an effective counter-discourse' (*ibid*.: 294) to the feminists and the physicians.

This text has swept through parts of the trans community and opened a door for what Stone called the 'multiple contradictions of individual lived experience' (*ibid*.: 297) and for the 'Emergent polyvocalities of lived experience, never represented in the [medical] discourse but present at least in potential' (*ibid*.: 293). Stone writes in order to draw recognition to those trans possibilities that the medical discourse has ignored or rejected, but also to create them. She makes room for transpeople who reveal their constructed selves; who show the seams of gender; who disrupt heteronormativity with their homosexual desires; and those who resist surgery or who answer that they can be content men or women without genital reconstructions. While Stone attends to the specificity of transgender work and to trans subjectivity, like Butler she has less tolerance for more 'traditional' transsexuals who pass (and who essentialize their identities in order to resist the idea that they are passing), or for heterosexual transsexuals, or for transsexual genital modification. Stone's queer appropriations have rescued trans-people from the trash can of feminist and queer theory, but only by appealing to the terms of absence. Also, Stone self-consciously writes from a male-to-female perspective about MTFs. A promised article on FTMs has not yet appeared.

Though Stone does not view transsexuals as third-sexers, but rather as mixed genres, the essays in Gilbert Herdt's *Third Sex, Third Gender: Beyond Sexual Dimorphism in Culture and History* (1994) provides this kind of framework for Anne Bolin's 'Transcending and Transgendering: Male-to-Female Transsexuals, Dichotomy and Diversity' (1994). This essay is perhaps the greatest artefact of and report on the changes that came to the trans community since Sandy Stone's article. In it, Bolin revisits the ethnographic scene of her work *In Search of Eve* and compares her conclusions from this earlier study (1982) to her observations in 1992.

> There has been a movement in which people of various gender-transposed identities have come to organise themselves as part of a greater community, a larger in-group, facing similar concerns of stigmatisation, acceptance, treatment and so on. This recognition of similarity fostered by a growing political awareness of gender organisations has facilitated the burgeoning of new gender options, such as the 'transgenderist'. *Transgenderist* is a community term denoting kinship among those with gender-variant identities. It supplants the dichotomy of transsexual and transvestite with a concept of continuity. Additionally, it highlights a growing acceptance over the past decade of non-surgical options for physical males wishing to live as women. (Bolin, 1994: 461)

Where Bolin had once observed a dichotomy between TSs and TVs, she now sees a continuity expressed by TG, which signifies a greater community awareness of similarity. As she later points out, 'transgender' is a term that is expanding to include the gays and lesbians who have gender-transposed styles. Bolin's earlier ethnography noted, like Stone, that the community self-image 'was refracted through the medical construction of transsexualism ... this was embodied in surgical and hormonal reassignment' (ibid.: 456). And, like Stone, Bolin observed that 'transsexualism was an identity to be outgrown as one eventually became a "whole" woman' (ibid.: 457).

She counts three major cultural shifts that account for the emergence of this pluralistic transgender community: (1) the closing of university-based gender clinics, (2) grass-roots organizing with political agendas, and (3) alternatives to traditional femininity spawned by feminism. The end of the gender clinics meant a much less regulated diagnostic and treatment regime, which allowed for greater diversity among trans-people and enabled greater freedom of choice in terms of treatment programmes. The politicization of the community emphasized the importance of coming out of the closet. The feminist critique of heterosexism and of beauty standards cracked open a space for trans lesbians and trans fags and provided legitimacy for trans women who preferred unorthodox female styles.

Obviously, several of these changes correspond directly to Stone's call for a new counter-discourse. And Stone, in turn, was influenced by the critiques of transsexualism in an earlier wave of scholarship (Butler, Kessler and McKenna). My immediate response to Bolin's essay was that my own transition had been enabled by these changes in the community and by reading the work of Butler, Kessler and McKenna. The more I read, the closer I got to approaching the line that divides women from men, until I finally crossed over it. My second response was more guarded. I am troubled by the inevitable invisibility of FTMs and more importantly, by the politicization of trans phenomena in the scholarship I have covered. My fear is not that 'pure' or 'objective' scholarship has been polluted by politics. Rather, my fear is that in the name of politics, those transsexuals who do favour surgery or who are not homosexual or who claim an essential identity (apart from what they tell their physicians) will be considered illegitimate transgender-ists. Like the butches and femmes from old gay life who were gradually considered backward and traditional (or worse) as feminism changed the face of the lesbian community, I have watched as queer theory and feminism have criticized and refigured transsexualism, in their own image. This is not to say that some versions of transsexualism are more 'true' than others, rather I want to highlight a dramatic shift in cultural identity and the possible effects of this shift on members of that community.

Where we stand today, at the dawning of an independent field of trans studies, the tensions between the terms of absence and the terms of presence that structured Garfinkel's work on Agnes have, for the most part, been foreclosed. The queering of transsexualism has privileged the terms of absence so that even calls for trans specificity avoid the differences between transsexuals, transvestites, cross-dressers, homosexuals, berdache, hijras and so on. Stone and Bolin are two trans scholars among many who have called for greater attention to trans subjectivity. But the bulk of published work is now framed in the terms of absence: FTM invisibility, gender ambiguity, critique, constructionism, instability of gender categories and the universality of gender performativity.

Changes in trans communities are dialectically related to this theorizing. Our communities and our scholarship are more pluralistic than they had been during the last 30 years, including a wider array of trans gender formations. This is partly the result of the feminist and queer critiques levelled by Butler, Kessler and McKenna. Without this, the field would be limited to the study of transsexuals only. It seems to me that the development of trans studies (forged in relationship to sociology, feminist and queer studies) made space for alternatives to a single transgender formation (forged dialectically with the medico-legal regimes that controlled our treatments). The next wave of scholarship is taking account of these new identities at both the community and individual levels.

Some of the new scholarship follows Stone's and Bolin's queer-inflected work, while another branch of trans studies is showing greater sensitivity to the good trans/bad trans binary that permeates queer and feminist studies. On the horizon we will see trans scholars examining essentialist narratives for the functions they serve some transpeople (Rubin, Prosser). The desire for realness or authenticity is being theorized, rather than critiqued (Singer, Stryker). In addition, there is an upsurge of work-in-progress by and about FTMs (Prosser, Singer, Rubin, Cromwell, Whittle, Hale). Trans scholarship will need to elaborate the specificity of transgender work, both in relation to non-transgender work and across the spectrum of trans variation. All of this work reinvokes the terms of presence, staying attuned to trans subjectivity.

This is a first step in the development of trans studies. Returning to the terms of presence provides a balance to the years of scrutiny and critique of trans phenomenon by queer and feminist scholarship. Scholarship that invokes the terms of presence takes transgender work on its own terms. Nonetheless, it seems to me that the long view must seek out a middle term between presence and absence. In the coming years, trans scholars must find a delicate balance that recognizes the legitimacy of trans desires for authenticity or realness while acknowledging the constructedness of our bodies and identities.

Notes

1. Esther Newton's *Mother Camp* (1972) remains a definitive account of drag culture with its emphasis on opposition between clothes and bodies. Gay drag performers reveal their male identities to their audiences by various means (what the performers call 'dropping the hairpin'). Also Newton notes that, even in 1968, the culture she studied was split between these individuals and those who chose sex reassignment and hormones. Those who chose SRS or hormones were stigmatized within the homosexual culture and were urged to exit (Newton, 1972: 102).
2. That Agnes was deemed 'convincingly female' according to her measurements (which are repeated more than once in the text) is problematized by the second wave of scholarship, notably Kessler and McKenna (1978).
3. It also spawned the notorious anti-transsexual, feminist manifesto *The Transsexual Empire: The Making of the She-Male* (1980) by Janice Raymond. Raymond's brand of essentialist feminism was deployed to delegitimate transsexual claims to authenticity and to assert that transsexualism was a plot designed by male physicians to infiltrate the women's movement and women's bodies. It also suggested that FTMs were dupes of the patriarchy, coerced to give up their female bodies in order to exterminate women. I considered including Raymond in this survey of trans scholarship and finally settled on this footnote where I could mention it without giving it the respect of my attentions. Sandy Stone's piece 'The *Empire* strikes back' (1991) effectively responds to Raymond. In general, I chose to focus on other feminist-inflected texts, which are more subtle in their approach and have had a greater influence on present trans scholarship.
4. Butler prefers the former term, once again revealing both the historicity of her text (prior to the cultural recognition of transgender) and the rhetorical power moves she uses to centre her analysis in a queer register.

References

Bogen, D. and M. Lynch (1991) 'In defence of dada-driven analysis', *Sociological Theory*, 9: 269–76.

Bolin, A. (1988) *In Search of Eve: Transsexual Rites of Passage*. South Hadley: Bergin & Garvey.

Bolin, A. (1994) 'Transcending and transgendering: male-to-female transsexuals, dichotomy and diversity'. In G. Herdt (ed.), *Third Sex, Third Gender: Beyond Sexual Dimorphism in Culture and History*. New York: Zone Books.

Bornstein, K. (1994) *Gender Outlaws: Men, Women and the Rest of Us*. New York: Routledge.

Butler, J. (1990) *Gender Trouble: Feminism and the Subversion of Identity*. New York: Routledge.

Butler, J. (1993) *Bodies That Matter: On the Discursive Limits of Sex*. New York: Routledge.

Garfinkel, H. (1984) 'Passing and the managed achievement of sex status in an "intersexed" person (part I)'. In *Studies in Ethnomethodology*. Cambridge: Polity Press.

Kessler, S. and W. McKenna (1978) *Gender: An Ethnomethodological Approach*. New York: John Wiley & Sons.

Lee, J. and J. Sasser-Coen (1996) *Blood Stories*. New York: Routledge.

Livingston, J. (1991) *Paris Is Burning*. San Francisco: Off White Productions.

Newton, E. (1972) *Mother Camp: Female Impersonators in America*. Chicago: University of Chicago Press.

Raymond, J.G. (1980) *The Transsexual Empire: The Making of the She-Male*. Boston: Beacon Press.

Stone, S. (1991). 'The *Empire* strikes back'. In J. Epstein and K. Straub (eds), *Body Guards: The Cultural Politics of Gender Ambiguity*. London: Routledge.

Terry, J. (1991). 'Theorising deviant historiography', *differences*, 3, 2: 55–74.

10

50 Billion Galaxies of Gender: Transgendering the Millennium

Gordene O. Mackenzie[1]

Introduction

Contemporary findings in astronomy and physics are blowing all of the myths we have lived by for thousands of years. From the discovery of black holes, the expansion of chaos theory, and the recent discovery inspired by the Hubble telescope that there are at least 50 billion galaxies, our traditional ways of seeing and existing are being challenged. Theories of hyperspace, to energy-sucking black holes, to theories that there are as many galaxies as there are visible stars in the night sky, are shaking up our ideas of the 'known' universe we live in. In a like manner transgender studies, an interdisciplinary body of work including theory, political practices, narratives, history, ethnographies and art, is bursting all the myths we have lived by for thousands of years. This time-bomb exploding the laws of gender is equivalent to the anarchist bomb the French physicist Poincaré set off when he challenged the Newtonian universe, claiming 'reductionism might be an illusion' (Briggs and Peat, 1989: 26). Although his charges were largely ignored for a century, he helped usher in chaos theory. And just as chaos theory in the nineteenth century disrupted reductionistic and mechanistic views of the universe, transgender theory as we near the twenty-first century is shaking up reductionistic and mechanistic ideas of the 'known' body we live in. Fixed ideas of gender bipolarism are wavering, forging a revolution on bodies and consciousness that embraces their complexity. From this new vantage the emergence of at least 50 billion galaxies of gender becomes a distinct possibility.

This chapter speculates about the future of gender, or more particularly the transgender future, through the lens of transgender studies. The approach of the third millennium provides an arbitrary date to assess personal, cultural and global debates, manifestations and representations of gender. Like feminist and queer theories, transgender theory is linked to a political movement to end gender oppression. As an emerging discipline and practice, transgender theory is raising important questions of how personal and cultural constructions of identity and desire are negotiated across gender, racial, ethnic, sex and class lines. In some respects transgender theory is to feminist theory and queer theory what Poincaré's theory of chaos was to the Newtonian universe, pushing the dialogue and practice of gender ever further. Progressive trans theory and practice represent a revolutionary paradigm shift that is shattering reductionist and essentialist identities, while simultaneously exploring social spaces where desire and identities intersect, resurrect, contest and transform. At the end of the twentieth century progressive feminist and queer theories and movements are crossing boundaries and building bridges to transgender theory. In the summer of 1997, after being lobbied by GenderPac and members of the National Lesbian Rights and other groups, the National Organization of Women (NOW) overwhelmingly passed a trans-inclusive resolution. One participant at the conference remarked that 'the transgender community is today's cutting edge ... of exposing artificial gender constructs and breaking down the stereotypes and barriers that divide us' (Wilchins, 1997: 221).

In the post-Newtonian universe where Hubble is expanding our vision, transgender theory and practice are tearing through the membranes of traditional sex and gender categories, creating new galaxies of gender. 'What is at stake is the very constitution of being – the ways we perceive ourselves and others, the modes of experiences that are available to us' (Olalquiaga, 1992: xi). Theorizing the expansion of the known gender universe necessitates that we question not only personal, cultural and global representations and manifestations of gender, but how race, ethnicity, sex and class filter those manifestations and representations. This requires pushing beyond personal fascination and/or horror at our own gender reflections in the mirror into cultural and global gender mirrors that reflect the daily struggles for survival, revealing the horrors and the injustices that transpeople are confronted with as their civil and human rights are systematically violated. Confronting these grisly reflections of gender bipolarism is crucial, particularly with the rise of the global police state where anything different is suspect. The root word for theory means 'to see'. In our quest for transgender theory it is vital to imagine new ways of 'seeing' the gendered body. However, it is also crucial that in doing so we never lose sight of the violent gender crimes enacted daily on trans bodies. As a field of inquiry, transgender studies combines trans-identified experiences, transgender activism and transgender theory in order to challenge the violent and rigidly policed boundaries of gender.

As we approach the year 2000 transgender studies is evolving into an expanding gender universe where ideas and images, many trans-produced, are exploding our traditional ways of seeing, doing and theorizing gender. This monumental interruption of conventional gender discourses, which include electronic representations, functions as a 'discourse interruptus' – the moment when dominant gender discourses and actions are interrupted by revolutionary discourses and actions that challenge us to rethink our current universe of gender.

In the late 1990s we are experiencing a global saturation of mass-produced commodified electronic and print images of transpersons. Many of these cultural artefacts offer corporately packaged gender images and discourses constructed to sell products. Most are not trans-produced. At this specific socio-historical moment as we wobble towards the third millennium, images of the gender ambiguous body translate into international currency. From US professional-basketball player Dennis Rodman's public appearances in matrimonial drag to promote his new book to the immense popularity of gender films including *The Crying Game, Priscilla, Queen of the Desert, Tu Wong Fu* and *Birdcage*, to the new 'ultrahip' British-based international make-up company MAC whose major spokesmodels are RuPaul and k.d. lang, to Ru Paul's VH1 talk show, to the Holiday Inn commercial featuring a transperson, which aired during the 1997 Superbowl, there seems to be an insatiable appetite to consume representations of the gender ambiguous body. However, consumption of an image does not ensure its full digestion. Even though corporate productions often place transpersons at the centre of discourse, they transmit conflicting messages. This is particularly evident in US gender films that generally offer more rigid gender performances than international productions. This raises questions of whether the increasing visibility and popularity of transpersons as popular icons reveal on one level a frustration with gender bipolarism and a longing for a new galaxy of gender. And what do these commodified representations have to do with the everyday lives of transpersons as we move towards the twenty-first century? Ken Plummer has observed that when private or personal stories enter the public arena it is because at that particular historical moment there is an audience ready to hear them (Plummer, 1996: 36–45). Plummer asserts that:

the stories we tell of our lives are deeply implicated in moral and political change, and the shifting tales of self and identity carry potential for a radical transformation of the social order. (*ibid.*: 45)

Discourse interruptus

The focus of this work revolves around three revolutionary sites of 'discourse interruptus' and 'discourse eruption' (the moment where new discourses and actions break through conventional paradigms of thinking and doing, thereby creating change). The three sites of transgender 'discourse interruptus' where new gender knowledge, practices and representations are breaking through are in trans-produced narratives and theories, many of which are combinations of fiction, autobiography and theory; in popular culture representations of transpersons, particularly in US and international films; and finally in the transgender liberation movement's fight for civil and human rights. As I mentioned earlier, all three sites are erupting simultaneously in the mid- to late 1990s.

Works authored by trans activists constitute a 'discourse interruptus' of modern Western medico-legal and psycho-clinical discourses. Many of these works continue the work of gender radicals in questioning hegemonic gender discourses and critically examining the historical and contemporary domination and subordination of transpersons. The emerging trans discourse advocates gender diversity and the disruption of static gender boundaries and borders. Many of these voices guide the trans liberation movement. However, there are competing popular gender discourses circulating in the public realm. The most visible are corporate-produced electronic media products like film and television, which have the potential to 'normalise as well as exoticise other cultures' (Shohat and Stam, 1994: 347).

Many of these productions, particularly those made in the US, flirt with gender diversity but also lock transpersons in antiquated and erroneous stereotypes. This results in contradictory messages being transmitted to the public. Some of the most liberating cinematic moments occur when trans representations move into a new space, smashing stereotypes and narrow gender categories, while interrogating desire. These moments function as a 'discourse interruptus' and often as a discourse eruption as new gender galaxies appear in dimensional windows. At the same time and often the same productions there are also media representations that mock and insult transpersons, reinforcing violence against the trans body. These representations and discourses require a closer reading of how popular culture reflects and shapes the culture and how we negotiate our identities through media representations.

In most instances the degree to which diversity is embraced in mainstream film productions varies from country to country. This work primarily focuses on liberatory moments in popular culture where traditional gender discourses are contested (discourse interruptus) and where new gender configurations emerge (discourse eruptions). Part of my intent is to examine and compare movement discourses and popular culture discourses. Both, I believe, have produced a discourse interruptus where traditional ideas about gender, identity, desire and transgender civil rights can be interrogated.

Changing the channel of discourse

> Where there is an 'I' who utters or speaks and thereby produces an effect in discourse, there is first a discourse which precedes and enables that 'I' ... the 'I' comes into being through being called, named ... (Butler, 1993: 225)

For too long transpeople have been named, otherized, and stigmatized by psychological, medical, legal, religious and media discourses. These institutional discourses have worked to disfigure, condemn, mortally wound and rob transpersons of their voices, while maintaining a dual gender order. However, as we near the third millennium a profound transformation is taking place as trans activists refute institutional categorizations. Trans activist Leslie Feinberg in discussing how hard it is to be differently gendered in a two-gender world observed 'we've always listened to "experts" tell us why we are, who we are'. S/he along with other gender activists argue that current gender pronouns are too small to hold the complexity of their identity.

From time to time in the history of ideas, a radical shift occurs in basic paradigms. Such a shift not only challenges the dominant discourse but calls into question basic conceptions of the world in which we live and the language we use to communicate. A revolutionary paradigm shift in gender is occurring now as dominant discourses about gender are being interrupted and challenged. A moment of 'discourse interruptus' took place on the *Joan Rivers Show*, a TV talk show that was broadcast during autumn 1993. During the programme Leslie Feinberg, a guest on the show, interrupted the clinical discourse of a therapist and asked if transpersons could speak for themselves.

Feinberg's 'discourse interruptus' subverted the dominant discourse on several levels. Foremost, the trans voice moved centre stage as transpersons were momentarily liberated from the clinical discourse in front of millions of viewers. And secondly, Feinberg as a working-class transperson interrupted the authoritarian therapeutic voice, challenging simultaneously the categories of gender and class. bell hooks astutely observes:

> Moving from silence into speech is for the oppressed, the colonised, the exploited, and those who stand and struggle side by side a gesture of defiance that heals, that makes new life and growth possible. It is that act of speech, of 'talking back,' that is no mere gesture of empty words, that is the expression of our movement from object to subject – the liberated voice. (hooks, 1989: 9)

Predictably, Feinberg's request that transpersons be allowed to speak for themselves was met by broadcast silence. However, many home viewers and audience members, off screen, were inspired or reinforced by Feinberg's courage to 'talk back'.

At long last, before millions of viewers, the formulaic TV presentation of transpersons controlled and colonized by medico-clinical discourses revolving around the 'illness' model was shattered by Leslie's dissenting and courageous voice. As Feinberg's brave words were electronically transmitted, something powerful occurred. For at least one brief televised moment the visual spectacle of transpersons that US television exploits took a backseat to what was being articulated, which was movement discourse. Leslie's words paralleled the ongoing contemporary struggle the transgender liberation movement was and still is waging with medico-clinical categorizations and stigmatizations of trans bodies and minds. Many transpersons witnessing Leslie's electronic dissent tell of how they, as viewers, vicariously felt empowered to speak of their own experience. Clearly, the media's capacity to both reflect and shape culture, particularly gender, requires further investigation. Feinberg's 'discourse interruptus' dramatizes the radical gender paradigm shift we are in the midst of as gender becomes increasingly liberated from medico-clinical jurisdiction. Suddenly, the freak show atmosphere on the *Joan Rivers Show* faded as audiences came face to face with real people. The formulaic presentation of transpeople being treated like circus animals (who are shamefully mistreated) was halted as the 'voice-overs' by the circus masters and 'experts' was questioned. For one brief historical moment the media-exploited, medically colonized, academically appropriated, and socially battered body of transpersons tuned audiences in the US and parts of North America into a different channel of discourse.

Gender liberation

Although transmission on this new channel of discourse is sometimes fuzzy and the volume still needs to be turned up, the new trans discourse encoded in the transgender liberation movement, novels, theories, autobiographies and popular culture is systematically smashing dominant ideas about sex and gender. This discourse has opened new debates that push gender boundaries ever further. What we thought was transgender is being re-imagined as identities mercurially change and transmute in space and time. In the last decade public ideas about transpersons have radically altered. With the gains of the contemporary transgender liberation movement gender complexity has been unleashed. Unfortunately, so has its opponent; the bigoted bipolar wardens of a closed and locked gender universe.

Recent writings and actions by trans activists are re-imagining and reshaping the known gender universe, suggesting that it is far more expansive and diverse than previously thought. Ideas of transpersons all being surgery-bound transwomen whose identity and desire is fixed have expanded to include numerous gender constellations as transmen, bigender persons, cross-dressers, drag kings/queens, gender queers, gender ambiguous and gender fluid bodies who are telling their stories about colliding with gender and gendered bodies and orbiting other bodies with desire. This is a departure from the formulaic trans autobiographies from the 1960s through the early 1980s that were often framed in medico-clinical explanations and frozen identities. At the century's end trans writing has morphed into hyperspace employing numerous dimensions including politics, autobiography, theory, art, literature, and so on into a single work, challenging reductionistic and mechanistic ideas about gender. These pieces have helped inspire struggles and negotiations towards gender liberation that are taking place on multiple levels; from the unravelling of the bipolar gender universe to the explorations of other sex and gender galaxies. Numerous gender struggles are being waged. All engage the terrain of the body and consciousness. Collective struggles are attempting to halt the institutional control and punishment of the trans body and consciousness, while other struggles explore the personal trans terrain of gender and/or how they intersect with sex and desire. These collective and personal gender negotiations in the late twentieth century are facilitated by the growth of trans communication in the form of activist groups, print and electronic media, including numerous Internet sites. In addition, we are bombarded with numerous popular cultural representations of transpersons, particularly in film.

Trans activist Riki Anne Wilchins combines numerous dimensions including electronic messages and newsletters in cyberspace, as well as a new book *Read My Lips*, to disrupt dominant discourses on gender. Wilchins's grass-roots organizing in cyberspace globally transmits 'discourse interruptus'. A 1996 posting by Wilchins called for support in picketing the American Psychiatric Association's annual meeting. The stated action was to protest the way the diagnosis of 'gender identity disorder' (GID) has been and is used to torture millions of gender variant children and adults. In her electronic message Wilchins acknowledges that the action is not unilaterally agreed upon in the trans community, largely because of insurance reimbursement for sex reassignment surgery (SRS). However, she concludes that while reimbursement is important the diagnosis routinely punishes gender difference. Wilchins's electronic post, like Feinberg's television appearance, exposes the power dynamics implicit in medico-clinical diagnosis. In a justified attack on the 'voices of authority' Wilchins urges that:

the APA has their *own* disorder – GenderPathoPhilia – which we define as 'an abnormal need or desire to pathologise any gender behaviour which makes you uncomfortable'. (Wilchins, 1996)

The electronic message places the issue of trans identity in a broad context where the complex negotiations between self and culture take place. As a result of the combined effort of activist groups like Transexual Menace, It's Time America, Queer Nation, TOPS, Lesbian Avengers and others, APA representatives held an hour-long meeting with demonstrators, discussing their concerns (Wilchins, 1997: 211). This type of activism holds out the hope of transforming a transphobic culture into a more trans friendly culture. It requires that we all examine our own gender identities, which are increasingly complex. Such public proclamations of the freedom to self-identify are paramount in the struggle for gender liberation.

Wilchins's 'discourse interruptus' invites everyone to join the fight against gender oppression and begin to examine our own personal and cultural gender negotiations. In a moving passage she asserts that the fight against gender oppression is not just one more civil rights struggle for one more narrowly defined minority. It is about all of us who are gender queer: diesel dykes and stone butches, leatherqueens and radical fairies, nelly fags, cross-dressers, intersexed, transsexuals, transvestites, transgendered, transgressively gendered, and those of us whose gender expressions are so complex they haven't even been named yet. (Wilchins, 1995: 4)

Wilchins believes that the gender revolution can halt gender-based oppressions that destroy all of us. For Wilchins and other trans activists/theorists fluidity is a cornerstone of gender liberation. As a result, identity is seen as fluid, not fixed; as a rallying point for contesting oppression, rather than an end in and of itself. Wilchins maintains that the gender liberation movement is not just about people murdered because of the way they express sexuality and gender. 'It is also about those who ... kill to preserve the regimes of gender' (Wilchins, 1997: 86–7). The gender movement, s/he argues,

> is also about the seventeen-year-old Midwestern cheerleader whose health is destroyed by anorexia because 'real women' are supposed to be preternaturally thin. It's about the forty-six-year-old Joe Six Pack who wraps his car around a crowded school bus ... because 'real men' are supposed to be heavy drinkers. It's about the unathletic and fat little boy ... attacked by his classmates every day ... It's about two lesbian lovers stalked and killed ... the ageing body succumbing to an unnecessary hysterectomy because certain ... bodies don't matter as much ... it's about the sensitive straight young man repeatedly raped ... in prison because ... he's perceived as genderqueer, genderdifferent, or simply gendervulnerable. (*ibid.*: 87)

Clearly, Wilchins's work as a gender revolutionary interrogates and contests traditional gender categories and imagines a much more complex gender universe.[2] Much of her work articulates how crossing the lines of gender is also crossing the lines of eroticism (*ibid.*: 120). It is at this fatal intersection between gender and sexuality that violence erupts in those so fearful of having their fixed identities shattered. It is also the same intersection that many popular US gender films avoid,[3] while international cinema seems interested in pursuing the relation between gender and sexuality in their gender films.

Using literature/theory as a 'discourse interruptus' in hir powerful 1993 award-winning novel, *Stone Butch Blues*, Leslie Feinberg eloquently interrogates gender categories, challenging readers to examine their own gender. Many students who have read the book report that their eyes have been opened to the horrors of gender oppression and the hope of gender diversity. The novel dramatically explores the horrors of gender prejudice in a wider context that reveals how it is interlocked with racism and classism. In the story Feinberg's main protagonist, Jess, a F2M (a category too small to hold the complexity of Jess's identity) transperson finds hir own voice and subsequently joins the fight for sex and gender liberation. Charting Jess's growing awareness that gender is more complicated than we have been conditioned to believe, we see Jess becoming more comfortable in hir own skin, as s/he falls in love with the drag queen, Ruth. The relationship between Jess and Ruth, beautifully portrayed by Feinberg, expands categories of desire as two transpersons passionately interact with one another, creating yet another galaxy of gender.

A key metaphor in the book is breaking the silence. Feinberg dramatizes how painful silence can be by having Jess's jaw wired shut. Moving from the personal narrative to the public narrative becomes a moment of liberation. After being brutally assaulted by 'white boys pumped up on chemicals' (Feinberg, 1993: 257) Jess's broken and bleeding jaw is wired shut. Recovering from the hate crime under the loving care of Ruth, Jess discovers that 'fear and silence had welded my jaw shut for more of my life than I'd realized' (ibid.: 264). Armed with this new awareness and self-acceptance, Jess reflects on hir former gender bigotry and tries to make amends. Here Feinberg's character becomes aware of perpetrating the horizontal hostility that so often occurs in oppressed groups. S/he apologizes to Frankie, a factory butch Jess long ago abandoned because at the time s/he could not understand Frankie's desire for other butches. When they meet, Jess, whose gender galaxy has expanded with hir desire for Ruth, another transperson, apologizes, admitting hir former bigotry:

> Frankie, I'm sorry. I always thought I was so open minded. But when I came up against my own fears, I tried to separate myself from you. I've done some growing up since then ... You know ... I thought I had it figured out: I'm a butch because I love femmes ... You scared me. I felt like you were taking that away from me. (ibid.: 273).

In a moving scene that explores the complexity of identity and desire, Frankie explains to Jess that he was never able to love himself until he allowed himself to love other butches. At the conclusion of the novel,

Jess, sick to death of silence, speaks out at a gay and lesbian demonstration against violence. Here the novel anticipates the mid to late 1990s coalition between some trans activists and lesbian and gay activists coming together to fight for an end to sex- and gender-based violence and discrimination. In the concluding pages of the novel Jess, who has moved from the private to public sphere, asserts:

> I'm a butch, a he-she. I don't know if the people who hate our guts call us that anymore . . . I know about getting hurt . . . And part of me feels so connected to you all, but I don't know if I'm welcome to join . . . We're getting busted and beaten up. We're dying out here. We need you – but you need us too. (*ibid.*: 296)

In the final moments of the novel Jess remembers the words of a union organizer friend who challenged Jess to 'Imagine a world worth living in, a world worth fighting for' (*ibid.*: 301).

'A world worth fighting for' is what many trans activists are struggling towards. A major nucleus of the US trans movement includes the International Transgender Law and Employment Conference and the political lobby groups It's Time America and GenderPac, along with activist groups like Transexual Menace, Transgender Nation, and growing transmen groups and numerous local and national organizations who are fighting for transgender civil rights. From the drafting of the gender bill of rights, to transgender lobby days at the Capitol in Washington, DC, to documenting violence against transpersons, to demonstrations protesting demeaning stereotypes and the hate crimes and murders of transpersons, the transgender liberation movement is creating a major 'discourse interruptus'. As the movement interrogates prejudice, a space is being created where new identities are erupting simultaneously as old categories are being turned inside out. Still the social order remains deeply inscribed upon our bodies. Nonetheless 'The social order constrains and oppresses people, but at the same time offers them resources to fight against those constraints' (Fisk, 1992: 157).

As a movement towards freedom we must first become aware of the cultural restraints and shackles placed on the body to confine its movement. Only then can we begin to re-imagine gender and desire and self-inscribe our bodies. Next in a movement towards gender freedom we need to influence other bodies. Some of the meanings for the word 'revolution' are to turn over or change movement of the body's orbit. While the term 'body' is used in this context to refer to stars and planets, I believe it also refers to our gendered bodies. As such, the transgender liberation movement is causing a 'wobbling orbit' where a smaller body (trans movement) is exerting a gravitational pull on a larger mass (society), causing the larger mass to change its orbit.

The 1995 International Transgender Law and Employment Conference, founded by long-time trans activist Phyllis Frye, challenged the closed and locked gender universe. This watershed event, reflective of what is happening in the gender world, saw F2Ms challenge the hierarchy of M2Fs in trans organizations. Conference participants vowed to be more inclusive of transmen and transpersons of colour and different classes. The 1995 conference had more international participation and began documenting the struggles transpersons in other countries face. By 1996 the International Transgender Law and Employment Conference in Houston included extensive workshops and presentations by transmen, transpersons of colour, extensive reports on international laws affecting transpersons, updates on states and municipalities adopting protective legislation for transpersons, and a keynote address on the relationship of feminism, race and transgender rights. All said, while there was much more diversity than before, most participants at this point were still white and middle-class transwomen. Much of the push towards inclusion and a recognition of gender variance, sexism, racism and classism is due to the increasing visibility of transmen in the movement. Many transmen who have been involved in feminist, lesbian and/or gay, bi and/or queer politics are bringing their politics with them.

Internationally, the courts are being challenged for legal recognition of transgender rights. While progress is slow, constructed ideas about gender are starting to wobble. In the US backlash initiatives financed by right-wing religious organizations are frequently launched to halt the civil rights initiatives that are proposed or passed in states and municipalities. In spite of these heavily financed attempts to halt civil rights, more states and municipalities are enacting civil rights initiatives for transpersons. Largely as a result of activist groups, the trans movement, as a smaller body, is starting to exert a gravitational pull that is changing the orbit of the larger culture, making it more of a world worth fighting for.

Electronic transgender colonization, transportation and transmutation in popular US and international films

Gender as a primary site where ideological and material realities are organized, based on perceived differences between the sexes, is undergoing a 'crisis of categories'. As gender theorist Marjorie Garber asserts:

> A category crisis is a failure of definitional distinction, a borderline that becomes permeable, permitting border crossings from one apparently distinct category to another. What seems like a binary opposition, a clear choice between opposites that define cultural boundaries, is revealed to be not only a construct but also – more disturbingly – a construct that no longer works to contain and delimit meaning. (Garber, 1992: xiv).

Our old ways of seeing and categorizing simply do not work as transpersons slip across boundaries and borders in gender skins that question monolithic categories of identity. Trans activist writings and struggles for freedom document how courageous gender nonconformists are mapping new terrains, attempting to carve a place to live. Some popular culture productions that place transpersons at the centre of the narrative capture fragments of this historic struggle, but often fall back on oppressive stereotypes that negate the complexities of personal and cultural struggles. Although mainstream US gender films contain liberatory moments, most ultimately reinforce the dominant gender order. This section decodes the role of transpersons in contemporary popular films, contrasting film stereotypes with transpersons' lives.

Identity categories can be liberating both personally and collectively for groups of individuals denied their basic civil and human rights. However, identity categories 'can also be too small to hold us' (Feinberg, 1996: Wilchins, 1997). Identity categories whose borders become narrow and policed confine and inhibit movement. These categories might best be viewed as a beginning in creating dialogue, not an end. The early 1960s conception of a transsexual is vastly different from the late 1990s conception of a transperson. For example, in the early 1960s transsexual identity was pathologized and policed by the psycho-medical establishment. By contrast, in the late 1990s while transgender is a much-contested political category it is also on one level an expanding, not contracting, universe. Brainwashed by gender propaganda from infancy to the grave makes thinking beyond two genders a complicated endeavour. But, as trans activists have observed, perhaps it is a failure of our imagination to think another way (Bornstein, 1996: Pratt, 1996). While there are progressive moments in gender films, many filmic representations of transpersons indicate a failure of imagination. Too often the celluloid trans images are electronically colonized in accordance with dominant gender ideology. Filming through bipolar ideological lenses of the culture often freezes transgender representations, making them one-dimensional and unable to transmute or reflect the vast diversity of the gender galaxy. This is particularly evident in US-made gender films.

'No image dangles in a cultural void' (Petchesky, 1994: 418). Rather, images are part of a complex system of symbols that reference the world around us and within us. In popular gender films, like other films, images frequently work to reinforce the status quo. This is often accomplished by mass-manufacturing traditional gender ideologies and images in the discourse of the film. Occasionally gender films contain revolutionary moments that affirm gender diversity. As image addicts, we are powerfully influenced by the images we receive. Much of our sex, gender and nationalistic identities are drawn from the bodies and discourses of our celluloid heroes and icons. Identity, as we move towards the third millennium, is largely shaped by the media. Film capitalizes on our most primary means of communication, employing visual images that move us deeply. The function of contemporary film is complex. While most popular films entertain us, they are also commodities produced for profit. Therefore vast sums of money are spent on analysing what gender images and discourses the public will purchase.

While representations of transpersons in cinema have long existed, the nature of these depictions changes as society changes. Gender film critic Rebecca Bell-Metereau (1995) in an insightful analysis of drag characters in film argues that the 1930s to 1950s depictions of drag characters as 'harmless asexual matrons' in such films as *Charley's Aunt* have largely disappeared. I must contest that assumption. Rather, I think in US films the asexual drag matron has not only been a staple of gender films but in popular contemporary US blockbuster films from *Tootsie*, to *Mrs. Doubtfire*, to *The Birdcage* the asexual M2F matron is becoming increasingly popular and is being positioned centre stage. The persistence of this gender stereotype in popular US gender films raises several questions. Why do most US gender films deny transpersons their sexual agency? Further, why is the asexual matron stereotype reincarnated, yet again, at this historical juncture when the fight for transgender rights is gaining public attention, even in the midst of a rising police state? And who are these films made for? Finally, what do these filmic images and discourses reveal about ourselves and our culture and the way gender, sexuality, race, class and ethnicity are negotiated, and/or mandated in the US?

Each decade's cultural anxiety and hope about gender is coded frame by frame in the celluloid representations of gender nonconformists. As I suggested earlier, there is a vast difference between most US and international filmic depictions of transpersons. International and independent films appear to be more progressive than their US counterparts. In a similar vein transgender rights in other countries are often far more progressive than in the US. In US gender films the asexual drag matron became a North American icon in Hitchcock's 1960s landmark film *Psycho*. In the film the main character, Norman Bates, a deeply disturbed and sexually repressed young man, drags out as his mother in order to murder women he is attracted to. *Psycho's* popularity created a formulaic stereotype of M2F gender nonconformists as homicidal maniacs 'dressed to kill'. This representation has been much imitated. Hitchcock's psycho-pathological sketch of a man in a dress on a murderous rampage was quickly reincarnated in such popular films as Brian DePalma's 1970s film *Dressed to Kill* and more recently in Jonathan Demme's 1992 Academy Award winning *Silence of the Lambs*. In the late 1960s through the 1970s numerous US films constructed gender ambiguous characters as objects of fear and scorn. This is in stark contrast to international cinematic productions, which during the same time period start to draw more sympathetic portrayals of drag and transpersons in such films as the Canadian *Outrageous*, and the French/Italian production of *La Cage aux Folles*.

One of the first major US popular films to evoke empathy for a drag character is the early 1980s smash hit *Tootsie*. Two other US films released around the time of *Tootsie*, *The World According to Garp* and *Come Back to the 5 & Dime Jimmy Dean*, feature M2F transsexuals. However, neither film achieved the popularity *Tootsie* did. Unlike *Tootsie*, the characters in these productions did not suddenly throw off their 'disguise' and become heterosexual gender conformists. During this time period most popular US gender films pretend that gender nonconformists don't really exist unless they are drag matrons who remove their disguise, or homicidal maniacs dressed to kill, or unhappy transsexuals.

As we approach the century's end popular gender films are flourishing. Most US films operate on dual levels, transmitting seemingly contradictory messages that offer something for everyone, guaranteeing large audiences. Film as cultural story-telling portrays subjects the culture wants to see. 'Stories have their time' and in order for them to flourish there must be audiences interested and waiting to hear them (Plummer, 1996: 36, 41). What are the current filmic stories about the gender-ambiguous body? The extreme popularity of recent gender films indicates a wide audience. But how audiences read the films is varied. Of interest here are progressive film moments in such films as *Priscilla, Queen of the Desert* and *Just Like a Woman* when the trans voice is heard and the political struggle for existence is revealed. In *To Tu Wong Fu with Love, Julie Newmar* several strengths of the film are its success in making the transphobic/homophobic sheriff Dollard look foolish and the filmic deconstruction of gender categories. These filmic representations function as 'discourse interruptus' and 'discourse eruptions', as silenced voices break into speech and new gender galaxies erupt. However, an overwhelming number of popular US films still feature transpersons for comic relief and/or as villains in sci fi/horror. In these genres the trans voice is absent and/or drowned out and the trans body is publicly humiliated and battered.

Two 1994 films that illustrate the transphobia implicit in many popular US films are the blockbuster hits *Ace Ventura, Pet Detective* and *Stargate*. Both films function on one level as the US response to the popular and award-winning 1992 Irish/UK film *The Crying Game*. In Neil Jordan's complex film about oppression and resistance, the IRA, sex and gender, Fergus, an IRA member, falls in love with Dil, a transwoman. The film explores the multiple emotions involved when Fergus discovers Dil is a woman with a penis. In the film's most talked-about moment when Fergus sees Dil's penis he freaks out and hits hir and then runs to the bathroom to throw up. The revelation that Dil has a penis also caused some audience members in cinemas across the US to exit.

Fergus does recover from the initial shock and ultimately takes the murder rap for Dil, who has killed his former lover and IRA associate, Jude. While the film resorts to the stereotype of transwomen as killers of women, overall the character of Dil, played by Jaye Davidson, is sympathetically drawn and represents a paradigm shift in how transpersons are depicted. Much of the film's message confirms that transpersons deserve of love and respect.

If *The Crying Game* expands the galaxies of gender and desire, the US response to the film *Ace Ventura, Pet Detective* contracts the known gender universe. In one of the most memorable and blatantly transphobic/homophobic scenes in the film, Ace Ventura, played by Jim Carey, upon discovering that the sexy female, Lieutenant Einhorn, who kissed him, is a M2F transperson, rushes into the bathroom where he loudly retches to the theme song of *The Crying Game*, sung by Boy George. Later he humiliates Einhorn in front of the police force, brutally disrobing hir to reveal s/he has a penis. Once again 'The

Crying Game' plays, acting as a cue for the police force to loudly and dramatically vomit in response to finding Einhorn is a transperson. The gender ideology transmitted here is that transpersons make us sick and it is OK to publicly humiliate and assault them. Unfortunately, vast audiences across the US responded to this scene with laughter. At the film's end Ace, now a hero, returns the animal mascot Einhorn stole to the football team. This act enshrines masculinity as a US institution, free of the threat of gender and sex variance. The trans voice in the film is drowned out.

The punishment of trans bodies is carried even further in the US film *Stargate*. Here Jaye Davidson, fresh from playing Dil in *The Crying Game*, plays the evil and extremely gender ambiguous Egyptian sun god, Ra, who enslaves persons on another planet. In response the US military moves in and literally nukes Ra/Davidson. Masculinity triumphs. Bipolar gender roles are restored and heterosexuality is valorized. Both of these films portray transpersons as dangerously malevolent, and deserving of humiliation, scorn, assault, incarceration and finally nuclear annihilation. This homicidal impulse ignited by transphobia and directed against a mixed-blood gender ambiguous body speaks volumes about US attitudes towards difference. On one level just having trans images in the media pool of images at least acknowledges transpersons exist. But, on another level, these negative portrayals 'participate in a continuum of prejudicial social policy and actual violence against disempowered people, placing the very body of the accused in jeopardy' (Shohat and Stam, 1996: 183).

Perhaps the predominance of matrons in drag in US gender films may be that they are less erotically threatening to mainstream US audiences' sense of identity. The asexual matron played by Robin Williams in the wildly successful film *Mrs. Doubtfire* concerns an estranged husband who drags out as an elderly nanny in order to be close to his children and wife. Like Tootsie, his 'disguise' is ultimately revealed and Mrs. Doubtfire is publicly unmasked and humiliated. Beneath the mask, the audience is assured, is a 'proper' gender identity and sexuality. The world is safe from the 'transgender menace'. In all fairness the film does have a few saving moments, particularly when Mrs Doubtfire speaks out about tolerance for 'different families' and 'difference' on her children's television show. But, overall, US gender films have a long way to go.

In the mid- to late 1990s global celluloid saturation of transgender images still primarily concentrates on M2F transpersons. With few exceptions, the existence of F2Ms is largely ignored. One notable exception is *The Ballad of Little Jo*, a film, drawn from several true stories, that places Josephine (Jo) living as a man in the late 1860s in the West at the centre of the cinematic discourse. Issues of homophobia, race and class are raised as Jo becomes erotically involved with a Chinese man s/he has hired to help hir. The film did poorly in cinemas, but seems to be gathering an audience through video rentals. A more negative portrayal of a transman, billed as comedy, *It's Pat* also failed at cinemas and was released in video. The lack of transmen in popular films may be a reflection of how until recently M2Fs have been far more visible in the public arena and at the forefront of the transgender liberation movement. Now as more F2Ms emerge publicly as strong voices in the gender movement, several films are in production that have an F2M protagonist. Here film can function as a historical guidepost. Both films, one an independent and one directed by a well known actress, draw from the life of Brandon Teena, a young transman who was brutally raped and murdered because he was a transperson. The gender community, savvy to the impact of representations, has expressed concern about how Teena will be portrayed to both directors. In addition there are rumours that Feinberg's book *Stone Butch Blues* will also be made into a film. Who these films will be made for and how the major characters are portrayed will certainly be a measure of current cultural gender attitudes. Overall, popular international cinematic representations of transpersons are more progressive than most popular US productions in that trans persons are drawn as more serious characters, meaning that audiences can identify with them. As audiences we can position ourselves in a new dimension of drag spectatorship. Most new international productions also avoid the mocking of gender diversity and punishment for gender difference that many US films ritually indulge in. The difference between US and international gender films becomes apparent if we contrast two recently released films: the Australian-made *Priscilla, Queen of the Desert* and the US-made *To Tu Wong Fu with Love, Julie Newmar*. Each film focuses on three M2F transpersons *en route* to physical and psychological destinations. The metaphor of a road trip provides a filmic space where the characters experience transformation as well as a sense that they are being transported to freedom. Vehicles of transportation, particularly buses, have historically symbolized liberation movements such as the Rosa Parks bus ride that helped ignite the civil rights movement, and Ken Kesey's 'Merry Prankster' bus, which symbolized the counter-culture's revisioning of the US, as well as Thelma and Louise's feminist ride to freedom in the Thunderbird.

Examining the cinematic road trips in the two films allows us to explore on symbolic levels where transpersons are travelling, personally and culturally. In other words, how is the trans image cinematically colonized? What spaces do transpersons occupy in the film? Using the metaphor of transportation, where are transpersons going? And finally how does the trans image transmute; how has the trans image changed in film? Though the modes of transportation range from the pink bus in *Priscilla* to the classic Cadillac convertible in *To Tu Wong Fu*, both vehicles experience a breakdown in rural areas, providing a filmic space that reveals transpersons interacting with each other, the local towns-people, and themselves.

Travelling in the fabulous pink bus through the outback, the Australian film *Priscilla, Queen of the Desert* explores the complexities of three transpersons *en route* to give a drag performance. While much of the film focuses on Tick, a TG/drag queen, coming to terms with hir role of being a father, as well as coming to terms with hir own desires, the film explores the life of the other characters as well. Bernadette, a M2F transsexual, explores a relationship with a man, while Adam the young drag queen encounters violence and hatred because of hir identity. Flashbacks in the film – revealing how Bernadette always wanted to be a girl, how Adam was molested by his uncle, and how Tick freaked out when hir son was born – serve to flesh out the characters, making it easier for audiences to identify with them. The Australian film triumphs in confirming that a drag queen, a transsexual and a transperson can form lasting bonds of friendship and support. Such a depiction is crucial at this historical juncture in the gender movement when, weary from battle, sometimes the thin borders of identity create horizontal hostilities directed against one another, instead of the real oppressors. This happens to all oppressed groups. By far one of the most positive messages in the film is that if Tick's son should grow up to be a transperson, so what! In a galaxy of at least 50 billion genders the expression of gender freedom is unlimited. Another break-through message in *Priscilla* and other international films such as *Just Like a Woman*, a British film released in 1992, is that transpersons are also sexual beings, with desires and the right to express them. *Just Like a Woman* portrays a M2F transperson's relationship with an older woman who is turned on by the protagonist's trans self. In the course of the film Monica begins to rethink her own sex and gender universe as they revel in each other's company. Many M2F's report that they found aspects of the film to be extremely erotic, particularly because Monica accepts Gerald/Geraldine, her M2F lover, as s/he really is. In neither film are the trans characters neutered or confined to the sanitized domain of asexual drag matrons. In *Priscilla* Bernadette and Bob become lovers. Additionally, Tick, at peace finally with hir identity in the film, starts to pursue hir desire for Adam, which appears to be mutual. Tick's son helps foster this as he casually asks his father whether s/he will have a boyfriend and indicates he hopes so.

Unfortunately, *Priscilla* also expresses some regressive and repressive moments that centre on racism and misogyny. Two scenes are problematic as Bob's Asian wife is portrayed in a stereotypical manner as an exotic exhibitionist prostitute, unworthy of him. Another problematic scene occurs when Bernadette, insulted by an older butch woman in a bar, drinks her under the table and tells her to light her tampon before inserting it, a put-down applauded not only by the bar patrons in the film but also cinema audiences. These scenes are all the more problematic in that the film confronts in a sympathetic manner the horrors and dangers of transphobia, specifically when Adam/Felicia is threatened with rape and the bus is covered with transphobic and homophobic graffiti. Are such stereotypical depictions in an otherwise ground-breaking film merely devices designed to make audiences feel more comfortable by retaining familiar prejudices? Or do they mimic the dangerous, hostile and often fatal formulaic interactions between transwomen and females that have sold popular films since *Psycho?* Ultimately, *Priscilla*, with the few exceptions mentioned above, is about liberation, becoming comfortable in your own skin and exploring the galaxies of gender. Is it any wonder that many of us want to enter the pink bus of gender and ride?

The popular US-made film *To Tu Wong Fu with Love, Julie Newmar*, directed by Beeban Kidron, and released shortly after *Priscilla*, provides an antidote for the formulaic portrayal of transwomen and females as deadly rivals, an idea which unfortunately is still being propagated by persons clinging to the idea of essentialist identities. Some of the more touching aspects of the film are the growing friendship/love and respect between Ms Vida and Carol Anne. In a memorable scene Ms Vida punches out Carol Anne's hideously abusive husband, Virgil, commenting 'that sometimes women need to hit back'. Sisterhood can be powerful!

To Tu Wong Fu, like most US gender films, contains contradictory messages. The film narrative on one level represents a flimsy attempt at multiculturalism. The story evolves as two drag queens, Ms Vida, a white upper-class TG drag queen and Ms Noxema, a black drag queen, tie for first prize in a local drag competition. Their prize is a trip to a national drag competition. Ms Vida and Ms Noxema trade in their plane tickets for a 1967 Cadillac convertible, so they can take Chi Chi, a young Latina working-class drag queen Ms Vida has taken pity on, with them on their cross-country trek. The film borrows images from *Thelma and Louise*, *Cinderella* and *Sleeping Beauty* to construct the queens' femme identities. On a lonely highway, the bigoted small-town sheriff Dollard pulls the car over and tells Vida he does not go for white girls 'riding with niggers and spics' and then attempts to fondle her. In a scene reminiscent of *Thelma and Louise*, Ms Vida shoves the racist trans/homophobic representative of the law away. Dollard lands on the asphalt. Thinking s/he has killed him, the trio flee, only to break down in a small town where Virgil, the town mechanic, has to order a part for their car. Meanwhile, Dollard recovers and finds Vida's size 10½ plastic slipper, reminiscent of Cinderella's glass slipper, and dedicates himself to finding 'the pervert' who lost it. Throughout the trip Chi Chi is coached on how to be a 'drag queen' by Ms Vida and Ms Noxema. Interspersed throughout the film are numerous racist references about Chi Chi running across the border, which many US audiences found amusing. With a little fabric, the three queens transform the drab town and its inhabitants. The use of wild and beautiful drag costumes in popular gender films may have a dual purpose. As feminist cultural critic Kaja Silverman perceives:

> clothing not only draws the body so that it can be seen, but maps out the shape of the ego, then every transformation within a society's vestimentary code implies some kind of shift within its ways of articulating subjectivity. (Silverman, 1994: 86)

Transpersons in *To Tu Wong Fu* and other gender films have emerged as subjects of filmic discourse. The use of imaginative clothing in *To Tu Wong Fu* functions as a challenge not only to dominant values, but also destabilizes gender and class. In one of the film's most liberating moments the bumbling sheriff Dollard roars into town with a bullhorn demanding that the drag queen that lost the shoe come out. A shrouded red bride appears on the empty streets. Audiences are set up to believe it is Vida. Even Carol Anne's daughter comments it's Ms Vida. However, the veil is dramatically raised to reveal it is Carol Anne who tells the sheriff, 'I believe that shoe is mine.' Inspired by Carol Anne's performance, one by one the entire town turns out, each proclaiming to be a drag queen and demanding that the now thoroughly confused Dollard give the shoe back. The entire town has come out in support of

Vida, Noxema and Chi Chi. In doing so, the category of drag queen has been skilfully deconstructed.

Such moments remind us of the potential of gender expression in all of us. At the conclusion of the film the outcasts are not the drag queens, who have been fully embraced by the community. Rather, it is the bigoted sheriff Dollard and the wife-abusing Virgil that the town has rejected. But although the film enlarges gender categories and explores transphobia, homophobia and sexism on some levels, it perpetuates racism. Although Chi Chi and Vida become deeply attached to Billy Ray and Carol Anne, respectively, they are prohibited from any erotic expression.

After decorating the entire town for the strawberry festival, Vida, Noxema and Chi Chi retire to a balcony like the three fairies in *Sleeping Beauty*, resigned to spreading their magic over the town's heterosexuals who have come to dance. Herein lie some of the problems. In most US films transpersons are tabooed from acting on their erotic desires. Their filmic position as asexual or celibate may be because trans desire is perceived as too threatening at this juncture for mainstream US audiences.[3] Certainly gender films like *The Birdcage* continue such censoring by never allowing a screen kiss to pass between the long-time couple Albert and Armand. *Birdcage* also constructs a right-wing senator as a sympathetic character in drag, dancing to the song 'We Are Family'. I don't think so. Even if the intent is to call attention to the horrors of prejudice, both US films ultimately reinforce racism. Not surprisingly, in both films the majority of the racist comments are directed towards Latina and Mexican queens. Clearly this mirrors US cultural anxiety that has inspired restrictive legislation passed in regard to borders and immigration. In *To Tu Wong Fu* Chi Chi is groomed by Ms Vida and to a lesser extent by Ms Noxema to assimilate into white ideas of beauty and behaviour. Ultimately, she wins the national drag queen competition looking like a white ingenue at a prom. Everything about her ethnicity has been whited out. And for this she is rewarded with the drag queen crown.

Although both *Priscilla* and *To Tu Wong Fu* are problematic, the films do transmit positive messages about where transpersons are going. Each production shows the characters becoming self-accepting and being accepted by the larger society. The objects of scorn in the films are not transpersons, but the bigoted transphobes who are made to look like fools. Additionally, transpersons are represented as being able to stand up for themselves and each other. While international cinema is more adept at dealing with the complexity of how gender and desire are negotiated, some US-made films and popular culture artefacts are starting to chart this course. Two weekly episodes of *Third Rock from the Sun*, a popular US television sitcom whose protagonists are aliens living in earth bodies, have focused on transpersons. Recently one of the major characters, Sally, was dumped by her gay boyfriend when he found out she was not a transperson. One of the subtexts is that transpersons are desirable and worthy of love and respect. Kate More[4] asked how would these visual depictions of transpersons be looked at in 30 years? Will we see them as historical (though fictionalized) markers – as visual records of private and public gender struggles? Or will we look back at these cultural depictions of transpersons in the electronic media the way we look at the media's historical treatment of women and persons of colour?

The gender revolution still has a long way to go. And the disparities between filmic representations and trans lives can be great. Trans activist Nancy Sharp was fired from the job she[5] held for many years by a transphobic boss who told her she was 'disgusting' for being a transperson. Later that day she saw her boss in a cinema viewing a gender film. She was horrified to see him laughing and enjoying the film. His response prompted Ms Sharp to ask if 'the recent explosion of images of gender nonconformity in the popular media' could be 'potentially harmful and exploitative?' She believes that the cinema is a safe place for those with gender anxiety to interact with 'those people' they are both attracted to and repulsed by – who in reality they want to distance themselves from (Sharp, 1996). Since film helps shape our identities and desires and can express our personal and cultural hopes and fears, it is crucial that more questions be asked about how gender films affect various audiences' perceptions of transpersons and their own identities.

At best film can be visionary. Perhaps one of the most inspiring moments in gender cinema occurs in *Priscilla* when Bernadette, Tick/Mitzi and Adam/Felicia climb the mountain in full drag make-up, feathers, sequins and hiking boots. Atop the mountain Bernadette, dazzled by the breathtaking view of land and sky, says 'Well we did it ... it never ends, all that space.' As gender stories move from the private and personal to the public in the gender liberation movement and popular culture a dimensional window is being opened giving us a glimpse of gender complexity. As we move towards the twenty-first century guided by the brave actions and words of trans activists, the images in popular culture affected by the culture around it will continue to transmute. All social movements for change necessitate a 'discourse interruptus' of the prevailing discourse and an emergence of voice like a battle cry, a 'discourse eruption' aware that 'gender becomes implicated in the conception and construction of power itself' (Scott, 1994: 45). Hopefully the increasing levels of discourse interruptus of the dominant gender code in trans writing, activism and popular film will reveal, as Kate Bornstein has observed, that 'there are as many types of gender . . . as could be imagined' (Bornstein, 1994: 30). A recent discovery in our own galaxy of a giant star, hidden by dust clouds, that reportedly has the energy of 10 million suns and is almost 200 million miles across reveals that our vision is being expanded. As we enter the next millennium embracing complexity with all of its ambiguities we will continue to discover forces hiding in our own gender galaxies. Perhaps we have only approached the first few dimensions of gender. As of yet, it may be impossible to fully visualize gender galaxies beyond our own. But we are getting glimpses.

Notes

1. *Acknowledgement: A politics of location.* I came of age during the sexual revolution and hope to help usher in the gender revolution. As a 'Louie', thinly veiled as an academic, I entered the gender community as an ally. In the early 1980s I co-founded the Albuquerque Cross-dresser and Transgender Support Group and the first local TG phone line. From the waist up I appear femme and from the waist down I appear butch. My gender presentation signifies my identity and desires, both of which I view as in a constant state of negotiation personally and culturally. And while I question locked-in categories of identity, I also strategically evoke them as sites of personal and cultural struggles and as potential launch sites of freedom. At this specific moment I define as a New Mexico desert rat, gender activist, feminist rebuking sexism, a bisexual rebuking heterosexism, and a person hovering on the trans cusp rebuking transphobia. My first attempt at shifting gender was at age five when I cut off my long braids and handed them to my mother. I believed short hair and my grey corduroy jeans and a plaid flannel shirt would transport me from the restrictive girl world into what I perceived as the freer boy world. I spent all afternoon on a swing singing over and over the words 'I'm a boy, I'm a boy.' I spent most of my high school years drag racing in my '57 Chevy, beating every male that challenged me. The journey into matter took me 25 years to conclude that I'm not totally a man or a woman, but a 'Louie' who travels through centuries of gender fabrics tunnelling through gender wormholes seeking dimensional windows. This work continues some of the ideas I first articulated in the late 1980s and early 1990s in Transgender Nation, in which I posited that identity is always in motion based on sociohistorical influences and personal and cultural negotiations. Part of my

goal is to deconstruct rigid gender and sex categorizations and the bigotry they inspire. Since the early 1980s I have been involved with the local, national, and to a lesser extent the international trans community. It is the place I feel most at home in, the community I am deeply indebted and committed to.

2. The use of inconsistent pronouns to refer to Ricki Anne Wilchins is due to her request that I 'scramble them'.

3. There are two notable exceptions. *Stonewall*, a powerful film about the role of transpersons at Stonewall, depicts the major protagonist as a transperson fully deserving to be loved and to love. The film is a collaborative UK and US effort. The 1997 film *Midnight in the Garden of Good and Evil* (a US production) also does a positive portrayal of the transperson Lady Chablis. However, in the film, even though s/he is clearly a sexual being, her own desire is sublimated to the white hetero couple.

4. In debate with the author (not referring to *Third Rock from the Sun*), Kate More wrote, 'Why for instance are today's films exciting, when e.g. the transvestite film-maker Ed Wood's *Glen or Glenda?* is perceived as laughable – are we going to be laughed at in thirty years' time for arguing that men go bald because they wear tight hats? Or is this a definite shift that puts us at the forefront of thinking? Will our chaos theory be forgotten for another 200 years? What of the radical drag movement after Stonewall/ with GLF? Why do we laugh at photos from then? Is it just the awful fashions, or are we so reactionary that we can't cope with moustached virility in a frock?'

5. Nancy Sharp requested that I use feminine pronouns when I refer to her.

References

Bell-Metereau, R. (1985) *Hollywood Androgyny*. New York: Columbia University Press.

Bornstein, K. (1994) *Gender Outlaw: On Men, Women and the Rest of Us*. New York: Routledge.

Bornstein, K. (1996) 'ABC's of Gender' panel at the Outwriters Conference.

Briggs, J. and D. Peat (1989) *Turbulent Mirror: An Illustrated Guide to Chaos Theory and the Science of Wholeness*. New York: Harper & Row.

Butler, J. (1993) *Bodies That Matter: On the Discursive Limits of Sex*. New York: Routledge.

Feinberg, L. (1993) *Stone Butch Blues*. New York: Firebrand Books.

Feinberg, L. (1996) 'ABC's of Gender' panel at the Outwriters Conference.

Fisk, J. (1992) 'Cultural studies and the culture of everyday life'. In L. Grossberg *et al.* (eds), *Cultural Studies*, New York: Routledge.

Garber, M. (1992) *Vested Interests: Cross-dressing and Cultural Anxiety*. New York: Routledge.

hooks, b. (1989) *Talking Back: Thinking Feminist, Thinking Black*. Boston: Southend Press.

Olalquiaga, C. (1992) *Megalopolis: Contemporary Cultural Sensibilities*. Minneapolis: University of Minnesota Press.

Petchesky, R. (1994) 'The power of visual culture'. In *Theorizing Feminism: Parallel Trends in the Humanities and Social Sciences*. Boulder, CO: Westview Press.

Plummer, K. (1996) 'Intimate citizenship and the culture of story telling'. In J. Weeks and J. Holland (eds), *Sexual Cultures: Communities, Values and Intimacy*. New York: St. Martin's Press.

Pratt, M.B. (1996) 'ABC's of Gender' panel at the Outwriters Conference.

Scott, J. (1994) 'Deconstructing equality versus difference; or, the uses of poststructuralist theory for feminism'. In *Theorizing Feminism: Parallel Trends in the Humanities and Social Sciences*. Boulder, CO: Westview Press.

Sharp, N. (1996) Personal correspondence.

Shohat, E. and R. Stam (1994) *Unthinking Eurocentrism: Multiculturalism and the Media*. New York: Routledge.

Silverman, K. (1994) 'Fragments of a fashionable discourse'. In *Theorizing Feminism: Parallel Trends in the Humanities and Social Sciences*. Boulder, CO: Westview Press.

Wilchins, R.A. (1995) 'Political activism against gender oppression', *In Your Face: Transexual Menace Newsletter* (Spring).

Wilchins, R.A. (1996) e-mail posted on *Transexual Menace*.

Wilchins, R.A. (1997) *Read My Lips: Sexual Subversion and the End of Gender*. New York. Firebrand Books.

11

What Does a Transsexual Want? The Encounter between Psychoanalysis and Transsexualism

Diane Morgan

B ack in the 1970s and early 1980s Freud's question 'What does a woman want?' was interpreted by some feminists, notably Kate Millett, as proof of his inability to understand a woman's needs. His refusal to hear how women were articulating their wishes was taken to illustrate further the patriarchal resilience of the psychoanalytical institution. A deaf ear was being turned towards the demanding voices of the woman while the law was being laid down elsewhere (in the form of castration and subsequent penis envy). The woman was mystified, turned into an enigmatic conundrum as a way of avoiding, thereby perpetuating, real political issues of (s)exploitation and discrimination. By way of contrast, Freud's question was understood by other feminists, notably by Juliet Mitchell, Jacqueline Rose and Sarah Kofman, to be open-ended, liberating, as evidence of the non-deterministic – descriptive rather than prescriptive – advantages of psychoanalysis for feminism.

The traditional complaints made against Freud are too well known: he is seen as defining female sexuality as inferior to male sexuality – the clitoris is a shrivelled-up version of the penis; as perpetuating the myth of female castration – the girl is represented as having to come to terms with the *fact* of her castrated state (Freud, 1977: 321 and 376); he is presented as subjugating women to male authority and its institutions – the girl has to give up her illusions of ever being able to become a boy, relinquish her hold on the pleasurable clitoris and resign herself to vaginal procreation. His theories are seen as determining women *biologically* and as slanted according to his male prejudices – that is, his starting point is that the girl envies the boy his 'far superior equipment' (Freud, 1991: 160). Psychoanalysis works with and for society by providing it with *normative* prescriptions about how women should be and must become.

What this account leaves out, so the counter-argument ran, is that psychoanalysis, rather than confirming society's assumptions, actually unsettles its certainties by revealing the sickness and pain at the centre of so-called civilization. It searches out the victims of the normalizing processes of repression and allows that grief to be enunciated. Instead of ideologically supporting the system, it focuses in on where that system breaks down. As Jacqueline Rose says in her essay 'Femininity and Its Discontents':

> What distinguishes psychoanalysis from sociological accounts of gender ... is that whereas for the latter, the internalisation of norms is assumed roughly to work, the basic premise and indeed starting point of psychoanalysis is that it does not. The unconscious constantly reveals the 'failure' of identity. Because there is no continuity of psychic life, so there is no stability of sexual identity, no position for women (or for men) which is ever simply achieved. Nor does psychoanalysis see such 'failure' as a special-case inability or an individual deviancy from the norm ... Instead failure is something endlessly repeated and relived moment by moment throughout our individual histories. It appears not only in the symptom, but also in dreams, in slips of the tongue and in sexual pleasures which are pushed to the sidelines of the norm. (Rose, 1986: 90–1)

There is a psychopathology of everyday life; symptoms are not at all seen as just the domain of stubborn and sick women, branded as hysterical because they will not fit into a society considered ideal, because it favours male domination.

At the end of the 1925 essay 'Some Psychical Consequences of the Anatomical Distinction Between the Sexes', Freud concludes:

> all human individuals, as a result of their bisexual disposition and of cross-inheritance, combine in themselves both masculine and feminine characteristics, so that pure masculinity and femininity remain theoretical constructions of uncertain content. (Freud, 1977: 342)

Psychoanalysis can be seen as undermining essentialist theories of sexuality (based on the assumptions that men and women are binary opposites, that one can be designated as known qualities, whose nature are obvious to the eye) and this allows psychoanalysis to be presented as a theory and practice that give an account of patriarchy and the exorbitant demands it places on individuals, both women and men.

Gender is regarded as a social construct – not as a biological given, forever there and determined. In the 1933 'Femininity' paper, Freud warns us of the misleading preconceptions we tend to have about the self-evident and absolute nature of sexual identity. I quote at length:

> When you meet a human being, the first distinction you make is 'male or female?' and you are accustomed to make the distinction with unhesitating certainty. Anatomical science shares your certainty at one point and not much further. The male sexual product, the spermatozoon, and its vehicle are male; the ovum and the organism that harbours it are female. In both sexes organs have been formed which serve exclusively for the sexual functions; they were probably developed from the same [innate] disposition into two different forms. Besides this, in both sexes the other organs, the bodily shapes and tissues, show the influence of the individual's sex, but this is inconstant and its amount variable; these are what are known as the secondary sexual characters. Science next tells you something that runs counter to your expectations and is probably calculated to confuse your feelings. It draws your attention to the fact that portions of the male sexual apparatus also appear in women's bodies, though in an atrophied state, and vice versa in the alternative case. It regards their occurrence as indications of *bisexuality*, as though an individual is not a man or a woman but always both – merely a certain amount more the one than the other. You will then be asked to make yourselves familiar with the idea that the proportion in which masculine and feminine are mixed in an individual is subject to quite considerable fluctuations. Since, however, apart from the very rarest cases, only one kind of sexual product – ova or semen – is nevertheless present in one person, you are bound to have doubts as to the decisive significance of those elements and must conclude that what constitutes masculinity or femininity is an unknown characteristic which anatomy cannot lay hold of. (Freud, 1991: 146–7)

Although Freud is not willing to leave the final word on sexual difference to science, he is content to use its findings – in Kofman's words – 'to shatter the pseudo-certainties of popular opinion' (Kofman, 1985: 112). Sexual identity does not meet the eye and instead of masculinity and femininity being considered as discrete categories, he makes use of scientific research to reveal a sliding scale of difference: the difference between the male and the female is one of dosage, 'a certain amount of one more than the other', it is quantitative rather than qualitative.[1] As Kofman puts it:

> Anatomical science . . . makes it possible to question popular opinion, the immediate certainty of a decisive opposition between the sexes: because the science of anatomy mixes up sexes and genres, it is troubling (*parce qu'elle mêle les sexes et les genres, elle trouble*) . . . (*ibid.*: 110)

Here it is anatomy that troubles gender rather than the gender troubling assumptions about sex.[2] However Freud proclaimed himself unwilling to pursue this line of research and laid out his position very clearly in a letter to Carl Müller-Braunschweig written in 1935:

> I object to all of you (Horney, Jones, Rado etc.) to the extent that you do not distinguish more clearly and cleanly between what is psychic and what is biological, that you try to establish a neat parallelism between the two and that you, motivated by such intent, unthinkingly construe psychic facts which are unprovable and that you, in the process of so doing, must declare as reactive or regressive much that without doubt is primary. Of course, these reproaches must remain obscure. In addition, I would only like to emphasise that we must keep psychoanalysis separate from biology just as we have kept it separate from anatomy and physiology. (quoted in Mitchell, 1975: 130–1)

Freud is right to call his reproaches to his errant disciples 'obscure', not immediately understandable, as fifteen years previously, in a sequence of footnotes added to the 1905 'Three Essays on Sexuality', Freud was indeed evidently intrigued by the revolutionary experiments taking place in the realm of biology. Despite being sceptical about their long-term significance, he describes the work of Steinach, who carried out pioneering research into the organic determinants of 'homo-erotism and sexual characters in general' (Freud, 1977: 58):[3]

By carrying out experimental castration and subsequently grafting sex-glands of the opposite sex, it was possible in the case of various species of mammals to transform a male into a female and vice versa. The transformation affected more or less completely both the somatic sexual characters and the psychosexual attitude (that is, both subject and object erotism). . . . In one case this transformation of sex was actually effected in a man who had lost his testes owing to tuberculosis. In his sexual life he behaved in a feminine manner, as a passive homosexual, and exhibited very clearly-marked feminine sexual characters of a secondary kind (e.g. in regard to growth of hair and beard and deposits of fat on the breasts and hips). After an undescended testis from another male patient had been grafted into him, he began to behave in a masculine manner and to direct his libido towards women in a normal way. Simultaneously his somatic feminine characters disappeared. (*ibid.*: 58–9)

Freud closes this 1920 footnote with the following reassurance, but also warning, to his readers:

It would be unjustifiable to assert that these interesting experiments put the theory of inversion on a new basis, and it would be hasty to expect them to offer a universal means of 'curing' homosexuality. Fliess has rightly insisted that these experimental findings do not invalidate the theory of the general bisexual disposition of the higher animals. On the contrary, it seems to me probable that further research of a similar kind will produce a direct confirmation of this presumption of bisexuality. (*ibid.*: 59)

Five years earlier, in 1915, Freud had also made clear that psycho-analysis was not at all interested in criminalizing homosexuals in 'separating [them] off. . . from the rest of mankind as a group of a special character' and subsequently felt the need in effect to distance himself and his movement from eugenicist crusades to forcibly correct imagined inversions of nature through surgical intervention (*ibid.*: 56).[4] However, this research is still compelling in its implications and does force us to question how far the body impinges upon the psyche orientating us sexually and behaviourally.

In the 1904 text of the 'Three Essays', before such research had been carried out, Freud was far more confident that psychoanalysis need not concern itself with such scientific speculation. Interestingly for us the case in question appears to be one of transsexuality *avant la lettre* in spite of the fact that Freud reads it as one of bisexuality:

The theory of bisexuality has been expressed in its crudest form by a spokesman of the male inverts: 'a feminine brain in a masculine body'. But we are ignorant of what characterises a feminine brain. There is neither need nor justification for replacing the psychological problem by the anatomical. (*ibid*.: 54)[5]

The psyche here, at this early stage, is definitely not to be upstaged by the biological even though, back at the turn of the century, science was not in the position to speculate on the determining characteristics of the feminine brain. Times have changed perhaps: for example, November 1995 saw the long-awaited publication in *Nature* magazine of details of the Swaab trial, the product of eleven years of work by the neurobiologists at the Netherlands Institute of Brain Research (More, 1996: 17). Tests done on the Bed Nucleus of the Stria Terminalis (BSTc) in the brain revealed differences in sizes between gay men, straight men, straight women and male-to-female transsexuals (there were no tests on female-to-male transsexuals, known lesbians or transvestites). For Freud such research was unimaginable until the 1920s when, as we have seen, he heard about the remarkable work done by Steinach on the organic groundings of sexuality. His reaction revealed him to be intrigued by its possibilities but anxious to preserve the specificity of his psychoanalytical movement and already wary of the uses to which such experimentation could be put.

It would seem that Freud backed away from biology and science more decisively in the late 1930s. Whereas in 1933 he was willing to use new evidence from biological research to deconstruct traditional notions of the naturalness of anatomy, by 1935 he was demanding an absolute (a 'clear and clean') separation of his movement from those of anatomy, physiology and biology and he showed no patience with his followers' dalliance with those disciplines. No parallelism or inter-connectedness between those domains and his can be tolerated. The rise of Nazism put an end to any dialogue, the subject became taboo.

The foreclosure of such a debate has had drastic consequence for transsexuals and our understanding of them. Instead of transgendered people being included as victims of Nazi eugenics, they have been presented as the monstrous offspring of that period. In a notorious and influential book, *The Transsexual Empire*, the separatist feminist Janice Raymond tells us that:

The Nazi doctors undertook many of their experiments in the name of science but for the purpose of supposedly gaining racial knowledge (e.g. how did skull measurements differ between Aryans and non-Aryans?). The doctors who treat transsexuals undertake many of their experiments in the name of therapy but for purposes of gaining sexual knowledge (e.g. is it possible to construct a functional vagina in a male body?). What we are witnessing in the transsexual context is a science at the service of a patriarchal ideology of sex-role conformity in the same way that breeding for blond hair and blue eyes became a so-called science at the service of Nordic racial conformity. (Raymond, 1979: 149)

Transsexuals are an insidious tool of the patriarchal system. They infiltrate women's circles and divide women against themselves. Raymond continues:

All transsexuals rape women's bodies by reducing the real female form to an artefact, appropriating this body for themselves. (*ibid.*: 104)

Her book was described by reviewers as being an 'accessible and deeply caring book', 'solid, unflinching and scrupulously fair'. To recap, transsexuals are deceptive parasites. Robin Morgan describes them as 'leeching off women' (*ibid.*: 85) who carry with them a lethal hidden sting. Raymond continues:

Loss of a penis ... does not mean the loss of an ability to penetrate women – women's identities, women's spirits, women's sexuality. As Mary Daly has noted, their whole presence becomes a 'member' invading women's presence to each other and once more producing horizontal violence. (Raymond, 1979: xix; and Millot, 1990: 42)

A male-to-female transsexual undergoes castration so as to become a big, even more powerful 'member': 'their whole presence becomes a "member"'. They lose the penis so as to become the phallus, or – in other (Lacanian) words – they lose the penis so as to become The Woman, 'more woman than all women, immune to castration';[6] this phallic woman represents an idealized and stereotypical view of femininity perpetuated by the media. In these last remarks Raymond is uncannily echoing the psychoanalytical position on transsexuality, despite Freud being one of the many on her hit-list and despite Freud undermining the very essentialism, a pure separatist feminist space, she is trying to preserve intact. This unhappy relationship takes us on to psychoanalysis's treatment of transsexualism.

Whereas Freud's question 'What does a woman want?' polarized feminists according to their understanding of psychoanalysis, our postulated question 'What does a transsexual want?' marks rather the absence of a debate, the failure of an encounter between psychoanalysis and transsexualism. Rather than being positioned as complex enigmas that no speculation can determine, analysts appear to have been all too confident of their assessments of transsexuals. Instead of an open-ended questioning, there has been a refusal to hear and the normative – and often final – judgement is passed on them: 'your anatomy is your destiny, accept it!' Whereas views on homosexuality have evolved, those held on transsexualism have been uncannily consistent.

In Freud's seminal 1911 study of the Schreber case the grounds were laid for future readings of transsexualism. The paranoid delusion of being transformed into a woman by God and His accomplices was the result of Schreber's inability to accept a homosexual attraction (to his father and in continuation to Flechsig). Schreber's phantasy of being humanity's redeemer, it being incumbent upon him to repopulate the world afresh, sprang from his psychosis, which had reduced the world around him to the unreality of 'fleetingly improvised men' leaving him to confront the Godhead head-on, in an unrelenting and totally unmediated fashion (Schreber, 1995: 143). This is what Lacan called Schreber's 'foreclosure of the Name-of-the-Father in the place of the Other' (Lacan, 1980: 215). The patient tries to sustain a dyadic imaginary relation to the God because the shift and displacement that an entry into the symbolic would involve cannot be negotiated. Language literally inscribes itself directly, in its full-blown unmediated violence on the subject's body as he denies its metaphoricity and contingency. He is too absolute in his demand for satisfaction.

The transformation of Schreber into a repressed homosexual was questioned by Ida Macalpine and Richard Hunter, the English translators of the *Memoirs*. This is the Mrs Macalpine who gets a chilling grilling from Lacan in 'On the possible treatment of psychosis' essay. She is peremptorily dismissed as forming one with the 'English diffusionist school' for her insistence on Schreber's birth fantasy as 'primitive' and 'asexual', that is not necessarily to be thought of from within the determining Oedipal structure – a son wanting to give a baby to daddy (Lacan, 1980: 191).[7] Lacan is absolutely resistant to her (their) idea of Schreber's fantasmatic contact with the eternally mutable 'life-substance' and dismisses it outright. In this he was giving a bad imitation of Freud's reaction to the proposition that there exists an 'oceanic feeling', an originary, pre-sexual 'feeling of being one with the external world as a whole'. Freud confessed that he found this idea 'strange' and a 'bad fit' with the psychoanalytical conception of the psyche. However, unlike Lacan, Freud did at least speculate what this bizarre notion might possibly mean for psychoanalysis, how psychoanalysis might reconfigure it into something more comprehensible for its mode of systematization (Freud, 1985: 252–3). As yet unaware of Lacan's scorn, Macalpine and Hunter go on to suggest that Schreber's psychosis was concerned with the origin of life: 'Whence life?'; 'Where do I come from?' (Schreber, 1995: 143). The same far-reaching questions are also asked in the Heine poem, called 'Questions', which Freud partially quotes in the 1933 'Femininity' lecture – however, this time like Lacan, Freud trims its preoccupations down to the question of what a woman is, limiting us once again to Oedipal, sexualized relations and thereby ignoring Heine's preoccupation with insoluble enigma and ambiguous cross-dressing (Freud, 1991: 146).

Battling against the odds, Macalpine and Hunter's is an attempt to win some recognition for the specificity of transsexuals. Their analysis was published in 1955 when the first publicized cases of 'sex change' operations were coming to people's attention (Schreber, 1995: 405). As psychiatrists they apparently felt the need to explain and justify their involvement in these cases, why they were lending their support to their patients' demands for surgical intervention – which others, even from within their discipline such as Charles Socarides, view as 'a sanctioning of the transsexual's pathological view of reality' (Socarides, 1979: 373). The opinion seems to be that if, after careful screening, help is given to transsexuals, if they are helped towards what they think they want, the professional is conniving with their madness, their deformed way of looking at the world. Although there is no question of Macalpine and Hunter suggesting surgery for Schreber – anyway he feels that it is already taking place – they do try to illustrate how they understand Schreber differently from the psychoanalysts and hostile psychiatrists: his so-called 'homosexuality' should be seen as being of a different order from a situation where man *qua* man desires sexual relations with another. In Schreber's case homosexuality arises only inasmuch as his birth sex as male would follow him to his apparently desired designation as woman. But this would not necessarily be a problem if he desired a man as a female – that is regardless of his birth sex s/he would then be heterosexual in orientation. One question which inevitably arises is what does this mean for a heterosexual male-to-female to desire a man *as a woman*? Psychoanalysis answers that this still means that s/he is homosexual (i.e. still a man) and, most disappointingly, the femaleness cashes out for them merely as passive homosexuality (Freud, 1979b: 182). The very equation passivity = female, which Freud repeatedly tried to trouble in essays such as the 1931 'Female Sexuality', comes back in his and other psychoanalytical readings of transsexuality.[8] What Macalpine and Hunter suggest as being of primary concern to Schreber is not his sexual orientation but instead his sexual identity *per se*: what is he, male or female?[9]

Lacan reads transsexuality as a psychosis. It is an inability to enter the symbolic, to take up a series of positions within the symbolic realm of language. Instead of asking 'What am I, male or female?' the question should run as follows:

> 'What am I there?', concerning his sex and his contingency in being, namely that, on the one hand, he is a man or a woman, and, on the other, that he might not be, the two conjugating their mystery, and binding it in the symbols of procreation and death. (Lacan, 1980: 194)

For this analysis transsexuals are not flexible enough; they refuse the contingency of sexual difference and obstinately stick to their story about being essentially one or the other or masochistically plague themselves with their indecision. Lacan makes the influential statement that transsexuals attempt to circumvent the FACT of castration – whether in the form of a *fait accompli* or as a threat – and gain quick access to the phallus. The male-to-female, for example, undergoes castration to avoid its threat, aims to be the Father's object of desire so as to steal the phallus from him and maybe even venture back the way he came; the female-to-male still refuses to believe that she is lacking and battles on in her impossible quest to compete directly with the Father and usurp his authority. Lacan associates these formulations of transsexual desire as the abolition of sexual difference:

> one is condemned to lacking both (sexes) when, in the hope of reaching them more easily, one wishes to ignore the symbolic articulation that Freud discovered the same time as the unconscious ... (*ibid.*: 191).

Macalpine and Hunter, the former ridiculed by Lacan, the latter suppressed completely, persist in their differing analysis. Far from denying sexual difference, Schreber is seen rather bewilderingly to belong to both sexes *as well as* to neither. They explain:

He was as much both (sexes) as he was neither. Thus he says 'that I have to imagine myself as man and woman in one person having intercourse with myself' and 'playing the woman's part in sexual embrace with myself'. (Schreber, 1995: 402)[10]

The mastermind engineering these scenarios is akin to the ghostly third person, the listener, described in 'A Case of Paranoia running counter to the psychoanalytical theory of the Disease' (Freud, 1979a).[11] For Macalpine and Hunter, psychoanalysts are unable to read this complexity in the case of transsexuals as they are too blinded by their 'adherence to the doctrine of libidinal wish-fulfilment as the basis of psychiatric symptom formation' (Schreber, 1995: 405), that is: they can only understand Schreber's abhorrence of Flechsig as repressed homosexual desire (for the father) since the unconscious knows no negation.

Freud's abandonment of the case of Schreber to the very people he claims are his oppressors (Flechsig, and before him, his father) is the reading given by Niederland (1984), Schatzman (1973) and more recently, Lothane (1992). In *My Own Private Germany*, Eric Santner also goes over the stakes of Schreber's difference with Flechsig (Santner, 1996). Flechsig was appointed to the position of professor of psychiatry at the University of Leipzig in 1882 despite having very little psychiatric experience – he had built up his reputation with his ground-breaking work on nerve fibres and the localization of nervous diseases. Lothane noted that his appointment marked a historical shift of paradigms in the history of psychiatry towards extreme medicalization. Schreber found himself in the hands of someone who was convinced that 'the most direct way to penetrate to the knowledge of the lawful relations between illnesses and brain anomalies' was through brain dissection and for this reason he hovered around the beds of those nearing death in the psychiatric clinic of the University Hospital (*ibid.*: 71).

Santner reads the Schreber case as deconstructing the symbolic structures informing authority, uncovering the instability of institutional foundations and the violence that at once allows them to lay down the law and produces its own deviance. Santner focused on why Freud could not take on board this aspect of Schreber's implicit critique of power and position:

Freud's study of the Schreber material was conducted at a moment in the history of psychoanalysis when the symbolic authority of that new institution was being strongly contested from within the ranks as well as from without – at a moment of institutional stress ... that made Freud particularly sensitive to the nature of Schreber's investiture crisis even though Freud never explicitly addressed it. (*ibid.*: 17)

In 1911, when Freud was writing about Schreber, he was also grappling with the dissenting voices of Adler and Jung within his own movement. He was busy trying to tighten the rules governing psychoanalysis and to explicate the party line to achieve consolidation. Unfortunately for Schreber and ultimately transsexuals, by so doing he sells out to the most *louche* forms of psychiatry.

In his open letter to Flechsig, written after the memoir, Schreber attempts to understand the 'soul murder' he still feels was practised on him by the psychiatrists independent of his psychotic delusions. He carefully surmises in the form of what he calls 'a mild reproach' that:

> you, like so many doctors, could not completely resist the temptation of using a patient in your care *as an object for scientific experiments* apart from the real purpose of cure, when by chance matters of the highest scientific interest arose. (Schreber, 1995: 34)

The legacy of Schreber's treatment by psychoanalysis has been that today's transsexuals are greeted on the one hand with the formulaic judgement of repressed homosexuality tending to psychosis and, on the other, with the prospect of being dependent on scientific research into brainsex or genetic determinism. Faced with one institution that refuses to think outside of Oedipalized libidinal drives and another that presumes to deal with psychosomatic crises as solely the result of organic malfunctioning, transsexuals have been trapped.

Just before he embarks on the interpretation of the Schreber case, Freud makes the following remarks:

> It will be an unavoidable part of our task to show that there is an essential *genetic* relation between [Schreber's transformation into a woman and his favoured relation to God]. Otherwise our attempts at elucidating Schreber's delusions will leave us in the absurd position described in Kant's famous simile of the *Critique of Pure Reason* – we shall be like a man holding a sieve under a he-goat while some one else milks it. (Freud, 1979b: 167)

There are, I suggest, several intriguing points to make about this passage: first the reference to the 'genetic' relation, the genesis of the relation between Schreber's sex-change and his particular relation to

God. The connection between these essential components of Schreber's nightmare possibly arises from the biblical condemnation of any tampering with the body. Indeed, as the performance artist, Orlan, whom we will come to later, states:

> Psychoanalysis and religion agree in saying 'Thou must not attack the body'. 'One must accept oneself'. These are primitive, anachronistic concepts. We react as if the sky would fall on our heads if we were to tamper with the body. (Orlan, 1996: 91)

To push our argument further: the 'genetic' relation as it regards transsexuality is what psychoanalysis does not even seem to want to know about, or to fight about. By contrast, Orlan, who describes herself as a 'woman to woman TS' declares:

> My fight is against the innate, the inexorable, the programmed, nature DNA (which is our direct rival as artists) and God. (ibid.: 16)

Lastly, Freud's reference to Kant is also strangely apposite. The analogy with the goat does not just refer to a case of mistaken sexual identity – the goat, presumed to be milkable, therefore female, but which is actually male – but also the section of the first critique from which it is taken treats the relation of truth to knowledge. Kant points out that one can have knowledge of an object without necessarily being able to give the truth about it, that is, one's knowledge of an object might not be convertible into a truth about it if it is not exclusive enough to differentiate that object's content from other objects' contents. Kant concludes that there is no truth (general criterion) of the matter of knowledge (Kant, 1781/1993: B82–3). I suggest that psychoanalysis's *refusal to know*, its refusal to debate scientific research into the organic causes of transsexuality, can be attributed to its attachment to this truth. The very institution whose founder taught that the truth is a lie,[12] wants to hold on to its truth, its generally applicable law for treating the abstracted, hollowed-out object, which is the transsexual it can deal with. Kant's section on logic is all about knowing what are the right questions to ask: one person is trying to milk the he-goat and another is holding a sieve in expectation because someone has asked the wrong question. This has led to a series of absurd and ludicrous answers.

Catherine Millot, a Lacanian psychoanalyst, published *Horsexe* in 1983 (it was translated in English into 1990). This book thinks it has the answers to transsexuality, but actually presents the reader with a scenario hardly less unseemly than that described by Kant. Completely unabashed, she quotes from Janice Raymond, the author of *The Transsexual Empire* mentioned above, to set the scene for her account of transsexuals: Male-to-female transsexuals feel themselves superior to 'Gennys' (genetic women) as they are not hampered by the burdens of menstruation and reproduction. 'The future is theirs!' (Millot, 1990: 14). Millot is complicit with Raymond's nightmare vision of infiltrating psychotics raping women's bodies (*ibid*.: 15 and 16). She suggests that 'transsexuality might appear to be one of the latest expressions of Malthusianism' (*ibid*.: 14). Here we are back in the world of fascistic projects of social engineering. She goes on to state that transsexuals have an image of women that is 'wholly conformist' (*ibid*.) though, in order to cement this monolithic account of these deviants, she has to travel to the TV/TS bars of Rio, dig out the Skoptzy sect, pack in anecdotal comments and apply a thick covering of Lacanian glue.

> Transsexuality, and above all male transsexuality, triggers in women the dream of understanding the conspicuously elusive essence of femininity, a question which confronts women with what is alien to themselves. Transsexuals who claim to possess a female soul imprisoned in a man's body are perhaps the only ones who can boast a monolithic sexual identity, one that admits of neither doubts nor questions. (*ibid*.: 15)

This scene of the genetic woman drawn to the male-to-female transsexual in her search for the ultimate answer to the elusive question 'What does a woman want?' irresistibly reminds me of the moment in Djuna Barnes's *Nightwood* (written in 1936 and chillingly clairvoyant about the fate of 'inverts' – gays, TV/TS and Jews – under fascism) when the lesbian Nora goes in desperation to visit the transsexual figure, Doctor Matthew Mighty O'Connor, in her quest for knowledge. 'His' response to her imploring question is: 'I tuck myself in at night, well content because I am my own charlatan' (Barnes, 1950: 139). Rather than passing over from one discrete identity to another, the transsexual body reworks the divide, spans the divide, destabilizing conventions and expectations rather than just attempting to conform to them. Even the doctor's room exudes sexual ambiguity, being described as a 'cross between a *chambre à coucher* and a boxer's training camp' (*ibid*.: 116). Fascinated with their horror it is the onlooker who petrifies the lengthy process that is transsexuality – remember, a transsexual wants to *become* the sex that s/he is, that is, the becoming is the opening of a process: however, all the eager onlooker wants to see, yet no further, is The Operation itself – the hacking off, the sealing off and the tacking on.[13] What is so special about being a woman or man that it merits that? The transsexual *must* perceive there to be something special to do that. One can imagine the disappointment when the answer can be heard: 'I am my own charlatan'.

Parveen Adams's article 'Operation Orlan' (1996) also builds on the horrified fascination with The Operation. It cannot be denied that Orlan's surgical performances are gruesome. However, what I find most insidious about this piece is the way transsexuals are used to advance an argument about art and representation.[14] The argument runs as follows: the artist, Orlan, proclaims herself to be a woman-to-woman transsexual and she is right to; transsexuals, however, want to change from one sex to the other so as omnipotently to deny sexual difference and become The Woman. This assertion is then confirmed through a footnote to Millot, who is drawing on Raymond. She continues:

> [the transsexual] urge to refiguration involves a wish not to become a woman, but to become The Woman. That is to *become* the phallus through castration. Clearly Orlan works differently. (Adams, 1996: 144)[15]

In that last sentence – 'Clearly Orlan works differently' – lies psychoanalytical theory's more or less consistently dismissive attitude to transsexuality. She continues: 'By becoming The Woman the transsexual is convinced that he will be complete' (*ibid.*). Mark the assurance of the generality – this is knowledge plus truth and we are still milking he-goats.

In the recent Orlan conference catalogue, Adams's article is preceded by a piece by the transsexual Sandy Stone. Stone worked for the progressive Olivia Women's Record Collective back in the 1970s and it was about her that the following remarks were written (quoted with approval by Raymond, who is used by Millot, who is used by Adams):

> I feel raped when Olivia passes off Sandy, a TS, as a real woman. After all his male privilege, is he going to cash in on lesbian feminist culture too? (Raymond, 1979: 103)

Here, twenty years later, she is still being called The phallic Woman out for the absolute. In this Orlan catalogue Stone writes:

From the trans perspective ... How do we reconcile our performative wanderlust with the reality of an oppressive structure of knowing, the issue of which is invariably injustice? (Orlan, 1996: 51)

Stone explains the transsexual dilemma: they are trapped between the desire to explore the possibilities of the performative gender bending and the need to fight for basic rights (for example equal opportunities, the right to privacy) for which they need to present a coherent, essentialist identity without ambiguity. It was exactly because of this conjunction of fantasy with the political that Rose encouraged feminism to engage with psychoanalysis. Unfortunately it does not look as if the same care and rigour will be applied to a debate between psychoanalysis and transsexualism.

Notes

1. This line of thought leads straight to the discovery that the difference between femininity and masculinity is one of (hormonal) *dosage*. See the reference to Eugen Steinach's pioneering work in the 1920s below.
2. In Kate More's interview with Judith Butler, the author of *Gender Trouble* rejects any dialogue with science. Biologists are seen to want indubitably to 'prove' a 'putatively pure sense of anatomy' proper to the female or the male. Butler regards such lines of enquiry as '[cauterizing] the ambivalence in the constitution of sex' in the name of 'logical', 'factual' certainty (see More, 1997: 4, 136). More's question about whether recent scientific experiments (especially the results of the Swaab trial, see below), are to be doubted or not and whether they are 'predicated on difference rather than the content of that difference', that is to what extent they are legislating for female and male modes of behaviour, is most apposite. Instead of rather stereotypically and hence dismissively characterizing those 'men of science, who have hard knowledge' (*ibid.*), science seen as an extension of patriarchal oppression, such scientific investigation throws up as many questions as it settles. For instance, Julian Huxley writing in 1923 on 'sex biology and sex psychology' – on the work being carried out by Steinach, Voronoff and Sand on endocrinological determinism – muses:

    What then has our rapid survey led us to? The actual origin of sex is lost to us in the mists of a time inconceivably remote. Its preservation once in existence, and its present all-but-universal distribution seem to be definitely associated with *the biological advantage of the plasticity which it confers*. Later the primary difference between male and female – their power of producing different sorts of reproductive cells – leads on to secondary differences. These differences may be biologically speaking non-significant, mere accidents of the primary difference. Or they may be in the nature of a division of labour between the sexes ... Or, finally, they may concern the more efficient union of the gametes; such differences may merely affect the ducts and apertures of the reproductive system and be more or less mechanical; or they may concern the use of these systems, in the form of still mechanical instincts, or they may be concerned in some way or other with the emotional side of the animals, and consist in characters or actions which stimulate the emotions of the other sex (Huxley, 1923: 117–18).

Even if at the level of 'primary' differences certain laws, albeit 'plastic' ones, appear to be laid down, all is up for grabs at the crucial 'secondary' level.

3. Steinach's work on the ductless glands made evident the physiological significance of the gonads for the differentiation of the sexes. However impressed Freud was by such amazing experiments, which could apparently change one's sex or bring back to life one's masculinity or femininity through hormonal 'rejuvenation', Freud resists the dominion of the 'organic'. In 'Some neurotic mechanisms in jealousy, paranoia and homosexuality' (Freud, 1979b: 205), Freud stakes out the residual terrain of the psychic. Still in relation to homosexuality and the implications of Steinach's research, he, about the same time, recognized that a three-tiered understanding of sexual 'identity' was necessary. He differentiates between sex, the 'physical sexual characters'; gender, the 'mental sexual characters'; and sexuality, the 'kind of object choice'. Steinach's work on sex glands appears to go a long way to explaining what constitutes one's overall sexual identity – he seems to master the mysteries of biological sex, whereas psychoanalysis is left with making inroads into sexuality. Psychoanalysis's task becomes that of 'disclosing the psychical mechanisms that resulted in determining the object-choice and with tracing back the paths from them to the instinctual dispositions' (ibid.: 398–400). Sandwiched in between these two domains is gender – 'masculine and feminine attitude'. Here biology leaves the field open for psychoanalysis thanks to the paucity of its understanding: masculinity reduces down to activity, and femininity to passivity, an equation that Freud finds wanting (ibid.: 399–400).

4. Despite the wish to distance himself from any ethically dubious applications of such experiments, Freud did succumb to their charms in 1923. Fighting with cancerous death, Freud allowed himself to be persuaded by von Urbantschitsch, one of Steinach's disciples, to undergo a 'rejuvenation' operation (see the Gay, Schur and Jones biographies of Freud). Freud hoped that a bolstered manhood, acquired through the ligature of the spermatic ducts, might increase his chances of staving off the onslaught of disease – he was disappointed. Such experiments are not unrelated to the eugenicist ideologies Freud elsewhere seems to be anxious about. Apart from its origins in the enforced sterilization of the insane and the criminal (see Kammerer, 1924: 68), such 'rejuvenating' operations

provide the tempting prospect of prolonging the richness of the race stock. In *The Theory and Practice of the Steinach Operation* (1924), P. Schmidt announced the vision of artificial selection apparently proffered by Steinach's research: 'the measures of rejuvenation afford us the possibilities of preserving or even of prolonging the life and working capacity of some men of peculiar value to mankind'. Such operations seem to pave the way for the worst medicalized excesses of the Third Reich. Nevertheless, the gesture of absolute rejection of such work because of its 1930s legacy would be inadequate. Steinach's research also opens up the field of hormone replacement therapy for menopausal women and presents sex as a matter of choice: 'The most important "decision" in the life of a creature, the "decision" whether it has to go through life as man or woman no longer appears so much a matter of chance. A decision can be made within the individual himself, he has the potential to develop towards either sex' (see Steinach and Loebel, 1940: 94–5). Any refusal of dialogue with science based on one aspect of its application is naïve, reductive and irresponsible.

5. Socarides begins his 1970 article 'A Psychoanalytical Study for the Desire for Sexual Transformation ("Transsexualism"): The Plaster of Paris Man' by citing this and the previous passage from Freud. The founder of psychoanalysis provides Socarides with the seal of approval for his subsequent treatment of transsexuality as a symptom of 'the delusional system of paranoid schizophrenics', unable to come to terms with their homosexual desires.

6. From Raymond's book we can seamlessly slip into C. Millot's *Horsexe* (1990: 42).

7. Macalpine and Hunter would have found allies in Deleuze and Guattari, who also rejected the restrictive 'Oedipal nursery', the repetitive 'family romances', of psychoanalysis. Their espousal of 'intense becomings, passages and migrations ... becoming woman' in *Anti-Oedipus* (1984: 84–5) corroborates Macalpine and Hunter's interpretation of the Schreber case. Their celebration of psychotic proliferation thwarts attempts to tie the case down to a standard one of repressed homosexuality. They suggest that such a reductive reading just touches the surface: 'We are statistically or molarly heterosexual, but personally homosexual, without knowing it or being fully aware of it, and finally we are transsexual in an elemental, molecular sense' (Deleuze and Guattari, 1984: 70). For the beginnings of an account of Deleuzian transsexuality see D. Beddoes, 'Deleuze, Kant and Indifference' in Ansell Pearson, 1997: 38–40.

8. See, for example, Freud, 1977: 383–4.

9. It is important to note that Macalpine and Hunter's attempt to think the difference between transsexuals and homosexuality is shared by today's transsexual theorists who are thinking their difference with queer theory – see, for example, Prosser, 1995: 483ff.

10. Compare with Deleuze and Guattari's affirmation of the schizophrenic in *Anti-Oedipus*:

It becomes nevertheless apparent that schizophrenia teaches us a singular extra-Oedipal lesson, and reveals to us an unknown force of the disjunctive synthesis, an immanent use that would no longer be exclusive or restrictive, but fully affirmative, non-restrictive, inclusive. A disjunction that remains disjunctive, and that still affirms the disjointed terms, that affirms them throughout their entire distance, *without restricting one by the other or excluding the other from the one*, is perhaps the greatest paradox. 'Either ... or', instead of 'either/or'. (Deleuze and Guattari, 1984: 76)

11. 'The patient's lover was still her father, but she herself had taken her mother's place. The place of the listener had then to be allotted to a third person' (Freud, 1979a: 154). Dr John Randall also attempts to close down the complicated circulation of transsexual desire and read it as basically indicative of homosexual panic. However, one of the cases he cites in 'Transvestitism and Transsexualism' (Randall, 1959: 1448ff) defies such simplicity, soliciting the distinction between homo- and heterosexual orientation, probing the limits of the TV/TS distinction. It is mind-blowing in its complexity:

> With one notable exception, the female patients were homosexually orientated. These 12 women had experienced homosexual attachments and the wish to take the male role in sexual intimacy with a Lesbian partner was the predominant and expressed reason advanced by those who wished for trans-sexualisation. The sole heterosexually orientated woman was both transvestite and trans-sexualist; she presented the unusual pattern of heterosexual seduction by a male transvestite (not her husband). At first revolted by the deviate practices into which she was initiated, she became conditioned to experience orgasm in such acts, and attempted without success to secure her husband's co-operation in similar behaviour. Depression supervened and she made three unsuccessful attempts at suicide. She is an attractive woman and has one child. (*ibid.*: 1450)

How should, can, we read this case history?

12. See the entry for 'truth' in the General Index to the Standard Edition of Freud's works. 'Truth, a lie' encapsulates the Cracow/Lemberg 'joke', in Freud, 1976: 161.

13. See Hemmings (1996) for a good analysis of an often-repeated fetishization of the transsexual operation by reductionist theorists.

14. Adams repeats Raymond's crime as analysed by Carol Riddell: '*The Transsexual Empire* is a dangerous book. It is dangerous to transsexuals because it does not treat us as human beings at all, merely as the tools of a theory' (Riddell, 1996: 184).

15. Adams's article explicitly engages Orlan against transsexuals. Orlan claims to be 'female-to-female transsexual'. In this Adams states that Orlan is not only 'exactly right' as far as her performances are concerned, but she also apparently demonstrates her sophisticated superiority to those other,

megalomaniacal, transsexuals who aim to abolish sexual difference with their will to power. Transsexuals are aiming for the 'triumph of completeness' (Adams, 1996: 145), they are misguidedly essentialist, whereas Orlan's performances demonstrate in graphic detail the 'emptiness of the image' (*ibid.*), that the 'image is a mask and that there is nothing behind it' (*ibid.*: 153). Not only is this reductionist reading of transsexuality highly problematic, but Adams's absolutist understanding of Orlan is also open to question: how sure can, *should*, we be about what Orlan is doing? What are her motives? Is she a sadomasochist? What is her relation to the cosmetic industry? Is what she does art? (see B. Rose, 1993). I would suggest that a crucial aspect of Orlan's work is the ambivalence she provokes: there is attraction, a wanting to see what she is having done to her; we are fascinated, yet we are also repulsed, dreading what is offered up to us for our perusal, unsure about what it is that is happening in front of us and how to situate ourselves in relation to it. By contrast, Adams is just too sure of herself, of the 'f-to-f' Orlan and of her knowledge about what those other ('power-craving', 'psychotic') transsexuals actually want.

References

Adams, P. (1996) *The Emptiness of Image: Psychoanalysis and Sexual Differences*. London: Routledge.

Ansell Pearson, K. (ed.) (1997) *Deleuze and Philosophy*. London: Routledge.

Barnes, D. (1950) *Nightwood*. London: Faber.

Butler, J. (1990) *Gender Trouble: Feminism and the Subversion of Identity*. New York: Routledge.

Deleuze, G. and F. Guattari (1984) *Anti-Oedipus: Capitalism and Schizophrenia*. Minneapolis: University of Minnesota Press.

Freud, S. (1976) *Jokes and Their Relation to the Unconscious*. Harmondsworth: Pelican Freud Library, Vol. 6.

Freud, S. (1977) *On Sexuality: Three Essays on the Theory of Sexuality and Other Works*. Harmondsworth: Pelican Freud Library, Vol. 7.

Freud, S. (1979a) *On Psychopathology*. Harmondsworth: Pelican Freud Library, Vol. 10.

Freud, S. (1979b) *Case Histories II*. Harmondsworth: Pelican Freud Library, Vol. 9.

Freud, S. (1985) *Civilisation, Society and Religion*. Harmondsworth: Pelican Freud Library, Vol. 12.

Freud, S. (1991) *New Introductory Lectures on Psychoanalysis*. Harmondsworth: Pelican Freud Library, Vol. 2.

Hemmings, C. (1996) 'Hausman's horror', *Radical Deviance*, July.

Huxley, J. (1923) *Essays of a Biologist*. Harmondsworth: Pelican.

Kammerer, P. (1924) *Rejuvenation and the Prolongation of Human Efficiency:*

Experiences with the Steinach Operation on Man and Animals. London, Methuen.

Kant, I. (1781/1993) *Critique of Pure Reason.* London: Dent, Everyman Library.

Kofman, S. (1985) *The Enigma of Woman.* London: Cornell University Press.

Lacan, J. (1980) *Ecrits: A Selection,* A. Sheridan (trans.). London: Tavistock.

Lothan, Z. (1992) *In Defence of Schreber: Soul Murder and Psychiatry.* New Jersey: Analytic Press.

Millot, C. (1990) *Horsexe.* New York: Autonomedia.

Mitchell, J. (1975) *Psychoanalysis and Feminism.* Harmondsworth: Pelican Books.

More, K. (1996) 'In bed with the Stria Terminalis', *Radical Deviance: A Journal of Transgendered Politics,* 2, 1 (March).

More, K. (1997) 'Excitable speech: an interview with Judith Butler on trans-sexuality', *Radical Deviance: A Journal of Transgendered Politics,* 2, 4 (May).

Niederland, W. (1984) *The Schreber Case: A Psychoanalytical Profile of Paranoid Personality.* New Jersey: Analytic Press.

Orlan (1996) *Orlan: This Is My Body ... This Is My Software.* Black Dog Publishing.

Prosser, J. (1995) 'No place like home: the transgendered narrative of Leslie Feinberg's *Stone Butch Blues*', *Modern Fiction Studies,* 41, 3/5: 483–514.

Randall, J. (1959) 'Transvestism and transsexualism', *British Medical Journal,* December: 1448ff.

Raymond, J. (1979) *The Transsexual Empire: The Making of the She-Male.* London: Women's Press.

Riddell, C. (1996) 'Divided sisterhood: the transsexual empire'. In R. Ekins and D. King (eds), *Blending Genders: Social Aspects of Cross-dressing and Sex-Changing.* London: Routledge.

Rose, B. (1993) 'Is it art? Orlan and the transgressive act', *Art in America,* February: 83ff.

Rose, J. (1986) *Sexuality in the Field of Vision.* London: Verso.

Santner, E. (1996) *My Own Private Germany.* New York: Princeton University Press.

Schatzman, M. (1973) *Soul Murder: Persecution in the Family.* New York: Random Press.

Schmidt, P. (1924) *The Theory and Practice of the Steinach Operation.* London: W. Heinemann.

Schreber, (1995) *Memoirs of My Nervous Illness,* I. Macalpine and R. Hunter (trans.). Folkestone: Dawson and Sons.

Socarides, C. (1970) 'A psychoanalytical study of the desire for sexual transformation ("transsexualism"): the plaster of Paris man', *International Journal of Psychoanalysis,* 51: 341ff.

Socarides, C. (1979) 'Transsexualism and psychosis', *International Journal of Psychoanalysis,* 7: 373ff.

Steinach, E. and J. Loebel (1940) *Sex and Life: Forty Years of Biological and Medical Experiments.* London: Faber & Faber.

12

Never Mind the Bollocks: 1. Trans Theory in the UK

Kate More[1]

A s we look forward, with some excitement, to the arrival of a new academic discipline – that newness reflected in the daring, the ridiculous and the downright wrong, dancing hand-in-hand together to make a monkey of the staid and the establishment – it is perhaps as well to take this breathless moment to see how far we have gone (and whether it's now possible to turn back!). Determinedly self-referential, this chapter uses the metaphor of my own writing as a method to summon or make a play of, some of the issues absorbing writers and activists doing theoretical work around transgender in the UK. The chapter also raises questions about how writing may negotiate the path between assimilation and resistance to greater credibility.[2]

Autobiography: trans-po(i)etics as subversion, reversion and aesthetic

> *There are also female transsexuals ...*
> *Theirs is not the star system.*
> (Millot, 1983: 105)

> *What is most true is poetic.*
> (Cixous and Calle-Gruber, 1997: 3)

KRISTEVA: *Before we started recording this, you mentioned that Lacan described male-to-female transsexuals as having a 'delirious manner' as if glorying in themselves, and you asked why transsexuals can never get beyond autobiography.*

KATE: *The first psychoanalyst I went to told me, after half-an-hour of assessment, that I was unanalysable, and that I wasn't a transsexual, I was a narcissist! 'You, me and Lacan', I thought, but I'd only read the Freud and believed that narcissism ends in dementia. It was a death-sentence – so it seemed. Add to this Carol-Anne Duffy, who was something of a hero, read a book of my fictional writing – which was deliberately grandiose and neurotic – as if straight, and it became clear that what I thought I was doing in terms of my creative work with the subject-in-process – with your work – for instance in my trans-feminist writing of masculinity as premature ejaculation, was at some level ... could be reduced simply to an overtly tumescent phallus.*

KRISTEVA: *These are strange admissions; how did you feel about the diagnosis of narcissism?*

KATE: *Well, I went to several other shrinks who were decently embarrassed by the first one, and to them I went dressed in stereotyped feminine clothes – my first clothes were boyish women's clothes. I still signified '1', I was a tomboy. Actually that's maybe too close to a medical discourse for me; I like the idea that TS surgery can be an opening-up of possibilities – three people think I was a 'woman in a man's body' – that the fourth doesn't, raises all sorts of other causalities. As the identity transsexuality, or rather the medicalized discourses connected with it, become passé, it's a way out, a collapse of patriarchal certainty. The fact that I only own transsexuality as a commonplace, remain distant, means I can't be pigeonholed.*

KRISTEVA: *But how did you feel?*

KATE: *I didn't mind the idea that wanting surgery was just acting-up, but the dementia business was a problem. I got to thinking how cheap life is, but also the politics. Faced with this text, 'narcissist', does one respond with more law? Or with poetry? Does one beautify the return until ... You read Millot and you think, given the lifestyle choice between being a pretty, narcissistic boy with psychotic episodes – dementia to come – and non-triggered psychoses: a healthy, happy tomboy, I know which I would choose to be ... but the question is, is that a radical choice, and in turn, has the hegemony got mental health covered?*

KRISTEVA: *This is why you feel more at home with transsexual 'murderers' and 'rapists' than academics?*

KATE: *Absolutely! Their diagnoses are just the same.*

KRISTEVA: *This is what? A Foucaultian mode?*

KATE: *Maybe then. Butler reading Althusser now. She may be too clever for her own good, ignoring the real and stuff, but her politics are better than most alternatives.*

KRISTEVA: *Than the Lacanians? Is there anything particularly trans-political?*

KATE: *Yes, to both I'm afraid. Žižek uses Hombach to critique, and then own, autopoiesis and trans-coding, which are the classic ways systems theory would answer the Lacanian cry of psychosis. Trannies rewrite their autobiographies as the opposite sex and they therefore become the opposite sex, a sort of, look no hands, it's all in the symbolic. And if that sounds familiar, it's me rethinking Sandy Stone. Other than Žižek, the Lacanians are a pain, and he would no doubt go along with the Master, if it were put to him he was talking about TSs. As for the other, for me trans-political praxis is often synonymous with bisexual flirting – gender allows you to play games with sexuality, and vice versa – how else does one put one's ambiguous gendering into play ... how else does one threaten the Maussian gift ideology of patriarchy if one is becoming woman, one makes ownership of oneself worthless, twoself, threeself. However, even if one becomes a 'normal', heterosexual woman, never repaying one's transition, one becomes a literal woman, and that's different.*

KRISTEVA: *I've heard it said that I am your god-mother [marraine]?*

KATE: *Absolutely! But the question is not whether you are my godmother, but whether I should name-drop you as such!*

Ahem. During these past few harassed, hurried and committed years my writing has often engaged with academic discourse – these ideas are the ones that frankly rule our society. However this practice positions me, as the author's 'article',[3] in a complicated relationship with the hegemony – in engaging, I, of necessity, adopt some of the symbolic structures with which I find myself at odds. This ownership is an exceptionally dangerous tool, so part of the project is to constantly undercut material you'll find in this chapter, with a textual stylistics (or properly poetics), which could not be read as irony.

Sometimes I have used as my model for academy the grandiosity of the transgender film *Glen or Glenda*, in which autobiographical excess constantly undercuts the documentary nature of the discourse. Both this film and some of my texts insert in visible ways the article's desire for the power of hegemony and in this way these become borderline texts, foreground the dangerous nature of discourse, and the agenda and agency of the article, while maintaining the otherness, reflect the abject status of the humble author. This could be seen as a method for using poetics to produce a gender nihilist position,[4] one in which a TS autobiography, by the very egoistic nature of the genre, collapses the authority of the text's attempt to construct gender in essentialist ways. Of course this is simultaneously a recognition of the impossibility of achieving identity.[5] I should make it clear that this type of discourse does not achieve the distance of irony and neither is it truly camp; these latter are both about summoning borders, not about showing up the weaknesses of the dominant discourse from within.

As well as presenting such a text, in the form of an article from *Radical Deviance*, itself presenting an article from *genderfuck*, citation of citation, this chapter also touches on the problematic raised by the question of introjecting guilt in what we could call these subversive poetics, via negativity[6] in Kristeva's politics and also via another discourse, that of Deleuze and Guattari, which similarly adopts the stylistically grotesque, also using poetics to interrogate the borderline nature of the desire it theorizes.

But first an introduction to the debate

The postmodern era has seen the rise of an unusual form of gender essentialist autobiography – the man-in-a-woman's-body discourse of the transsexual (Prosser, 1998). Paradoxically, it has also seen a vigorous defence of biological determinism from sections of the women's movement (More, 1996a). This defence perceived such bodily reconstructions to be anti-essentialist, to be a 'rape', for turning the real woman's body into an artefact (Raymond, 1980). One might argue that these very protestations led in turn to Baudrillard's famous declaration that there are no transsexuals, and conversely that we are all transsexuals, that transsexualism means an end to 'any real sexuality or any type of real otherness' (Baudrillard, 1994). Since then, modernist discourse, in the form of neuroscience, has claimed that male-to-female transsexuals have femaleness hardwired into their brains (Swaab *et al.*, 1995), and the debate goes on ...

In the UK, transsexuals faced ridicule in the press, in post-Lacanian and, as we shall see, in queer theory texts; a dramatic loss of civil rights followed successive court cases after 1970 (More, 1995a); and in 1980 inclusion in diagnostic manuals categorized the community as mentally-ill. They responded to the state with trans-activism and to the women's movement with a new form of cultural discourse, an often anti-essentialist trans-theory. This latter, analogous to queer theory, promises to shed new light on both sexual dissidence and women's studies. For me, however, there are some obvious aporia in the current debate: where for instance, do labia-possessing female-to-male transsexuals work their difference from the 'labial feminism'[7] of Irigaray? Where is the situated, political response to post-Lacanian texts such as Millot's *Horsexe* (1983)? If transsexuals are indeed socialized/constructed as one sex, but essentially the other, does an internal dialectic result which collapses bipolar gender paradigms? Does this unique position enable us to produce an *écriture hors-genre* à la Cixous? Moreover, are men in women's bodies always going to be read as reactionary within postmodern constructionist discourse and is the appropriate political response to write them in terms of post-postmodern reconstruction?

One can see these as literalisms, but as we've seen, even the phallus bears some relationship with/to a penis.

On *being*[8] and *having* gender

Central to these questions is the issue of essentialism versus constructionism – which is also pivotal in the relationship between modernism and postmodernism. In this section I contextualize the issue using two books, Somer Brodribb's *Nothing Mat(t)ers*[9] and Diana Fuss's *Essentially Speaking*. The first is a development of the 1980s feminist debate epitomized by Raymond, as can be witnessed by the author's acknowledgement of Raymond's support and her repeated use of the jibe that a given male theorist is an intellectual transvestite. Included here are Derrida for writing as a woman, Deleuze for the 'becoming-woman', Lacan for the displacement of the phallus discussed below and, for a literary style based on 'hysterics', Nietzsche for 'using female fetishes to affirm male motherhood ... He dresses as a woman to fool the devouring abyss, to pass' (Brodribb, 1993: 68–70) and associated with this practice is the idea that transvestism is evidence of misogyny.[10] The second book questions the pat nature of the essentialist versus constructionist divide in a rigorous attempt to deconstruct it.

It could be argued that in spite of the declaration on the back cover, Brodribb's book is deconstructive also, if only in the simple tabloid sense of trying to ridicule her postmodernist victims' work with aspects of their non-theoretical lives, bringing the margins centre-stage. But whereas she uses an essentialist position as whiter-than-white 'Woman' to deconstruct the work of postmodern theorists as whole people,[11] Fuss's, for Brodribb, 'romantic thralldom', operating from a post-structuralist standpoint, may even be working to 'undo postmodernism homeopathically by the means of postmodernism: to work at dissolving the deconstruction by using all the instruments of deconstruction itself'.[12]

'The possibility of any radical constructionism', Fuss says, 'can only be built on the foundations of a hidden essentialism ... [Derrida] deploys essentialism against itself, lean[ing] heavily on essence in its determination to displace essence' (Fuss, 1990: 12–13). This is a recognition of the key agenda – there is no going back on either the collapse of essentialism, or the advent of postmodernism. If society is to not collapse in on itself we must look to a play between essentialism and radical constructionism to do some positive 'construction work' on our society.

Diana Fuss hits an even more important note for transsexualism, when she says, 'Irigaray's reading of Aristotle's understanding of essence reminds me of Lacan's distinction between *being* and *having* the phallus: a woman does not *possess* the phallus, she *is* the Phallus. Similarly, we can say that, in Aristotelian logic, a woman does not have an essence, she is Essence. Therefore to give "woman" an essence is to undo Western phallomorphism and to offer women entry into subjecthood' (*ibid.*: 71). The parallel, in my thinking about trans-sexualism, is not with the Lacanians, for transsexualism is not about becoming the Woman as a transcendental signifier, but with Irigaray's Aristotelian essence, writing our entry into subjecthood as about 'being' women, the performative rather than having/owning woman.[13] The true 'dupes of gender' are those like Hausman who underestimate the importance of the strategic use of essence and categorical resituation (Hausman, 1995: 140).

Along with the relationship the sexes produce between the social desire and the specular, this doubling, this being and having of the phallus, as we shall see, makes the Lacanian one of the most sophisticated analyses of gender and also one of the most conservative.

As for Brodribb, her relationship with Kristeva's concept of being is perhaps as instructive as any; among these important cross-dressing 'male' postmodern theorists, there is this 'woman'. Brodribb, quoting Kristeva, says:

> Julia Kristeva, the self-styled 'father of semiotics' has brought us the phallic mother: the phallus becomes the mother of us all in Kristeva's magical replacement of male supremacy. Her work is tied to the Lacanian formula of desire and/for female aphasia: *On a deeper level, however, a woman cannot 'be'; it is something which does not even belong in the order of being.*

KRISTEVA: *I'm still here, Kate.*

KATE: *Of course the translation's provocative, 'Mais, plus profondément, une femme, cela ne peut pas être: c'est même ce qui ne va pas dans l'être' – the translators use the impersonal pronoun in the sentence,* 'On a deeper level, however, a woman cannot "be"; it is something which does not even belong to the order of being' *which is technically correct:* 'cela' – *to which the word* 'même' *refers, being translated as* 'it' *rather than* 'that' *because referencing an indefinite subject like* 'a woman' – *the translation seems more provocative in a culture where objectification of women, is so foregrounded. Less grammatically accurately, one could do without that sort of extraposed subject, so,* 'But, most profoundly, a woman is that which is powerless to be: woman is that which is excluded from being.'

It follows that a feminist practice can only be negative, at odds with what already exists so that we may say 'that's not it' and 'that's still not it'. In 'woman' I see something that cannot be represented, something that is not said, something above and beyond nomenclatures and ideologies. There are certain men who are familiar with this phenomenon; it is what some modern texts never stop signifying: testing the limits of language and sociality – the law and its transgression, mastery and (sexual) pleasure – without reserving one for males and the other for females, on the condition that it is never mentioned. (Brodribb, 1993: xxi)

KATE: *It doesn't matter to Brodribb[14] that Kristeva's is a thetic subject, produced as a wannabe (Kristeva, 1974, 1984: 131) and that her political praxis is to break down identity (ibid.: x), or that analysis is a relationship in which the analyst is seen to process from subject to object, that in some sense, an analyst is a becoming woman for that relationship,[15] or at a wider level, that postmodernism is only characterized by its sense of the crisis of our society, the irrelevance of these petty concepts, 'man' and 'woman', for a time when, after the Hitler regime we can no longer believe in the old truths that Goebbels peddled so well. Of course, Brodribb ignores Tante Julia's prefatory remarks to this statement, that the concept 'woman' is almost as meaningless as the concept 'man',* almost *because even for, erm, Kristeva, there are certain rights to be won, abortion, contraception, state-provided day care, job recognition and so on. Therefore the only place for some sort of provisional use of these identity constructs, is political. Compare this to Janice Raymond's continued concentration on 'patrochemical' attacks on women with the morning-after pill, used by the separatist women's movement to prevent pregnancy in rape victims. The pill is, like the transsexual, black and white, made by men, to destroy women (Raymond, 1993).*

KRISTEVA: *I've just flipped to the Butler interview. How are people supposed to achieve/not achieve identity at a personal level?*

KATE: *Will you please! Some of us are trying to talk about Brodribb ... Brodribb fails to understand the critique of positivism, the crisis of identity that a TS as quiet and simple as myself, in adopting my grandmother's patronymic, Moore, and excising a vaginal 'o', can put into play. Could there be more of a crisis/identity than one which names our one and only truth, desire, and in fixing it as a black hole of identity, naming the death (mort) that forms it? Such is the lack of comprehension that created the concept 'gender dysphoria'. For Kristeva, that a woman cannot 'be' is a statement of the greatest praise.*

What have I done, Tante Julie? I have cooked myself![16] *I've reified my subject! Stop the tape, we must do this again, new iteration, new identity. Now remember – Lacan and the delirious manner? How about 'Kate Plus'? More or Less ...? Plus personne, Katerin'ya Plus?*

Perhaps, in my writing at least, this nihilism about all essences, especially identity and the authority of positivist science, can best be seen in the irritatingly notorious 'Stone Femme' article from *genderfuck*. This read 'transsexual' as being as absurd and meaningless as Kristeva reads the concept 'woman' – a construction for use only in political struggles against the ruling discourse. Kristeva's yardstick is negativity in relation with ethics – 'Ethics should be understood here to mean the negativising of narcissism within a *practice*; in other words, a practice is ethical when it dissolves those narcissistic fixations (ones that are narrowly confined to the subject) to which the signifying process succumbs in its socio-symbolic realisation' (Kristeva, 1974/1984: 233) – you'll have to decide yourself if the article fits the rule! The interesting thing about this article is that people couldn't decide whether to take it seriously or not. Some queer theorists were offended because it was clear to them that I was deliberately reducing their arguments to absurdity, others took the material seriously, but decided the article was badly written and totally incomprehensible. At least one person has seemingly adopted the neologism 'Stone Femme' for their identity and is either trying to single-handedly collapse hetero-hegemonic gender bipolars using the article's ideas, or taking the whole identity game with a pinch of salt. *Radical Deviance*, never fighting shy of controversy, decided to print a new ten-times longer version/defence of the original article. Here it is:

The Stone Femme Piece 2[17]

Subjective, situated, prefatory: When it was suggested that we reprint my short 'stone femme' piece from *genderfuck* (More, 1995b) in this more academic journal as a way of reminding people about G&SA's original call to radicalize the transsexual community and its politics, I had second thoughts. I wasn't convinced that this is where we find ourselves 16 months on; the key project then, after all, was to refute the belief that transsexuals were reactionary to queer's radical. The publication of Hausman's book attacking transsexuals[18] showed queer stooping as low as everyone else. At a personal level, the 'stone femme' piece has been my version of Halberstam's ill-received *Lesbian Postmodern* essay.[19] My feeling is, 'reprint it, yes, – I can add in footnotes – but place the article within another, within the wider debate.'

The Stone Femme Piece 1

At one level, many people know what transgender is: it is about TSs and TVs and drag queens all getting together to fight for common issues. But what people don't know is where transgender is coming from; originally, for instance, transgender designated everyone who wasn't a transsexual (the latter argued that their gender remained the same, that didn't transition – nor were the others gendered – they operated at the level of sexuality). Did TSs then batter down the transgendered door to be allowed into this seemingly progressive paradise?

No, transsexuals were included because of the arrival on the scene of a new theoretical project, queer theory. Queer holds some strangely contradictory positions – queer theorists often deify Butler as their founder, yet Butler regards it to be originating with De Lauretis.[20] Even within Butler's work, the subjectlessness of what's called performativity combines with the idea that one must create coalitions by acknowledging one's differences.[21] If postmodernism is about blurred boundaries, then its queer theory subset argues that by circumventing divisive subject positions such as 'transsexual' and 'transvestite' and by concentrating on what these groups do in common, e.g. dress up in the opposite sex's clothes, one allows wider alliances to concentrate on the real enemy, governments, the conservative right and so on.

So where are queer's roots? Queer isn't actually a US invention, or at least performativity isn't[22] – Mary McIntosh, of Gay Liberation Front fame, did the major groundwork in London in 1968 and with the anti-psychiatric campaigner, Elizabeth Wilson and others founded what became known as Deviancy Studies. De Lauretis used the excuse of a conference in 1990 to coin the term 'Queer Theory'; present were people with a number of influences, notably postmodernists like Donna Haraway and several strongly influenced by the French critical theory of the 1970s.[23]

But look at what the movement away from subjectivity does – there is no longer a distinction between gender and sexuality – in the performance which is femininity, who can say where femininity – as being about performing/producing one's gender-identity stops, and where it is about signalling one's sexual attraction through difference?

The questions that need to be asked are: who sets the transgender agenda, and how within that coalition, when subject positions are overridden by performance, does one assert one's difference? Again if there are no subject positions, which group loses and which gains? Although everyone I've so far connected with queer has been an out lesbian, many of the main players, Weeks, Dollimore, Sinfield and others are nominally gay men, and theirs is certainly the most noticeable agenda.

Again it is instructive to see how this Gay Liberation Front generation dealt with transsexuals. From anecdotal evidence McIntosh seems to have been hostile, and theoretically she rejected the biologically determined categories TSs have espoused. Wilson clearly attacked the medicalized model, indeed anything she felt to be dependent on psychiatry, and GLF as a whole split over drag queens – unlike the drag of Butler and Jameson, parody was perceived by lesbians (as by many TSs) to be misogynistic (Power, 1995).

Transsexuals would now agree, I think, that Wilson, like Raymond, was right about psychiatry – much of what goes on there is about patriarchy taking power over the deviant. But while queer and postmodernism now espouse gender parody, the anti-parodic mode has almost defined the transsexual – we can't laugh at ourselves, the sense of our opposite-genderedness is too precious and this isn't a surprise, given the fight we have for the right to our gender – the transsexual project has been, in this sense, about producing gender as opposed to reducing it. In their historical avatars transsexualism is therefore anti-queer and anti-postmodern. So what would a version of transgender that includes transsexuals look like?

To some extent gay and lesbian subjectivities remain unthreatened by transgender – there is a normalizing aspect to performativity in practice; they have indeed managed to remove drag queen activity from the realm of sexuality, and given it a different name and ownership. Transgender is a different performance – and so this could be portrayed as sexuality at work on gendered subjectivities, and in this – cynic's view, it is another imperialist project aimed at cracking the transsexual nut.

One answer is to refuse to let this be a one-way project. No one likes the medicalized concept 'transsexual' – it is a pact with the devil, simply a name for the relationship between cross-gendered individuals and psychiatry. If there is no coherent distinction between performative gender and sexuality, then dropping or reclaiming that category in non-surgical, non-medicalized ways enables us to rewrite sexuality in our own terms.

We all know m-to-fs who consider themselves to be 'asexual lesbians'.[24] By this sub-group claiming itself in sexuality terms as stone femmes, one integrates transsexuals into the lesbian continuum by referencing an acknowledged lesbian group at the opposite end of the continuum, stone butches. At the same time this pulls apart medical distinctions that transgendered groupings with 'low sex drive' who are biological females count as lesbians and are not transsexuals, and the idea that transsexuals need surgery. This is a statement that transsexual/lesbian distinctions are arbitrary and that there will always be a play between transsexual and homosexual, between gender and sexuality that will never be settled and must be owned, uncomfortably or no, by both groups. A similar gender-identity-based sexuality continuum stretches from drag queen to transfag. This transgendered praxis allows our desire to produce gender to create genetically male lesbians and genetically female gay men – the effects of re-writing sexuality, on feminism and naturalized bipolar gender constructs would be pronounced.

The Stone Femme Piece 2 (continued)

Brief discussion

That article used a form of transgressive reinscription to provoke political realignment; looking at it now I can see how it could be read in terms of infiltration and subversion. Perhaps this should tell us something important about life after performativity. It needs, I think, to be read in the light of Butler's words, 'the political construction of the subject proceeds with certain legitimating and exclusionary aims, and these political operations are effectively concealed and naturalised by a political analysis that takes juridical structures as their foundation. Juridical power inevitably "produces" what it claims merely to represent; hence politics must be concerned with this dual function of power: the juridical and the productive' (Butler, 1990: 2) – as an example, the basis of our rape crisis campaign can be read as queering juridical structures – the centres produce/legitimize an internally coherent/essentialist concept of Woman, by judging their rape victims, excluding men and transsexuals.

What the article attempted to do was to demonstrate that attempts like Butler's to privilege parodic drag – which Sinfield has argued to always be recuperable (Sinfield, 1994: 202) – over subjective concepts of gender, could be overturned, and that subjectivities and seemingly reactionary practices such as 'producing' gender are always situated, can themselves be used counter-hegemonically.

Aside from the article, I'm inclined to agree with Sinfield – as Mark Blechner argues of homosexuality (Domenici and Lesser, 1995: 284), Freud's shift from biology to psychology was perceived as liberating and yet when LeVay and others moved it back that was also liberating, because the oppressive hegemony had moved, as it always will to crush the new ground. This is the problem with having one causality, which is why I've argued the need for a multiplicity of strategies: transvestism, transsexualism and others. It also shows up the truth about how power operates, discursively; each person's oppression is different, and their answer to their situation will be specific to their issues, hence my worries about the loss of transsexual autonomy within transgender. If we are not careful transgender will mean the end to sex-change surgery.[25]

Others, however, were not convinced, felt the piece was integrating transsexuals, or creating a bipolar opposition, or in the gay community, stealing lesbians; my continuums polluted gender, contained sexuality with cross-dressing bookends. Most resistance from the TS community, however, surrounded the idea of a gay male continuum: drag queens to transfags. One or two argued that this was just wordplay: my style was too academic or merely pseudo-academic, the gay community already absorbed gay and lesbian TGs.

All those progressive strategies

Before defending the piece I ought perhaps to outline the options it sketches over and others that aren't mentioned. Almost all of these re-writings of the transsexual subject originate as responses to Janice Raymond's famously offensive lesbian separatist work, *The Transsexual Empire* (1980). There have actually been three ways that transsexuals have responded to these attacks, (1) by trying to reclaim the word 'transsexual' either as is, as the word 'gay' has been reclaimed, or as Susan Stryker has done, by making it complex, excessive, or as G&SA have done, by arguing against medicalized versions of the word based on surgery, seeing surgery as a part of body-morphing for those who want it or as a way of fixing the TS as a metaphor of transition – I don't think anyone has seriously taken up the option I'd suggested in the 'Stone Femme' piece, (2) by becoming post-transsexuals along postmodern cyborgian lines à la Allucquère Rosanne Stone; and (3) by adopting transgender – and I shall talk about these three projects.

Reclaiming the transsexual

As this piece is mostly about queer, perhaps I should take my examples from queer theorists. Here's Sinfield: '[Genet's] strategy was that "to every charge brought against me, unjust though it be, from the bottom of my heart I shall answer yes". So he "owned to being the coward, traitor, thief and fairy they saw in me", and thus, by embracing the conditions of repression, discovered strength through abjection' (Sinfield, 1994: 196). The problem with this strategy of reversing discourses is about becoming complicit; if psychiatry says one is mentally ill, and one says, okay, I'm mentally ill, now give me surgery, one becomes mentally ill because one is accepting categories and becoming dependent on them. This is the trap I'll argue Virginia Prince, the US pioneer of non-op transsexualism, fell into.[26]

Susan Stryker is a well-known trans theorist and TS activist in the United States, but not here. Her magnus opus, *Trans: Changing Sex and Other Ecstatic Passages into Postmodernity*, due from Oxford in New York, promises to be the next Dollimore's *Sexual Dissidence* they publish. As I read the lecture versions of the chapters, Stryker looks at individual transsexuals' lives, giving them weight beyond the stereotype, beyond the autobiography, and situates them historically, letting the individual write their own version of the word 'transsexual', and by juxtaposing difference Stryker fragments the word until it refuses to be coherent. This is what I'd call a neo-transsexual approach, but there is also a *post-transsexual* school.

Post-transsexuals

The writings of two feminists have played a major role in Sandy Stone's life: Janice Raymond, who attacked Stone in *The Transsexual Empire* when she worked as a recording engineer for Olivia Records, a women-only record label; and Donna Haraway, who theorized the Marxist, postmodern feminist cyborg manifesto, whose half-man, half-machines would be anathema to technophobic Raymond, and which stubbornly rejects essentialist concepts like 'woman'. Stone took the cyborg manifesto and produced a post-transsexual manifesto which instead of fragmenting the word 'transsexual' aims at fragmenting the transsexuals' conception of themselves as coherent, natural beings, because nothing is natural. For Stone, traditional transsexual autobiography – in the form, woman-in-a-man's-body – is complicit with gender oppression; we must, she says, 'seize upon the textual violence inscribed in the transsexual body and turn it into a reconstructive force' (Epstein and Straub, 1991: 295). Our cyborg autobiographies are of men with breasts, women with male voices; we should take Raymond's adage that ' "Transsexuals divide women", beyond itself, and turn it into a productive force to multiplicatively divide the old binary discourses of gender – as well as Raymond's own monistic discourse'. (*ibid.*: 296).

Qualifying this strategy, we perhaps need to remember Brenda Polan's words, quoted in *Backlash*, 'Post-Feminism is the backlash. Any movement or philosophy which defines itself as post whatever came before is bound to be reactive. In most cases it is also reactionary' (Faludi, 1992: 15). Are there disadvantages with feeling oneself to be incoherent?

Transgender and queer

Talking about transgender, I have to return to queer theory and the way transsexuals have been read, and return to that first paradox, that Butler doesn't think she's a queer theorist and that Sinfield, who clearly is, radically disagrees with her valorization of drag. Butler argues it subverts gender constructs, Sinfield, and Dollimore to a lesser extent, argue this subversion is recuperable, is ineffective. I should state that there are many queer theories and many overlaps in their theoretical origins, which coincide only in this idea that one should leave homo- and hetero- behind and concentrate on -sexual.

However while generalizing about queer is not easy, looking at the agendas behind what essentialists could see as a denial of the self, is a possible project. It is my belief that Butler and her followers are firstly feminists focused on gender, this traceable from McIntosh through Adams to Butler; Sinfield *et al.* have a gay male agenda, arising from Foucault, which talks about sexuality – this latter is the queer agenda. If this seems familiar in that old GLF rift, then perhaps it's comforting that the lesbians now support genderfuck, and the gay men are trying to ignore it.[27]

As to the way TSs have been read, as you can see from Sandy Stone's example, the women's movement is split over transsexuals, between those who think we are regressive, like Raymond, and those who think we are transgressive, like Haraway. While I thought I was out on a limb saying that we were being discursively produced in this bipolar way, Clare Hemmings at York and Henry Rubin at Harvard have both been arguing the same. Almost a consensus.

However, to argue the split is between intelligent pluralist, postmodern feminists and the old reactionary essentialist ones is too neat. Is it a surprise that the separatist violence against transsexuals on the grounds that we break down the category woman,[28] has been continued by their enemies within the women's movement, who argue the opposite?[29] Neither group latches onto the idea that by re-situating themselves categorically, transsexuals are less recuperable than a drag queen who can be dismissed by society as a perverted/misogynistic man. Male-to-females are clearly neither perverted nor misogynistic, because (a) they are doing what comes 'naturally' and (b) they become women, so their presumed hatred of women is acceptable, because it is self-hatred.

Transsexuals use their upbringing to create categorical excess in the opposite gender, because, as we shall see, it is that category which is the crucial thing.

Both groups of feminists refuse to feel happy with the idea that male-to-females reject their lives as men by arguing that they are still patriarchs; perhaps the reason for this lack of comfort is the contradictory position that female-to-males reject their lives as women, and hence from some vantage points, feminism. These feminists, like patriarchs, have an investment in their gender which is entirely unquestioned; transsexuals have questioned the gender assumptions of their biologically determined gender, found them flawed, and then acted, but not by creating a bipolar opposition, instead by foregrounding the constructed nature of the whole system. This is what I mean when I talk of doing work on a limitrophic hegemony. The second group of feminists, whom some *Deviance* TSs have rather cruelly nicknamed the 'M-sur-Ref' school[30] would, I think, mostly agree with Chantal Mouffe's argument that feminism should be seen as a 'struggle against the multiple forms in which the category "woman" is constructed in subordination', whose very multiplicity necessarily implies that feminist goals depend on many feminisms, and that 'any attempt to find the "true" form of feminist politics should be abandoned' (Mouffe, 1993: 88).

The problem and bonus of, in effect, disembodying feminism, is that this in itself universalizes rather than specifies the site of antagonism from which a given set of oppressions originate. We hide the agenda and in doing so we allow both separatist and pluralist feminism to make reactionary attacks on male-to-females' categorical excess as women, by naming it as belonging to men.

The radical/reactionary paradigm is of course flawed, partly because people read 'transsexual' simply and in isolation, and not in terms of deforming the social fabric – what about the wives who suddenly become lesbians, the husbands who become gay men, the children who have two parents to call mother, the families and families-in-law who become out-laws, who have to confront a schism between sex and gender, a foregrounding of society's assumptions. Within the present legal system male and female tick boxes are not adequate to cover the case of someone who is legally female but who lives and identifies as male, the transsexual has to choose between outing themselves or breaking the law. Far from being a site of antagonism who hangs her high-heels up at the end of the day, and signs a male name on the bottom of her life insurance policy, transsexuals have process, are not a point, but a locus, of antagonism that is forcing the government to change gender-biased legislation.

I've said elsewhere that I don't think queer is really interested in gender, and I hope people are beginning to see where I'm coming from. You cannot dismiss transsexuals as Dollimore does with a quote from the infamous Altman, 'the transvestite ... and even more the transsexual, seem the ultimate victim of ... stigma ... so conditioned into the male/female role dichotomy that the only way they can accept their own homosexuality is by denying their bodies ... My personal belief (hope?) is that transvestism and transexism [*sic*] would disappear were our social norms not so repressive of men who exhibit "feminine" traits and vice versa' (Dollimore, 1991: 296). Countering this is easy: transsexuals are of all orientations, indeed, transsexuals who were straight become lesbians and gay men, so irrelevant is the issue of taboos around sexuality. That Altman can make this elementary mistake in 1972 is sad, and he was diabolized for it – that Dollimore can replicate his findings in 1991, after other *causes célèbres* like Raymond, Jeffreys and Socarides had attacked TSs, sounds far more suspicious.

Perhaps we can read Sinfield's Altman against Dollimore's Altman: Sinfield says, ' "As long as society is based on competitiveness and sexual repression," Denis Altman observes, "there will be a need to demarcate it into categories, to maintain socially induced repressions by stigmatising heavily all those who fall outside the norm." ' (Sinfield, 1994: 187). Does Dollimore's Altman stigmatize transsexuals for falling outside Dollimore's norm? Yes, clearly. A corollary exists: is that normative homosexual society so fêted by Teresa de Lauretis[31] based on competitiveness and sexual repression? If one is a transsexual, it would seem so, and if the gay identity is being produced as we've seen rape crisis centres produce that of women, then restrictions on one's sexuality to same-sex relations, clearly are repressive.[32]

One of the divisions I suspect is evidenced between queer feminists and queer men surrounds psychoanalysis. Both groups in theory argue for 'the decentred subject', but where de Lauretis, Butler, Merck *et al.* and the pre-queer Adams take up Lacan and Freud, and its predicating of the conflicts between individual and society, I'm not sure the men do. Jeffrey Weeks argues notably, with Deleuze and Guattari, that psychoanalysis is 'both discoverer of the mechanisms of desire and the organiser of its control' (Weeks, 1985: 174). After a long critique of the medical model and its ability to internalize people's shame and guilt, including the argument that the Oedipal triangle is hetero-centric, this is what Sinfield has to say: 'It is not that I do not believe in psychic life, or that I would not like to have a theory of it. The trouble is, the plausible conceptual space for that exploration has been occupied, for our time, by Freudianism, which deploys fail-safe, double-bind, double-take and self-defence mechanisms of a subtlety undreamt of in Marxism or Christianity – the main alternative faiths of the century. So it is very difficult to envisage other terms with which to think our emotional processes' (Sinfield, 1994: 171–2). This is again a switch from the 1970s when the key GLF lesbians were extremely anti-psychiatric.

Queer and gender

Sinfield's study of effeminacy, *The Wilde Century: Effeminacy, Oscar Wilde and the Queer Movement*, manages to avoid using Altman to attack transsexuals, and like all these queer theory books is a very useful book that we can learn from, but I suspect it ignores Altman's transsexual by ignoring the issue of effeminacy. Perhaps I should explain: Sinfield's book historically details confusions between gender and sexuality through the various economic classes. He denounces some gay men's tendency towards effeminacy as being complicit with what he calls a *cross-sex grid*, the attempt to fit people into masculine/feminine, active/passive binaries and argues that effeminate gay men are belittled by allowing themselves to be produced discursively as women, who in our misogynistic society are perceived as lesser beings. He sees that receptive sex isn't necessarily feminine, that in Rictor Norton's words, 'if one partner gets fucked, he is not necessarily expected to make the breakfast next morning' (Sinfield, 1994: 46). But what he doesn't contemplate is that gender may have a place in the scheme of things in its own right as separate from sexuality, that for instance Molly Houses may have been produced because of gender oppression, and just became a safe haven for gay male sexuality as secondary. The cross-sexed grid is a classic example of a queer discourse structurally excluding 'trans'. Sinfield's general category for cross-dressing is effeminacy. 'Effeminacy is founded in misogyny' (*ibid.*: 26) he says. We know no better, we have to presume that m-to-f TSs are misogynists for Sinfield then. So much for Butler's definition of coalitions – do the gay and lesbian community acknowledge our difference?

I don't want to portray the queer women as being good and queer men bad; after all Bernice Hausman calls transsexuals, the 'dupes of gender' (Hausman, 1995: 140). However, some things queer dykes are saying might be extremely useful to us. Mandy Merck's description of how butch lesbians, such as Radclyffe Hall in the 1920s, constructed themselves within the terms of late nineteenth-century sexology as men in women's bodies, 'inverts',[33] allows us to read Hall's classic novel *The Well of Loneliness* as a parallel to transsexual autobiography, a fiction carrying a justificatory moral. This process queries both lesbian and transsexual identities, for, as non-op TS Virginia Prince says of m-to-fs, the desire for a vagina can be to use it for sex or to validate anatomically femaleness,[34] and while Prince limits us to just three possible uses for constructing a vagina, in my view erroneously, she is clearly right that this dichotomy points up the equivalence between gender and sexuality.

Radclyffe Hall may have been a lesbian constructing herself in what we now perceive to be transsexual terms, colluding with TS historians' attempts to reclaim her, but she may have been a proto-TS constructed by the lesbian community as a dyke; similarly, à la Prince, transsexuals may be gender transsexuals or sexuality transsexuals, or both, in the same way we can talk of gender lesbians and sexuality lesbians as I have implied with my writing of stone butches/femmes. What Merck disproves is the argument that transsexuals are constitutionally reactionary in comparison with lesbians' transgression, or that we can be discrete with gendered categories and sexuality-based categories.

Writing our own categories

Whether it delineates power juridically or not, psychoanalysis is one of the best analyses of social power we have, but we can also learn from queer's adoption of Deleuze and Guattari – especially those 'pioneers', like Virginia Prince, of the category 'non-op TS', attempting a similar realignment to the stone femme one.[35] One problem with Prince's adoption of medicalized terminology for her new term, 'pseudotrans-sexual', is that she reduced the excess of non-op transsexuals within Benjamin's new medical category. Pseudo-TSs still needed the category to provide hormones, and so this wasn't a category for us, but one for them. It is quite clear from Prince's ridicule of TS autobiography and her terminology on which side of that 'us versus them' border she situates herself. Anyone calling herself a pseudotranssexual, as she did, is indeed seriously self-oppressing – unless in doing so she gained points from the hierarchy, which this paper clearly does; my feeling is that most pseudo-TSs would want to be the real thing, such are the hierarchies around the word 'pseudo,' but it gets worse if you *are* one of the '5% to 10%' of non-pseudo-TSs who Prince believes suffer from what seems suspiciously like Goffman's spoilt identity syndrome.

What Prince, who starts her paper with an awareness that transsexuals construct themselves within psychiatric texts, was doing was to use psychiatric causation to justify non-operative transsexualism as a category – this at the expense of people wanting surgery; real transsexuals define themselves as sexually inadequate people with spoilt identities – surgery is appropriate for them. It's not even a case of saying 'she's muddling up cause and effect', it's a case of saying, 'don't collude with psychiatry'. Instead of justifying the non-op boundary position between the sexes, as many queer theorists argue TSs should do, she, in effect, stigmatizes both groups – all the excess between 'transvestite' and 'transsexual' is placed in a third medical category.

Prince's paper gets worse. For all her distinction between sexuality and gender, she falls back on desire for her diagnosis,[36] and the indexes she uses to judge between the two categories – the Kinsey scale of orientation, and the TS's experience of sex – would lead those seeking surgery to reject bisexuality, sexual experimentation and to abstain from sexual relationships. Transsexuals are safely neuter. Transgender via queer, on the other hand, doesn't care about causation – you don't need to have a spoilt identity, or to have had surgery, and it is too young and diverse a category to have acquired heavy accretions of pejoratives and establishment power play – thus, in Blechner's terms, we own it, it is liberating.

Limitrophic hegemony

Although I've read it as a plus, one problem with performativity is that not only can our agenda be lost in the transvestite's but we also become gay men and lesbians. In the TS's subjectless fight against gender, the Rhodesian mercenary-become-Soho prostitute scenario, we are signifying in similar ways to the butch/femme, to Sinfield's machismo/effeminacy of the lesbian and gay communities. Similar, but perhaps not the same, the distinction between producing gender and reducing it implies that transsexuals previously existed in a gender limbo, as in some way neutral, outside of male/female, hetero- and homo- sexual domains.

But in saying this, surely the movement from gender neutral is reactionary? No, sadly, the life experiences of TSs have shown that neutral gender is not read as such. At least in the UK, it is read as sexually uninterested, and even in the case of stone femmes, that's not true. But note if someone wants to become involved in sexual activity they need to signify through the peacock's tail of gender. Nor is drag an excess of femininity – the more feminine one is, the more turned on one appears, because one is still in productive mode. A reductive mode isn't a communication of sexuality to others, but rather to oneself, the peacock admiring his tail. Thus we are back, sadly perhaps, to the Oedipal versus the narcissistic, or worse, rejecting psychoanalysis.

One reason why some gay community discourses are as oppressive to our community as the straight, is because they read/write us as transparent in essentialist terms to the hetero-hegemony; this after all privileges their own transgression of the sexuality taboo, however we indeed present ourselves as desirous of being transparent to the patriarchy. Clearly someone brought up as male and living as female cannot be transparent, 'we want to be patriarchs we say' with our deeply queer voices. But too many bits of the gay community just want to see us selling out.

This has other implications: if camp for Dollimore is 'the pervert's revenge on authenticity' then his production of the gay communities' most characteristic performative mode is as inauthentic – this seems dangerously close to introjecting guilt. Sinfield argues that all lesbian and gay strategies are bound to be reactive to the dominant hegemony because they are defined by it (Sinfield, 1994: 203). Transsexual strategies of integration, however, are not reactions against the dominant, they attempt to integrate, but in the wrong place, and in the process show the dominant hegemony to be reactive. An example: for someone who is legally male by normative standards but living *and passing* as a female, all the efforts of the law are seen to be aligned against her – in pleading patriarchy she, with the aid of a fascinated media, shows the law to be reactionary; eventually, if G&SA, and similar groups, gets their way all male/female tick boxes may have to be removed from forms, all statements about sex from birth certificates, and as for marriages ... Gender will cease to be a label of the state. This strategy is about using your opponent's own weight against it – for queer to admit our transgression would be to admit its own 'us versus them' binary, worse that in comparison, its champion, drag, is banging its head against a brick wall.

One can see how this works – feminism won the moral argument, but then couldn't move beyond this position of power as the Other. Transsexuals will hopefully take this a stage further, by getting real equality through the law, a clear step towards making gender irrelevant to the state. However, until feminism stops colluding with patriarchy in its construction of women as victims, we will go no further in rectifying the problems of the rest of society. Here too, transsexuals have their place: in queering what a woman *is*, in being as much the victim of the women's movement as they are of patriarchy, transsexuals break down this limitrophic hegemony and there is a paradigm shift – the issue moves onto that of gender.[37]

Since the first article was written, a series of debates have taken place on the Internet in which the mood is to attack these poor stone femmes as a sort of trans-lesbian equivalent of fag-hags – they have no sexuality of their own, rather living through the desires and relationships of other women. Some of these writings remind me disturbingly of Moustapha Safouan's well-known piece on male-to-female transsexuals. For Safouan, my use of stylistics would be evidence not of my being a (subject position) woman, but of my psychotic desire to avoid being the phallus; my desire to destroy my penis was an attempt to escape from my castrating mother (who probably sexually abused me as a child) to a place where my desire could function 'normally'. If Lacan had, for Roudinesco, a fear of mothers, this also says something to me about Safouan's relationship with women – for, as in the work of Millot, these psychotic castrated male-to-female transsexuals are the only 'true' women.

The Lacanian constructions of transsexuals as psychotic are profoundly important, partly because it's useful to see what an intellectual, a philosopher would make of some of the raw material produced by Stoller, Money and others, and partly because of their influence in the French-speaking and academic worlds, which is considerable.

As well as the Schreberian comments and diagrams of Lacan, we have, among others: writing by Safouan, the infamous Millot, the regretfully compliant Mladen Dolar, Parveen Adams of course; Nicole Kress-Rosen's and Agnes Faure-Oppenheimer's attacks on Stoller, and why not the 'traumatic object-stain' in, sadly, Žižek's own writing of Hitchcock's *Psycho*? There Norman Bates's psychosis is predicated on the collapse of his own identity in favour of the return of his acousmatic (M)Other. A mother-in-a-man's-body, Norman is, of course, not a transsexual, but nevertheless perhaps we could see, to appropriate Michael Chion's phrase, these texts as interpellating a psychotic transsexual as product of an acousmatic-machine. All of these Lacanian dramatizations of the transsexual object of desire, if one buys that line, can be seen in relation to the 1956 transsexual-as-psychotic doctoral thesis of Jean-Marc Alby,[38] and all of whose work turns on the idea, not that the sexes are themselves essential, but that sexual difference is irreducible, Cixous puns on the initials of '*différence sexuelle*' and *déesse*, the sound the initials make in French, D.S. is transcendent, the goddess,[39] and so I am going to devote the rest of this section to look at this issue via another post-Lacanian, Joan Copjec – who, for a change, doesn't talk about transsexuality.[40]

EKATERINA PLUS: *Last night I dreamed of sexuation tables. The trannies were playing shuffleboard, reading the phallus as passing, flinging it down the tables. Would it go imaginary, symbolic or real?*

Copjec is interesting because she attacks Butler, as Millot attacks transsexuals, by backing up her arguments using the Lacanian sexuation tables. So we have an, admittedly dislocated, confrontation between the two most sophisticated sets of writings on transsexuality. These tables, or rather the accompanying algebra, are taken from Lacan's Seminar XX (1972–3), *Encore*. Like Ama Ata Aidoo, Copjec argues, via Kant, that Butler basically reads the theory wrong – far from being a mere symbolic/imaginary construction (to do with the social, language, and the seduction of images), sexual difference for Lacanians, she says, is in the real, is principally to do with the unconscious and the unpredictable nature of desire.[41]

EKATERINA PLUS: *Waking, there was Copjec at the end of my bed. A bubble left her mouth inscribed with the word, '$\forall x.\Phi x$' [all men have the phallus], for it to have been a close encounter, I should have returned the interpolation, '$\exists x.\overline{\Phi x}$' [but not all men may be castrated]*

Copjec's argument is that the Lacanian system is a more radical construction than Butler's, on the basis of this absolute contradiction held within the algebra. However, we have seen exactly how radical the system is, allowing Millot to write transsexuals as nasty psychoperverts. Copjec's arguments around this contradiction are extremely powerful for me, but what I read as aporia in her text are revealing. Lacan's sexuation tables are based on the speaking subject, and so the phallus is represented by a capitalized phi, Φ, positioning sexual difference in the symbolic – the phallus in the real is written, Π, and in the imaginary, ϕ. In trying to hold together Kant, Lacan and Butler, Copjec faces a return of the Lacan, does he actually mean that sexual difference is in the symbolic? I'm afraid so; elsewhere, in his Seminar IV, *La relation d'objet* (1994a: 153) Lacan follows a discussion of the fantasized body in fetishism with:

C'est en tant qu'il (le phallus) est là ou qu'il n'est pas là, et uniquement en tant qu'il est là ou qu'il n'est pas là, que s'instaure la différenciation symbolique des sexes;

that is, he specifically distinguishes between the fantasized body in the real and imaginary[42] and the institution – by the presence and absence of the phallus – of sexual differentiation uniquely in the symbolic. And further in the same place he repeats:

C'est en tant que la fille n'a pas ce phallus, c'est-à-dire aussi en tant qu'elle l'a sur le plan symbolique, c'est en tant qu'elle entre dans la dialectique symbolique d'avoir ou de n'avoir pas le phallus, c'est par là qu'elle entre dans cette relation ordonnée et symbolisée qu'est la différenciation des sexes, relation interhumaine assumée, disciplinée, typifiée, ordonnée, frappée d'interdits, marquée par exemple de la structure fondamentale de la loi de l'inceste.

Sexual differentiation is part of a symbolic dialectic, of having and not having *ce phallus*, the symbolic one, but note how easily Lacan goes from 'différentiation des sexes' to 'relation interhumaine'. For Lacan there is very little difference between sexual differentiation and the sexual relation between the sexes, whereas for a lesbian or gay man that might not be so simple. But to the point, even fifteen years later in *Encore*, Copjec's source, Lacan is still very clear that the tables apply to any speaking being whatsoever, and on the nature of sexual difference, 'Ce champ est celui de tous les êtres qui assument le statut de la femme' (Lacan, 1975: 75) – all those beings who *assume* the position of woman, and note this is not 'tous les gens', all those people, but, 'tous les êtres', all those who *be*. And we remember, via Kristeva, earlier, those male writers who assume such a position.

As we know, the real is that which resists symbolization absolutely, is 'that domain which exists outside of symbolisation' (Lacan and Wilden, 1984: 280). However, maybe there is something else in Copjec other than this sliding of sexual difference, via Kantian logic, into the real, a sliding between 'rapport sexuel' and 'différentiation des sexes'. A subtle difference in Lacan because he perceives the sexual rapport as gendered *per se*. This is also a very subtle trace in Copjec so I will only briefly touch on it with her introduction to this argument in *Encore*. 'In this seminar', she begins, 'Lacan reiterates the position of psychoanalysis with regard to sexual difference [*sic*]: our sexed being, he maintains, is not a biological phenomenon, it does not pass through the body, but "results from the logical demands of speech" ' (Copjec, 1994: 213), but by the end of the paragraph she quotes him saying, ' "There are two ways for the affair, the sexual relation, to misfire. . . . There is the male way . . . [and] the female way.' The phrase Lacan uses at first is *'L'être sexué de ces femmes'* (Lacan, 1975: 15) ('the sexed being of these women') and the second begins *'Il y a donc . . .'* the 'donc' referring to the famously misconstrued statement, 'il n'ya pas de rapport sexuel' (*ibid.*: 53). In the first we talk about 'being' and in the second about the relationship in gendered sexuality. 'Sex', as in sexuality, is clearly in the real, but sexual differentiation is in the symbolic. Sexual 'difference' is not mentioned in these passages quoted from Lacan. This positioning of sexual difference into sexuality, this positioning even of the real as synonym for desire, found in most Žižekians, feels like the heterosexual imperative; the real is caused by the *objet petit a* in the imaginary – the other ('autre', from which the letter 'a' derives) doesn't equal male versus female – sexual rapport isn't *per se* sexual difference.

Another problem Copjec has, however, is mostly shared by Lacan. On entry into language the child is ordered by language, (the nom/non du père) and, as we know, positioned by it in terms of sexual difference – when the child becomes a subject, it is always already a sexed subject. This privileging of gender over other differences is really problematic in Copjec: 'sexual difference is unlike racial, class or ethnic differences. Whereas these differences are inscribed in the symbolic, sexual difference is not: only the failure of its inscription is marked in the symbolic' (Copjec, 1994: 207). Unhappy with negated inscription in the symbolic, Copjec places difference as if a positive, without argument into the real. She then goes forward to predicate individual sovereignty and the failure of determinism on sexual difference, as if sexual difference were arbitrarily transcendent.[43] If this is not evidence of an essentialized difference based, I suspect from the other Žižekians, on anatomy, I'm not sure what is, and yet conversely, when someone walks into a room the first things I notice about them are their sex and skin colour, i.e. the visual, I am hit by the imaginary, whereas in Copjec there is an undervaluing of the imaginary in favour of the real.

We could see this as being in the Lacanian tradition, however, in so far as Lacan devalues the imaginary ego (and hence conscious agency) in favour of the symbolic subject. Copjec brings in political correctness to rescue the Lacanian position, but only succeeds in raising the spectre of Millot's transsexual: 'It is only when the sovereign incalculability of the subject is acknowledged that perceptions of difference will no longer nourish demands for the surrender of difference to processes of "homogenisation," "purification," or any other crimes against otherness with which the rise of racism has begun to acquaint us' (*ibid.*: 208). One only has to remember Millot's use of Raymond to realize that transsexualism, and probably Butler's writing, are 'crimes against otherness'.

Delouse and Gabbana: a final leg to trans-theory's English table

Finally then, to this last venue on our whistle-stop tour of UK trans theory. We are left with everyone's favourite weirdoes, Deleuze and Guattari. The venue for this paper was the First UK Radical Transgendered Politics Forum run by Sheffield University (July 1996). It's notorious because a couple of activists, who had been straight white men a few short years ago, and who were now radical lesbian separatists, objected to the forum being chaired by G&SA's straight white male HIV worker. 'He should be "torched"', one declared. For me it was most memorable because over half the audience walked out at my oblique paper, leaving me confused as to quite what I was doing. A shame, because psychosis is perhaps extreme, but it is a way of solving the problem of introjected guilt – which bedevils the debate around Harawayan/Sandy Stone's post-transsexual discourses.

I think of this D&G piece as a site, an edge where empirical and pomo discourses meet, but to some extent this is mitigated by the realization that *Capitalism and Schizophrenia* is systems philosophy, D&G as much cybernetians here as Stafford Beer or Niklas Luhmann. I also want to introduce doubt or ambivalence about/into my work; yes, the TS community have faced assaults more or less equally from both 'patriarchs' and 'feminists', but Merl Storr has argued that the stone femme piece(s) we've just heard, and the Lacan-to-D&G paper, *Limitrophic Hegemony and the 3rd Sex*, part of which we are about to visit, which looks at the way the Rape Crisis Centre's relationship with patriarchy allowed it to interpellate transsexuals as both rapists and rape victims – that these papers 'transsexualise feminism into a paternal/oedipal figure. Which is not by any means to condemn [Kate More's] account, but merely to say that it, like the RCC idea of woman, has its own effects and productions of desire'. Clearly we need to go further into the limitrophic hegemony debate to see where this criticism takes us.

Limitrophic hegemony

Introduction

We are set several problems by Raymond and Millot, and UK trans theory tries to examine some of them. Raymond through Haraway and Stone is proving to be a saviour rather than an avenging angel. But Millot, Adams *et al.*? One of the things the TS community needs to work on is simply understanding Millot's exceptionally complex Lacanian arguments. How can transsexuals be psychotic, what does it mean to be psychotic for Lacan and his schools? After all, for erm, Kristeva, lesbianism is psychotic.

Avoiding the issue of introjected guilt here, of taking on perhaps the juridically constructed identity of psychoses, there are questions about psychosis that seem valid and not about stigmatization. Why do we apparently perceive our gender identities to be essentialist, when for Lacan this means foreclosure of language and psychoses? How do we explain that the Nazis during the Second World War could be caring fathers, brothers, boyfriends and husbands and yet were able to go about the work of gassing hundreds of thousands of seemingly innocent Jews? This is a situation where the abject Jewry weren't psychotic, and the soldiers were, to all intents and purposes, normal, but in retrospect, perhaps that society, constructed above all from a bipolar between the abject and the blond-haired, blue-eyed normative, was, yes, psychoticized by acts of war, but the structure must, for Lacan, already have been latent. Psychiatrists condemn the psychotic – by denying them agency, physically and chemically, and by defining the term psychotic. For me this is the most dangerous situation for any identity, for clearly for those with power but not agency, madness follows. This is a familiar situation for medicalized transsexuals. One question for me is, while maintaining agency for the individual, can one construct a juridical identity in which individuals are not pathologizable as psychotic, but which by the nature of juridical identity gains power from the potential for psychosis, from the energy source which is the black hole foreclosure of the name of the father?

These are questions that led me first to Lacan's reading of the *belle âme*, which proved useful in theorizing both trans-activism and separatist feminism, and then to the work of Deleuze and Guattari (D&G), another of the butts of Brodribb's humour. D&G adopted schizoid logic to theorize power from the perspective of the psychotic. Their work is perhaps the most eccentric off-shoot of Lacanian psychoanalysis, rebelling against the Père himself, though staying strangely within Lacan's understanding of the psychotic as a foreclosure of the name of the father, the source of all repression.[44]

In preamble I ought to mention again D&G's concept, the 'becoming woman', to reinforce how this is a becoming psychotic because sexual difference, for Lacanians, is irreducible. I would mention this idea in Irigarayan terms, to show how the move from phallocentric sexuality is replaced by a multiplicity of touching and re-touching. I want to show how complex the relationship with transsexuality would be for Irigaray if sexual difference weren't irreducible, but is irreducibility my problem?

The war being too far away for me to summon/examine adequately, I found myself returned to the poor abject transsexual and the normative counsellors and psychiatrists, to look for gas chamber parallels (you will remember Raymond's statement that sex change surgery was not created in the concentration camps, but this is what the Nazis did there, and wasn't it similar? So forgive me for wreaking this return of the barely repressed on the separatist women's movement).

EKATERINA PLUS: *Perhaps a TS is a man who walks into a woman-making machine, or a woman who walks into a man-making machine and comes out as if schizophrenic. The TS who goes into a man-making machine has the 'I am' of a man, but the history and socialization of a woman. Perhaps the world sees someone who says 'I can be a man "and" a woman' instead of 'I can be "either ..."' a man "or" a woman', and this is the reason TSs are perceived to be psychotic. Perhaps a TS is performatively schizo, sometimes operating as men and sometimes as women ...*

D&G (IN CHORUS): It might be said that the schizophrenic passes from one code to the other, that he deliberately scrambles all the codes, by quickly shifting from one to another, according to the questions asked him, never giving the same explanation from one day to the next, never invoking the same genealogy, never recording the same event in the same way ... The schizo maintains a shaky balance for the simple reason that the result is always the same, no matter what the disjunctions. (Deleuze and Guattari, 1996: 15)

On rape crisis centres (RCCs)

For D&G it should be impossible to turn desiring-production into an assemblage without the presence of a BwO (a body without organs – a psychotic 'space' where difference is undifferentiated). A rape crisis centre could not, in deleuzoguattarian terms, be a BwO simply because its difference *is* differentiated – it is a single-sex venue. In this section, however, I want, in positing that an RCC *is* a BwO, to problematize D&G, to raise the possibility of the impossible, non-molar gender-creating binary machines.[45] This is an examination of the sort suggested by Butler[46] at the beginning of *Gender Trouble*, to establish how much of the gender/sex debate is 'prediscursive', i.e. written in molar ways (Butler, 1990: 7).

In doing this I do not intend to say that RCC workers are psychotic, I intend to say that the system they participate in, as read by D&G, is psychotic. For D&G psychosis is an incredible compliment. This in itself poses a problem for me.

The right term for an RCC is 'RCC', that anonymizing acronym, those connotations surrounding Catholicism even, but when meaning is established, 'Rape Crisis Centre' and 'Rape Crisis Collective' are interchangeable – the body and the assemblage are at some level indivisible, the assemblage is, or is mapped onto, the body without organs. I started trying to analyse RCCs by thinking of individuals I've known, but found myself repeatedly being returned to either the collective body, or if determinedly reading people as individuals, to Lacan's reading of Hegel's concept, the *belle âme*. Appropriately for D&G this is a classic schizoid position.

Desiring production

RCCs are machines for collectivizing people, they are machines for constructing the identity 'Woman'; they are process, from the anonymous 'Hello, Rape Crisis', the break : flow of the initial telephone conversation, to the mechanics of an Egan-based or Rogerian counselling process. Using these methods, telephone counselling can even be reduced to a Samaritans-style 'a-ha', followed by an occasional précis of the caller's statements; all individuality on the part of the counsellor is minimized, all thought has been freed into process; the client is where it's at – the counsellor is not in her individual body at all, for she has none, but at the far end of the telephone becomes a function of the client's disjunctive relationship with the assemblage. It is hypnotizing telephoning an 'a-ha' machine; one soon slots oneself into a desperate desire to get beyond the a-ha, one sucks oneself dry telling this machine whatever it needs to hear, each correct sentence is registered (*enregistrement*) in an appropriate pause by an a-ha, the counsellor's function being merely to witness/record, and the production is predicated on the desire to make some sort of relationship based on our common experience – one needs to become a part of that collective identity.

> D&G: Desiring-machines are binary machines, obeying a binary law or set of rules governing associations: one machine is always coupled with another. The productive synthesis, the production of production, is inherently connective in nature: 'and ...' 'and then ...' This is because there is always a flow-producing machine, and another machine connected to it that interrupts or draws off part of this flow (the breast – the mouth). (Deleuze and Guattari, 1996: 5)

EKATERINA PLUS: *Autopoiesis?*

Being a member of an RCC implies having experienced trauma at the hands of patriarchy, a regression, a becoming childlike, that one is called to talk about, and perhaps this is why the cogs in an RCC adopt a semi-anonymous mode. Such a mode allows a slippage of identity, only one piece of baggage is brought into play. To the client, the telephone counsellor often has no name at all, she is the noise of the machine, the sound of the voice of the hidden RCC.[47] If the client is suitable for absorption into the body without organs of the RCC, and visits the centre for face-to-face counselling, counsellors may be distinguished from one another by use of the first name, but even fellow counsellors contrive, often, to be unaware of their colleagues' surnames, the name of the father if you like. In the same way the RC Centre is not announced – they are often ordinary terraced houses in anonymous streets, workers keep the whereabouts secret, there is seldom a sign on the door and sometimes collectives go to extremes to hide it. One centre I know arranges a nearby street-corner as meeting place, this overlooked from a room used by the centre. The centre operates a car, and counsellor, driver and, well, 'bodyguard' drive around the block and the one diagonally opposite. The counsellor and bodyguard get out of the car and walk to the client. The driver leaves the car engine running. The two plus client walk back to the car, which is physically in the opposite direction from the centre, and they drive away continuing to vet the client until, once accepted, the client is taken to the centre, via the back streets. Understandable given the nature of rape, but again adding a disjunctive element. This is, yes, partly about confidentiality, but also because of separation/deterritorialization – the rules of the RCC are to be distinct from the outside. Inside is women-only space, empowerment is perceived to be about displacing the male ideology – which has forced itself physically, territorially, onto the client – with a Woman-centred one.

This flow of clients, this juncture, is critically important in the Lacanian model, working in three ways, for the client, the rapist and the TS. D&G say, 'A machine may be defined as a system of interruptions or breaks (*coupures*). These breaks should in no way operate along lines that vary according to whatever aspect of them we are considering ...' (Deleuze and Guattari, 1996: 36–7), yet two of our three groups of people are banned.

'The disjunctions characteristic of these chains', say D&G, 'still do not involve any exclusion. ... exclusions can arise only as a function of inhibitors and repressors that eventually determine the support and firmly define a specific, personal subject' (ibid.: 38–9), that is, this disjunctive should not be a line of flight, but rather molar – indeed we can see at this point the construction both of the identity 'Woman', and of the identity 'Rapist'. Yet we saw from our example the creativity that goes into breaking the rapist from his territory, the woman – the refusal to even allow police*men* into some RCCs. This is a line of flight that has molar effects; the transsexual woman who has been raped is turned away, because as we've seen (More, 1996a), she is in some ways contiguous with, and in other ways metaphorically, the rapist.

It seems to me that there are several peculiarities about this particular assemblage/BwO. Clearly (as should be the case), most of the people in the collectives are undifferentiated, a few of the more commercial centres have a centre-manager, but even the admin. staff in the RCCs I know best, have had to go through counselling-training and have experienced rape or child sexual abuse. Sometimes the workers were even produced as clients of the body without organs in which they work. The assemblage is achieved, I suspect, by yet more hypnosis: all the women in the body without organs are one, they are processed/ connected up by counselling and being counselled, but moreover, by hearing and re-hearing, speaking and reiterating the litany of the raped. It seems to me that the product 'Woman' is productive of more 'Women', in that the women she meets, sees and emulates emerge into society apparently caring and wise, having a professional and first-hand understanding of trauma, and trained to detect deceit in people's body language and the Rogerian methods of desiring-production. She is 'strong' because she has become essentialized. In Kristevan terms she has become a walking, talking pheno-text, the genesis of her signification has been closed by its relationship with the ideology which produced it;[48] at some level rape crisis centre and collective, body without organs and assemblage, replicate itself and the woman becomes essentialized, the machine. Clearly when RCCs took to the streets in the US in the 1970s and here in the 1980s to 'Reclaim the night', the sense of people's unity as women was extraordinary.[49]

But perhaps this is a feature of all desiring-machines. What strikes me as particular to the RCC is the way the interface/counselling works. For me normal psychoanalysis is what the Barthes of *Mythologies* would call a wrestling-match; it is a structured game, a performance in which the actor and the audience test the boundaries of various identities, and if it works, the actor has found a place to safely go about the business of rewriting her identity. However, whereas in normal psychoanalysis there is transference and counter-transference – in the Rogerian and Egan-based counselling used by RCCs there is no transference, the actor does her bit, but the audience is a machine which says 'a-ha.'[50] In other words, there is a one-way system in operation – for the counsellor she is a part of the desiring-machine/body without organs, but the situation for the rape survivor is merely that of desiring-production. Does not Freud say that the schizo, unlike the paranoid, is 'incapable of achieving transference' (Deleuze and Guattari, 1996: 23).

I ask myself if we have an understandably paranoid clientele connected to what is arguably a schizoid RCC. As we know, flow-producing machines connect to other flow-producing machines that interrupt or draw off part of the flow (*ibid.*: 5) – perhaps the RCC-machine is interrupted by the rapist-machine, and the flow of rapists/TSs drawn off. It is easy through psychoanalysis to see how denial (lack) creates desire, indeed the RCC could be seen as a return of the repressed, the woman's cathected 'no' triggering the rape, the RCCs' 'no' triggering the rapist's need to destroy the sanctity of the women-only space. For the TS, the juridical denial by these authorities of her identity as 'woman', as 'rape victim', creates more trauma, more introjection of the label, 'rapist'. This label was commonly ascribed to TSs of both sexes by the 1980s women's movement (More, 1996a). But for D&G there is a problem, there is no Freudian concept of repression, indeed identity itself is formed through boundaries and is thus by definition, reactionary.

For me the interface with the assemblage/BwO is unusual because the deterritorialization is based on the metaphysics of gender as much as on ideology or geography (there are only one or two places in D&G

I've found where the endless stream of metaphysics overtakes anti-essentialist production of undifferentiated difference, particularly, surprise, surprise, sexual differentiation and the becoming-woman. For instance, D&G say, 'Does a girl have a peepee maker? The boy says yes, and not by analogy, nor in order to conjure away a fear of castration. It is obvious that girls have a peepee-maker because they effectively pee: a machinic functioning rather than an organic function. Quite simply, the same material has different connections, different relations of movement and rest, enters different assemblages in the case of the boy and the girl (a girl does not pee standing or into the distance)' (Deleuze and Guattari, 1993: 256). Here sexual difference is clearly posited on biological function and then removed from biology to something else, 'machinic' rather than 'organic'. Being perhaps rather than having? Perhaps, perhaps not, but clearly something of that order. 'There is a mode of individuation very different from that of a person, subject, thing or substance. We reserve the name *haecceity* for it' (*ibid*.: 261) and this is what little girls are made of. 'What is a girl, what is a group of girls? Proust has shown us once and for all that their individuation, collective or singular, proceeds not by subjectivity but by haecceity, pure haecceity' (*ibid*.: 271). Rather familiarly, women are not subjects, but D&G go on to state through Proust's narrator, Swann, that boys are. According to Braidotti this point had been raised before: 'Deleuze deferred to the superior knowledge of women on this matter' (Braidotti, 1996: 5). Of course, if it weren't for male rape victims and the unfortunate TS, we could argue that rape and rape crisis centres were predicated upon the potentiality that one could be raped, upon the biology of the female anatomy, but in reality, it seemed, denial happens.

The next place this thinking took me is very uncomfortable, perhaps for D&G the essentialists, the separatists were right – in some way to do with the nature of Oedipus and patriarchy – only 'real' women can be raped. That there is some qualitative universalized difference that makes men and TSs rapists rather than rape victims. That the RCC's is not a 'true' exclusion, just a line of flight from the fascist. Of course it is our old friend sexual difference.

If I am right, through this metaphysical deleuzoguattarian quirk, desire and identity can be created juridically, by gate-keeping – men and those women, such as trans-women, who fail the metaphysical test, are refused entry to the body without organs, are refused the right to produce the identity 'Woman'. But notice, as I've remarked before, the rape crisis centre doesn't allow men to change for the better, even by becoming women – it enforces patriarchy, even the becoming-woman is rejected.

Perhaps we should have presumed that an exception to the rule of undifferentiated difference might occur when it is realized that D&G's becoming-woman is so obviously predicated on a metaphysical opposition, but clearly this shows us a form of machinic coupling that D&G failed to foresee: linked, binary desiring-machines working symbiotically, acting to produce in effect repression of a third, the transsexual. This is what I call a limitrophic hegemony, a shakily balanced schizoid mechanism constructing identity via people living in and feeding on the oppositions in society. A limitrophic hegemony is performative, it only exists when both machines operate to crush a third, in this case the TS, who is both raped and turned away as the rapist. If the trans-sexing case were not crushed it would otherwise be a position that has the potential to decouple the bipolar machine.

D&G say that the nature of desire is that desiring-machines will always link together as binaries, forming a linear series (Deleuze and Guattari, 1996: 5) and of course this implies that this trinary linkage of the limitrophic hegemony may only exist if the third party may oppose the other two, in this case is both male and female.

It seems to me that producing RCCs as a cult of the Déesse and TSs as psychotics is a long way to go to bypass the difficulty of the already sexed subject and the relationship of that sexing with essentialism. I do, however, think that for some cultures psychotic social structures are at play in the construction of gender.

CIXOUS: ... *I have noticed that there are actually national forms of inscription of all those problems. I was in Greece two years ago, I was completely struck because I had never taught there – I gave a lecture and met with young people, transsexuals, people who had, for instance, taken Deleuze as a kind of prophet ...*

KATE: *Becoming Woman?*

CIXOUS: *Yes, they were becoming butterflies and things like that, it was totally imaginary! I just asked, 'Has Deleuze ever done that, has he become another being than being a man', that was paper! It was not real. But in Greece you know they lived according to that. So of course it was a specific situation, it could not be exported.*

KATE: *You see it as a literalism?*

CIXOUS: *Absolutely.*

JAY PROSSER: *Of writing?*

Conclusions

Millot says Flaubert says conclusions are silly. They certainly aren't a pomosexual thing, but sometimes being silly is the most important thing. As Fuss has shown us, it is almost impossible to produce essentialist discourses without also summoning constructionism and vice versa, so perhaps we should be no longer playing this bipolar game and start looking at a situation where postmodernism is taken as read, as almost universal throughout today's discourse, as a part of the Real, indivisible, for with acceptance, perhaps we can get past the negativity, the anger and start to build a society out of the chaos.

In arguing that a TS is provisionally both male and female I recognize the risk of essentialism, but I also recognize that in my recategorization as female I am simultaneously essentializing woman and constructing her, as Merl Storr points out, from a transsexed male/femaleness. My feeling is that this essence of woman is both male and female, that is by categorically resituating itself, TS woman becomes neither sex. Rather like Irigaray's woman, a TS is always plural, always both and neither metaphor and metonymy, always a community, never an essence.

KATE MORE: *Hah! You just think stone femmes individuate themselves by opting out of altérité!*

Shhhh ... closure ... closure ...

Notes

1. *Acknowledgements:* Thanks to Sarah Gasquoine who put me up/put up with me, during endless trips to various London libraries. Thanks to the young black librarian who chased after me in the Round Reading Room with my lost floppy disk containing this chapter. Thanks to Leroy White and Tim Jordan, dear friends, for totally confusing me between them with contradictory advice – and letting me talk D&G at them! 'Limitrophic Hegemony and the 3rd Sex' was my fault, not theirs! I owe special thanks to Diane Morgan for going to the extreme of buying *Séminaire IV* when I couldn't find it, for drawing my attention to Jonathan Dollimore's unindexed quote and for just being there. Professor Hélène Cixous

appears courtesy of a forthcoming interview undertaken by myself and Jay Prosser for *Radical Deviance* after her recent visit to the ICA. Many thanks to Professor Cixous (and to Helena Reckitt for help with those arrangements).

2. Much of the work on the borders between identities is also being done in the US. We owe much of our re-thinking to Judith/Jack Halberstam, Jacob Hale and Jay Prosser whose dialogue, borrowing from Butler, has removed it from Kristeva's and other post-structural theory, where most of us had left it stagnating. See Prosser's paper in this book (Chapter 4) and the Halberstam/Hale paper in the Transgender issue of *GLQ*. For a simpler, more textbook approach to gender acentricity see Gesa Lindemann, *The Body of Gender Difference* (1996): 'In contrast to Laqueur's two-sex model, this acentric explanation of gender distinction brings together three moments into one form of distinction whose immanent coherence is otherwise hard to comprehend: (1) acentric gender distinction does not have a gender-defined centre, and inasmuch it permits the notion of women gradually attaining the same equality with the generic that men already have; (2) at the same time, the distinction appears from the perspective of the male pole as a qualitative difference; and (3) it remains a hierarchical polar contrast of opposites from the female perspective' (p. 346). Those from the UK community making significant contributions – whose work is not mentioned here include: Zach Nataf with an interest in film, race and in popularizing transgender theory; Carol Riddell, with a long-time involvement in the women's movement; closest to my own work in some ways perhaps, Sue/Johnny Golding, and my co-editor, Stephen Whittle, rapidly being accepted as paterfamilias to the UK community, specializing in law, but with interests including cyber-gender.

3. See Jean-Louis Baudry, 'Écriture, Fiction, Idéologie', *Tel Quel*, 31, (1967): 22, 'Déjà le pseudonyme est le phénomène daté de l'écrivain en tant qu'il est créateur et propriétaire de son "œuvre". Pleynet l'a bien montré à propos de Lautréamont, ce n'est pas un "auteur" qui signe une "œuvre", *mais un texte qui signe un nom'*.

4. See the forthcoming text by Diane Morgan, *'An Angel on All Fours':* *'Inverts' and Their Dogs*. For me one of the most impressive things about the excitement of trans-theory is that philosophical contradictions, for instance in this paper, nihilism working with Deleuze and Guattari, regularly appear in the same sets of discourses.

5. See the *Radical Deviance* interview (More, 1997) with Judith Butler in this book (Chapter 13).

6. Kristeva has argued that negativity is the fourth term in the Hegelian dialectic, in our discussion of Butler; perhaps we should recall her discussion of Derridean deconstruction where she writes, 'Negativity is inscribed in arche-writing as a constitutive absence: the "absence of the other"'; 'irreducible within the presence of the trace'; '*différance* is therefore the formation of form' (Kristeva, 1984: 141).

7. This term is coined I think by the excellent Dave Boothroyd, University of Teesside.

8. This is an extremely complicated philosophical concept Lacan borrows from his friend Heidegger. One trap is to see 'being' and 'existence' as synonymous, when actually the subject (which exists, but doesn't *be*) is brought into existence by the desire to be. Lacan says in *The Psychoses* that one feature is irreducible in being – the copulatory function (Lacan, 1993: 301).

9. I've been criticized for wasting my time reading this book, and I concede that it is full of literalisms and is hardly rigorous. My response is that my interest is in separatism as a borderline state, and Brodribb seems to be one of the first full-length texts engaging at a conscious level with postmodernism.

10. See Brodribb, 1993: xvii, 17, 59–70, 72, 81–4, 97, 111, 118, 128 and 145–6. An interesting comparison is in Fuss (1990: 12), where she argues that Lacan also spoke as woman, as Derrida tried to do.

11. Althusser's insanity and murder of his wife is covered in depth (Brodribb, 1993: 2–4 and 10, about half of the discussion about him); Sartre's description of women as holes and slime (*ibid.*: xvi); poor Deleuze apparently describes women as bodies without organs (*ibid.*: xvi. For Deleuze whose philosophy in *Capitalism and Schizophrenia* was based on the logic of schizophrenia, becoming a body without organs was a stage in revolutionary actions not just for women, but for both people and groups.); Baudrillard's statement about taking a woman to the desert to sacrifice her (*ibid.*: 16, interesting because it is the last thing we hear of Baudrillard whereas the rule is that we hear about the misogyny before the theory); postmodern feminists suffer 'romantic thralldom' (*ibid.*: xvi) to the dragged-up gods of postmodernism.

12. Apologies to Fredric Jameson, whose actual quote was, 'undo postmodernism homeopathically by the means of postmodernism: to work at dissolving the pastiche by using all the instruments of pastiche itself', quoted in Brodribb, 1993: 13. For Žižek, in his writing of anti-postmodernist Habermas, Habermas is king of pomo and Derrida merely the most rigorous of modernists (Žižek, 1992: 142), but more of these slippages later.

13. Far from dismissing political fictions as some sort of Grand Guignol, we rather need to find ways of authorizing them. My hope is for theory to open out practice and I feel that this writing of Aristotelian essence could be a very profitable political project, provided our puppets were of the sort Rosi Braidotti writes of in her book *Nomadic Subjects*; what could Winkte theorists (Native American berdache) do with a bit of strategic literalism? With a text like Deleuze and Guattari's *A Thousand Plateaus* to stimulate nomadic becomings, the kachina dolls of the Hopi, which some might read simplistically as literalized animist spirits, others as bits of kitsch for the tourist market, could indeed exceed the prosaic,

and, for example, the spirit of the wind could be inhabited, could be gendered, could become complex, in turn making gender more complex.

14. Nor to Catherine Clément, whose piece, 'Enslaved Enclave' precedes Kristeva's in the book of translations Brodribb uses. Ann Rosalind Jones précises Clément's question, 'Do not feminine delirium, hysteria, ecstasy finally support the order that tolerates such states as temporary or finally imprisonable deviations?' (Jones, 1987: 4) Where does that leave my trans-questioning of my/the male ego? To which my reply is that there is absolutely a question over these strategies, as there is over the 'colluding in male discourse' strategy, but this isn't something we can afford to construct a bipolar over. Some people's oppression will just not allow them to fit in with hegemonic control. We need all strategies, the unconscious/ desire is absolutely a defence mechanism against external control, and is often recognized as such, as in anorexia and narcissism even. In defence of ecstasy, (a) Kristeva's praxis is not that simple, is to break down bad identities like 'Woman' – which is where she sites the problem; (b) ecstasy is only easily recuperable as a monolithic margin, only when it is voiceless, when ecstasy is not articulated – mass, critically and strategically articulated ecstasy would be a different situation; and (c) to an extent owning two categories through a third, 'transsexual' allows me to elide, certainly the category 'man' which I am critiquing with my narcissism discourses. Unlike the Carol-Anne Duffy situation before I was labelled 'transsexual' by my surgery, no one would now take me as a 'man', would read the discourse straight, nor do I come across as narcissistic because I read as female. In effect I play one category's difference off against the other's – as a textual practice.

15. One can see this becoming-woman of analysis in H.D.'s account of the end of hers. Freud is reduced to pleading for the importance of the father, hammering on the headpiece of the couch, at his lack (H.D., 1971: 22–3). H.D.'s response in her poem 'The Master' (quoted in Brodribb, 1992: xv) is to reduce his deity to the more important state, woman.

16. 'Cuit' from Derrida, 'Dès qui'il est saisi par l'écriture, le concept est cuit', as soon as a concept is seized it is cooked/lost.

17. Written in a fit of pique, this article adopted the very same line as my opponents, but rather than begin to wonder how they could be so appropriated by irresponsible postmodernists ('In critiquing Butler have I just made a return to Kristeva?'), and challenge me with 'But we said that!', they remained silent. The article's anti-parodic mode reference Sèméiotikè (Paris: Seuil, 1969b – see, e.g., p. 91, where Kristeva's position is that the parodic mode is, in fact, only pseudo-transgressive, reinforcing the law it refuses to engage with). The article's subject also projected its embodiment into the symbolic, i.e. came to be in discourse – but this, of course, is better known Kristeva from La Révolution du langage poétic (Paris: Seuil, 1974). As one can tell (by my basing authority on self-citation), we are not dealing with the real Kristeva, but a flüchtig-hingemachte-Kristeva.

18. Reviewed by Clare Hemmings, *Radical Deviance*, 2, 2 (1996): 59–60.
19. Halberstam, 'F2M: the making of female masculinity', in L. Doan, *The Lesbian Postmodern* (1994) – for a discussion of this conflict see Halberstam's forthcoming article in the *GLQ*, Transgender Special Issue (1998).
20. In Interview *Radical Philosophy*, 67 (Summer 1994).
21. In *Gender Trouble* Butler (1990: 24–5) talks of gender being a performance that creates the subject, a doing, but 'not a doing by a subject who might be said to pre-exist the deed' yet this quasi-Kantian metaphysics of substance (see Kant, 1991: 191–2) doesn't seem to allow for differences within coalitions (Butler, 1990: 14) which aren't based on doing, such as the desire for, or predication of action upon, surgery, which arguably separates transvestite from transsexual, or those that separate lesbians from gay men, nor does it take into account their different positions in the hierarchy and the relationship this has with discourse – compare the following: 'There is a paradox in synergy. The paradox is that the creativity and innovation which are needed for synergy to happen usually come from thinking about things differently. This is usually achieved in groups where there is a high degree of difference among people. It is this very difference which can generate inter-personal conflict. As said earlier, the higher the difference, the higher the variety of the system, and this combination of high variety and inter-personal conflict can be explosive. On the other hand getting into rapport with and being able to work easily with others comes from the similarities people share. It has been found that people most naturally like others who look, sound and behave like they do. Thus the paradox' (Team Syntegrity, *Guide to World Syntegrity*, 1993).
22. See Fuss, 1990: 107–8; Merck, 1993: 1; Bristow and Wilson, 1993: 6; Power, 1995. Having commented with Bristow and Wilson and the American, Merck, that performativity grew up in London, one might see McIntosh's performativity prefigured in Foucault, 'There is being only because there is life ... the experience of life is thus posited as the most general law of beings ... but this ontology discloses not so much what gives beings their foundation as what bears them for an instant towards a precarious form' (Foucault, 1966), though an even earlier version arises through the performative speech acts of Austin.
23. The register of those present can be found in *differences*, 3, 2 (1991) xvii.
24. According to G&SA's equal ops policy we keep a record of these identifications, and asexual lesbians comprise 8 per cent of the membership. There is also some discussion in the medical texts: e.g. Bentler, 1976, and Hoenig and Kenna, 1979.
25. Which is given on the grounds that gender dysphoria is a mental disorder as defined in DSM IV and ICD 10. There are plenty of studies showing that surgery relieves many of TSs' problems – do we have a right to play God in the name of political correctness? See, e.g., Lothstein, 1984 and Mate-Kole *et al.*, 1988.

26. See also Sinfield, 1994: 161–75, on adopting guilt.

27. I don't want to portray this as a regressive move: GLF lesbians were suspicious of the gay men's motives in adopting gender as an issue in genderfuck; this was perhaps because they didn't obviously benefit from doing damage to gender, being (a) men and (b) gay, not having to compromise their patriarchy in the application of desire. Nor was this because the men didn't attempt to be feminist, this was just read as political correctness (see More, 1996b). As I've argued elsewhere, there is a great deal of investment in the male–female binary which neither patriarchs nor feminists want to give up. To get beyond the frisson, the production of identity in the female-versus-male hegemony, we need more than women, 52 per cent of the population, to work on gender.

28. Or reify and problematize 'woman' as a category, as seen throughout Janice Raymond's text *The Transsexual Empire* and as exemplified in her famous call to arms, 'All transsexuals rape women's bodies by reducing the real female form to an artifact, and appropriating this body for themselves', (Raymond, 1980: 104).

29. Parveen Adams, Ann Bolin *et al.* argue that far from moving from Butler's valorized position of parody or a position where one is read as a man 'pretending', to a genuine categorical re-situation within which a number of often excessive positions are adopted, we attempt to become either transparent as women or in the Lacanian school's case as The Woman.

30. The pun being a mimesis of m-to-f; the separatists being the Ref school, after the common Women's Aid abbreviation for refuge, and the latter after the prominent post-Barthesian psycho-feminist journal, *m/f* so associated with the Lacanian Parveen Adams. For Adams's view on transsexuals see Morgan, 1996: 70.

31. In her introduction to the foundational texts of queer theory as a term, *differences*, 3, 2 (1991) iii.

32. This piece on Rape Crisis Centres is 'Limitrophic Hegemony and the 3rd Sex', part of which concludes this chapter. Sinfield references Trumbach and G.S. Rousseau to argue that there was a move from bisexuality evident around 1700 (Sinfield, 1994: 37–8).

33. Merck writes of Hall's heroine in *The Well of Loneliness*, 'If Stephen Gordon is an effort at lesbian self-portraiture, she serves to remind us just how constructed such portraits are. This brings us back to photography and Hall's efforts to construct her own image (efforts which extended to having the luxuriant curls of her childhood portrait obliterated in conformity with Ellis's theory of congenital gender reversal)' (Merck, 1993: 89; see also pp. 86–100).

34. The third use being to give birth. In Prince, 1978: 265.

35. The most recent edition of *Chrysalis*, 2, 3, is dedicated to Prince and Benjamin's 'pioneering' work in creating the two categories, pseudotrans- sexual and transsexual.

36. See Diane Morgan's (1997) paper on the failures of this approach (and reprinted in this book, Chapter 11).
37. This paper first appeared as: Kate More, 'Radical [a]genders: stone femme, effeminacy & the English queer', *Radical Deviance*, November 1996.
38. This section, argument and references, come from my forthcoming 'Contre Lacan?' in *Radical Deviance*.
39. In *rootprints* (1997: 54), but Cixous is not new. Lacan says, 'je mettais entre l'homme et la femme un certain Autre qui avait bien l'air d'être le bon vieux Dieu de toujours' (Lacan, 1975: 64), roughly, I put between man and woman (wife) another that has the manner of that good old god of old.
40. Thanks to Mandy Merck for referring me to Copjec's book – the section I am working with is Copjec, 1994: 201–38.
41. Copjec, 1994: 207, 'Sexual difference, in other words, is a real, and not a symbolic difference'.
42. It doesn't affect my point, but I'm being controversial in positioning fetishism in the imaginary and the real, Lacan's attribution of it to the symbolic raising considerable debate (see Gamman and Makinen, 1994: 101–3). I prefer Kristeva's formulation: fetishism is a substitution in the symbolic, 'which consists in denying the mother's castration, but perhaps goes back even further to a problem in separating an image of the ego in the mirror from the bodily organs invested with semiotic motility' (Kristeva, 1974/1984: 63), i.e. the symbolic is shifted into the imaginary and the real. The debate is that if the penis is fetishizable then most women are fetishists through their lack. Bizarrely, as I see it, this may help us explain why m-to-f transvestites are sometimes sexualized by their clothing while m-to-f TSs seldom are – the TSs often don't achieve sexualization until after surgery, when the operation to produce lack allows them to fetishize the penis in others.
43. See the Butler interview in Chapter 13 – 'What does that mean – "difference?"'
44. Roudinesco records that Lacan believed he had invented the 'desiring machines', and the body without organs seems to bear a terminological resemblance to the Lacanian Real. *L'étourdit*'s 'becoming woman' was in 1973.
45. It seems that for Deleuze and Guattari the concept of becoming is a breaking away from the molar writings of the 'great bipolar machines'.
46. In an almost autopoietic, if misreading of Maturana, kind of way!
47. Centre is physically hidden geographically, Collective in another way. Bea Campbell in *Unofficial Secrets* (Campbell, 1988: 99), quotes workers at Tyneside Rape Crisis Centre recalling that for public purposes they all used to call themselves 'Beryl Thompson', their anonymity perhaps named after the supposed ex-wife of the Tyneside comic, Bobby Thompson, a queasy portrayal of northern masculinity.
48. See Kristeva, 1969a: 35–6. For those who read French it goes: 'Le texte

n'est pas un *phénomène* linguistique, autrement dit il n'est pas la signification structurée qui se présente dans un corpus linguistique vu comme une structure plate. Il est son *engendrement*: un engendrement inscrit dans ce "phénomène" linguistique, ce *phéno-texte* qu'est le texte imprimé, mais qui n'est lisible que lorsqu'on remonte *verticalement* à travers la genèse: 1) de ses catégories linguistiques, et 2) de la topologie de l'acte signifiant. La signifiance sera donc cet engendrement qu'on peut saisir doublement: 1) engendrement du tissu de la langue; 2) engenderment de ce "je" qui se met en position de présenter la signifiance. Ce qui s'ouvre dans cette verticale est l'opération (linguistique) de génération du phéno-texte. Nous appellerons cette opération un *géno-texte* en dédoublant ainsi la notion de texte en phéno-texte et géno-texte (surface et fond, structure signifiée et productivité signifiante).'

49. Merl Storr (forthcoming) notes that there was much dissent from black women; although this is a valid criticism, some of this I feel was retrospective, and at that time RCCs were predominantly white organizations, i.e. it would be against white RCC unity.

50. 'As we examine our clinical experience in client-centred therapy and our recorded cases, it would appear to be correct to say that strong attitudes of a transference nature occur in a relatively small minority of cases' (p. 199 continuing on to p. 214 explaining) 'why a dependent transference does not tend to develop in client-centred therapy' (Rogers, 1951).

References

Barthes, R. (1986) *Mythologies*. London: Paladin.

Baudrillard, J. (1994) *Plastic Surgery for the Other*, *http://www.ctheory.com/ a33-plastic_surgery.html*

Baudry, J.-L. (1967) 'Écriture, fiction, idéologie', *Tel Quel*, 31.

Bentler, P.M. (1976) 'A typology of transsexualism: gender identity, theory and data', *Archives of Sexual Behaviour*, 5: 567–84.

Braidotti, R. (1996) *Radical Philosophy*, 76, 5 (March/April).

Bristow, J. and A. Wilson (1993) *Activating Theory: Lesbian, Gay, Bisexual Politics*. London: Lawrence & Wishart.

Brodribb, S. (1993) *Nothing Mat(t)ers: A Feminist Critique of Postmodernism*. Melbourne: Spinifex Press.

Butler, J. (1990) *Gender Trouble: Feminism and the Subversion of Identity*. London: Routledge.

Campbell, B. (1988) *Unofficial Secrets: Child Sexual Abuse: The Cleveland Case*. London: Virago.

Cixous, H. and M. Calle-Gruber (1997) *rootprints: Memory and Life Writing*. London: Routledge. Translated by Eric Prenowitz.

Clément, C. (1990) *Vies et légendes de Jacques Lacan*. Paris: Grasset.

Copjec, J. (1994) *Read My Desire: Lacan against the Historicists*. Cambridge, MA: MIT.

Deleuze, G. and F. Guattari (1993) *A Thousand Plateaus: Capitalism and Schizophrenia* (Volume 2). Minneapolis: University of Minnesota.

Deleuze, G. and F. Guattari (1996) *Anti-Oedipus: Capitalism and Schizophrenia* (Volume 1). Minneapolis: University of Minnesota.

Dollimore, J. (1991) *Sexual Dissidence*. Oxford: Clarendon Press.

Domenici, T. and R.C. Lesser, (1995) *Disorienting Sexuality: Psychoanalytic Reappraisals of Sexual Identities*. London: Routledge.

Epstein, J. and K. Straub (1991) *Bodyguards: The Cultural Politics of Gender Ambiguity*. London: Routledge.

Faludi, S. (1992) *Backlash*. London: Chatto & Windus.

Foucault, M. (1966) *Les Mots et les choses*. Paris: Éditions Gallimard.

Fuss, D. (1990) *Essentially Speaking: Feminism, Nature and Difference*. London: Routledge.

Gamman, L. and M. Makinen (1994) *Female Fetishism*. London: Lawrence & Wishart.

genderfuck (1995–6) G&SA transzine. Middlesbrough.

Halberstam, J. (1994) 'F2M: the making of female masculinity', in L. Doan, *The Lesbian Postmodern*. New York: Columbia University Press.

H.D. (1971) *Tribute to Freud*, with an introduction by Peter Jones. Oxford: Carcanet Press.

Hausman, B. (1995) *Changing Sex: Transsexualism, Technology and the Idea of Gender*. Durham, NC: Duke University Press.

Hoenig, J. and J.C. Kenna (1979) 'EEG abnormalities and transsexualism', *British Journal of Psychiatry*, 134: 293–300.

Hombach, D. (1990) *Die Drift der Erkenntnis*. Munich: Raben Verlag. (Cited in Žižek, 1991.)

Jones, A.R. (1987) Introduction to C. Clément, *The Weary Sons of Freud*, (N. Ball, trans). London: Verso.

Kant, E. (1991) *The Critique of Pure Reason*. London: Everyman.

Kristeva, J. (1969a) 'L'engendrement de la formule', *Tel Quel*, 37, Printemps.

Kristeva, J. (1969b) *Sèméiotikè: Recherches pour une sémanalyse*. Paris: Seuil.

Kristeva, J. (1974/1984) *Revolution in Poetic Language*, trans. M. Waller. New York: Columbia University Press.

Lacan, J. (1975) *Le Séminaire Livre XX. Encore*. Paris: Seuil.

Lacan, J. (1977) *Écrits: A Selection*, trans. A. Sheridan. London: Tavistock.

Lacan, J. (1981) *Le Séminaire Livre III. Les psychoses*. Paris: Seuil.

Lacan, J. (1993) *The Psychoses: The Seminar of Jacques Lacan*, trans. R. Griggs. London: Routledge.

Lacan, J. (1994a) *Le Séminaire Livre IV. La relation d'objet*. Paris: Seuil.

Lacan, J. (1994b) *The Four Fundamental Concepts of Psycho-analysis*. Harmondsworth: Penguin.

Lacan, J. and A. Wilden (1984) *Speech and Language in Psychoanalysis*. Translated with notes and commentary by Anthony Wilden. Baltimore: Johns Hopkins University Press.

Lindemann, G. (1996) 'The body of gender difference', *European Journal of Women's Studies*, 3: 341–61.

Lothstein, L.M. (1984) 'Psychological testing with transsexuals: a 30-year review', *Journal of Personality Assessment*, 48: 500–7.

Mate-Kole, C. *et al.* (1988) 'Aspects of psychiatric symptoms at different stages in the treatment of transsexualism', *British Journal of Psychiatry*, 152: 550–3.

Maturana, H. and F. Verela (1980) *Autopoiesis and Cognition: The Realisation of the Living*. London and Dordrecht: D. Riedel.

Merck, M. (1993) *Perversions: Deviant Readings*. London: Virago.

Millot, C. (1983) *Horsexe: essai sur le transsexualisme*. Paris: Point Hors Ligne.

More, K. (1995a) 'The law, the ass and the transsexual', G&SA leaflet (reprinted in *genderfuck* March, 1996).

More, K. (1995b) 'So what is transgender?', *genderfuck*, August: 3–4.

More, K. (1996a) 'TSs and the radicalness of separatism', *Radical Deviance*, 2, 1: 6–14.

More, K. (1996b) 'Coalitions, common issues and hate crime: a conversation with Angela Mason', *Radical Deviance*, 2, 2: 48–9.

More, K. (1996c) 'Limitrophic hegemony and the 3rd sex', paper given at First UK Radical Transgendered Politics Forum, London, July.

More, K. (1996d) 'Radical [a]genders: stone femme, effeminacy and the English queer', *Radical Deviance*, 2, 3: 96–103.

More, K. (1997) 'Excitable speech: an interview with Judith Butler', *Radical Deviance*, 2, 4: 134–43.

More, K. (forthcoming) 'Contre Lacan?', *Radical Deviance*.

More, K. and J. Prosser (forthcoming) 'An interview with Hélène Cixous', *Radical Deviance*.

Morgan, D. (1996) 'Passovers: of postmodernism and transsexuality', *Radical Deviance*, 2, 2: 69–70.

Morgan, D. (1997) ' "What does a transsexual want?": the encounter between psychoanalysis and transsexualism', *Radical Deviance*, 2, 4: 153–60.

Morgan, D. (forthcoming) ' "An angel on all fours": "inverts" and their dogs'. In C. Blake and G. Banham, *Evil Spirits: Nihilism and the Fate of Modernity*. Manchester: Manchester University Press.

Mouffe, C. (1993) *Return of the Political*. London: Verso.

Power, L. (1995) *No Bath But Plenty of Bubbles*. London: Cassell.

Prince, V. (1978) 'Transsexuals and pseudotranssexuals', *Archives of Sexual Behaviour*, 7, 4.

Prosser, J. (1998) *Second Skins: The Body Narratives of Transsexuality*. New York: Columbia University Press.

Radical Deviance: A Journal of Transgendered Politics. (Continuation of *genderfuck*, 3/1996–; G&SA, 6–9 Cynthia Street, London N1 9JF).

Raymond, J. (1980) *The Transsexual Empire*. London: Women's Press.

Raymond, J. (1993) *Women as Wombs: Reproductive Technologies and the Battle over Women's Freedom*. New York: HarperSanFrancisco.

Roudinesco, E. (1997) *Jacques Lacan*. Oxford: Polity.

Rogers, C.R. (1951) *Client-centred Therapy: Current Practice, Implications and Theory*. London: Constable (1951/1993).

Sinfield, A. (1994) *The Wilde Century: Effeminacy, Oscar Wilde and the Queer Movement*. London: Cassell.

Storr, M. (forthcoming) In T. Jordan and M. Storr, 'On stone femmes', roundtable discussion, *Radical Deviance*.

Swaab, D.F. *et al.* (1995) 'A sex difference in the human brain and its relation to transsexuality', *Nature*, **378** (2 November): 68–70.

Team Syntegrity (1993) *Guide to World Syntegrity*. Toronto, Canada.

Weeks, J. (1985) *Sexuality and Its Discontents*. London: Routledge and Kegan Paul.

Žižek, S. (1991) *For They Know Not What They Do: Enjoyment as a Political Factor*. London: Verso.

Žižek, S. (1992) *Looking Awry: An Introduction to Jacques Lacan through Popular Culture*. Cambridge, Mass.: MIT.

13

Never Mind the Bollocks: 2. Judith Butler on Transsexuality

An interview by Kate More

I n the following interview for *Radical Deviance*, which took place in London on 13 May 1997, Kate More (KM) talked to Judith Butler (JB). We would like to thank Professor Butler herself, the Institute of Contemporary Art[1] who scheduled her and provided the facilities, and her publishers Routledge for their support. For obvious reasons *Radical Deviance* asked Kate to footnote freely.

KM: In the interview as a whole I want to ask a couple of general questions about yourself and your politics; I then want to go through the books, introducing them and asking questions to help unpack them a little, and then go on to see what room there is for a Lacanian reading which doesn't follow the line of Millot[2] and Adams.[3] Maybe I shouldn't talk about your own subject positions given your writing on performativity ... ?[4]

JB: No, I think you should do that, everyone's going to want to know!

KM: I think it's probably because of your comments in *Bodies That Matter*[5] about people calling you 'Judy', situating/feminizing you after you wrote *Gender Trouble*;[6] I was really interested when someone suggested you might see yourself as, quote, 'a butch dyke' unquote. I wondered how – whether – you constructed yourself juridically,[7] and if you do anything with your own portrayal of gendered norms?

JB: I see, yes, something I never write about! I'm trying to think how I would answer this question – see I told you to ask me the question and

I'm not sure what response I have! What's clear is that I have an uneasy relationship to categorization, I accept that categories exist and I even use them, and yet the point of my work is not to figure out a proper or adequate mode of description for myself and I would hope I never come up with such a thing. I think it might be a certain kind of death to have actually achieved identity. On the other hand I tell a little narrative about myself which uses categories, and I say that I came out when I was sixteen, and situated myself in relationship to butchness in my early twenties – I'm 40. And I've had an active and complicated relationship with both butch–femme discourse and S/M discourse probably for almost 20 years, which is not to say that I would identify myself fully within any of those terms. How can I say this? I'm engaged by them and that I negotiate my identity in terms of them.

KM: Transgender?[8]

JB: I think transgender has always been there for me as an issue and that I feel great affiliation with transgendered communities and feel that my work, although it hasn't always been explicitly linked to those issues, strikes me as at least theoretically very sympathetic. I think that one of the points I try to make to people on this issue is that there is a lot of transgendering that goes on in mundane heterosexuality, and it is not just this identity over here that's more marginalized, that's different from normative identities, but it actually underwrites normative identities, that there is a kind of spectre of transgendering that heterosexuals work with all the time, and that gay people do, and that it actually haunts any stable gender identity. I don't mean to globalize transgender, that is, make it into something everybody is, but I want to say that it's an issue that people deal with all the time. Have you heard about the Ellen episode in the US?

KM: Go on ...

JB: There's this sit-com in which this woman comes out as lesbian and the next day everybody walked around with these buttons, 'I'm one too!' I was asked to wear such a button, but I can't really do that ontological moment. Be out – it makes me really nervous, but I don't deny it either, I wouldn't go around saying I'm not one. I'm kind of somewhere in the middle.

KM: A presence and absence? If I go on to situate your books? Your first, often forgotten book, *Subjects of Desire*,[9] interests me, I imagine it to read Hegel's master/slave dialectic[10] via Lacan;[11] the ideas that the master needs the slave, the distinction between *being* and *having* that Lacan takes on with his ideas that the woman *is* the phallus and the man *has* the phallus.[12] This seems like an origin for your central concept of performativity. How does *Subjects of Desire* prefigure *Gender Trouble* and *Bodies That Matter* and is this where performativity comes from?

JB: I don't know, it may be. I think that my work has been about the problem of recognition and that Hegel introduced me to that problem, the idea that a subject not only requires recognition, but that a subject actually can't come into being without recognition of a certain kind. So I suppose one could say that recognition exercises a performative effect, that one *is* to the degree that one is recognized, to the degree that one realizes that modes of recognition are in discourse; there is a Foucaultian[13] twist to that Hegelian formulation which then suggests that what we are is a function of the discursive categories that are available for recognition. So I think my work continues to be concerned with that issue – that even the hate speech book[14] is about the whole problem of what it is to recognize oneself in language that may also be injurious, but which also leads one '*to be*' in some socially significant sense. On 'Lordship and Bondage': I still think it's brilliant, I love it and teach it, I think the whole question of how identity is purchased at the expense of another, and the question of self-loss at the core of identity is something Hegel gives us.

KM: *Gender Trouble* was immediately an intellectual best-seller, arguably founding both queer theory and subsequently the new transgendered politics. However, it has also perhaps provoked a split in TG politics between the parodic deconstruction of gender with drag and the more anti-parodic constructionism of transsexuals. The title *Gender Trouble* has been seen as a phrase de-medicalizing the transsexual syndrome – *gender dysphoria* – yet contains just 50 words on transsexuality – may I read them? '*Transsexuals often claim a radical discontinuity between sexual pleasures and bodily parts. Very often what is wanted in terms of pleasure requires an imaginary participation in body parts, either appendages or orifices, that one might not actually possess, or, similarly, pleasure may require imagining an exaggerated or diminished set of parts.*'[15] And I was interested in the relationship here between the imaginary[16] and transsexuality; the debate's been read in two different ways? Millot talks about TSs being duped by the imaginary.

JB: Can you explain more about what the two ways have been?

KM: Reading it the way that it seems as though you're writing, and according to Prosser,[17] sex is constructed through the imaginary, in which case transsexuality is there at the cutting edge, almost, politically, but for Millot that participation in the imaginary, presuming it happens, means TSs have an idea of becoming The Woman and ...

JB: ... This is tricky! I hate these positions! [laughs] No, it isn't 'The Imaginary', OK, I'm not using imaginary here in a strictly Lacanian sense and that's really important, and I think if I were using it in that way I'd talk of the imaginary. I think in fact, if we were speaking in a more properly psychoanalytic vein, there is no sexuality without a phantasmatic,[18] which I think is the term I then use in Bodies That Matter to describe something similar, so here 'imaginary' is being used in a very untechnical sense and as for transsexuals being at the cutting edge, I think what's crucial is that that slippage between what we might understand as a sense of anatomy outside of the phantasmatic and of an phantasmatic anatomy – that that kind of sense of slippage is actually constitutive of sexuality and to the extent to which transsexuals expose it or work it, or own it or make it graphic, that that's making graphic a structure that is also happening within the most normative modes of sexuality. The discussion in Gender Trouble that you cite is about intersexuality, but I think the Herculine Barbin chapter is also about a certain kind of transsexuality, it could be read that way.

KM: Briefly, because it's about to come up again in a new study. In Gender Trouble[19] you talk of David Page's attempt in Cell magazine to reassert the biology of sexual differentiation over the gendered body. How do you read the Swaab[20] paper from Nature magazine's arguably much more successful attempt to do this?

JB: I haven't actually read it.

KM: What that's saying is that there's a bit of the hypothalamus, called the central bed nucleus of the Stria Terminalis which is not only sexually dimorphic, but that male-to-female TSs are 'female' when read by this standard. I guess the question really is: if biological gender dimorphism is proven to be determining, where do we go politically from there?

JB: Proven?! I don't think it can be proven. I am actually permanently suspicious of any such proofs on logical grounds. What is meant by 'female'? It seems to me that there is an enormous semantic equivocation at that moment. What is being stated? Is it some putatively pure sense of anatomy that's being stated? Is it a sense of gender? Is it a sense of sexuality? What are the attributes? What are the characteristics? It's either semantically empty, at which point the proof could be valid without having any meaning whatsoever, or it's using an utterly fictitious construct as if it were valid. I'd love to look at this paper, I'm sorry I don't know it, but I bet I could destroy it, and I would seek to do so!

KM: It seems to be predicated on difference rather than the content of that difference,[21] there seems to be some space for play there ...

JB: What does that mean, '*difference*'? Without an attribution of any specificity? It strikes me as either the smuggling in of a semantic specificity under the rubric of pure fact or structure – or just bullshit. I'm unequivocally hostile to such explanations.

KM: OK, [*laughs*] let's go back to *Bodies That Matter*!

JB: [*laughs*] Sorry!

KM: No, seriously! There are times when these things can feel liberating, and other times when it can be terribly constricting ...

JB: ... Sure, but that's another question entirely: What's the desire for biological explanation? What is the desire for biological determinism? And what do we imagine to be its satisfaction? Do I want desire to be beyond my choice at some point and ontologically constitutive, to be proven by men of science, who have hard knowledge? What does that do? It's a kind of fabulous release from the anxieties and the ambivalences that go on with being sexed, it cauterizes the ambivalence in the constitution of sex and I actually think there is no way round that. I can understand why we might want it, but I think that to accept it as explanation, is to sacrifice everything that is dynamic and important about the categorization of sex and its possibility of being revised and re-worked and re-lived and unless we live it as a social category I think we are in a lot of trouble.

KM: In a way that's the problem of transsexuality, isn't it, a Catch-22, you have to give ground to the medical people to get surgery ...

JB: I think that's a question, but I think there are ways to negotiate that, you don't need to understand medicine as the final authority in your life. It can be one instrument or resource to be deployed.

KM: That's my view too, we need all options, politically. [pause] Ahem! Bodies That Matter [laughs] tries to set limits on the excitement caused by Gender Trouble, it rather turns to the materiality of the body, to sex rather than gender. What do you think of Kate Bornstein's comment that there is no sex only biological gender?[22] Would you put that into the 'misreading of Gender Trouble' category?

JB: Kate Bornstein's very interesting and I actually have a fair amount of sympathy with what she does. What she means about biological gender is not about determinism. It seems to me that for her transsexuality is all about a possibility of self-transformation which she understands as constitutive of gender itself, so when she's talking of biological gender she's not talking about it as something which fixes and determines, she's talking of a scene of transformation. And because she's committed to a notion of becoming and transformation, as the end in itself, she's not trying to go from one gender to another and then to arrive. And I would totally buy that, it's not a teleological view of transsexuality. And there's another German scholar called Gesa Lindemann who does this as well, in a really brilliant way, in a book called The Paradoxical Sex.[23]

KM: Do you think that TSs' bodily recategorization closes down possible interpretations of the text in almost the constative way that Hausman[24] reads them doing in TS autobiography? [pause] I'm interested in why TSs are so literalized in academic texts, like in the Hausman itself.

JB: Yes ... but what text do you mean? The text of transsexuality? How would that be? Are you asking me if there's a dominant interpretation of transsexuality as a process of literalization, that it is a process of literalization or that it somehow becomes the occasion for highly literal interpretation?

KM: The last, I think. But I'm wondering if transsexuality is in some way complicit with that, beyond writing medicalized texts for surgery.

JB: Give me an example of what you're worried about ...

KM: I suppose I'm thinking of Adams's reading of Orlan,[25] the French performance artist, you know, who sticks cheekbones on her forehead so that she shouldn't be read in a metaphysical way as The Woman. She should be something other, and TSs are criticized for not fixing their transition. Maybe I'm not making very much sense?

JB: It depends on which transsexual perspective you take; some do try to achieve a certain truth of the ontology of gender, to approximate as far as possible an idealization of gendered norms. And yet others that seek to be disruptive. Bornstein for instance. Jan Morris[26] tends to accept a certain kind of gender essentialism which probably would be taken as a literalization, but even to take something as a literalization is still not to take it for granted as the literal truth. It's still to perform and act a literal version, and so to undermine something of the literalness that is being achieved. Even in the supposedly more literal version of transsexuality, the very fact that it's constituted undoes its claim... part of the excitement is... there's an ambivalent relationship to passing, and there are people who argue that the point is not about going from man to woman or woman to man, but from one category to being a transsexual. Right?

KM: Right! A shifter, a self-indexing thing?[27]

JB: Yes. And that seems to be a more radical move; it doesn't precisely make the transition that it indicates, it becomes in a peculiar way an allegory of the process which it undergoes.

KM: That's interesting, it sounds good to me. Would it help to outline what *Bodies That Matter*'s view on transsexualism is?

JB: There are students of mine who are writing on this, and perhaps it would be better coming from them. I do think that the point of *Bodies That Matter* is not so much to pose the materiality of the body as a counter to the excitement of *Gender Trouble,* though I can see that. But to suggest that when we approximate a gender norm that it's not just a role we take on, but it actually has to do with a fundamental crafting of the body, that norms are materialized on bodies, and that what we take to be the materiality of the body is in some ways the action and effect of a set of norms. But those aren't simply composed *on* the body, but they also produce bodies, and if you can accept that at some level, then it seems that we have to think about transsexuality rather differently. We wouldn't talk about a given body that then gets subjected to a new set of gender norms, but about one normatively construed body that renegotiates its relationship to the norms that constitute it. So transsexuality would not necessarily be the move from a descriptively female body to being a normatively male body, but rather the transition from one set of norms to another set of norms. And surely the transition and the incongruity that is constitutive of those norms, so what do we say about this? The living body, the lived body, is the matrix of gender norms, that there is no recourse to a biological fact that is not already construed normatively as the sex and 'biology' of the situation. Transsexuality may challenge all the ways of describing biological sex. I would so much prefer that transsexuality be a radical epistemic challenge to reigning biological descriptions than an acceptance of received biological descriptions.

KM: OK! Your new book *Excitable Speech* is, in a way, a return to Lacan and his concept of the parlêtre[28] – a return to speech and the law of the father. In *Gender Trouble* I looked for the subjectivity behind the performative as a deconstructive strategy and it struck me, moving to *Excitable Speech*, that you have refocused subject positions, if you like, from privileging parody to examining what it is like to be parodied; ridiculed in language. Do you see this – and how has your position re deconstruction versus constructionism changed between these books?

JB: Good question. The way I would see it … It's interesting, I don't think that Lacan makes much of an overt presence in *Excitable Speech*, or maybe it does[29] … I'm not sure it's the Law of the Father though, I don't think I buy that Law of the Father stuff, I think what I accept is that one is certainly constituted in a language that exercises a power that is not the same as the power of the subject, the power which constitutes the subject, that precedes the subject. Because *Gender Trouble* was interpreted as a highly voluntarist text by some, and by others as a very determinist text, I thought I needed to reapproach the question of agency within discourse. I thought I needed to work on what it is to be constituted by the various names that one is called, and at the same time how one might begin to use those very names, injurious though they are, to respond to that call, and to refigure it in ways which allow for agency within discourse. The book is an effort to explicate how agency is possible in the field of the discursive constitution of the subject. Certainly it is a book about being parodied by others, insulted, injured, gendered, raced, but it is also about deriving an agency from that situation, and about how that agency is riven with ambivalence, irreducible to a sovereign notion of agency. So agency is about the repetition of norms and I would say that *Gender Trouble* is about the repetition of norms, and *Bodies That Matter* is about the repetition of norms and one might even go back to Hegel and say that the phenomenology does nothing but repeat a certain scene seeking to alter it fundamentally through its repetition. So I think I'm still working on this problem of agency and repetition.

KM: Early on when I was myself transitioning, somebody I'd walked past on an estate asked me, 'Have you got the time, Miss?' – flushed by my success in passing I turned back to hear her add a sarcastic '-ter' on the end, 'You got the time, Miss-ter?' Not a question, a summoning of the closet followed by an outing of me from it. How does *Excitable Speech* see these acts of hate speech operating?

JB: Isn't it tricky? What I find really interesting is the way in which people tend to apologize as if they've insulted you massively when they get your gender wrong, and the idea that mistaking your gender is understood as being a really basic insult. People get flustered, they get embarrassed, they get mortified by making this mistake and I gather that the assumption is that they presume you will feel that way, insulted by the mistake. I find this very interesting, as if something very fundamental about one's integrity is bound up with being addressed in the proper gender. Of course what that misses is the interpellative[30] issue of what it is to be addressed through the proper gender, where being properly gendered through address is its own massive insult. You were in fact being normalized, you were being recognized in the first syllable, as one who had departed from a proper gender norm, and then being brought back under the norm by the second syllable. So I find it a very interesting speech act, because it acknowledges the faltering of its power and then it recuperates its power. Why don't people apologize for portraying 'proper' gender norms? Although what I get is, the 'Judy' joke, what was meant in jest, or, if I brought attention to it, it was taken as a sign that I was humourless. People 'Judy' me, 'You're just a girl – like the rest of us, Juuu-dy!' There is a certain kind of anxiety that maybe I'm not just a girl like the rest of them, an acknowledgement of it, but what they do is see this as just the structure of a certain kind of misbegotten fantasy on my part, 'Oh there's Judy, she thinks she's not a girl! Poor self-deluded girl!' And that's a self-delusion that girls undergo and the very fact that she engages in self-delusion is proof that she's a girl because girls are deluding themselves all the time by that fiction. But I think that it's also an attempt to regender me and to allay a certain anxiety that they have that I've actually departed in some fundamental way from the norm and that there is no possibility of me ever returning to girl, to the girls, which is that active and threatening interpolative moment.

KM: You become a strange sort of transsexual in some way!

JB: I think I psychically and culturally signify as such in some quarters! And that in some ways my identification with transsexuality is rather seamless, which I'm happy to avow, though that's not the same as having an identity. That's just because I have problems with identity!

KM: How much do you think we can read academic texts like Janice Raymond's *Transsexual Empire*[31] and Catherine Millot's *Horsexe* as hate speech?

JB: I think so, why not! I think they're horrible![32]

KM: What I was thinking was that because they seem to use the cultural weight of academe to invert and invoke transsexuals' victim status – we are part of the patriarchal rape machine for Raymond, and clearly *Horsexe*'s cleverness as a title is partly its reference to the English 'Whore Sex'?

JB: I feel that it will be some time before the general academic audience comes to understand that those texts are as pernicious and as hateful as overtly misogynist and racist texts are. They work in different ways. I think Raymond's text is part of a homophobic radical feminism, but also one that can only understand gender trespass and gender transitivity as appropriation, as if something's been stolen from them. Gender is itself a transferable property, it doesn't belong to anyone, and the idea of figuring it as non-transferable property is just a massive mistake. In the case of Millot I think that she appeals to the sexual conservatism in orthodox Lacanianism that seeks to install sexual difference in a fairly unambiguous and normative sense as the condition of the intelligibility of the symbolic[33] itself. I think there are other ways of reading Lacan which suggest that any sexed position is in itself split and non-unitary, but I think that what she does is shore up a certain kind of normativity of sexual difference, and also of heterosexuality, a kind of naturalizing sexuality which allows many Lacanians to feel that they can occupy a patronizing and diagnostic mode in relationship to transsexuality by which they want to figure the perverse as such and I really find it nauseating.

KM: I find it actually difficult to read TSs in the way Millot and Lacan seem to ... I don't see any evidence for TSs being psychotic for a start and I think non-triggered psychoses to be extremely convenient when it's only Lacanians who still believe the psychosis argument. I see *Horsexe* as a text to be predicating its academic machinery on a rather nasty melange of anecdotal moralizing in the introduction ...

JB: I couldn't agree with you more.

KM: ... and I almost see this idea of TSs being fooled by the Imaginary into wanting to become 'The Woman' as almost deconstructing itself, it sees TSs as being so transparent, but I don't really know where to go from there. What are the more progressive ways of reading through Lacan? [*pause*] Nasty question?!

JB: Good question, and a very hard one for me. I think that in many ways the possibility of a sexually progressive Lacan rests on the rearticulation of the relationship of the symbolic and the imaginary. I think what has to happen is that the symbolic law cannot be seen as exercising its force apart from the demands of the social. Those who claim that there is a symbolic law that's not reducible to socially produced regimes of power and that that symbolic law establishes sexual difference and its irreducibility, establishing the position of the father, the mother, naturalizing Oedipalization, are clearly wrong. I think that that framework has to be made subject to a radical reworking, that what are finally kinship relations that appear to be ultimate and constitutive of law actually get recast as rearticulated norms. I think the symbolic has to be made more vulnerable to temporal lapse, has to be vulnerable to a sort of radical rearticulation and I think the imaginary also has to be understood not simply as that which fixes the object and mistakes the object, dupes the subject, but the Imaginary is also a space for the rearticulation of the symbolic, it's why, to return to the passage from *Gender Trouble*, I'm using the imaginary in a much more active and productive sense than a Lacanian would, I don't understand the imaginary as inevitably subordinate to the symbolic, nor do I understand it as that which escapes from the symbolic on a given occasion but then always comes back under its law. I actually think that the Imaginary can be a scene in which the symbolic gets substantially revised, so I would actually like to see a refocusing on the imaginary. I also think the real,[34] which is linked to the psychotic in Millot's work and some of the most recent Lacanian work that I've seen gets used in many ways to figure socially abject[35] positions. You know, Kristeva did that, with lesbians, she said lesbianism was necessarily psychotic. These are ways of deradicalizing, keeping certain kinds of social possibilities unthinkable as part of the intelligible world. And I find that to be prescriptive in the worst sense, because they don't say, 'This is wrong!', 'I disagree with it', or 'I can't stand it!' What they say is, 'Transsexuality is not possible!', 'It's not real, it's psychotic!', 'It's not liveable!' So I think the real question for me is, whether a sexually progressive Lacanianism can expand and extend what we think of as a culturally intelligible existence.

KM: You almost seemed to be heading towards Deleuze and Guattari there, but then they adopt the psychotic.

JB: I don't go that far, they don't take prohibition seriously and I do. I just don't think it's cast in stone, but they override it methodologically and that I take to be an automatic response that doesn't actually work it through.

KM: It's interesting, the criticism to Deleuze and Guattari is almost the same as that of performativity, which is that difference is undifferentiated, it's almost too machinic a method, and there is no way 'forward' politically in inverted commas.

JB: I'm not sure I know which criticisms you're referring to, as 'machinic', no one's told me that, but I'm ready to listen to it.

KM: When you get to the stage where there is no category which is 'stable' it is very difficult to build a 'future'; all of these are modernist terms which may be reusable if postmodernism is perceived to be a fashion which we really want to get rid of! Where do we go if performativity is just deconstructive and doesn't enable us to be reconstructive?

JB: Well, it's always been a question of being reconstructive for me. You know maybe the way to handle this is to return to the example of drag, 'cause I've had to rethink that a lot, under pressure! And I think what is actually reconstructed, to borrow a term from surgery, has to do with the way in which the question of reality gets posed; the mimetic approximation of the so-called real, wasn't just a vain failure, to approximate the truly real, but itself was part of the constitution of what will be real. There's a kind of forward moving effort to reconceive and redefine what counts as real. So for me the performative theory of gender was not about putting on a masquerade that hides a reality, or that is derived from a higher reality, but it's actually about a certain way of inhabiting norms that alters the norms and alters our sense of what is real and what is liveable. That's my affirmative and forward-looking view and it remains my view, it's in fact the question I pose about hate speech as well; how does one inhabit it and situate it, feel able to change it and rework it and subvert its injurious power, lessen it so the lives which are rendered unliveable by it become liveable in some new way. I'm really interested in this whole problem about what it is to become intelligible. Probably a previous generation of feminist theorists were interested in finding radical spaces outside of the symbolic, inhabiting the psychotic or the hysteric, or the imaginary to some degree which would be in permanent disruption of the symbolic, but I think I'm interested in disrupting the symbolic in order to rearticulate it in more expansive ways. Some people say that's selling out, but I think it's about finding a way to live.

KM: You are turning out to be much more pragmatic than I thought. Finally then, *Excitable Speech* was out a couple of weeks ago, you have another, a new book out from Stanford soon, out here in October, perhaps you could say something about that?

JB: *The Psychic Life of Power*. It's about trying to reconcile a Foucaultian notion of the subject as posited within discourse with a theory of the psyche. Trying to figure out whether and how social norms are organized psychically and dealing with questions of internalization, and melancholia. There's an extended discussion of gender melancholia in the text. I'm trying to figure out what it means when social norms seek to constitute the subject and also seek to obliterate the subject, when that particular moment is lived at a psychic level. Anyway it's the same issue as *Excitable Speech*, only not focused on speech, focused on the psyche and the social.

Notes

1. Butler undertook another much longer interview at the ICA for *Radical Philosophy*, 67 (Summer 1994). As time was limited I concentrated on the obvious gap in information surrounding transsexuality, there being so much on drag already.

2. Catherine Millot, *Horsexe* (New York: Autonomedia, 1990). See the discussion in Diane Morgan's ' "What does a transsexual want?": the encounter between psychoanalysis and transsexuality', *Radical Deviance*, 2, 4; reprinted in Chapter 11.

3. Parveen Adams, 'Operation Orlan', in *The Emptiness of the Image* (1996). See Diane Morgan's 'Passovers: of postmodernism and transsexuality', *Radical Deviance*, 2, 2: 69–70.

4. Butler's ideas turn on an understanding of people taking up subject positions in terms of identity categories such as 'transsexual' or 'Lesbian', which are created by setting up boundaries against others. She argues against this practice in favour of constructing oneself (and therefore one's politics) performatively, through one's actions.

5. See Judith Butler, *Bodies That Matter: On the Discursive Limits of 'Sex'* (London: Routledge, 1993): ix–x.

6. Judith Butler, *Gender Trouble: Feminism and the Subversion of Identity* (London: Routledge, 1990).

7. To construct oneself 'juridically' is a phrase Butler uses to imply that we have to police these boundaries socially to maintain the distinction between, e.g., 'man' and 'woman'. It is interesting to note how close Butler is to her adversary, Kristeva, in her writing of this identity.

8. For a description of transgender politics including a discussion of Judith Butler see the 'Stone Femme' articles in the central section of the previous chapter.

9. In the last couple of years credit for invention of performativity (at least in my own work) has been regularly revised backwards, notably from Mary McIntosh's 'The homosexual role' to Foucault's *Le Mots et les choses* two years earlier, and not having managed to get hold of a copy of her first book, I wanted to know if her use originates from Lacan or even Hegel. Austinian performativity, from J.L. Austin's *How To Do Things with Words* (Cambridge, MA: Harvard University Press, 1962), has proved to be a source in *Excitable Speech*. Butler's first book is *Subjects of Desire: Hegelian Reflections in Twentieth-Century France* (New York: Columbia University Press, 1987). She was very gracious not to point out that it

contains a much wider survey of contemporary French thinking than just Lacan.

10. Hegel's *Phenomenology of Spirit* in many ways prefigures Freudian as well as Marxian thinking, including perhaps concepts such as splitting that we credit to later authorities, Janet, Klein, and others. His master/slave dialectic, *belle âme*, and so on are notably taken up in the early Lacan.

11. Lacan is most easily understood as the father of postmodern psychoanalysis. His works are perhaps the most difficult primary texts critical theorists have to encounter, combining psychoanalysis, linguistics, algebra, graphs and schematic diagrams and, perhaps, surrealist poetry. I can't possibly do justice to this material simply in footnotes, so perhaps the best secondary text introducing his work is by Slavoj Žižek, *Looking Awry: An Introduction to Jacques Lacan through Popular Culture* (Cambridge, MA: MIT, 1991).

12. The Lacanian phallus is not the biological penis, but closer to the role played by the penis in the desires constructed by each sex.

13. Michel Foucault theorized the relationship between knowledge and power, and is best known for his *History of Sexuality*. The interviews in *Power/ Knowledge: Selected Interviews and Other Writings 1972–77*, edited by Colin Gordon *et al.* (Harvester) are some of the easiest primary texts to tackle.

14. Judith Butler, *Excitable Speech: A Politics of the Performative* (London: Routledge, 1997).

15. See *Gender Trouble*, pp. 70–1.

16. Lacan talks of the imaginary realm of the psyche as being created at the mirror stage. At this stage the child starts off unindividuated from its mother, but seeing itself for the first time in a mirror recognizes itself joyously as a whole and coherent independent being, which of course it is not, thus the imaginary realm is the realm of seductive images. The imaginary is one of three interlinked Lacanian realms, the symbolic, the imaginary and the real, which delineate the way in which the psyche works. As an example, Lacan says, 'within the phenomena of speech we can integrate the three planes of the symbolic, represented by the signifier, the imaginary, represented by meaning and the real, which is discourse that has actually taken place in a diachronic dimension' (*The Psychoses*, London, Routledge, 1993: 63).

17. This interpretation was perhaps unfair on Jay, being almost certainly too simplistic a view, absorbed as it was from conversation during a meal with him. His will be a complex and impressive book, but at the time of the interview it was still at manuscript stage. For a more detailed view please read Jay Prosser, *Second Skins: The Body Narratives of Transsexuality* (New York: Columbia University Press, 1998).

18. The phantasmatic isn't a Lacanian term, rather deriving from Laplanche and Pontalis, 'Fantasy and the origins of sexuality' in Burgin *et al.*, *Formations of Fantasy* (London: Methuen, 1986). The idea according to

Hausman, quoting Butler, is that gender identity is a kind of ' "literalising fantasy" that is "established through a refusal of loss that encrypts itself in the body and that determines, in effect, the living versus the dead body" ' (Bernice Hausman, *Changing Sex: Transsexualism, Technology and the Idea of Gender* (Durham, NC: Duke University Press, 1995: 190). In this way it relates to Butler's more extensive later writings on gender melancholy.

19. See *Gender Trouble*, pp. 106–11.

20. See D.F. Swaab, *et al.*, 'A sex difference in the human brain and its relation to transsexuality', *Nature*, **378** (2 November 1995): 68–70. The human complexity of this situation is felt when one realizes that the Swaab paper has been used in almost all of the successful civil and human rights court cases on transsexualism in the UK since its publication. Its sequel is believed to be an *in vivo* study measuring the size of the central subdivision of the bed nucleus of the Stria Terminalis (BSTc) and if successful it is argued that this might reduce or even eradicate the use of the much-criticized psychiatric assessment as the basis of surgery, while restricting surgery to the few whose brain measurements and whose desires/needs/fantasies coincide.

21. See the discussion on 'difference' in the previous chapter. One question that none of the literature seems to have mentioned, but which interests and appals me about the Swaab debate, is the possible collapse of the gender/sexuality binary, and a return to the early Freud. Swaab is a study extrapolated from work on rabbits. If one removes the BSTc from a rabbit it loses interest in sex. If male-to-female TSs have a smaller, female-sized BSTc, then maybe what is going to be argued next is that gender difference is to be once more predicated on an active/passive continuum and gender is ultimately a function of biology via sex drive.

22. See Kate Bornstein, *Gender Outlaw: On Men, Women and the Rest of Us* (London: Routledge, 1994): 118.

23. Gesa Lindemann, *Das paradoxe Geschlecht. Transsexualität im Spannungs-feld von Körper, Leib und Gefühl* (Frankfurt: Fischer, 1993) has my vote too. Will somebody please translate and publish this excellent book – way beyond any other text with a 'sociology' rubric. But please with a less irritating cover!

24. See Hausman, *Changing Sex*, p. 147.

25. My critique of Orlan almost reverses Adams's praise: Orlan's tools are radical, but her use is ultimately reactionary; her performance has taken on transsexualism's gendered figuration of the body, but instead of a transfiguration of gender she opts for a re-figuration – this is the problem with postmodern pastiche. She reinforces gender stereotypes; hers is a cosmetic surgery of the worst type. Orlan started her performance career with transvestism, as the early medical viewpoint stated TSs are supposed to begin, then she went on to make a performance out of having cosmetic surgery, declaring herself to be a female-to-female transsexual, but the problem is that she still occupied the female gender, she was contiguous,

not in the role of metaphor, so eventually she had two cheek implants affixed above her eyebrows, and when all the surgery is finished, she intends to mimic French transsexuals in their fight for the right to a change of name. While the transsexuals fight the French state and courts for the right to define themselves, Orlan is to change her name to that of another artist, the name to be decided by the public. She intends for her dead, preserved body to go not to science, but to an art gallery, embalmed as the centre of an installation. Her body will be a text as pernicious and hateful as Butler later describes Raymond and Millot's texts as being.

26. See Jan Morris, *Conundrum* (Harmondsworth: Penguin, 1974). The interesting thing here is how Butler summons the by-now-traditional radical/reactionary divide common to discourse about transsexuality, only to show how the reactionary side fails to live up to its bipolar promise.

27. This is a concept Lacan seems to have borrowed from C.S. Peirce, an American who, many decades earlier and in several ways, prefigured the 1968 generation of French thought. Lacan uses the term to explain the strange behaviour of the personal pronoun, I, which always points to the person who is physically speaking; here I was using the term to suggest the 'embodiment', within the symbolic realm, of transition.

28. Parlêtre is a Lacanian term/concept meaning to be-in-language.

29. Of course I didn't mean a literal return to Lacan, but something more provocative. Lacan talks of speech as invocation and this is an idea we see again in Althusser, and thence cited by Butler. Lacan does appear more explicitly in the text's margins, briefly in the end section and in the footnotes.

30. 'Interpellation' is an Althusserian term borrowed by Butler in *Excitable Speech* from his paper 'Ideology and ideological state apparatuses' (see *Excitable Speech*, p. 165). Although I replace the term in the interview with 'summon' or 'invoke', this is perhaps a bit sloppy. Terry Eagleton says something like 'all ideologies hail or interpellate concrete individuals, transforming them into subjects'.

31. J. Raymond, *The Transsexual Empire* (London: Women's Press, 1980).

32. Saussure makes a seminal distinction, that between speech and writing, 'langue' and 'actes de parole', see chapters III and IV of the *Course in General Linguistics* (Fontana, 1974). I think this is an amazing intervention, which threw me totally at the time. I had presumed, through Bourdieu, Foucault even, that there was a different relationship to power, perhaps just that there was a cultural capital attached to the printed word. For Kristeva, writing may correspond to speech (*Revolution in Poetic Language*, New York: Columbia University Press, 1974: 87). 'Writing represents – articulates the signifying process into specific networks or spaces; *speech* (which may correspond to that writing) restores the diacritical elements necessary for an exchange of meaning between two subjects (temporality, aspect, specification of the protagonists, morpho-semantic identifiers, and so forth).' However, from a Lacanian perspective at least, texts are not the

same as speech, their materiality connects them solidly with the real, and the relationship with the symbolic within Butler's discourse was to be a follow-up question. What is the difference that makes speech excitable?

33. The symbolic is the realm of language, of signifiers, and what Lacan calls the No/Name of the Father (it is through language that we are ordered).

34. The real, the third Lacanian realm, is not the same as reality, but rather a more essentialized version. I would have said the real is that realm of desire which principally opposes the seductive imaginary, merely finding its difference from the symbolic: being-in-itself rather than being-in-language. When I first heard of Butler's work I naïvely thought hers was the former, a politics of the real, a politics of being-in-itself.

35. The 'abject' was influentially theorized in Julia Kristeva's *Powers of Horror* (New York: Columbia University Press, 1982). For Butler's usage, see *Bodies That Matter*, footnote 2, p. 243: that which is cast out and hence founds its subject through foreclosure. Butler works her difference from Lacan's usage of foreclosure as a term connected with psychosis.

Index